The SENSE of
BEING STARED AT

The SENSE of
BEING STARED AT

and Other Aspects of
THE EXTENDED MIND

RUPERT SHELDRAKE

CROWN PUBLISHERS ✷ NEW YORK

Published by Crown Publishers, New York, New York.
Member of the Crown Publishing Group, a division of Random House, Inc.
www.randomhouse.com

CROWN is a trademark and the Crown colophon is a registered trademark of Random House, Inc.

Printed in the United States of America

DESIGN BY BARBARA STURMAN

Library of Congress Cataloging-in-Publication Data
Sheldrake, Rupert.
    The sense of being stared at : and other aspects of the extended mind /
    Rupert Sheldrake.
Includes bibliographical references and index.
    1. Extrasensory perception.   2. Extrasensory perception in animals.
    I. Title.
    BF1321 .S48   2003
    133.8—dc21   2002009943

ISBN 0-609-60807-X

10 9 8 7 6 5 4 3 2 1

First Edition

IN MEMORY OF

William Barrett, Henry Sidgwick, Frederic Myers, Edmund Gurney, Eleanor Sidgwick, John Dunne, Joseph and Louisa Rhine, and other pioneering investigators of unexplained human abilities.

Contents

Preface

There is much we do not understand about human and animal nature. This book grows out of a conviction that if we only open our minds and make an effort to understand, we will be vastly rewarded with our new knowledge. Clues lie disregarded all around us. For generations, prejudices rooted in the thinking of seventeenth- and eighteenth-century philosophers have inhibited research and inquiry. As a consequence, there is still much for us to discover about the biological nature of humans and animals.

As I showed in my books *Seven Experiments That Could Change the World* (1994) and *Dogs That Know When Their Owners Are Coming Home* (1999), relatively simple experiments can yield very large returns in this new phase of scientific exploration.

In this book, I argue that unexplained human abilities such as telepathy, the sense of being stared at, and premonition are not paranormal but normal, part of our biological nature. In *Dogs That Know When Their Owners Are Coming Home*, I showed that these unexplained powers are widely distributed in the animal kingdom. They are exhibited by some of the animals we know best, such as dogs, cats, horses, and parrots. Although we ourselves are generally less sensitive, we share these abilities with many other species. We have partly lost or neglected these aspects of our evolutionary heritage.

By investigating these abilities, rather than dismissing them, we will come to understand more about the nature of our minds and the invisible connections that link us to each other and to the world around us. In this book I concentrate on unexplained human abilities, but I build on the investigations of animal powers discussed in *Dogs That Know When Their Owners Are Coming Home*.

This book differs from other accounts of unexplained human abilities in several ways. First, it is grounded in biology and animal behavior, and treats telepathy and other unexplained abilities as aspects of our biological, animal nature.

Second, some books either bring together collections of stories or are rigorously experimental, excluding anything that has not been tested in the laboratory. I believe in combining both approaches. This book starts from the natural history of personal experiences, but wherever possible discusses experiments that can shed light on what is happening.

Third, I show that scientific research on unexplained human powers can be done quite simply, and in Appendix A, I outline a variety of ways in which readers can take part in this research themselves.

Fourth, although the phenomena I discuss are currently unexplained, I do not think that they are inherently inexplicable. I argue throughout this book that the exploration of these abilities could lead to a new understanding of the nature of human and animal minds. Instead of thinking of minds as confined to brains, I suggest they involve extended fields of influence that stretch out far beyond brains and bodies.

This book summarizes research in which I have been engaged for more than fifteen years, and in which I have been helped by many people.

More than 5,000 correspondents have contributed case histories to my databases, based on their own experiences and on their observations of animals. Hundreds of people, including animal trainers, farmers, veterinarians, naturalists, hunters, wildlife photographers, pet owners, surveillance officers, soldiers, detectives, teachers, and martial-arts practitioners, have helped in this research through participating in interviews with me or my research associates. More than 1,600 people have responded to my random household surveys, and a further 2,000 have helped in my research by filling in questionnaires about their own experiences. In addition, more than 20,000 people have participated in experimental tests. I thank all those people for their help. I quote some of them by name in this book.

My research associates and I have organized many experiments directly. Many others have been conducted by dozens of independent researchers, mainly in schools and colleges. Also, more than fifty students have carried out research projects based on experimental designs suggested in my books and on my website. I thank all those who have kindly sent me reports and raw data from their experiments.

I am greatly indebted to my research associates, who have carried out surveys and interviews, conducted experiments, and collected all sorts of information on my behalf. Pam Smart, in Lancashire, has had the primary responsibility for maintaining my computerized databases, for responding to the many e-mails that come through my website, and for coordinating hundreds of experiments on telephone telepathy. Jane Turney and Katy Barber have helped me in London, as has my secretary, Cathy Lawlor. Susanne Seiler has worked for me in Zurich, David Jay Brown in California, Helen Robinette in New York,

Nina Nikolaeva in Moscow, and Socrates Seferiades in Athens. I thank them wholeheartedly.

Jan van Bolhuis, assistant professor of statistics at the Free University of Amsterdam, has advised me on statistical methodologies and carried out numerous statistical analyses for me. I much appreciate his patience, thoroughness, and kindness.

Matthew Clapp set up my website, www.sheldrake.org, in 1996 when he was an undergraduate at the University of Georgia, and served as my webmaster until the beginning of 2002, when his professional duties finally became too demanding for him to continue. All this time he gave his services freely, as has my German webmaster, Helmut Lasarcyk, in Hamburg. Helmut has also translated hundreds of case histories and other communications for me. I am very grateful for their help.

The research described in this book was made possible by financial assistance from the late Ben Webster, of Toronto, by grants from the Lifebridge Foundation in New York, the Institute of Noetic Sciences in California, the Bial Foundation in Portugal, the Fred Foundation in the Netherlands, and by gifts from Evelyn Hancock, of Old Greenwich, Connecticut. I gratefully acknowledge their generosity.

In the course of this research I have had many stimulating discussions, and benefited from the comments, criticisms, and advice of many people. In particular, I would like to acknowledge the contributions of Ralph Abraham, Hunter Beaumont, John Beloff, Dick Bierman, John Brockman, Christopher Clarke, Larry Dossey, Lindy Dufferin and Ava, Brenda Dunne, Leni Erikson, Sally Rhine Feather, Peter Fenwick, Jan Fjellander, David Fontana, Mathew Fox, Robert Freeman, Alan Gauld, Franz-Theo Gottwald, Anne Harrison, the late Renée Haynes, Bert Hellinger, Myles Hildyard, Rupert Hitzig, John Hubbard, Nicholas Humphrey, Francis Huxley, Diana Issidorides, Theo Itten, Robert Jahn, David Lorimer, Betty Markwick, Katinka Matson, Robert Matthews, Elizabeth Lloyd Mayer, the late Terence McKenna, John Michell, Guido Mino di Sospiro, Aimée Morgana, Robert Morris, Roger Nelson, Charles Overby, John Palmer, Guy Lyon Playfair, Dean Radin, Anthony Ramsay, John Roche, Miriam Rothschild, Janis Rozé, Edward St. Aubyn, George Sassoon, Gary Schwartz, Marilyn Schlitz, Stephan Schmidt, Giuseppe Sermonti, Ian Stevenson, Harris Stone, James Trifone, Barbara Valocore, Mario Varvoglis, Ian and Victoria Watson, Zofia Weaver, and Goetz Wittneben. In addition, my wife, Jill Purce, and our sons, Merlin and Cosmo, have helped me in many ways, not least as the participants of first resort in trying out new experiments.

I thank all those who gave me their comments and suggestions on drafts of this book, especially David Christie-Murray, Ted Dace, Montague Keen, Aimée Morgana, Guy Lyon Playfair, George Sassoon, and Pam Smart. And I could not have hoped for a better editor than Kristin Kiser of Crown Publishers, in New York.

I am grateful to Merlin Sheldrake for drawing the diagrams in Figures 11.5 and 18.2, and thank the following for permission to reproduce illustrations: Aimée Morgana (Figure 1.1), the estate of E. N. Willmer (Figure 10.2), Max Velmans and Routledge Publishers (Figure 13.2), Dean Radin (Figure 17.1), and Dick Bierman (Figure 17.2).

The SENSE of

BEING STARED AT

Introduction

The Seventh Sense and the

Extended Mind

For a long time, I have had a feeling of telepathy with my two daughters who I am very close to. I start thinking about them just before the phone rings. It happens too with friends. I'm always saying "I was just thinking about you" when I answer the phone to them. ⊙ JANET WARD

Leto Seferiades was sleeping in the same room as her baby daughter.

I suddenly woke up, fully awake and expectantly alert. I could see my six-month-old daughter sleeping peacefully in her cot under the window. Then I seemed to hear an imperative inner voice telling me to check that she was all right in her cot. When I reached her cot, the voice urgently, like an order, told me to move the cot instantly away from the window. I grabbed that cot and moved it a step back into the room just before the entire heavy wooden curtain box and rails collapsed, falling onto exactly the position where the cot had been!

William Carter was leading a patrol of Gurkhas on an antiterrorist operation in Malaya in 1951 when they came across a camp that had obviously just been abandoned.

While we were examining the bits and pieces left lying around, I had an uncanny feeling that someone was watching me. I had this sense of danger. I felt the sensation of something almost gripping me at the back of the neck. I turned around and there, about twenty yards away, was a chap in uniform with a red star on his cap gazing hard at me. He was bringing his rifle up and I knew one of us was going to be killed. I shot him before he shot me, so I have lived to tell the tale.

He says he does not doubt the existence of a sense of being stared at. "But for it, I wouldn't be alive today."[1]

◇◆◇

Telepathy, premonitions, and the sense of being stared at are currently unexplained in scientific terms. Indeed, their very existence is controversial. They *appear* to happen, but if all possible kinds of forces, fields, and information transfer are already known to science, then they ought not to exist. Is our scientific understanding of fundamental principles already more or less complete? Have all the big questions been answered? Some scientists believe they have.[2]

On the other hand, if these phenomena do in fact occur, they show that current science is incomplete. When they are taken seriously within the scientific community, the effects will be revolutionary. They will enlarge our ideas about minds and brains, about animal nature and human nature, and about space and time.

In this book I discuss a large body of evidence and summarize recent research that shows that telepathy, the sense of being stared at, and precognition occur both in nonhuman animals, such as dogs and cats, and in people. They are not "paranormal" or "supernatural." They are normal and natural, part of our biological nature.

Different groups of people refer to these phenomena by different names. Some call them psychic, implying that they are related to the psyche, or soul, or call them psi phenomena, for short. Some describe them as forms of extrasensory perception, or ESP, meaning forms of perception beyond the senses. (Here the word *extra* means "beyond," in its original Latin sense, not "additional" as in the modern English sense.) Some prefer to call them paranormal, meaning beyond the normal (the Greek *para* means "beyond"), or parapsychological, meaning beyond psychology. Other people think of them as aspects of a "sixth sense," over and above the five familiar senses of seeing, hearing, smelling, tasting, and touching.

The fact that so many different terms are used is confusing. And all these terms carry different implications. *Psychic* implies a dependence on the psyche, or soul. This shifts the problem back one stage, because no one knows how the psyche could account for these experiences. To do so, it would have to stretch out beyond the brain. But how?

The term *extrasensory perception* restates the problem in different words. It tells us that these phenomena cannot be explained in terms of the known senses, but says nothing about how they *can* be explained.

The word *paranormal* raises the question of what is normal. The sense of being stared at and telepathy are normal in that they are common. Most people have experienced them. But they seem paranormal from the point of view of the materialist theory of the mind, still taken for granted within institutional science. According to this theory, the mind is just an aspect of the activity of the brain. A mind confined to the inside of the head cannot account for psychic phenomena. Hence, from a materialist point of view, they ought not to happen. But what if science took a broader view of the mind?

As science progresses, it continually changes the boundaries of the scientifically "normal." Television and cell phones would have seemed miraculous to an eighteenth-century physicist, knowing nothing of electromagnetic fields. Seeing things at a distance or hearing the voices of people far away would have seemed like the work of witches or the delusions of lunatics. Now they are everyday experiences, thanks to television, radio, and telephones.

Likewise, hydrogen bombs would have been unthinkable for nineteenth-century physicists. In the age of steam and gunpowder, such devices would have sounded like an apocalyptic fantasy. Lasers would have sounded like mythic swords of light. They only became conceivable for twentieth-century physicists through the scientific revolutions wrought by relativity theory and quantum theory.

These enlargements of science did not contradict or invalidate what was already known, but built on it. The recognition of electromagnetic fields in the nineteenth century supplemented rather than overthrew classical Newtonian physics. The twentieth-century revolutions in physics brought about by quantum and relativity theory and modern cosmology did not destroy the achievements of nineteenth-century physicists, but added to them. In biology, Darwin's theory of evolution illuminated rather than eclipsed the classification of living organisms by the great eighteenth-century biologist Linnaeus.

Historians of science, most notably Thomas Kuhn,[3] have recognized that at any given stage in the history of science, phenomena that do not fit into the prevailing model or paradigm are dismissed or ignored or explained away. They are anomalies. Yet to the embarrassment of the reigning theories, they persist. Sooner or later science has to expand to include them.

To cite one of many examples, meteorites were anomalies in the eighteenth century. In the perfect mathematical universe of Newtonian physics, there was no possibility of stones falling from the sky seemingly at random. So when people claimed to have seen such things happen, scientists felt they had to deny them, explain them away as illusions, or dismiss them as superstitions.

In one celebrated example, on September 13, 1768, in Maine, France, several villagers heard a noise like a thunderclap, followed by a whistling sound, and saw something falling into a meadow. It turned out to be a stone too hot to touch. A local priest sent part of it to the Academy of Sciences in Paris for identification. The chemist Lavoisier ground it up, did some tests, and claimed he had proved it had not fallen from the sky, but instead was an ordinary stone that had probably been struck by lightning.[4] He told the academy, "There are no stones in the sky. Therefore stones cannot fall from the sky."[5] Now, of course, meteorites present no theoretical problem, and their existence is no longer disputed.

Materialism as a philosophy keeps evolving as scientific ideas about physical reality change within science. The boundaries of the "normal" are not fixed, but shift according to changes in scientific orthodoxies. In the course of the twentieth century, materialism "transcended itself" through physics, as the philosopher of science Karl Popper remarked.[6] Matter is no longer the fundamental reality, as it was for old-style materialism. Fields and energy are now more fundamental than matter. The ultimate particles of matter have become vibrations of energy within fields.

The boundaries of scientific "normality" are shifting again with a dawning recognition of the reality of consciousness. The powers of the mind, hitherto ignored by physics, are the new scientific frontier.

THE SIXTH SENSE AND THE SEVENTH SENSE

Of all the terms used to describe such phenomena as telepathy, "sixth sense" seems to me a better starting point than any of the others. This has a more positive meaning than "ESP" or "the paranormal," in that it implies a kind of sensory system over and above the known senses, but a sense just the same. As a sense, it is rooted in time and place; it is biological, not supernatural. It extends beyond the body, though how it works is still unknown.

An even better term is "seventh sense." The sixth sense has already been claimed by biologists working on the electrical and magnetic senses of animals. Some species of eels, for example, generate electrical fields around themselves through which they sense objects in their environment, even in the dark.[7] Sharks and rays detect, with astonishing sensitivity, the body electricity of potential prey.[8] Various species of migratory fish and birds have a magnetic sense, a biological compass that enables them to respond to Earth's magnetic field.[9]

There are also a variety of other senses that could lay claim to being a sixth sense, including the heat-sensing organs of rattlesnakes and related species, which enable them to focus heat and track down prey by a kind of thermographic technique.[10] And there is the vibration sense of web-weaving spiders, through which they can detect what is happening in their webs, and even communicate with one another through a kind of vibratory telegraph.[11]

The term *seventh sense* expresses the idea that telepathy, the sense of being stared at, and premonitions seem to be in a different category both from the five normal senses, and also from so-called sixth senses based on known physical principles.

EVIDENCE

The first and most fundamental kind of evidence for the seventh sense is personal experience. And there are many such experiences. Most people have sometimes felt that they were being stared at from behind, or thought about someone who then telephoned. Yet all these billions of personal experiences of seemingly unexplained phenomena are conventionally dismissed within institutional science as "anecdotal."

What does this actually mean? The word *anecdote* comes from the Greek roots *an* and *ekdotos*, meaning "not published." Thus an anecdote is an unpublished story.

Courts of law take anecdotal evidence seriously, and people are often convicted or acquitted thanks to it. Some fields of research—for example, medicine—rely heavily on anecdotes, but when the stories are published they literally cease to be anecdotes; they are promoted to the rank of case histories. Such case histories form the essential foundation of experience on which further research can be built. To brush aside what people have actually experienced is not to be scientific, but unscientific. Science is founded on the empirical method; that is to say, on experience and observation. Experiences and observations are the starting point for science, and it is unscientific to disregard or exclude them.

Isaac Newton's insights about gravitation started from observations of such everyday phenomena as apples falling to earth and the recognition of a relationship between the Moon and the tides. Almost all of Charles Darwin's evidence for natural selection came from the achievements of plant and animal breeders, and he drew heavily on the experience of practical people. My favorite book of Darwin's is *The Variation of Animals and Plants Under Domestication*, first published in 1868. It is full of information he collected from naturalists, explorers, colonial administrators, missionaries, and others with whom he corresponded, all over the world. He studied publications like *Poultry*

Chronicle and *The Gooseberry Grower's Register*. He grew fifty-four varieties of gooseberry himself. He was interested in the observations of cat and rabbit fanciers, horse and dog breeders, beekeepers, farmers, fruit growers, gardeners, and other people experienced with animals and plants. He joined two of the London pigeon clubs, kept all the breeds he could obtain, and visited leading fanciers to see their birds.

In a similar way, people's personal experiences form the essential starting point for research on the reach and powers of the mind. The founders of psychic research in the 1880s started by carrying out large-scale surveys of people's seemingly psychic experiences, as well as investigating whether they could be explained in conventional scientific terms. They pioneered the use of statistics, in order to examine whether chance coincidence could provide a plausible explanation for the experiences they were studying. They also developed "blind" experimental techniques, and psychic research was one of the first fields of scientific inquiry where such techniques were routinely used.

But despite an impressive accumulation of evidence, psychic research has never been accepted within institutional science. It has been kept on the margins as a result of powerful taboos against the "paranormal." As a result, the phenomena of the seventh sense have largely been ignored within universities and scientific institutes and academies. In spite of the dedicated work of the small band of psychic researchers and parapsychologists, this field of investigation is still the Cinderella of the sciences.

I am impressed by what psychic researchers and parapsychologists have already discovered, and admire their bravery in pursuing a field of research that has exposed them to so much adversity and even hostility. And I appreciate the way in which they have pioneered the use of rigorous methods of experimental research.

I myself am not a parapsychologist, but a biologist. I am interested in the seventh sense because it has much to teach us about animal nature and human nature, about the nature of the mind, and indeed about the nature of life itself. My own approach is more biological than that of parapsychologists and psychic researchers, who have almost entirely concentrated on human beings. I see the seventh sense as part of our biological nature, which we share with many other animal species.

In my own research I have used three complementary approaches. First of all, I have investigated the natural history of unusual perceptiveness in people and in animals. I have appealed for information through radio, television, magazines, and newspapers in Europe, Australia, South Africa, and North America, asking people about their own experiences, and also about observations of pets and wild animals suggesting the existence of unexplained sensitivities. My associates and I have also interviewed hundreds of people whose professions provide opportunities to observe the seventh sense in action, including soldiers, fighter pilots, martial-arts practitioners, psychotherapists, security officers, private detectives, criminals, photographers, hunters, horse riders, animal trainers, and pet owners.

In these ways we have built up a computerized database of more than 5,000 case histories of apparently unexplained perceptiveness by people and by nonhuman animals. These case histories are classified into more than 100 categories. When many people's accounts point independently to consistent and repeatable patterns, anecdotes are transformed into natural history. At the very least, this is a natural history of what people *believe* about their own perceptiveness and that of animals.

Second, I have carried out surveys in Britain, Germany, Switzerland, the United States, and Argentina about various kinds of unexplained perceptiveness and the conditions under which they operate. In addition, through questionnaires I have investigated in detail the experiences of more than 1,600 people. My associates and I have also surveyed more than 1,500 randomly selected households in Britain and the United States by means of telephone interviews.

Third, over a period of more than ten years we have done a variety of experiments on the sense of being stared at, and on different aspects of telepathy in animals and in people. I will summarize the results in the following chapters, and will give the technical details in Appendix B.

WHY THIS SUBJECT IS SO CONTROVERSIAL

The research described in this book is harmless in itself, and deals with subjects that many people find interesting. Yet it can provoke surprisingly intense emotions. Some people become angry at, or scornful of, anyone who takes these phenomena seriously.[12] Why?

Some people find psychic phenomena of no interest, which is fair enough. Most people are not very interested in the scientific study of the behavior of cuttlefish, or research into the genetics of mosses. Yet no one becomes emotionally antagonistic to cuttlefish or moss research.

Is it simply a matter, then, of hostility to new ideas? This may be a partial explanation, but some areas of contemporary scientific speculation seem far more radical, and yet excite little or no opposition. Some physicists, for example, postulate that there are countless parallel universes besides our own.[13] Few people take these ideas seriously, but no one gets angry about them. Even speculations about time travel through "wormholes" in space-time are considered a legitimate field of inquiry within academic physics, rather than a branch of science fiction.[14]

Could it be that psychic researchers are particularly disreputable, or that this field is rife with fraud and deception? There are well-documented cases of fraud in most branches of science and medicine,[15] including paleontology (for example, the hoax "missing link" fossil known as the Piltdown Man), and even in botany.[16] There have also been two well-publicized cases of fraud in psychic research, unmasked by fellow psychic researchers.[17] But no one would dismiss all medical or botanical research because a few people within those disciplines have cheated, nor can psychic research or research in any other field be dismissed in its entirety because there have been a few dishonest researchers.

In fact, psychic research and parapsychology may be less prone to fraud than most other branches of science, precisely because the former are subject to more skeptical scrutiny.[18] In an insightful study of fraud and deceit in science, William Broad and Nicholas Wade concluded that fraud is most likely to be successful in mainstream, uncontroversial areas of research such as immunology: "Acceptance of fraudulent results is the other side of that familiar coin, resistance to new ideas. Fraudulent results are likely to be accepted in science if they are plausibly presented, if they conform with prevailing prejudices and expectations, and if they come from a suitably qualified scientist affiliated with an elite institution. It is for lack of all these qualities that new ideas in science are likely to be resisted."

The only remaining explanation is that the existence of psychic phenomena violates powerful taboos. These phenomena threaten deep-seated beliefs, especially the belief that the mind is nothing but the activity of the brain. For people who identify science and reason with the materialist philosophy, they arouse fear. They seem to threaten reason itself; if they are not kept at bay, science and even modern civilization seem to be endangered by a tidal wave of superstition and credulity. Hence they have to be denied outright, or dismissed as unscientific and irrational.

In addition, some opponents of "the paranormal" have strong personal fears about invasions of their own privacy. "I would not care to live in a world in which others had the telepathic power to know what I was secretly thinking, or the clairvoyant power to see what I was doing," wrote Martin Gardner, one of the most implacable deniers of psychic phenomena.[19] Worse still, says Gard-

chapters.indigo.ca

ner, is psychokinesis, the influence of mind over matter, or PK for short. "PK opens up even more terrifying possibilities. I am not enthusiastic over the possibility that someone who dislikes me might have the power from a distance to cause me harm."[20] In the background lurks an archaic fear of witchcraft.

These taboos are strongest among intellectuals, and are actively upheld by many academics. Otherwise reasonable people can be surprisingly prejudiced when it comes to phenomena such as telepathy. Although people with these attitudes usually call themselves skeptics, they are not genuine skeptics. They are usually believers in a worldview that excludes psychic phenomena. Some try to deny or debunk any evidence that goes against their beliefs. The most zealous behave like vigilantes policing the frontiers of science. The Greek word *skepsis*, the root of our word, means "inquiry" or "doubt." It does not mean denial or dogmatism.

The effect of these taboos has been to inhibit research and to suppress discussion in the academic world in general, and within institutional science in particular. Consequently, although there is an enormous public interest in psychic phenomena, there is virtually no public funding for psychic research and parapsychology, and very few opportunities for doing this kind of research within universities.[21]

I believe it is more scientific to explore phenomena we do not understand than to pretend they do not exist. I also believe it is less frightening to recognize that the seventh sense is part of our biological nature, shared with many other animal species, than to treat it as weird or supernatural.

THE MIND BEYOND THE BRAIN

If the seventh sense is real, it points to a wider view of minds—a literally wider view, in which minds stretch out into the world around bodies. And not just human bodies, but the bodies of nonhuman animals, too.

In this book I suggest that minds really are stretched out; they extend through fields that link organisms to their environment and to each other. These fields can help to explain telepathy, the sense of being stared at, and other aspects of the seventh sense. But more important still, they also help to explain normal perception. Our minds are extended into the world around us, linking us to everything we see.

If I look at someone from behind, and she does not know I am there, sometimes she turns and looks straight at me. And sometimes I suddenly turn around and find someone staring at me. Most people have had experiences like this. The sense of being stared at should not occur if attention is inside the head. But if attention stretches out and links us to what we are looking at, then our looking could affect what we look at.

I suggest that through our attention, we create fields of perception that stretch out around us, connecting us to what we are looking at. Through these fields, the observer and the observed are interconnected.

Mental fields that extend beyond the brain may also help explain telepathy. In the modern world, the commonest kind of telepathy occurs in connection with telephone calls, as will be discussed in chapter 6. Many people say they sometimes know who is ringing before answering the phone.

Telepathy seems to be widespread in the animal kingdom and is part of our biological nature, though our own telepathic powers are generally poor compared with those of dogs, cats, horses, parrots, and other species of mammals and birds. I have discussed a large body of evidence for telepathy in non-human species in my book *Dogs That Know When Their Owners Are Coming Home*. Although the present work is primarily concerned with the human seventh sense, I shall also summarize the evidence for the seventh sense in animals, and look at additional evidence from my ongoing research. Only by viewing the human seventh sense in its broader biological context can we begin to understand it, and begin to see how it is related to the nature of human and animal minds.

Telepathy, like the sense of being stared at, is only paranormal if we define as "normal" the theory that the mind is confined to the brain. But if our minds reach out beyond our brains, just as they seem to, and connect with other minds, just as they seem to, then phenomena like telepathy and the sense of being stared at seem normal. They are not spooky and weird, on the margins of abnormal human psychology, but are part of our biological nature.

Of course, I am not saying that the brain is irrelevant to our understanding of the mind. It is very relevant, and recent advances in brain research have much to tell us. Our minds are centered in our bodies, and in our brains in particular. I suggest, however, that they are not *confined* to our brains, but extend beyond them. This extension occurs through the fields of the mind, or mental fields, which exist both within and beyond our brains.

The idea of fields around material bodies is already familiar. Magnetic fields are centered in magnets; gravitational fields are centered in material bodies such as Earth. The field of a magnet is not confined to the inside of the magnet, but stretches out beyond it. Earth's gravitational field stretches out far beyond its surface, holding satellites and the Moon in orbit around it.

Magnetic fields, like electrical and gravitational fields, are invisible yet capable of bringing about effects at a distance. Likewise, the fields of our minds are not confined to the insides of our skulls, but stretch out beyond them. I suggest that our mental activity depends on invisible fields that can also bring about effects at a distance. I will discuss more about these mental fields and how they work in chapter 19.

IMAGES OUTSIDE OUR HEADS

Look around you now. Are the images of what you see inside your brain? Or are they outside you — just where they seem to be?

I suggest that your mind reaches out beyond your brain and into the world around you. Vision involves a two-way process, an inward movement of light and an outward projection of images. By contrast, according to the conventional theory, there is only a one-way process: light moves in, but nothing is projected out.

The inward movement of light is familiar enough. As you look at this book, reflected light moves from the book through the electromagnetic field into your eyes. The lenses of your eyes focus the light and form upside-down images on your retinas. The light falling on your retinal cone and rod cells causes electrical changes within them, and these trigger changes in the nerves that connect the cells to the brain. Nerve impulses move up your optic nerves and into the brain, where they give rise to complex patterns of electrical and chemical activity. So far, so good. All these processes can be, and have been, studied in great detail by neurophysiologists and other experts on vision and brain activity.

Then something very mysterious happens. You consciously experience what you are seeing, the pages of this book. You also become conscious of the printed words and their meanings. From the point of view of the standard theory, there is no reason why you should be conscious at all. Brain mechanisms ought to go on just as well without consciousness. Then comes a further problem. When you see this book, you do not experience your image of it as being inside your brain, where it is supposed to be. Instead, you experience the image of the book as being located about two feet in front of you, where the book itself is. The image is outside your body.

For all its physiological sophistication, the standard theory has no explanation for your most immediate and direct experience. All your experience is supposed to be inside your brain, not where it seems to be.

The basic idea I am proposing is so simple that it is hard to grasp. Your image of this book is just where it seems to be, in front of your eyes, not behind your eyes. It is not inside your brain. Your mind is projecting it outward to where it seems to be.

The images we project outward when we see something usually coincide very well with what we are looking at. If they did not, we would not be able to walk, or ride bicycles, or drive cars without bumping into things all the time. Fortunately, illusions or hallucinations are relatively rare. Accurate connections between our perceptions and the surrounding world are of obvious advantage to us, as they are to any species. They are no doubt strongly favored by natural selection.

All of our senses, not just sight, are deeply rooted in evolutionary history. The history of how we see can be traced back not only through our human past, but through the evolutionary history of mammals, reptiles, and fish, which see as we do, in that they see images. Other, independent evolutionary histories are found in cephalopods, like octopuses, which have eyeballs, lenses, and retinas comparable to our own. The compound eyes of insects have yet another evolutionary ancestry. All these histories stretch back over hundreds of millions of years. And if human vision involves an outward projection of images, it seems likely that countless other species also project images outward in the process of vision, and have done so ever since eyes evolved.

Our minds connect us to the world around us, just as they seem to do. This connection, through our sense organs, links us directly to what we perceive. What you see is an image in your mind. But it is not inside your brain. Your brain is within the confines of your cranium. Your mind is extended in space, and stretches out into the world around you. It reaches out to touch what you see. If you look at a mountain ten miles away, your mind is stretching out ten miles. If you look at a distant star, your mind is extending over literally astronomical distances.

THE ASTONISHING HYPOTHESIS

As we have seen, vision, according to the conventional theory, is a one-way process. Light moves into the eyes, from which impulses travel up the optic nerves, initiating complex patterns of activity in the visual cortex and in other parts of the brain. Then somehow images appear and are subjectively experienced inside the brain. Our visual images are inside our brains, even though they *seem* to be in the world around us.

It is easy to forget how much this theory conflicts with our own experience, how much it leaves unexplained, and how little evidence there is for it. After all, no one has ever observed an image inside a brain. Most of us accepted the mind-within-the-brain theory before we ever had a chance to question it. We took it for granted, and it seemed to be supported by all the authority of science.

In his study of children's intellectual development, the Swiss psychologist Jean Piaget found that before about the age of ten or eleven, most of the European children he tested were like "primitive" people in that they did not know that the mind was confined to the head. They thought it extended into the world around them. But by about the age of eleven, most had assimilated what Piaget called the "correct" view: "Images and thoughts are situated in the head."[22]

Perhaps it is because no one wants to be thought stupid, childish, or primitive that this "scientifically correct" view is so rarely questioned in public by educated people. Yet it inevitably conflicts with our most immediate experience every time we look around us. It also leads to a dogmatic denial of the existence of unexplained phenomena such as telepathy.

The materialist theory violates our experience yet further by asserting that our consciousness does not actually do anything. Either it is an "epiphenomenon" of brain activity, rather like a shadow, or it is identical with brain activity. An epiphenomenon is a merely incidental result of a process, but does not influence the process itself. From this point of view, consciousness is merely an incidental accompaniment to patterns of physical and chemical activity in the cerebral cortex, with no purpose or function.

The identity theory says that mental activity is nothing but the subjective experience of brain activity. Francis Crick, a Nobel laureate and one of the founding fathers of molecular biology, has called this the Astonishing Hypothesis: " 'You,' your joys and your sorrows, your memories and your ambitions, your sense of personal identity and free will, are in fact no more than the behavior of a vast assembly of nerve cells and their associated molecules. . . . This hypothesis is so alien to the ideas of most people alive today that it can truly be called astonishing."[23]

Crick is surely right. This is indeed an astonishing claim. Even though it is the standard, orthodox view within institutional science, it goes against all our most immediate experience. It is alien to most people's ideas and to common sense. It makes nonsense of our social and legal systems, which hold that sane adults are responsible for their actions. In practice, people cannot be treated as mere automata with no choice or free will, nor do most people really think of themselves as choiceless mechanisms. All systems of political democracy are based on ideas of choice, free will, and responsibility, as are most religions. From religious, political, legal, social, and personal points of view, we are not merely the automatic activity of vast assemblies of nerve cells and their associated molecules. As Carl Sagan liked to say, "Extraordinary claims demand extraordinary evidence." Where is the extraordinary evidence for the astonishing claim that the mind is nothing but the activity of the brain?

There is very little. No one has ever seen a thought or image inside some-one else's brain, or inside their own.[24] We experience images outside ourselves, not just in our heads. We experience our bodies as occupying space. My experience of my fingers is in my fingers, not in my head. Direct experience offers no support for the extraordinary claim that all our experiences are inside our brains. Direct experience is not irrelevant to the nature of consciousness; it *is* consciousness.

All we find is evidence for some kind of relationship between mental activity and brain activity. When I decide to stand up or sit down, changes occur in my brain and in the nerve impulses transmitted to my muscles. Con-sciousness affects the brain. And the brain affects consciousness. Changes in the brain brought about through the senses, or by drugs, or through electrical stimulation or brain damage, can lead to changes in consciousness. Everyone agrees that the mind and the brain are closely interconnected. But this does not prove the mind *is* the brain.

Drivers are closely interconnected with their cars. A change in one can affect the other. But they are not identical. Likewise, pianists are closely con-nected with their pianos. The activities of their fingers are closely linked to the sounds the piano makes. But this does not mean that pianists *are* their pianos, or mere epiphenomena of them, like incidental apparitions.

For a less dualistic analogy, think of a television set. The pictures on the screen and the sounds it produces are closely connected with the pattern of electrical activity inside the receiver. But there is more to it than that. What you see and hear depends on influences moving through invisible fields from distant transmitters, picked up by the aerial. These pictures depend on what channel you are tuned to and on what program is being broadcast. The pic-ture also depends on your response. If the program does not engage your attention, you may change the channel, or stop looking, or turn the set off.

It is true that some conscious experiences are associated with particular activities in particular parts of the brains. Modern scanning techniques show how particular parts of the brain "light up" when particular mental activities are going on. But it is also true that the pictures on the screen of the television set and the sounds coming from the speakers depend on the patterns of electrical activity inside the receiver. It is also true that different parts of the electrical circuitry are involved in the production of images and sounds. But this does not prove that everything you hear and see on television originates inside the receiver, and is nothing but the activity of the receiver.

In short, the fact that the mind and the brain are related to each other does not prove they are the same. The idea that they are the same is no more than an assumption. If we follow Francis Crick in treating this assumption as a scientific hypothesis, rather than as a philosophical dogma, then it should be testable. Indeed, it should be refutable.

What might refute it? First, direct experience. We do not see things inside our brains, but all around us. But believers in the Astonishing Hypothesis are not impressed by evidence of this kind. It is by definition subjective, not objective, and they therefore feel free to dismiss it.

Then what about evidence for the seventh sense? Wouldn't the effects of attention and intention at a distance seem to contradict the Astonishing Hypothesis? They would. That is why telepathy and other aspects of the seventh sense are so controversial.

As we will see in the following chapters, there is a great deal of evidence that attention and intention can extend far beyond the brains in which they are centered.

THE EXTENDED MIND

The idea that minds or souls reach out beyond bodies is found in traditional societies all over the world, and is taken for granted in most religions. It corresponds with experience, and is part of traditional common sense. Philosophers, both ancient and modern, have also advocated it. I discuss this historical and philosophical background in chapter 13 and Appendix C.

All of us have known about the extended mind from our childhood, although we may never have formulated it in words, and have forgotten what we once took for granted. The idea of the extended mind is also implicit in our language. The words *attention* and *intention* come from the Latin root *tendere*, to stretch, as in *tense* and *tension*. Attention comes from *ad* + *tendere*, literally meaning "to stretch (the mind) toward." Intention comes from *in* + *tendere*, "to stretch (the mind) into." And extend, from *ex* + *tendere*, means to stretch out.

But the idea of the extended mind is not simply a philosophical theory. It is a scientific hypothesis that leads to testable predictions. It is already supported by a large body of evidence both from people's spontaneous experiences and from controlled experiments.

In the first three parts of this book, I explore the evidence for the existence of a seventh sense, and hence for the extended mind. Part I discusses telepathy in people and in animals; Part II explores the sense of being stared at; and Part III examines remote viewing, premonitions, and precognition. I show how the idea of the extended mind can be tested and explored scientifically.

Finally, Part IV discusses what the extended mind is, how it works, and how it helps to account for the seventh sense. I suggest that the mind stretches out through mental fields. Through these fields, animals and people can both sense things at a distance and act at a distance.

What do mental fields consist of, and how do they work? I propose that mental fields are kinds of morphic fields. These are a new kind of field, in addition to the gravitational, electrical, magnetic, and quantum matter fields already recognized by physics. The word *morphic* comes from the Greek word *morphe*, meaning "form."

As I describe in my book *The Presence of the Past*, other kinds of morphic fields include morphogenetic fields (from *morphe* + *genesis*, the coming-into-being of form) involved in the development of animals and plants, shaping the forms into which they grow. Behavioral fields organize the behavior of animals by patterning the activities of the nerve cells within their brains. Social fields link together the members of social groups and help to coordinate their activities in such a way that the society acts like a single organism, as in ant colonies, flocks of birds, schools of fish, or packs of wolves. Morphogenetic fields, behavioral fields, social fields, and mental fields are all different kinds of morphic fields. All morphic fields share common properties, and all contain an inherent memory given by a process called morphic resonance. In chapter 19, I summarize this hypothesis of morphic fields and show how it can help in the understanding of such otherwise unexplained phenomena as telepathy and the sense of being stared at.

Part 1
TELEPATHY

1 PICKING UP
THOUGHTS AND INTENTIONS

Telepathy comes from the Greek *tele*, "distant," as in telephone and television, and *pathe*, "feeling," as in empathy and sympathy.[1] It literally means "distant feeling."

Telepathy is classified by psychic researchers and parapsychologists as a kind of ESP, or extrasensory perception—a form of perception beyond the known senses. Alternatively, it can be seen as an aspect of the sixth or seventh sense.

Telepathy and other psychic phenomena contradict the assumption that the mind is confined to the brain. Therefore, from the materialist point of view, they are impossible, and dogmatic skeptics dismiss them as illusory. Nevertheless, many people claim that they themselves have had telepathic or other psychic experiences.

In one national survey in the United States, 58 percent of those questioned claimed personal experience of telepathy. In another national survey, in 1990, 75 percent said they had had at least one kind of paranormal experience, and 25 percent had had telepathic experiences.[2] In recent random household surveys in Britain and the United States, 45 percent of the respondents said they had had telepathic experiences. In a large newspaper survey in Britain, 59 percent of the respondents said they were believers in ESP.[3]

The figures vary, but they show clearly enough that many people in western Europe and the United States claim to have experienced telepathy, and most people believe in the reality of psychic phenomena.

THE TWO MAIN KINDS OF TELEPATHY

There seem to be two main kinds of telepathy, the first of which is exemplified by thought transference, and usually occurs between people who are nearby, each aware of the other's presence, and already interacting with each other. Although thought transference is most common between people who know each other well, it can also occur with others with whom they are currently interacting. I discuss this kind of telepathy in this chapter and the next.

In the second kind of telepathy, which I will discuss in chapters 3 through 6, one person picks up a call, intention, need, or distress signal of another at a distance. This results in thinking about the other person, or seeing an image of that person, or hearing his or her voice, or experiencing a feeling or impression. In this kind of telepathy, someone's attention is attracted, just as it is by hearing one's own name called, or by seeing an alarm signal, or by hearing the telephone ring. A connection or channel of communication is opened up. This kind of telepathy typically occurs between people who are closely bonded.[4]

The same principles apply to telepathy between people and animals.

PETS PICKING UP THEIR OWNERS' INTENTIONS

Many people who keep pets have noticed that their animals respond to their thoughts and intentions. In surveys of randomly chosen pet owners in Britain and the United States, on average 48 percent of those with dogs, and 33 percent of those with cats, thought that their animals were sometimes telepathic with them.[5]

Many cats, for instance, seem to know when their owners are planning to take them to the vet, and disappear. For example:

I was always most careful to give my cat no clues when we were due to visit the vet, but from the moment I got up in the morning she viewed me with suspicion. She was very wary of me (not her usual loving self) and as the time to leave home approached she would try to escape. ◇ JEAN SEGAL, LONDON

There are hundreds of similar stories on my database. And in a survey I described in *Dogs That Know When Their Owners Are Coming Home*, my research associates and I asked all the veterinary clinics listed in the North London Yellow Pages whether they ever found that some cat owners canceled appointments because the cat had disappeared. Sixty-four out of sixty-five clinics had cancellations of this kind quite frequently. The one exception was a clinic that had abandoned an appointment system for cats, because cancellations had been so frequent. People simply had to show up with their cats, and so the problem of missed appointments had been solved.

One of the commonest ways in which dogs seem to pick up their owners' intentions is by anticipating walks. No one thinks this is strange if the walk is at a routine time, or if the dog sees its person picking up the leash, or putting on outdoor clothes. But some dogs anticipate walks at nonroutine times, even if they are in a different room.

Tammy, our Maltese, always knew when we were going for a walk even though she was sleeping in the garage when we made our decision and would come racing in to the bedroom all excited, jumping up and down. We could never figure out how she knew, as it wasn't a regular thing at a regular time or day. We wouldn't have changed our shoes or clothes but she always seemed to know. ◇ GILLIAN COLEMAN, QUEENSLAND, AUSTRALIA

There are more than a hundred such stories on my database. Of course, the fact that many people think their dogs are reading their minds, rather than picking up subtle sensory cues, does not prove that they really are doing so. But I take seriously the opinions of people who know their animals well and have had years of experience in observing them. Nevertheless, the most convincing evidence is that which comes from experimental tests specifically designed to eliminate explanations in terms of sensory clues and routine.

In *Dogs That Know When Their Owners Are Coming Home*, I describe an experiment in which dogs were shut up in an outbuilding and videotaped continuously. At randomly chosen times, their owner, who was inside her house, silently thought about taking them for walks for five minutes before actually doing so. In most of these tests, during this five-minute period the dogs went to the door and sat or stood in a semicircle around it, some with their tails wagging. They remained in this state of obvious anticipation until their owner came to take them for their walk. They did not wait by the door in this way at any other times.

Many dogs and cats seem to know when their owners are intending to go out and leave them behind, especially when they are planning to go away on a journey or holiday. This is one of the commonest ways in which domestic animals seem to pick up people's intentions. In random household surveys in

Britain and the United States, an average of 67 percent of dog owners and 37 percent of cat owners said their animals knew when they were going out before they showed any physical sign of doing so.[6] Some parrots do this, too. Robbi, an African Grey belonging to Michael Fallarino, a New York writer and herbalist, often announces that she knows when Michael is about to leave the room or go out of the house by saying, "Bye-bye, see ya later! Have a good day," then whistling plaintively.

> She even knows ahead of time when I am going to leave the house when she cannot see me; for example, when I am upstairs and she is downstairs. Once after working at my upstairs desk for hours I stopped and simply thought, "It's time to run some errands." No sooner had I thought this than she (downstairs) began uttering her plaintive cries of protest. I'm utterly convinced that her knowing is intuitive and beyond any form of sensory perception.

Some animals seem to read their owners' minds by knowing when they are going to be fed. No one thinks this strange if it happens at a routine time, or if the animal sees, hears, or smells the person getting out the food. The most striking examples concern unscheduled treats or snacks. And many blind people with guide dogs have noticed that their animals seem to pick up their intentions in a seemingly uncanny way. Sometimes dogs even respond to thoughts the owners are not planning to put into action immediately.

Among dog trainers, telepathic abilities are often taken for granted. "No one in their senses disputes them," said the well-known British dog trainer Barbara Woodhouse.

> You should always bear in mind that the dog picks up your thoughts by an acute telepathic sense, and it is useless to be thinking one thing and saying another; you cannot fool a dog. If you wish to talk to your dog you must do so with your mind and willpower, as well as your voice. . . . A dog's mind is so quick at picking up thoughts that, as you think them, they enter the dog's mind simultaneously.[7]

HORSES AND RIDERS

Some riders experience a close connection with their horses and find that the horse seems to respond to their thoughts.

It is like being one. What you think immediately gets picked up by the horse. It is almost as if the horse becomes part of yourself. So if you think of something the horse will do it. ◇ PAUL HUNTING, HAMPSHIRE

I am certain that Chip and I have a telepathic link. When I ride Chip I only have to think of something and he responds. I have tested out thinking things and making sure that I am not giving the slightest move. For example, I think we'll go down to the end of the field and canter back, he immediately starts going to the end of the field and then canters back to the same point where I had the thought. ◇ ANDREA OAKES, CHESHIRE

But precisely because the horse and the rider are in such close physical contact, it is difficult to disentangle mental influences from unconscious body signals, such as small changes in muscular tension.[8] It remains an open question how such impressions of experienced riders can be explained. Unfortunately, experiments that rule out slight movements would be practically impossible while the horse is being ridden. As in so many cases of apparent thought transference, telepathic influences may often work together with communication through the recognized senses. In real life it is hard to tease them apart. That is why it is necessary to carry out formal experiments to find out whether telepathy really happens. Here is one example.

EXPERIMENTS WITH A LANGUAGE-USING PARROT

After *Dogs That Know When Their Owners Are Coming Home* was published in 1999, I received more than a thousand additional accounts of perceptive animals. Some of the most surprising of these concerned parrots. I heard over and over again about parrots that responded to their people's moods, feelings, and intentions by making appropriate comments. In some cases this ability seemed to be telepathic.

Some parrots seem to pick up their owner's intentions to go out, as described above. Some seem to know when their owners are coming home, and announce their arrival beforehand (see chapter 5). Others seem to know when particular people are calling on the telephone before the phone has been answered, announcing the caller by name (chapter 6). They ignore calls from insurance salesmen and other strangers.

The fact that parrots can use language meaningfully has been established beyond reasonable doubt by Dr. Irene Pepperberg, now at the Massachusetts Institute of Technology. She has spent twenty years training her African Grey parrot, Alex, who now has a vocabulary of around 200 words. Through meticulous experiments, she has found that Alex is capable of abstraction, and can grasp such concepts as "present" and "absent" and use the words for colors appropriately, whatever the shape of the colored object.

Before Pepperberg's research, within institutional science it was generally assumed that parrots were mere mimics, "parroting" words with no understanding. Most scientific studies of human-to-animal communication were carried out with apes, using sign language. Pepperberg has succeeded in showing that parrots, although literally bird-brained, rival apes in the ability to use thoughts and concepts, and of course have the huge advantage of being able to speak. She has summarized her research with Alex and other parrots in a monumental book titled *The Alex Studies: Cognitive and Communicative Abilities of Grey Parrots.*[9]

Pepperberg's pioneering work has inspired a number of other people to do research on the meaningful use of language by parrots. One of this new generation of researchers is Aimée Morgana, an artist who lives in New York City. Her African Grey, N'kisi (pronounced "in-key-see"), had a vocabulary of around 700 words by January 2002, even though he was only four years old. Aimée taught N'kisi to use language as if he were a human child. He has learned the contextual meanings of words, and is able to use his understanding of language to make relevant comments. He speaks in sentences, of which Aimée Morgana has now recorded more than 7,000 different ones.

Although Aimée's primary focus is on the meaningful use of language, she soon noticed that N'kisi often seemed to say things that referred to her thoughts and intentions. He did the same with her husband, Hana. After reading about my research on telepathy in animals, in January 2000 she contacted me by e-mail through my website, summarizing some of her observations.

What she told me was off the end of the scale of anything I had heard of before. Although many companion animals like dogs and cats seem to pick up their owners' thoughts and intentions, N'kisi's enormous vocabulary meant that he was capable of many different specific responses. Aimée wrote, "N'kisi regularly comments when we are thinking about eating, going out, or taking a shower, even if we are sitting quietly in another room and he sees no body language and hears no audio cues. At these times he will say, for example, 'You want some yummy,' 'You gotta go out, see ya later,' or 'You wanna take a shower.' "

In January 2000, Aimée began keeping a detailed log of seemingly telepathic incidents, and has continued to do so. At the time of this writing, two years later, there were 630 such incidents on record. Here are a few examples:

"I was thinking of calling Rob, and picked up the phone to do so, and N'kisi said, 'Hi, Rob,' as I had the phone in my hand and was moving toward the Rolodex to look up his number.

"We were watching the end credits of a Jackie Chan movie, edited to a musical soundtrack. There was an image of [Chan] lying on his back on a girder way up on a tall skyscraper. It was scary due to the height, and N'kisi said, 'Don't fall down.' Then the movie cut to a commercial with a musical soundtrack, and as an image of a car appeared, N'kisi said, "There's my car." (N'kisi's cage was at the other end of the room, and behind the TV. He could not see the screen, and there were no sources of reflection.)

"I read the phrase 'The blacker the berry, the sweeter the juice.' He said, 'That's called black' at the same instant.

"I was in a room on a different floor, but I could hear him. I was looking at a deck of cards with individual pictures, and stopped at an image of a purple car. I was thinking it was an amazing shade of purple. Upstairs he said at that instant, 'Oh wow, look at the pretty purple.' "

Of all the various incidents, the ones I found most remarkable occurred when N'kisi appeared to have responded to dreams. For example: "I was dreaming that I was working with the audio tape deck. N'kisi, sleeping by my head, said out loud, 'You gotta push the button,' as I was doing exactly that in my dream. His speech woke me up." (N'kisi usually sleeps by Aimée's bed.) On another occasion, "I was on the couch napping, and I dreamed I was in the bathroom holding a brown dropper medicine bottle. Kisi woke me up by saying, 'See, that's a bottle.' "

It soon became clear to me that if what Aimée told me was true, this would be the most remarkable case of human-to-animal telepathy that I had ever come across.

In April 2000, I visited Aimée and N'kisi in Manhattan, and was immediately impressed by their remarkably close relationship, and the way in which N'kisi used language meaningfully. Of course, after hearing about so many remarkable incidents, I was interested in seeing for myself if N'kisi really could pick up Aimée's thoughts, and we decided to do a simple test then and there, replicating a situation in which N'kisi had appeared to demonstrate telepathy spontaneously. Aimée and I went to another room, where N'kisi could not see what we were doing, and I watched as Aimée looked at several different images. When she picked up a picture that showed a girl, and concentrated on it for a moment, we heard N'kisi say with unmistakable clarity, "That's a

Figure 1.1 *Aimée Morgana and her African Grey parrot, N'kisi.*

girl." Since we were in a different room, and had not spoken about the image, there was no possibility of clues being transmitted through any of the normal sensory channels.

Clearly it was important to try to test this apparent telepathic communication in controlled experiments. Yet the whole point of Aimée and N'kisi's interactions was that they took place in the context of their life together. It would have been out of the question to transplant Aimée and N'kisi to a clinical laboratory environment and expect the parrot to behave normally.

Together we developed a procedure that would be rigorously scientific and would also work fairly naturally in N'kisi's familiar environment. Aimée had noticed that N'kisi seemed to respond to moments of discovery. As she put it, N'kisi seemed to "surf the leading edge" of her consciousness. Therefore, methods of testing for telepathy that used repetitive images, like card-guessing tests, were not likely to work. In order to preserve an element of surprise, we designed an experiment in which Aimée would open sealed envelopes one at a time. Each envelope contained a different photograph. These photographs were selected by a third party, who sealed each of them in a thick, opaque envelope. He then numbered them in a random order. Neither Aimée nor I knew what pictures he had selected, or what order they were in.

In each trial, Aimée opened an envelope in numerical order and looked at the picture for two minutes. Two synchronized cameras recorded Aimée and N'kisi, who were in separate rooms on different floors of the house, with the doors closed. Of course they could not see each other, nor could N'kisi hear Aimée. In any case, Aimée said nothing, as confirmed by the audio track recorded by her camera.

Subsequently, three separate people independently transcribed the tapes of N'kisi's comments. They did not know what pictures Aimée had been looking at. The transcripts were in very good agreement with one another. They were then compared with the images Aimée was looking at in the synchronized videotapes.

In many cases, N'kisi's comments corresponded to the images Aimée was seeing. For example, when she was looking at a picture of flowers, he said, "That's a pic of flowers." When she was looking at picture of someone talking on a cell phone, he said, "Whatcha doin' on the phone?" and made a series of noises like a phone being dialed. When she was looking at a picture of two people on a beach wearing skimpy swimming gear, he said, "Look at my pretty naked body."

N'kisi was right far more often than he would have been if he had simply been talking at random. In more technical terms, we considered it a "hit" when he said a predefined key word that corresponded to an image representing that key word. He scored 23 hits out of a total of 71 trials. The statistical analysis of the results showed that his "hits" were far more frequent than would have been expected by chance, and his "errors" far fewer. The results were highly significant statistically. (For technical and statistical details of this experiment, see Appendix B.)

In brief, these tests confirmed what Aimée had already noticed on hundreds of occasions, namely, that N'kisi picked up her thoughts far more often than would be expected by chance.

N'kisi has continued to respond to Aimée's thoughts and intentions in a seemingly telepathic manner. He has also continued to enlarge his enormous vocabulary.[10]

KNOWING WHAT SOMEONE IS ABOUT TO SAY

Just as domesticated animals sometimes seem to "read the minds" of those they are close to, so do people.

Many people have found that others seem to pick up their thoughts or intentions, even when they are close enough to communicate verbally or visually. A common way in which this happens is for one person to say what the other is thinking. These experiences occur most commonly between husbands and wives, between parents and children, and between lovers. They can also occur between friends and between colleagues, and in other situations where people are closely attuned.

Here are some typical statements: "On many occasions my husband would start thinking about something and I'd put it into words, or he'd express my thoughts." "Frequently I'd be thinking about something and my husband would start talking about it, and vice versa."

The same can happen with friends. For example, a woman in Massachusetts who took part in one of my surveys recalled: "My best friend in middle and high school and I developed the habit of speaking the exact same words in unison, without preparation ahead of time." Some lovers have this experience in a particularly striking way, like this young woman in California: "My boyfriend and I are very in tune with each other. We communicate without words; all we do is look at each other and we catch the gist of what the other is thinking. Sometimes we complete each other's sentences, and sometimes one will do something that the other was just thinking about doing."

My surveys have shown that these experiences are common. Probably many readers of this book have experienced similar incidents themselves.

But is this really telepathy? When people know each other well, perhaps they just tend to have the same thoughts at the same time in response to things they've just seen or heard, without being aware of the external trigger for their thoughts. Or maybe they have a "mental concordance" through their shared experience, which results in similarities of thought that seem telepathic when in fact they are not.

No clear answers to these questions are possible at present. Such incidents would not make convincing evidence for telepathy if there were no independent evidence when people were beyond the range of sensory communication. But given that such evidence exists, as discussed in the following chapters, it is an open question what is going on when one person says what another is thinking.

In any case, "mental concordance" and similar responses to external stimuli may not be alternatives to telepathy, but just different ways of talking about it. When people are "in tune" with each other, there may be a resonance between their thoughts that is indeed telepathic. Indeed, telepathy may play a major but unsuspected role in normal communication.

PICKING UP TUNES

As well as people saying what others are thinking, it is also quite common for people to sing or hum a tune that their companion has in mind. For example: "On several occasions I've thought of a tune or song while my husband has been in another room. How amazed I've been to hear him whistle or hum the same tune!" (Elizabeth Monaghan, Egremont, Cumbria, England). Here is another example: "With my wife I have experienced having a tune in my mind or humming a tune, and having her exclaim that the same tune was in her mind" (Alfred Bryant, London).

Such experiences seem to happen most frequently between husbands and wives, and between parents and children, even with very young children.

One day, when my daughter was about two and a half, we were driving in the car and I saw some colorful flowers in a window box. This prompted me to think of the rhyme "Ring Around the Rosy." I am sure I did not sing or hum the tune aloud. A second later my daughter started to sing the very same rhyme. I asked her, "What made you think of that song, honey?" She replied, "You did, Mommy." "Did I sing it or was I thinking it?" "You were thinking it, Mommy." ✧
NADINE HAYDUCHOK, WESTHAMPTON, NEW JERSEY

Again, in instances such as these, it is by no means clear that telepathy is at work, since both people may have thought of the same tune because of the same external stimulus. But as we have just seen, these arguments are ambiguous. The tendency to react to the same stimulus in the same way could be a result of telepathy rather than an alternative to it.

In some cases, however, such explanations do not apply. Here is a Victorian example, recorded by Sir Lepel Griffin:

Colonel Lyttleton Annesely, Commanding Officer of the 11th Hussars, was staying in my house some time ago, and one afternoon, having nothing to do, we wandered into a large unoccupied room, given up to lumber and packing cases. Colonel A was at one end of this long room reading, to the best of my recollection, while I opened a box, long forgotten, to see what it contained. I took out a number of papers and old music, which I was turning over in my hand, when I came across a song in which I, years before, had been accustomed to take part, "Dal tuo stellato soglio." . . . As I looked at this old song, Colonel A, who'd been paying no attention whatever to my proceedings, began to hum "Dal tuo stellato soglio." In much astonishment I asked him why he was singing that particular aria. He did not know. He did not remember having sung it before; indeed I have not ever heard Colonel A sing, though he is exceedingly fond of music. I told him that I was holding the very song in my hand. He was as much astonished as I had been, and had no knowledge that I had any music in my hand at all.[11]

This phenomenon may be related to an experience that several people have described to me, namely, thinking of a tune and then turning on the radio and hearing it playing. This could be coincidence, and, of course, popular tunes are frequently played. It could also be a form of precognition, anticipating what will be heard when the radio is turned on. But it could also be telepathic, with an influence from the many people who are already listening to the tune on the radio, possibly including some to whom the person is closely bonded.[12]

PICKING UP THOUGHTS

Many married couples and partners say they can often tell what the other is thinking, and even answer questions that have not yet been spoken. The same is true of many parents and children.[13] Again, this could be a matter of "mental concordance." But sometimes it happens at a distance and can serve a useful function. For example, Jeanne Salzman of Sonoma, California, says that "with my husband I can almost always telepathically send him a message of what to bring home from the market."

My own experiences of picking up thoughts have mainly occurred with my children. Some of these could have been due to common interests or external stimuli, but others seem too improbable to be explained in that way. For example, one day I was traveling in a cab with my two sons through the Little Venice area of London when I looked out of the window and saw a plaque on a building saying that Alan Turing had lived there. I thought of mentioning it to the children. But then I realized that they would probably never have heard of Alan Turing, so I said nothing. To my surprise, about a minute later my elder son, then aged twelve, said, "Daddy, what's the name of the man who helped crack the Enigma code at Bletchley Park during the

Second World War?" "Alan Turing," I replied. I asked him why he had asked, and he said that he had seen a TV program about a week before on the codebreakers at Bletchley Park, and had been discussing it with his friends at school. But only at that moment had he thought of asking me about it. When I saw the plaque, he was playing with his brother in the back of the car, and was most unlikely to have noticed it himself. Also, he has no recollection of seeing it. I myself had passed that house many times before without noticing it.

Sometimes this kind of communication is frequent. For example, according to Teri Woods, of Washington State, "When my children were between four and eight, I didn't have to say things to them; they would answer me or come in from playing before I called them, or asked things of them. I did this with my own mother a lot until I was in high school. I could 'see' what she was thinking. If she'd bought me something from the store, I would see her carrying it before she came in."

Claire Boyd, who lives in England, has such experiences quite often with her nine-year-old daughter: "If I'm thinking about something, she will often answer out loud my question. She frequently will bring up a subject I am thinking about. On one occasion we both had the same dream at the same time, involving a passenger plane landing in the back garden!"

Dr. Berthold Schwarz has carried out by far the most detailed study of parent-child telepathy, together with his wife and two children. Schwarz, a psychiatrist, and his wife, Ardis, who lived in New Jersey, kept detailed notes on all possible telepathic episodes between themselves and their children, Lisa and Eric, from birth onward. By the time the children were fourteen and twelve respectively, they had recorded a total of 1,520 such incidents. In his book *Parent-Child Telepathy: A Study of the Telepathy of Everyday Life*,[14] Schwartz gives details of all 524 incidents up to the children's ages of nine and seven. Here are two examples, the first when Eric was three, the second when Lisa was eight, both involving their father:

After breakfast, Eric and I remained in the kitchen. Eric was at his blackboard with his back to me. I felt cold, but suppressed the desire to briskly massage my arms and back. Eric suddenly turned around and vigorously rubbed his arms and back.[15]

I was comfortably seated in an easy chair looking at a topographic map, with Lisa standing beside me. I noted on the map for the first time Stickle Pond. . . . [It] was quite intriguing. I thought, "Hmm, a natural lake, must be beautiful." Hardly had these fleeting thoughts occurred to me when Lisa burst out, "Stickle Pond, is that a natural pond or not?" There are at least seventy-five ponds, of which more than thirty-five appear on the U.S. Government topographical map. Lisa, who was behind me, could not see my eyes.[16]

Schwarz was, of course, aware of the difficulty of knowing whether incidents such as these really were telepathic, or involved subtle cues, or similar associative memories, or were mere chance coincidences. In fact he thought many of them lay on a spectrum between "uncontaminated telepathic events at one end of the band and the usual means of sensory perception at the other."[17]

Indeed, in most cases of possible telepathy between people who are physically and emotionally close to each other, it is difficult to distinguish between ordinary thought processes and thought transference by telepathy. Usually this is taken to weaken the case for telepathy, on the assumption that similarities of thought between people who know each other well require no special explanation. Yet we know very little about the transmission of thoughts, and it could well be that telepathy plays a major role in perfectly ordinary communication, even where its importance is quite unsuspected.

Words can, of course, be used to convey thoughts, and they do so best if the thoughts are essentially verbal. But when someone is trying to communicate an image, words are often inadequate. We do not have a direct means of communication for transmitting images from mind to mind, except perhaps through pointing to similar things, or using pictures or drawings. Some people have found that they can communicate more effectively by somehow transferring images directly. For example, a young man in London told me that he had quite often tried unsuccessfully to describe something in words to a friend. "Then I think in a picture. The person says, 'Ah!' and understands completely." A woman in Buenos Aires told me that several times when someone was talking to her about a film, but had forgotten its name, she received "an image of the film, and could put a name to it." Perhaps this happens frequently. Rather than trying to explain many instances of apparent telepathy in terms of ordinary communication, it might be more appropriate to explain many cases of ordinary communication in terms of telepathy!

If the telepathic transfer of images occurs in human communication, then it may well do so in communication between nonhuman animals. We generally assume that the barking of dogs or the calls of birds are themselves the means of communication. But what if they are mainly a way of attracting attention, and of opening a channel through which telepathic communications then occur? The sounds may serve to tune in the hearer to images in the mind of the animal that is making the sounds. There could be much more to animal and human communication than meets the eye or ear.

The importance of this principle becomes particularly apparent in relation to the transfer of mathematical ideas.

TELEPATHIC MATHEMATICIANS OR PLATONIC MATHEMATICIANS?

Many mathematicians think visually and have what Francis Galton, Charles Darwin's cousin, called "mathematical landscapes" in their minds.[18] They "see" mathematical processes and understand ideas through a kind of visual intuition. For those who do not have such landscapes, mathematics is often difficult to understand or follow. Mathematical symbols fail to convey anything of the mental imagery of visually gifted mathematicians. A musical analogy would be the attempt to communicate a piece of music to someone who was deaf, simply through a sheet of printed music. Some people who are exceptionally musical can read written music and "hear" it with an "inner ear." But for most people this is not possible, and for them musical notation does not communicate the music itself.

For mathematicians who think visually, the role of mathematical symbols is an aid to transmitting thoughts, but the thoughts themselves seem to be accessed in a way that goes far beyond visual or verbal signs.

Many leading mathematicians and mathematical physicists are Platonists, and believe that the world of mathematics inhabits an eternal realm of Ideas that go far beyond any individual human mind. (In the Platonic tradition, these transcendent Ideas, with a capital I, are distinguished from merely human ideas, which are more limited and fallible.) For the founding fathers of modern science, such as Copernicus, Kepler, Galileo, Descartes, and Newton, mathematical forms were Ideas in the mind of a mathematical God, and many mathematicians still persist in this way of thinking. Even those who no longer believe in God still think of mathematical Ideas as existing in a transcendent mental realm beyond the normal world of time and space.

Perhaps one reason mathematicians are so attached to this way of thinking arises from the way that mathematical ideas are grasped. The communication of these concepts seems to go beyond the capacities of ordinary human language. Roger Penrose, a well-known Oxford mathematician, has given a particularly vivid description of this process:

Almost all my mathematical thinking is done visually and in terms of non-verbal concepts. . . . Often there are simply not the words available to express the concepts that are required. . . . A common experience, when some colleague would try to explain some piece of mathematics to me, would be that I should listen attentively, but almost totally uncomprehending of the logical connections between one set of words and the next. However, some guessed image would form in my mind as to the ideas he was trying to convey—formed entirely on my own terms and seemingly with very little connection with the mental images that had been the basis of my colleague's own understanding—and I would reply. Rather to my astonishment, my own remarks would usually be accepted as appropriate, and the conversation would proceed to and fro in this way.[19]

Penrose goes on to describe how an image could be communicated in spite of the inadequacy of the words, and says it was "a puzzle to me how communication is possible at all according to this strange procedure." In trying to explain it, he did not consider the possibility of telepathy. Rather, he stayed within the conventional framework of science, which offers only two options. One is the materialist approach of trying to explain everything in terms of physical communication through the known senses and physical processes in the brain. The other is Platonism, the other side of the coin of scientific materialism. Although in mechanistic science, all physical processes are supposed to occur mechanistically through causes of material and energetic nature, the whole of nature is assumed to be governed by mathematical laws that transcend time and space, more like Platonic Ideas than things. This is the notion that Penrose adopts to account for the communication of mathematical ideas:

I imagine that whenever the mind perceives a mathematical idea, it makes contact with Plato's world of mathematical concepts. (Recall that according to the Platonic viewpoint, mathematical ideas have an existence of their own, and inhabit an ideal Platonic world that is accessible via the intellect only.) When one "sees" a mathematical truth, one's consciousness breaks through into this world of ideas, and makes direct contact with it. . . . [T]his "seeing" is the essence of mathematical understanding. When mathematicians communicate, this is made possible by each one having a *direct route to truth*, the consciousness of each being in a position to perceive mathematical truths directly, through this process of seeing (indeed, often this act of perception is accompanied by words like "Oh, I see!"). Since each can make contact with Plato's world directly, they can more readily communicate with each other than one might have expected.

Perhaps many mathematicians share Penrose's view, though few would want to defend this rather mystical position in public. But for most nonmathematicians this is a very surprising theory. Penrose has adopted it because he has taken the trouble to think about how mathematical communication takes place, and has found the conventional explanations in terms of symbolic and verbal communications inadequate. But Platonism is not the only alternative. Telepathy is another possibility. Rather than mathematics being a unique and special case, it can be seen as one aspect of the more general problem of communication of nonverbal images, and it may be that telepathic thought transference plays a major role in mathematical and nonmathematical communication alike.

TELEPATHY BETWEEN THERAPISTS AND CLIENTS

Quite often, psychotherapists and their clients form close emotional bonds, particularly when they meet frequently and intensively, as in Freudian psychoanalysis. These bonds are often referred to as *transference* and *countertransference*. Transference is defined by Freudians as "the displacement of feelings and attitudes applicable toward other persons (usually one's parents, but also siblings, a spouse, etc.) onto the analyst."[20] Countertransference involves the analyst's projections onto the client, or, more generally, an emotional involvement with the client.

This situation provides not only good conditions for telepathic thought transference, but also good conditions for it to be noticed, since therapists and clients often pay more attention to thoughts, dreams, and emotions than do people in more casual relationships. Telepathy may well occur quite commonly in this situation, but therapists, who are subject to the same taboos as other intellectuals, are often reluctant to acknowledge or admit it.

Sigmund Freud himself was interested in psychic phenomena, and was a member of the Society for Psychical Research. In papers circulated only to his inner circle of followers, he provided several striking instances of thought transference that could not easily be explained by any other means.[21] But at the same time he was anxious to establish the scientific credibility of psycho-analysis. He was only too aware of the taboo against psychic phenomena within institutional science and among intellectuals in general. And he was worried that any public endorsement of "occult phenomena" would have a serious negative effect not only for psychoanalysis but also for mechanistic science as a whole:

There is little doubt that if attention is directed to occult phenomena the outcome will very soon be that the occurrence of a number of them will be confirmed; and it will probably be a long time before an acceptable theory covering these new facts can be arrived at. But the eagerly attentive onlookers will not wait so long. At the very first con-firmation the occultists will proclaim the triumph of their views. . . . They will be hailed as liberators from the burden of intellectual bondage, they will be joyfully acclaimed by all the credulity lying ready to hand since the infancy of the human race and the childhood of the individual. There may follow a fearful collapse of critical thought, of determinist standards and of mechanistic science.[22]

Given such dire fears and the fervent aspirations of Freud and many of his followers to scientific respectability, it is not surprising that they preferred not to mention thought transference in public, and even tried to avoid thinking about it. Nevertheless, analysts mention possible telepathic experiences in dozens of publications.[23] But things are now changing.[24] Since the 1990s a growing number of psychoanalysts have been ready to admit, at least to each other, that telepathy really seems to happen, and they are open to thinking more about it, and even to exploring it with their patients.

A leader in this movement is Elizabeth Lloyd Mayer of Berkeley, Califor-nia, who has published and discussed a number of vignettes from her own experience. In one of these a patient was describing his uncle's new girlfriend, remarking how charming, graceful, and bright she was. Mayer comments, "I noticed an image of ripe, fresh peaches flitting across my mind. . . . My patient then mentioned to me that the girlfriend had four younger sisters. . . . She was from Georgia, my patient went on to explain. At that point, my patient added that the girlfriend's father had been so proud of his five daughters that he'd always called them his five Georgia peaches."[25]

Mayer does not regard her vignettes as particularly unusual, but as "rather ordinary clinical experiences," and acknowledges that they are not in them-selves sufficient to demonstrate the existence of telepathy. But she thinks they "beg for explanation" and feels that they need to be seen in the larger context of research into psychic phenomena.[26]

Some of the most striking vignettes to be published by a Freudian analyst are contained in a paper titled "Telepathic dreams?" by Robert Stoller, who taught at the University of California, Los Angeles. This paper, written in 1973 and published posthumously in 2000, contains many instances of apparent telepathy between Stoller and his patients. For example, a male patient told him of a dream from the previous night: "A man explained to me a new invention. It was a new way to build and market homes. What he showed me was a big, central concrete pole. On this could be hung individual rooms that one could buy at the store, in any number and in any style." The patient had few or no associations with the dream, and the details were different from any in his previous dreams, and never recurred. But the dream was closely related to an actual event in Stoller's own life: "The previous day, a friend had visited from San Francisco and told me of a conversation with an architect who was trying to market a new idea: one would build a central concrete core upon which could be hung prefabricated rooms of any size and number."

In spite of the fact that such seemingly telepathic episodes happened repeatedly, Stoller was very uncomfortable with them: "Besides finding the whole subject alien to my scientific beliefs, I have also hesitated to write this up because of not knowing if something right or wrong is going on in me. If, someday, it is found that such experiences reflect an ordinary enough function of human psychology, it will seem quaint that I was uneasy."[27]

Psychotherapists of the Jungian school have generally been less fearful about telepathy and other psychic phenomena, following Carl Jung himself.[28] For example, Jung published an account of a dream of his own that occurred when he was sleeping in a hotel. At that time he was worried about a particular patient who he thought might be suffering from depression. He awoke with a start at about 2:00 A.M., feeling that someone had come into the room and put on the light, but no one was there. "I tried to recall exactly what had happened, and it occurred to me that I had been awakened by a feeling of dull pain, as though something had struck my forehead and then the back of my skull. The following day I received a telegram saying my patient had committed suicide. He had shot himself. Later, I learned that the bullet had come to rest in the back wall of his skull."[29]

As telepathy comes to be seen as "an ordinary enough function of human psychology," probably more psychotherapists will feel free to record and investigate the telepathy between themselves and their clients. Research by psychotherapists could shed much light on the workings of telepathy, and, in particular, help to illuminate the relationship between telepathic thought transference and the communication of thoughts by normal sensory means.

TELEPATHY IN GUESSING GAMES

When they are playing guessing games, some people seem to react telepathically to thoughts in others' minds. Katie Campbell, who lives in Minnesota, summarized her experience as follows: "My mom and I are very connected — she can read me, and I think I'm better at sending out signals. If we're playing guessing games and I ask her a question (or someone else asks a question) and I know the answer, then she will be able to answer it. But if I don't know the answer she is less likely to get the correct answer. Also, if I deliberately think of the wrong answer, then she usually can't answer the question either."

One game in which this seems to occur quite commonly is Trivial Pursuit, a board game in which players have to answer general-knowledge questions printed on cards.

Trivial telepathy is my secret weapon when playing against my husband, though the very idea of it only makes him cross! I have noticed that if he hesitates before answering, and I look at the answer, he always gets the right answer. If, however, he hesitates and I think of all sorts of other answers, he fails to find the right answer. But despite these devious tactics he still beats me. Sadly I can't read his much more well-equipped mind! ◇ EIRWEN DALLAS, ALFORD, LINCOLNSHIRE

One of the games that seems to produce the most striking examples of telepathy is Pictionary, in which two teams compete against each other to discover the word, person, or object drawn by a member of their team. The two people doing the drawing, one on each team, each see the same card with a word or object on it. Each has to draw it, while the other members of their team have to guess what it is. In one family containing identical twins, when the twins were on the same team they almost always won, because "one could guess what the other was drawing almost as soon as he started."

Of course, in situations such as these it is impossible to be sure that telepathy really is at work, as opposed to subtle cues, body language, similar associative memories, and so on; but again, these are not really alternatives. Telepathy may well work together with these other means of communication. To sort out the relative contribution of telepathy, special experiments would be necessary.[30]

TEAMS AND OTHER GROUPS

Michael Murphy, the founder of the Esalen Institute in California and a pioneering researcher on human potential,[31] has argued convincingly that sports
are one of the commonest ways in the modern world in which people experience altered states of consciousness, and even mystical experiences. In his
book *The Psychic Side of Sports* (coauthored with Rhea White) he argues that
in team games, "it may be possible that in addition to 'luck' or coincidence
and picking up on subliminal sensory clues, there is an element of extrasensory perception, or ESP."[32]

For example, Walt Frazier, the former basketball star of the New York
Knicks, said of his ability to anticipate Bill Bradley's passes: "Sometimes he has
passed the ball before I've taken the first step. It's like telepathy. We look each
other in the eye and he knows the mischief I'm thinking about." But as Murphy and White commented, "[As] long as they look each other in the eye, sensory clues cannot be ruled out, even if they were neither deliberately given nor
consciously received. It *is* like telepathy, but we can't say that it actually is."[33]

Jayne Torvill and Chris Dean became the most famous ice dancers of
their generation, and were well known for their extraordinary rapport. Their
two bodies "moved as one." As Dean himself commented, "We are telepathic
on the ice. There's simply no other way to explain it."[34] Again, sensory clues
must have played a large part in their rapport, but there could well have been
more to it, just as Dean said.

The famous Brazilian soccer player Pelé went further: "Intuitively, at any
instant, he seemed to know the position of all the other players on the field,
and to see just what each man was going to do next."[35] No doubt this is partly a
matter of alertness and concentration, and also of good peripheral vision, but
more may be involved as well. As we have already seen, telepathy and the normal senses are not mutually exclusive, but may often work together.

Bonding between members of a group is of enormous importance in the
armed forces, and military training programs are usually designed to inculcate
team spirit. Joint combat experience does this even more.

Teams are social groups in which the individual members work together
like a single organism to achieve common goals — including the scoring of lit-
eral goals. The bonds between them can serve as channels for telepathic
communication, as in other social groups. But this is not to say that the individuals are always bonded effectively, and that all teams function well as
organisms. Even within a well-established team whose members have had
much shared experience, this state may come and go. It comes as a conta-

gious confidence spreads through the team; it goes when the members are tired or demoralized. Michael Novak, another perceptive writer about sports, has expressed it as follows:

> When a collection of individuals first jells as a team, truly begins to react as a five-headed or eleven-headed unit rather than as an aggregate of five or eleven individuals, you can almost hear the click: a new kind of reality comes into existence at a new level of human development. . . . For those who have participated in a team that has known the click of communality, the experience is unforgettable, like that of having attained, for a while at least, a higher level of existence.[36]

Similar experiences occur in many other kinds of group activities, including the playing of music. For example, Catherine Baker, a professional bassoonist, says that musicians playing together use nonverbal communication all the time, sometimes including telepathic links between players, as well as between players and conductors. "It does seem that when a chamber group orchestra gets this psychic 'link' in a performance, the audience genuinely knows that it has been part of something special (as do the players!)." Other musicians who play in folk music and jazz groups have told me much the same. So have actors who work in theater groups, especially when they are improvising together. And so do people who dance together.

Probably in traditional societies such linkages most commonly occur through singing and dancing, and may well play a vital part in group activities such as hunting. But little is known about the possible role of telepathy in social groups. Obviously normal sensory communication, including body language and subtle cues, plays a major role, as do memory and implicit expectation. Once again, telepathy would not be an alternative to other forms of communication and to memory, but would work with them. For example, it is one thing to see or hear what another member of the group is doing; it is another to interpret this information and respond appropriately. Telepathy in human groups is part of our evolutionary heritage and is rooted in the way that animal groups are coordinated through social fields, as will be discussed in chapters 7 and 18.

2

THOUGHT TRANSFERENCE

IN THE LABORATORY

Most research on telepathy has concentrated on the first kind of telepathy, thought transference, as opposed to the second kind involving the attraction of attention from a distance, as in telepathic telephone calls.

Thought-transference experiments typically involve guessing what cards another person is looking at, or guessing what she is drawing, seeing, or thinking.

By contrast, there has been little experimental research on the detection of calls or intentions at a distance. My own experiments with dogs that know when their owners are coming home provide one example, and my experiments on telephone telepathy (see chapter 6) provide another.

Some of the earliest and most fascinating experiments on telepathy explored the connections between hypnotists and their subjects.

TELEPATHY BETWEEN HYPNOTISTS AND THEIR SUBJECTS

In the early nineteenth century, hypnosis became both fashionable and controversial, although at that stage it was not called hypnosis but "animal magnetism" or "mesmerism," after Franz Anton Mesmer (1734–1815), who popularized the phenomenon in France. By the 1840s a number of surgeons were using hypnotism to induce anesthesia in their patients, with remarkable success.[1] Some of these doctors noticed that when their patients were hypnotized they developed a

41

"rapport" or "sympathy" with them, as a consequence of which there was a "community of sensation."[2] The subject seemed able to smell, taste, or feel what the hypnotist was smelling, tasting, or feeling.

Some of the earliest experiments concerned the transfer of tastes and smells. One of the pioneers was a Scottish doctor, James Esdaile, a government surgeon in Calcutta, India. In the 1840s he carried out more than 3,000 operations using hypnotism to anesthetize his patients, and had remarkable success not only in anesthesia, but also in the success of his surgery.

In one of Esdaile's experiments, the subject was a young Indian man on whom he had carried out a successful operation under hypnotic anesthesia. When the patient came to pay his respects after his recovery, Esdaile asked him to take part in a test. He put the man into a trance, and blindfolded him. Then he asked his assistant to put various substances, including salt, gentian, brandy, and a lime into his (Esdaile's) mouth, in any order. The first thing he put in was a slice of half-rotten lime. "Having chewed it, I asked, 'Do you taste anything?' 'Yes, I taste a nasty old lime': and he made a wry face in correspondence. He was equally correct with all the other substances."[3]

Similar experiments were carried out by other doctors, with similar results, and also by several clergymen. One of them, the Reverend Andrew Gilmour, of Greenock, Scotland, mesmerized one of his servants every evening until he could put her into a trance in less than a minute. "She is able to tell what I taste, such as soda, salt, sugar, milk, water, etc., though not in the same room with me. When my foot is pricked, or my hair pulled, or any part of my person pinched, she feels it, and describes it, unerringly."[4] The biologist Alfred Russel Wallace, who, together with Charles Darwin, put forward the theory of evolution by natural selection, tried out experiments of this kind when as a young man he was a schoolmaster in Leicester, mesmerizing some of the boys, and even the headmaster himself.[5] He found he seemed able to "merge his mind" with that of a hypnotized subject. And when he put some sugar or salt in his own mouth, or when somebody pinched him or pricked his skin, the schoolboy seemed to react in sympathy at a distance.[6]

Some subjects also picked up the hypnotist's private thoughts. A clergyman's daughter in Bury St. Edmunds, Suffolk, England, found that she could alleviate the chronic ailments of one of the parishioners through mesmerism, and called on her regularly to do so. After a while she noticed that this woman somehow knew what she was thinking. One day, for example, her patient started speaking about a young man in India. Unknown to her patient, she had just gotten engaged, in secret, to a young man who was joining the Indian Civil Service.

No one in the town knew anything about it then . . . yet I had no sooner magnetized my patient than she began talking as if all the facts were perfectly familiar to her. "India is a long way off, isn't it, dear?" In fact for months she could talk of little else when mesmerized and knew my husband's name, age, and appearance, but was as ignorant as the rest of the world in her natural state.[7]

Although in most cases the hypnotists and their subjects were in the same room, some tried to see if their influence could also be exerted at a distance. One such was Captain Battersby, of Enniskillen, Ireland, who regularly hypnotized his mother-in-law to relieve pain. He found that she could taste what he was eating or drinking, feel sensations, such as a hair tickling his forehead, and answer questions in foreign languages, as long as he himself knew the answer. Sometimes he mesmerized her from his own house, half a mile away.

On such occasions she was able to tell what I had been doing and would generally go to sleep. The sensation she described was that of a hand pressed on her forehead. Though able thus to send her to sleep, I was unable to keep her so, as she would waken again the moment my attention wavered. The means used were stretching out my hand towards her house, and bringing my will sharply to bear.[8]

One of the first lines of inquiry taken up by the newly formed Society for Psychical Research in the 1880s was to see if the experiments by mesmerists could be reproduced without the need for hypnosis. Working with sensitive subjects in a normal state of consciousness, they found that "community of sensation" could indeed occur with respect to tastes and smells. They also explored the telepathic transmission of pain. In one noteworthy experiment, carried out in Liverpool, the subject was seated and blindfolded, while the experimenters sat behind her. Each of them was equipped with a pin. In response to silent signals, all the psychic researchers simultaneously inflicted pain upon themselves in the same way; for example, by pricking their left wrists or right knees, or by biting the ends of their tongues. "In 10 out of the 20 cases, the percipient localised the pain with great precision; in 6 the localisation was nearly exact."[9] These discoveries helped to convince them that community of sensation could happen in normal states of consciousness, and not just in a state of hypnotic rapport.

The other source of inspiration for experimental research on telepathy was a parlor game, popular in Britain and America in the 1870s, called the "willing game."

FROM GAMES TO SCIENTIFIC TESTS

In the willing game a member of the group left the room and closed the door. The rest then chose a simple action that he was to perform, or hid an object that he was to find. The person was then called back, and one or more of the "willers" took his hand or touched his shoulders lightly. Often the person quickly performed the willed action or found the hidden object. I recently tried this game myself with my family and friends, and was surprised how well it worked.

But such games by themselves, however impressive to participants, could not prove the existence of telepathy. As Edmund Gurney put it in 1886, "Even when the utmost care is taken to maintain the light contact with absolute neutrality, it is impossible to lay down the limits of any given subject's sensitivity to such slight tactile and muscular hints."[10]

Sir William Barrett, an eminent physicist, led the way in doing experiments to find out what was really going on in willing games. He found that "willing" could still work even when there was no physical contact between the willers and the subject, and even when the willers were sitting still. But the possibility remained that they could still be picking up clues from people in the room, or that someone in the room would deliberately cheat by giving signals, so he carried out tests to rule out such possibilities. This is how he described one particular set of experiments. The subject, a vicar's daughter, was sent out of the room and the door was closed. She had been told to bring the object that the people in the room willed, and not enter the room again until she had found it.

I thought of some object in the house, fixed upon at random; writing the name down I showed it to the family present, the strictest silence being preserved throughout. We then all silently thought of the name of the thing selected. . . . After a very short interval the child would enter the sitting room, generally with the object selected. No one was allowed to leave the sitting room after the object had been fixed upon: no communication with the child was conceivable. . . . In this way I wrote down, among other things, a hair brush; it was brought: an orange; it was brought: a wine-glass; it was brought: an apple; it was brought: a toasting fork; failed on the first attempt, a pair of tongs being brought, but on a second trial it was brought.[11]

The next step in this experimental research involved asking the group to concentrate on a particular playing card, using written instructions. The subject was then asked to name this card. The procedure was repeated over and over again. The subjects were right far more often than would have been expected by chance. In the early 1880s, Barrett and other psychic researchers were already using statistical analysis to find out whether the results they obtained could be attributed to coincidence, long before statistical tests became standard practice in other branches of science.

From this modified version of the willing game, it was a short step to the realization that experiments with cards provided a simple way in which any pair of people could carry out tests for telepathy. Even if the subjects were not particularly sensitive, with a sufficiently large number of trials, small deviations from the results expected by chance could be statistically significant. By 1886, more than 17,000 trials of this kind had been done in which the subject guessed the suit of each card, either hearts, spades, clubs, or diamonds. There was one chance in four of guessing correctly by chance; hence, the success rate that would be expected without thought transference would be 25 percent. In fact the average success rate was 26.5 percent. Although not a very impressive figure, with such a large number of trials, this result was very significantly above the chance level according to statistical tests.[12] Telepathy experiments with cards became one of the favorite procedures for psychic researchers and parapsychologists, and are discussed in more detail below.

Another kind of experiment grew out of the willing game: tests involving the use of pictures or diagrams. One person drew a simple picture or diagram, out of sight of the subject, usually in another room, and continued to concentrate on this image. Meanwhile, the subject tried to draw it. There was quite often a remarkable correspondence. This became a favorite kind of test among amateur psychic researchers, and was often strikingly successful.[13] The American writer Upton Sinclair carried out one of the most impressive series of trials with his wife. Lying in semidarkness with her eyes closed, she was frequently able to pick up images corresponding to drawings that Sinclair or other family members were concentrating on in another room, or even in a house forty miles away, and she then drew them. Many examples are given in Sinclair's book *Mental Radio*, published in 1930.[14] But although the successful matches are very clear, the trouble with this type of experiment is that it is difficult to quantify or to analyze statistically.

EXPERIMENTS WITH CARDS

Between the 1880s and 1939, dozens of investigators all around the world published 186 papers describing a total of 4 million trials involving card guessing. Most of these gave positive, statistically significant results, which is to say that more guesses were correct than would be expected by chance. When the results of all of them were combined together (using a statistical procedure called meta-analysis), the odds against these positive results arising by chance were more than 10^{21} (10 with 21 zeros after it) to one.[15]

A standard objection raised by skeptics against such impressive arrays of data is that researchers may tend to publish only their positive findings, while nonsignificant results may remain buried in laboratory files. No doubt the tendency to publish positive results and ignore the rest is true of most areas of science. But, in my experience, psychic researchers are far more aware of this problem than scientists in more conventional fields of research. Also, the papers published in this field include those by skeptics, who have an interest in drawing attention to negative results. Nevertheless, this so-called file-drawer effect needs to be taken seriously, and it is possible to calculate how many unpublished unsuccessful studies there would need to be to bring down the astronomical odds in favor of positive psi effects to chance levels. It turns out that file drawers would need to contain 626,000 unpublished reports on card-guessing tests. Put another way, there would have to be 3,300 unpublished unsuccessful reports for every published report. This is obviously highly implausible.

The positive results from the card-guessing tests implied that there had been a transfer of information that could not be explained in terms of the normal senses.[16] But although the pioneers of psychic research focused mainly on telepathy, it soon became clear that telepathy alone could not explain the data. In some experiments the cards were placed in sealed envelopes, and subjects scored above chance in guessing what they were, with no one looking at the cards. In other experiments the experimenter merely picked up one card after another from the top of a shuffled pack without turning it over and looking at its face, and still the subjects' scores were, on average, above chance levels.

The best-known experiments with cards were the ESP card tests carried out at Duke University, in North Carolina, by Professor Joseph Banks Rhine and his colleagues, from the late 1920s to 1965. Rhine introduced the term *parapsychology* to distinguish his approach from that of previous psychic research, which was, as he put it, conducted "on a broad and tolerant approach to unusual mental phenomena."[17] By contrast, he wanted to make parapsychology into a regular laboratory science, with "strictly experimental methods," carried out by professional scientists in an academic setting.

Rather than using ordinary playing cards, Rhine and his colleagues invented a special pack, called Zener cards, with five different kinds of card, each with a different symbol: square, circle, wavy lines, star, and triangle. Each pack contained twenty-five cards, five of each kind. The packs were shuffled by hand or machine, and subjects had to guess the sequence of cards in the pack, either when an experimenter looked at them one by one, or when no one looked at them. By chance, the subjects would be right about one time in five; thus on average their scores would be 20 percent correct if they were just guessing at random. Rhine and his colleagues took elaborate precautions to prevent cheating or the transmission of subtle sensory clues; for example, by having experimenters and subjects in different buildings. They proved that the shuffling of the packs really did produce random sequences, and successfully replied to a barrage of technical criticisms put forward by skeptics. Moreover, other investigators replicated their positive results.

But although the Duke card-guessing experiments gave significant results, the effects were small. On average, the percentage of correct guesses was around 21 percent, only just above the chance level. Because there were hundreds of thousands of trials, however, this difference was highly significant statistically.[18]

Rhine and his colleagues tried to find unusually sensitive subjects, and did indeed find some who were spectacularly successful for a while.[19] But even the best subjects' scores fell off as the experiments were repeated. This was called the "decline effect," and the most probable explanation was boredom. Guessing random sequences of meaningless cards is tedious to start with, and after hundreds of trials it becomes very boring indeed, for both the experimenters and the subjects.

In spite of the fact that these experiments were so artificial, so boring, and so unrelated to the way that psychic phenomena occur in real life, they succeeded in proving that *something* was going on. Moreover, Rhine and his colleagues showed that different kinds of ESP were closely related.

If people could guess above chance levels a sequence of cards that someone was looking at, then this could be called telepathy. When no one was looking at the cards, this would be clairvoyance. And when people could guess which cards the experimenter would look at later in time,[20] this would be precognition. But then these distinctions began to break down. For example, in the clairvoyance tests, in which people guessed cards that no one was looking at, could the effect in fact be due to precognitive telepathy? Perhaps the subject picked up what would be in the experimenter's mind when he later examined the sequence of cards to see if the guesses were correct or not.

The researchers at Duke tried to tease apart these different kinds of ESP; for example, by trying to separate telepathy from clairvoyance. In the standard telepathy tests, a "sender" looked at the cards. But could the "receiver" be picking up what card he was looking at by clairvoyance, without the need for a transmission from the sender's mind? In this situation it was not possible to differentiate between these different kinds of ESP. So instead of such "general ESP" tests, they tried doing "pure telepathy" experiments, where the sender merely *thought* of cards in random sequences, rather than looking at actual cards. (To make sure the sequences were in fact random, the senders were given lists of random numbers, which they had to translate into sequences of cards using a code that was also kept in their minds and not written down.) Only after the subjects had written down their guesses did the senders record the symbol they had been thinking of. These experiments worked. As Rhine put it, "The result of all the comparisons was that there was no essential difference in the scoring rate, whether the pure telepathy type of test or the old-style procedure of undifferentiated ESP was used."[21]

Another important discovery in this card-guessing research was that some people's scores were *below* chance levels. These negative scores implied that ESP was at work, but that the subjects were somehow denying or negating its effects. The phenomenon was called "psi-missing" as opposed to "psi-hitting." Rhine first noticed it when one of his star subjects was working unwillingly, under stress. He also found that another subject could obtain significantly negative results on request: "He *never* goes below chance unless we ask him to. When we do ask him to go below chance and deliberately miss the cards, he can do so, sometimes scoring zero."[22] Another parapsychologist, Gertrude Schmeidler, working in New York, found that psi-missing was related to people's beliefs about the possibility of ESP. Before asking them to do standard ESP card-guessing tests, she asked her subjects whether they believed in ESP. She found over and over again that skeptics ("goats") scored negatively, at levels significantly below chance, while the others (whom she nicknamed "sheep") tended to score positively.[23]

Rhine was working in an era when the dominant fashion in university psychology laboratories was behaviorism, an extreme form of materialism, which dismissed consciousness as irrelevant, at best a mere epiphenomenon of physical processes in the brain, like a shadow. The business of psychology, according to this approach, was simply to study glandular secretions or measurable muscular actions. Ironically, Rhine's own approach was influenced by this arid academic fashion. Probably he would have had no chance of achieving scientific credibility otherwise. Nevertheless, he regarded the positive findings of parapsychology as evidence against the materialist theory of the mind. "The psi researches have established the occurrence of a mode of reaction of a living being that is both personal and nonphysical. The result is to provide psychology with its first clear deed to a distinctively *mental* domain of reality."[24] Nowadays the fortunes of behaviorism have waned, and most academic psychologists are no longer so hostile to talking about consciousness and the reality of personal experience. But most are still materialists, and locate all mental activity inside the head.

The sharp dualism between the physical and the mental that Rhine thought he had established scientifically is blurred by a field theory of the extended mind. Telepathy and clairvoyance provide evidence that minds are extended in space. Precognition shows that they are also extended in time. We will return to a discussion of clairvoyance and precognition in Part III.

DREAM TELEPATHY

In the 1960s a new generation of researchers became disenchanted with the boring, repetitive card-guessing tests that had dominated parapsychology since the 1920s. They wanted to do experiments that were more interesting and closer to real life. Many spontaneous psychic phenomena take place during dreams.[25] In order to study dream telepathy experimentally, from 1966 to 1972 a group of researchers at the Maimonides Medical Center in Brooklyn, New York, led by the psychiatrist Montague Ullman and the psychologist Stanley Krippner, carried out a remarkable series of experiments with sleeping subjects. The subject first met the sender, who was one of the researchers, and then spent the night in a soundproofed dream lab. The researchers attached electrodes to her head to measure brain waves (EEG) and eye movements. She was then left alone, and went to sleep. Meanwhile her brain waves and eye movements were continuously monitored. When her eyes began to move rapidly, indicating that she was probably starting to dream, the sender opened a sealed packet containing a picture that had been selected at random from a pool of eight possible targets. He concentrated on the target picture with the aim of influencing the subject's dream telepathically. In some trials the sender and receiver were up to forty-five miles apart.

Toward the end of each dreaming period, the subject was awakened by means of a buzzer and asked to describe any dream she might have experienced. Her comments were tape-recorded and later transcribed. Then a panel of independent judges compared the transcript with all eight pictures in the pool of possible targets, and ranked them. They were not told which picture was actually used in the test.

In some cases the correspondence was very striking. For example, one subject dreamed about going to Madison Square Garden in New York and buying tickets for a boxing match. The target picture was a painting of a boxing match. Sometimes the connection was more symbolic, as when a subject dreamed of a dead rat in a cigar box. The picture was of a dead gangster in a coffin.[26]

From all 450 dream telepathy trials reported in scientific journals about this series of experiments, the overall hit rate was 63 percent, compared with the 50 percent expected by chance.[27] The statistically calculated odds against this result being due to chance are 75 million to one.[28]

THE TELEPATHIC TRANSMISSION OF IMAGES

In the mid-1970s, several young parapsychologists thought of a new kind of telepathy experiment, with the subjects in a state of mild sensory deprivation. Previous research in parapsychology had shown that receivers tended to perform best when relaxed, and the dream telepathy research had shown that telepathy could occur in dreams. The new procedure was designed to make subjects more receptive to telepathic influences in the waking state. These experiments proved successful, and versions of them are still being carried out today.

A subject was taken to a special room, asked to sit in a comfortable reclining chair, and put on headphones playing continuous white noise, like the static between radio stations. Translucent hemispheres, made from halved Ping-Pong balls, were placed over her eyes, and a red light was shone on her face. This soft, unpatterned sound and light created a state of sensory deprivation called the *ganzfeld*, from a German word meaning "whole field." In addition, in some tests a ten-minute relaxation tape was played through the headphones before the test began.

Meanwhile, the sender was in another room, and was given a photograph in a sealed envelope randomly selected from a pool of four possible images. Or else he was shown a short video selected from a pool of four possible videos. When both sender and receiver were shut up in their soundproofed chambers, the sender tried to "send" the image to the subject. Meanwhile, the subject spoke about her impressions, and what she said was recorded.

At the end of the fifteen- or thirty-minute test session, the subject was shown all four images in the pool from which the target had been selected. These images were shown in a random order. She was asked to rank them, putting first the one that corresponded most closely to her experiences during the test period. If the actual target image was indeed ranked first, this counted as a hit. Since there was a one-in-four chance of picking the right target by chance, the expected hit rate if she was guessing at random was 25 percent.

In addition, the transcripts of the subjects' impressions were compared with the images. Some showed a remarkable correspondence. In one test, for example, the target was a video clip of a collapsing suspension bridge, which first swayed back and forth and bent up and down. The subject's impression: "Some kind of ladder-like structure but it seems to be almost blowing in the wind. Almost like a ladder-like bridge over some kind of chasm that's waving in the wind. This is not vertical, this is horizontal. . . . A bridge, a drawbridge over something."[29]

One of the leaders in this field of research was Charles Honorton, who had earlier been involved in the Maimonides dream telepathy project. In 1982 he collected together the results of twenty-eight separate ganzfeld studies conducted in several different laboratories, and found that the overall hit rate was 35 percent, very significantly higher than the chance rate of 25 percent. The odds against this result being due to chance were more than 10 billion to one.

Skeptics of course challenged his analysis, and one of them, Ray Hyman, analyzed the data himself. To his surprise, he came up with the same result. Unable to dismiss the actual data, Hyman and other skeptics tried to find faults in the way the experiments had been designed and executed. Hyman and Honorton then worked together to produce a joint statement on improved procedures that could eliminate such possible flaws. They set out mutually agreed-upon criteria, so that neither side could move the goalposts.[30]

In response to these new guidelines, parapsychologists in several different labs carried out new, computer-controlled versions of the ganzfeld experiment, called the autoganzfeld. By 1989, ten different autoganzfeld studies had been completed. The overall hit rate of 32 percent was highly significant statistically.

Skeptics then tried to find new flaws, arguing, for example, that clues might still have passed from the sender through air-conditioning ducts, false ceilings, and so on. They tried to fault the researchers because they did not know all the architectural details of the buildings in which they carried out their tests.[31] Others argued that the videos that were shown repeatedly during tests might have become scratched, and subjects might have picked these out because of their lower quality, rather than because they had identified them telepathically.

Once again the ganzfeld researchers tightened up their procedures; for example, by using duplicate copies of videotapes to show to the subjects. Overall they still continued to obtain positive, statistically significant results.[32]

Not all individual experiments did so, however.[33] For example, in one test there were no senders, but only images displayed to an empty room. If the receivers had been able to pick these up, they would have had to do so by clairvoyance rather than telepathy. In fact their scores were no better than chance.[34] But under the usual procedures for testing telepathy, combining the results from dozens of new, ever more rigorous ganzfeld tests, the hit rates were still very significantly above chance levels.[35] In a review published in 2001, the ten most recent studies had an overall hit rate of 37 percent.[36]

This long series of ganzfeld studies has not only provided yet more evidence for the existence of telepathy, but has shed light on factors affecting its occurrence. For example, Marilyn Schlitz and Charles Honorton explored the possibility that artistically gifted people do better as receivers than others. They tested students from the Juilliard School in New York, a renowned conservatory for the performing arts. Sure enough, the students had an exceptionally high success rate, on average scoring 50 percent, twice the chance expectation of 25 percent.[37] Kathy Dalton, working at Edinburgh University, confirmed this finding with both musicians and artists.[38] She also found that when sender and receiver knew each other well—for example, when they were best friends, or mother and daughter—the scores were often far higher than those obtained when senders and receivers were strangers. Other researchers also found that sender-receiver pairs who were emotionally close, especially parent-child and sibling pairs, scored exceptionally high hit rates.[39]

Ganzfeld telepathy experiments have thus been performed under ever more rigorous conditions over twenty-five years. Over and over again, well-informed skeptics have done their best to fault them and have failed.[40] The experiments have proved repeatable; they have been independently replicated in several different countries; and they are continuing to give impressive results. They provide some of the strongest evidence to date for telepathy under laboratory conditions.

THE UNCONSCIOUS DETECTION
OF MENTAL INFLUENCES

In the late 1970s, William Braud and his colleagues at the Mind Science Foundation, in San Antonio, Texas, began a new type of experiment, which proved remarkably successful. As in ganzfeld experiments, the sender and receiver were in separate soundproof rooms and could not communicate by any of the known senses. But instead of the sender trying to convey images, he or she simply focused attention on the receiver during randomly chosen periods, thirty seconds long. In the control periods, called "calm" as opposed to "active" periods, the sender did not attempt to influence the receiver. The periods of concentration and the control periods took place in a random sequence, and between each trial there was a rest period.

Meanwhile, the receiver tried to keep his or her mind in an "open, flexible" state, and tried to avoid getting involved with any particular train of thought. The receiver's emotional state was monitored continuously by means of electrodes placed on the fingers, measuring changes in skin resistance, as in a lie detector. Changes in emotional arousal lead to changes in sweating, which in turn affect skin resistance. The receiver does not have to make any guesses or try to pick up any images. The purpose of the experiment was to find out whether there was a significant difference in emotional arousal when the sender was concentrating on the receiver. There was. The overall result from fifteen separate studies in San Antonio was highly significant statistically. These experiments were replicated in nineteen studies at different laboratories in the United States and Europe, and again the overall result was positive and highly significant statistically.[41]

In some experiments the receivers not only had their skin resistance monitored, but also were asked to guess when the senders were concentrating on them and when they were not. Their guesses were no better than chance. But their skin resistance was significantly different in the active sessions compared with the calm sessions, showing that they were detecting the senders' intentions unconsciously, without knowing it.[42]

Parapsychologists usually refer to these kinds of effects as "direct mental interactions with living systems," or DMILS. The responses of the receivers demonstrate a kind of unconscious telepathy. They make it particularly clear that this aspect of the seventh sense does not depend on the conscious mind; rather, it is based on emotional arousal, physiologically measurable. These experiments remind us that telepathy literally means "distant feeling."

TELEPATHY BETWEEN A MOTHER AND HER MENTALLY RETARDED SON

Although the dream telepathy, ganzfeld, and DMILS experiments represent a big improvement on the card-guessing tests, they are still very artificial, bearing little relationship to telepathy in everyday life. But they do show that these phenomena can be investigated rigorously in the laboratory, and that the overall results are positive and highly significant statistically, with enormous odds against chance. But while academic parapsychologists have generally confined their attention to laboratory experiments, psychic research has continued to espouse "a broad and tolerant approach," to use J. B. Rhine's phrase, starting from real-life cases.

A good example of open-minded scientific investigation concerns a mother and her mentally retarded son who lived in Cambridge, England. Not a well-known case, it is one of many that have been published in research journals, but it is of particular significance for me because it is the first such report I ever read.

When I was doing research in the Department of Biochemistry at Cambridge University, I used to enjoy talking with Sir Rudolph Peters, a former professor of biochemistry at Oxford, who had retired to Cambridge and worked in our lab, still doing experiments. He was charming, his eyes sparkled, and he had more curiosity about the world than most people half his age. One day we were talking in the laboratory tea room and the subject of telepathy came up. I dismissed it with the knee-jerk skepticism I had absorbed as part of my scientific education. To my surprise, he told me that he had actually investigated a case of apparent telepathy, and concluded there was something to it. He gave me a copy of his paper, summarizing the tests he and two colleagues had carried out together. He also lent me tape recordings of the experiments so that I could study the details for myself.

This case concerned a mother and her son with complex needs. The boy was born with impaired vision, was partially paralyzed, and was also mentally retarded. When an ophthalmologist tested him at regular intervals, starting when the boy was five, he was surprised to find that the boy did much better in standard eye tests than his very limited vision would have allowed: "I was amazed when trying to estimate his visual acuity by his astonishing guesswork when asked to identify letters, etc. It gradually dawned on me that this guesswork was peculiarly interesting; and I came to the conclusion that he must be working through his mother." The boy could read the letters only when his mother was looking at them. This discovery raised the possibility that they were somehow communicating telepathically.[43]

Peters and his colleagues did some preliminary experiments at the family's home. The mother and son were separated by a screen, so no visual clues were possible, and in any case the boy was almost blind. The mother was shown a series of written numbers or words of one syllable, and in many cases the boy guessed correctly what they were.

The next experiments were carried out over the telephone and were tape-recorded. The boy was nineteen years old at the time. The mother was taken to a laboratory in Babraham, six miles from Cambridge, while the boy remained at home. The experimenters prepared cards on which numbers or letters were written, and these were piled up, facedown, in a random sequence. One of the researchers turned up the first card and showed it to the mother. The boy, six miles away, then guessed what it was. The mother responded to his guess by saying "right" or "no." Then he guessed the next card, and so on. Each test lasted only a few seconds.

Out of 58 tests with numbers, the boy guessed 20 correctly the first time (34.5 percent), and 19 correctly on the second attempt (32.7 percent). The numbers 1 through 10 were used, hence there was a 1-in-10 chance of guessing correctly by chance (10 percent). The boy's actual result was far above chance, and was highly significant statistically, with odds against chance of 50 million to 1.[44]

In the tests with letters there were 45 trials, and the boy guessed right the first time in 17 (37.8 percent) and the second time in 12 (26.7 percent). Here the probability of guessing correctly by chance was only 1 in 26 (because there are 26 letters in the alphabet), and the odds against this result being due to chance are greater than 10^{16} (10 with 16 zeros after it) to 1.[45]

Peters and his colleagues carried out further tests over the telephone, with similar results. In a total of 479 trials with numbers, the boy was right 32 percent of the time on his first guess, with astronomical odds against chance of 10^{27} to 1. In a total of 163 tests with numbers, on his first guess he was again right 32 percent of the time; the odds were even more astronomical, 10^{75} to 1.

The telepathic communication between this mother and her son was vastly superior to anything observed by parapsychologists in standard laboratory experiments. In most of their tests, the senders and receivers hardly knew each other, and the telepathic communication between them served no biological or emotional needs, other than a desire to do well in scientific tests. By contrast, this mother and son were very close emotionally, and their communication served very practical needs on a day-to-day basis. As Peters remarked, "In every respect the mother was emotionally involved in trying to help her backward son."[46]

Of course, many parents are emotionally involved in helping their children. The telepathy between this Cambridge woman and her son may differ only in degree from that between more ordinary parents and children. Perhaps many parents influence their children telepathically, as well as communicating by facial expressions, body language, words, and other recognized means. At the same time they may be entirely unaware of this telepathic connection. We will return to a discussion of these ideas in chapter 7.

3

TELEPATHIC CALLS

Before the invention of the telegraph and telephone, telepathic calls were the only way in which people could instantly alert others at a distance to their needs, or summon them from afar. Such telepathic communications probably served an important role in pretechnological societies, and may also be of great significance in many animal species. In chapter 7 we will return to a discussion of the evolution of telepathy.

In one way, telepathic calls resemble the sense of being stared at, in that one person is focusing attention on another. But the sense of being stared at is primarily spatial, while telepathic calls are not. A look involves focusing attention on a particular person in a particular place. But calls do not generally depend on knowing where the person is located. Ordinary vocal calls are, of course, sounds, and therefore we can respond to them from any direction. Our sense of hearing gives us all-around awareness, and all-around vigilance if need be. And we all instinctively respond when we hear our name called, whatever direction it comes from. A call opens a channel of attention.

Telepathic calls share the quality of ordinary vocal calls, in that they seem to be detectable from any direction. However, although they are sometimes experienced as sounds, this is not necessarily the case. Sometimes they enter consciousness as a visual image, and sometimes as a feeling or an impression. In most cases people who pick up telepathic calls know whom they are from.

The frequency of telepathic calls has probably increased in recent decades as a result of the widespread use of telephones, which permit us to call other people in a nontelepathic way no matter how far away. Most people do not intend to call the other person telepathically as well, but the very act of calling someone by phone involves focusing intention on that person. Telepathic connections often seem to occur just before telephone calls, as a kind of by-product. We will return to this subject in chapter 6.

The clearest examples of calls that do not involve telephones occurred before most people had telephones in their homes. Luckily, psychic researchers built up large collections of case studies of telepathy before telephones were widespread, starting in the late nineteenth century, and there are many well-authenticated examples of people seemingly reacting to calls or needs at a distance. The most impressive are those in which people actually acted upon their intuitions. Here is a typical example, taken from the 1893 *Proceedings of the Society for Psychical Research*, and attested by several independent witnesses:

A Mrs. Hadselle had just boarded a train to go to Williamstown, New Jersey, when something quite unexpected happened.

> I sprang to my feet with the force of an inward command, "Change your ticket and go to Elizabeth [New Jersey]. *Change your ticket and go to Elizabeth.* Change your ticket" . . . I did go, and in a moment more was on my way to Elizabeth, though I had not before even thought of such a thing. . . . [O]n reaching my friend's house, she threw her arms around me and sobbed out: "Oh, I have wanted you so." Then she led me to a room where an only and beloved sister lay in life's last battle. In an hour it was ended. My poor grief-stricken friend declared then — declares now — that my sudden change of purpose was a direct answer to her repeated though unspoken demand for my presence.[1]

One of the most extensive databases, containing thousands of cases of telepathy and other psychic phenomena, was built up at the Parapsychology Laboratory at Duke University, in North Carolina, starting in the 1930s. In her analysis of these cases, Louisa Rhine found many examples in which one person deliberately called another. In some the call was made vocally.

For example, a girl in Ohio was baby-sitting one night in an upstairs apartment. Everything seemed peaceful. She had dozed off. Suddenly she awoke to hear a drunk stumbling and cursing up the stairs toward the door. Sitting upright and putting both hands to her mouth, she called in a whisper, "Mother, oh Mother." But then she realized that the drunk was not heading for her apartment, but for the one next door. Soon after, she heard her mother, who lived three blocks away, at the bottom of the stairs calling her.

She went down to let her in, and her mother asked what was wrong. When the girl explained, her mother said she had been sitting in her rocking chair dozing, but awoke to "see" her daughter before her, sitting upright and calling "Mother, oh Mother," with her hands to her mouth.[2]

This telepathic call did not involve a great distance, but some such calls seem to work over thousands of miles. In another case published by Louisa Rhine, a girl in Los Angeles one night heard her mother call her as if from the next room. She turned and answered "Yes" before she had time to think. But then she realized that her mother was 3,000 miles away. A few days later she received a letter from her mother saying that that night "I was so lonesome for you that I stood in the doorway of your room and called to you."[3]

Some calls do not involve anything said aloud, but only silent thoughts, as in the following episode described by the British psychic researcher Rosalind Heywood. She and her husband, Colonel Frank Heywood, were on holiday. He had gone out to practice golf on a grassy area by some sand dunes. Meanwhile, Rosalind was lying on her bed, enjoying a chance to relax. After about half an hour,

I began to fuss. "Frank has put his foot in a rabbit hole. He may have sprained his ankle. I ought to go and look for him." I must make it clear that the impression was only of putting his foot in a hole. The ankle-spraining was my deduction from it. I got up, very restless, not knowing what to do. . . . Finally, I compromised between my imagination and a bit of me which didn't want to go, by deciding that if he was not in by dinner time I would go. In fact he came in quite happily as usual for dinner. I said first, "I've been fussing, I thought you'd put your foot in a rabbit hole." He laughed and replied, "I did put my foot in a rabbit hole. And I sent you a message to tell you so." I asked, "What do you mean by that?" "Oh," he said, "just that I thought of you as I fell." I suspect that the answer here is that as he fell, being an old man, he was frightened of hurting himself and automatically wanted me to come to his help.[4]

Sometimes people do not have any image or idea of what is wrong; they say they just have the feeling that a particular person needs them. And sometimes, like Mrs. Hadselle on the train to Williamstown, they just know they are needed in a particular place.

Psychic researchers have documented hundreds of cases in which people acted on such telepathic calls, even when they had no clear idea why they were doing so. I, too, have collected dozens of reports from people who have experienced being called telepathically, most of them of types similar to those already published. But sometimes the person hears the call without knowing why it is being made, and may not even realize that it is subjective, and not a real call that others can also hear. This was the case with Dr. William Grierson when he was boy growing up in England.

My mother used to be ill a great deal. One time when she was sick in bed I went off on my bicycle to visit relatives forty miles away. When I got back, the house was dark and I could not find my mother. Alarmed, I went from room to room and out in the garden calling for her. She had got up and, though sick, had ridden her bicycle to the church, a couple of miles away, for Evensong. On her return, she reproached me for embarrassing her by making such a fool of myself calling for her outside the church. She repeated, word for word, my worried calls for her. "Fortunately, everyone was very polite and pretended not to hear you."

Some of the commonest examples of telepathic responses to calls involve mothers and young children. The physiological and emotional links between mother and baby built up in the womb, and continuing through nursing, often seem to establish psychic bonds that persist as the child grows up.

In some families the ability of the mother to respond to a child's calls and needs at a distance is taken as a matter of course. For example, Lisa Shendge, of London, who was frequently ill as a child, told me:

I had an "arrangement" to "call" my mother, and wherever she was, she would come home. For instance, one time my mother was at the theater. It was a first night or something, and she turned to her husband and said she had to come home. At about the same time I turned to my grandmother at home and said, "Don't worry, she is on her way home now." This was something that I totally took for granted.

Sometimes mothers not only feel that something is wrong, but also visualize some of the details. This was the case with Mrs. Joicey Hurth, of Cedarburg, Wisconsin. Her five-year-old daughter, also named Joicey, had gone to meet her father at a nearby movie. Quite suddenly, "an awesome feeling" came over Mrs. Hurth. "For some unexplainable reason I knew Joicey had been hit by a car or was going to be." She telephoned the movie theater and learned that the accident had just happened. Fortunately the girl was not badly injured. "Joicey remembers that at the time she was hit, she called, 'Mama.' She remembers sitting on the curb crying and calling, 'Mama, Mama, I want my Mama.' "[5]

In cases such as the above, there was an explicit call from the child to the mother, but the call itself may not be essential. As we shall see in chapter 4, telepathic influences from people who are in distress or even dying are sometimes associated with explicit calls, and sometimes not. What is important seems to be the emotional bond between the people involved.

I now turn to the most fundamental and biological of all human calls, the call of a hungry baby for its mother.

TELEPATHIC CALLS FROM HUNGRY BABIES TO NURSING MOTHERS

Babies cannot speak, but their cries announce their hunger or distress in no uncertain terms. Parents in general, and mothers in particular, usually respond by going to them and doing what is needed. Responding to the cries of an infant is undoubtedly instinctive, and has been favored by natural selection for many millions of years of evolutionary history, both human and prehuman.

In nursing mothers, breast milk becomes available for feeding the baby through a physiological process called the letdown reflex, mediated by the hormone oxytocin, produced in the pituitary gland. As the letdown occurs, many women experience a tingling sensation in their breasts, and often the nipples begin to leak. This reflex takes only a few seconds and is usually triggered by the stimulation of the nipple by the baby, by the sound of the baby crying, or even just by thinking about the baby.[6]

Many nursing mothers claim that when they are away from the baby, they often know when it needs them because their milk lets down.[7] Here are three examples, taken from dozens I have received in response to appeals for information on this subject.

When my youngest son was a baby, I had the experience of my milk "letting down" when I was away from him. This was accompanied by a "knowing" that he needed me. When I would phone home, the sitter would always confirm that he had just awakened. Since he nursed on demand, he was never on a schedule. ◇ CAROLE TYRA, ARLINGTON, WASHINGTON

I have seven children; the eldest is now twelve and the youngest seven months. I have fed six of my children and each time have experienced the "letdown reflex" when I leave them. I know when my baby cries when we are apart. The very second I think she may be crying, I leak. When I get home, she has usually been crying at the time I have leaked. My husband says that my boobs are like antennas. I'm sure I can pick up their crying for miles. ◇ PAM BRIGGS, BLACKBURN, LANCASHIRE

I'm a professional actress. When my son was four to five months old, I left my son with my mother and went to the theater. In the middle of the performance I felt the milk coming intensely (though I thought I left quite a lot for my son at home, and it wasn't a time when he would be hungry). My costume was soaking in milk, and I couldn't remember my lines. I could hardly wait until I could leave the stage, and as soon as I did, I rushed to call my mother. My son was crying for food on the balcony of our apartment, and my mother couldn't hear him. She thought he was sleeping. ◇ TATYANA SHIRAYKINA, MOSCOW, RUSSIA

Most women who have had this kind of experience seem to take it for granted, and assume that it depends on a psychic bond. If they are right, this would imply a form of telepathy more physiological and fundamental than the kinds of ESP usually investigated by parapsychologists and psychic researchers.

There are two main alternatives to the telepathic hypothesis. First is the possibility that the phenomenon is an illusion caused by a combination of coincidence and selective memory. Milk letdown can occur when women are away from their babies for reasons unconnected with the babies' needs, including the breasts being full after a long period away from the child, hearing other babies cry, or thinking about feeding the baby. On the occasions when this letdown coincides with their baby's needs, the mothers may remember it, and forget all the times they were wrong.

Second, it is possible that the letdown occurs as a result of physiological rhythms shared by the mother and baby, thus accounting for the synchronization of the baby's crying and the mother's letdown reflex, even when they are far apart. I have found that the synchronized-rhythm hypothesis is not usually taken very seriously by nursing mothers themselves, either because they feed on demand and do not have a fixed schedule, or because they try not to leave the baby when it is due for a feed. But practically no research seems to have been done on this subject.

As a first step toward a systematic investigation of this phenomenon, I carried out a survey of 100 mothers who had recently had babies. My main purpose was to find out how common it was for lactating mothers to experience the letdown reflex when they were away from their baby, and how many of them had noticed that this seemed to coincide with their baby needing them.

The women in this survey had all attended the Active Birth Centre in Highgate, North London, which promotes yoga and natural childbirth, and encourages breast-feeding. Most were first-time mothers. Some were so devoted that they practically never left their babies, or did so too briefly for milk letdowns to occur when they were away from the baby. But out of the sample of 100, 62 women said they remembered their milk letting down when they were away from their babies, and 16 out of this group (26 percent) said that the milk letdown coincided with their babies needing them. Most of the others did not know whether the letdown happened when their babies needed them. Interestingly, the women who said that they had noticed the letdown coincided with their babies' needs were generally those who had breast-fed longest.[8]

Far from these results supporting the idea that mothers tend to make exaggerated claims about their telepathic bonds with their babies, most seemed not even to have considered the possibility. Those most experienced in breast-feeding were significantly more likely to have noticed a link between milk letdown and their baby's needs, perhaps because they had more opportunities to do so. It may well be that mothers who have had several children are more likely than inexperienced mothers, like most of the women in this survey, to be aware of this phenomenon. Further surveys with more experienced mothers should be able to test this idea.

I then carried out an investigation in order to find out in more detail how often milk letdowns coincided with a baby's needs and how often they did not. Again, the women who took part were recruited through the Active Birth Centre, and most were first-time mothers. Katy Barber, an experienced midwife, carried out this research for me. Nineteen women took part in the study. Each was given two notebooks that she undertook to fill in for a period of eight weeks, during the period she was breast-feeding. The mother carried around one notebook when she was away from her baby, to record the times at which her milk let down, and any other comments about her feelings. The baby-sitter kept the other notebook, and noted in it the times at which the baby cried, seemed hungry, or showed other signs of distress. By comparing the two sets of notebooks, I could then determine whether the letdowns occurred when the baby was distressed.

I found that the letdown reflexes did in fact coincide with the babies' needs far more often than would be expected by chance (for the details of this study, see Appendix B). But there were still a fairly high number of false alarms. In future studies, it would be preferable to work with more experienced mothers, less prone to anxieties about leaving their babies, and also to videotape the baby continuously during the mother's absence to obtain a more accurate record of its behavior than is possible with people making notes.

The evidence thus far supports the claims of many mothers that their breasts sometimes seem to respond telepathically to their baby's need, even when the baby is far away and even when it is not a usual feeding time. Just as the mother and baby can remain physiologically connected for months after birth through breast-feeding, so they can remain psychically connected.

MOTHERS WAKING JUST BEFORE THEIR BABIES

Another very common observation by nursing mothers, and also by mothers who feed with bottles, is that they often wake up in the night just before their baby starts crying, even if the baby is in another room, and even if they cannot hear the baby stirring. For example:

My babies always slept in another room, so I could not hear the stirring, etc. I know that their cries did not wake me, as all was silent on waking. I got used to it—would get out of bed to prepare the feed, before the baby cried.

There is only one "thing" in the world that wakes me up and that is our son. I know when he wakes up; I can just feel it. I feel when he is tossing around in his bed. I wake up immediately and run to his room. It has happened since the first moment I started to nurse him.

Some mothers experience this connection the other way around, and attribute the baby's awakening to their own.

During the first four months or so after his birth, my younger son could be counted upon to wake up in the night just moments after I awoke in anticipation of nursing him. I used to dread waking up because I knew he would also. When the time came to get him to sleep through the night, I tried to will myself not to wake up.

◇ CAROLINE JOHNSON, PHILADELPHIA

Do these kinds of experiences depend on telepathic connections, or synchronized rhythms? Or maybe presentiment on the mother's part, a feeling that something is about to happen? No one yet knows. Fairly simple research could shed light on these questions (see Appendix A).

TELEPATHIC CALLS TO ANIMALS

Many people who keep dogs and cats have noticed that their animals seem to respond telepathically to their thoughts and intentions. One way in which they do so is by coming when called. I described a wide range of examples in *Dogs That Know When Their Owners Are Coming Home*, and have subsequently heard of many more cases. For example, Teresa McKenzie of Carmel Valley, California, spent a lot of time training her dog until she noticed, to her surprise, that the dog was responding to her thoughts.

The test that really convinced me was this: After an exhausting day hike my dog was sound asleep in the living room on her bed, even snoring a little—out for the night. I was in the bathtub, and I decided to "call" her with "mind pictures." I imagined her far away from me outdoors, and I stood calling. I was careful not to move or make a sound, even though the dog and I were in completely different rooms, not visible to each other. To my astonishment, I heard her get up in the living room, and shake off her sleepiness. She walked into the bathroom, came up next to the tub, yawned and stretched, and looked at me as if to say, "You rang?"

This call took place over a short distance, but sometimes dogs seem to react from miles away. When he was working with elephants in the jungles of Burma, J. H. Williams deliberately trained his dog, Molly Mia, to respond to his silent calls. At first he did it when she was in his hut with him, then he tried from farther away: "I started about a hundred yards from camp, out of sight, and as far as possible out of scent. It was uncanny because she came to me as fast as I'd called her and she already knew where I was." He found she could still respond to his silent calls from as far as two miles away in dense jungle. He then tried an even more arduous experiment: "I synchronized my watch and my camp clock and at 6:00 A.M. set off for my forest work, first crossing the river and then recrossing it. At noon, when I was at least four miles away, I sat down and concentrated hard on Molly. Within half an hour I heard her ranging somewhere near me, and towards me, and sure enough she came bounding in a minute or two. The most interesting thing about this was that my servant Aung Net told me that at noon Molly Mia had suddenly dashed off exactly as if she had heard me call; but she did not cross the river."[9] So she knew not only when her owner called but where he was, without needing to follow a scent trail.

The ability to respond to silent calls and to locate other members of the group may be of considerable value to wild animals. The ancestors of dogs are, of course, wolves, and there is evidence from the observations of naturalists that wolves in the wild communicate telepathically with each other, and can find each other over many miles without following scent trails.[10]

Many cat owners have also found that they can call their cats mentally. Here is just one example from more than thirty similar cases on my database: "I don't have to call my cats when they are outside, I just visualize them, concentrate and think on them, and yes, there they are" (Christine Schülte, Kapellen, Belgium).

Experimental research on silent calls to cats will be discussed in Appendix A.

ANIMALS CALLING PEOPLE

Not only do people call animals telepathically, but animals call people. Some of the most striking cases involve horses. In the case of Pat Westwood, of Largs, Ayrshire, Scotland, her horse's calls turned into a regular occurrence. She worked with horses, and kept her own horse, which had been her close partner for fifteen years in the stables where she worked.

> I had a few days off, and had gone home. Round about the third or fourth day, I had this compulsion to drive back to work. On entering the yard, I was struck with the noise of a horse kicking the walls with great purpose and yelling its head off. It was mine, and the distraught staff had been about to phone me, as nobody could get near her. I spoke her name quietly. Instant silence, a gentle whinny, a big sigh, and then she began to pick at her hay as if nothing had happened. This performance would be repeated if I abandoned her for more than three or four days at a time, but the staff left her to make her own "phone calls." As she became older and stiffer, she found it a useful talent.

Jane Strick, who raises ponies and keeps sheep in Aberdaron, near Pwllheli in North Wales, found that she could tell when there was something wrong with a mare that was foaling, and noticed that her intuition came into play with sheep as well. "At lambing time, when I am going round, I get the feeling and change my route and find something is wrong. I wasn't always right when I got that feeling, but I should say I was right about 75 percent of the time." Some people have had comparable experiences with cows.

It would be of great interest to know how common such experiences are among farmers and shepherds, especially among those who still farm on a small scale and know their animals well. Obviously the ability of animals in need to attract human attention is of survival value to the animal, and when the farmer is out of earshot, telepathic calls can clearly save lives. Equally, it is useful for farmers to respond to their animals' calls when they are needed, if only for the sake of saving valuable livestock.

Some dogs appear to call their owners telepathically on a regular basis, especially when they are outdoors and want to be let in. So do some cats. Curiously enough, while I was writing this chapter, this happened with our own cat, Allegra. She was out at night, since my attempts to call her in before I went to bed had failed. At about 3:00 A.M., my wife, Jill, suddenly woke up and saw Allegra's face very close to her own, looking her in the eyes. But the cat was not there. She tried to go back to sleep, but could not, and after about a quarter of an hour she got out of bed and went downstairs to find Allegra's face pressed against the glass of the French window, waiting to come in.

The most dramatic calls from cats occur when they are lost or injured and they somehow summon their owners to rescue them. Sometimes their owners "see" where they are, like Bonnie Kutsch: "I have an orange tabby who sends me pictures of where he is when he gets lost or locked in someplace. It has happened every single time he's been missing for several days." But clearly cats are not always able to call their owners; otherwise we would not see so many notices about lost cats.

As we have seen in this chapter, and will see again in the following two chapters, the great majority of telepathic communications occur between people who have strong emotional bonds, or between people and animals with strong emotional bonds. Members of the group continue to be linked by these bonds even when they are far apart. The bonds are elastic; they stretch, like invisible rubber bands. Or, to use another metaphor, they are like channels through which influences can flow. In chapters 7 and 19 I'll discuss in more detail the nature of these connections.

4 DISTANT DEATHS
AND DISTRESS

On the morning of October 27, 1879, being in perfect health and having been awake for some considerable time, I heard myself called by my Christian name by an anxious and suffering voice, several times in succession. I recognised the voice as that of an old friend . . . who had not been in my thoughts for many weeks, or even months. I knew he was with his regiment in India, but not that he had been ordered to the front, and nothing had called him to my recollection. Within a few days I heard of his death from cholera on the morning I seemed to hear his call. The impression was so strong I noted the date and fact in my diary before breakfast. . . . I was never conscious of any other auditory hallucination whatever.[1]

This report, from a lady of "thorough good sense, with no appetite for marvels," was published in 1886.

In the last quarter of the nineteenth century, in the context of an intense debate about the possibility of the soul surviving bodily death, such apparitions of the dying took on special significance.

On one side were materialists, who denied all possibility of conscious survival. They believed that subjective experience was nothing but an aspect of the activity of the brain. Hence, when brain activity ceased at death, so did consciousness. All memories were erased as the brain decayed. Seemingly supernatural powers, such as thought transference, were simply impossible. Belief in them was mere superstition.

On the other hand there was widespread religious faith in survival after bodily death, and also a growing popular interest in spiritualism, with séances, mediums, rappings, table turnings, and ectoplasmic materializations. Many mediums turned out to be frauds, preying on the credulous. Yet some eminent scientists investigated a number of reputable mediums and found seemingly genuine phenomena that seemed inexplicable in current scientific terms. These open-minded investigators included the physicist Sir William Crookes and the biologist Alfred Russel Wallace.

There was also much contemporary interest in hypnotism, which was being recognized within the medical profession as a natural phenomenon rather than an occult one, and was no longer subjected to the scorn that "mesmerism" had attracted for decades.[2]

This was the context in which psychic research as a scientific discipline was born. The founders of the Society for Psychical Research in London in 1882 summarized their aim as follows: "[T]o examine without prejudice or prepossession and in a scientific spirit those faculties of man, real or supposed, which appear to be inexplicable on any generally recognised hypothesis." (This summary is still printed in every issue of the *Journal of the Society for Psychical Research*.)

One of the first projects was to investigate apparitions of the dying. If the dying really did appear to people who could not otherwise have known of their deaths, then this might imply that their souls had left their bodies at death, and hence support belief in survival.

These pioneering researchers soon found that not all apparitions were of dying people. Many were of people who had had accidents or were seriously ill or in other kinds of distress. And some were not in danger at all. They called these apparitions "phantasms of the living," as opposed to phantasms of the dead, such as ghosts. They took the word *phantasm* to "signify any hallucinatory sensory impression, whatever sense—whether sight, hearing, touch, smell, taste, or diffused sensibility—may happen to be affected."[3]

The results of their inquiries were summarized in a two-volume, 1,300-page book, *Phantasms of the Living* (1886), by Edmund Gurney, Frederick Myers, and Frank Podmore. (The first two were Fellows of Trinity College, Cambridge.) They launched widespread appeals for information, and analyzed thousands of reports from the people who responded. They checked up on these reports, and obtained signed statements from witnesses who could corroborate the claims of their informants, using methods similar to those that would be used in a legal investigation. They weeded out all cases that could reasonably be attributed to natural causes, and also rejected accounts that lacked precision. But that still left 702 cases that they described in detail in this monumental work.

They came to several important conclusions, perhaps the most important of which was that apparitions of the dying were only one type of a much more general kind of unexplained communication, for which Myers coined the term "telepathy." This word rapidly caught on, and entered ordinary English usage. Myers deliberately chose a word that included emotions and impressions, rather than just visual apparitions or the transfer of thoughts. He defined it as "the communication of impressions of any kind from one mind to another, independently of the recognised channels of sense."[4]

Some cases of telepathy were visual, but at least as many involved the hearing of calls and other sounds, both in dreams and while awake. A few even involved smells. And some telepathic communications were devoid of sensory hallucinations, but simply involved a feeling of alarm or concern about someone, without knowing why.

For example, when at work one day, the foreman of the masons at Winchester Cathedral felt an intense urge to go home. He was reluctant to do so, not wanting to lose any pay or incur his wife's ridicule. But eventually he did so, and when he arrived, his wife's sister answered the door, and asked him how he knew. His wife had been run over by a cab and was seriously injured. She had been calling for him piteously.[5]

In some cases the telepathic impression took the form of a bodily sensation, as in the case of the wife of the artist Arthur Severn. One morning in 1880, she woke up in her bedroom near Coniston Water, in the Lake District of England, feeling that she had had a sharp blow on the mouth. She looked at her watch, and found it was seven o'clock. Her husband was not in the room, and she assumed he had gone out sailing on the lake. When he came into breakfast, she noticed he sat farther away from her than usual, and kept putting his handkerchief furtively up to his lip.

> I said, "Arthur, why are you doing that?" and added a little anxiously, "I know you've hurt yourself! But I'll tell you why afterwards." He said, "Well, when I was sailing, a sudden squall came, throwing the tiller suddenly round, and it struck me a bad blow in the mouth under the upper lip, and it has been bleeding a good deal and won't stop." I then said, "Have you any idea what o'clock it was when it happened?" and he answered, "It must have been about seven."

Sometimes the bodily sensations were more general, as when a Cambridge University undergraduate was overcome by a sense of extreme illness, cold, and misery from eight to eleven o'clock one evening, when, unknown to him, his twin brother lay dying miles away at home.[6]

The early psychic researchers called the person who received the impression the "percipient," and the person who was the source of it the "agent." They found that the majority of their percipients (58 percent) were females, but that most agents (63 percent) were males. "The preponderance of male agents is probably to be accounted for by the fact that men are more liable than women to accidents and violent deaths, and that a larger proportion of them die at a distance from their nearest relatives and friends."[7]

When they analyzed the relationship of the percipients to the agents, they found that most were within the same family (53 percent of the total). Parent-child cases were commonest (23 percent of the total), followed by brothers and sisters (15 percent), cousins, uncles, et cetera (9 percent), and husbands and wives (6 percent). Among nonfamily pairs, 32 percent of the total number of cases were between friends, and 11 percent between acquaintances. Only 4 percent occurred with strangers, and of these almost half took place when the percipient was with someone who knew the agent intimately and who also had a telepathic experience with the agent: a so-called collective case.[8]

HALLUCINATIONS AND COINCIDENCE

The existence of telepathy and other psychic phenomena was as controversial in the nineteenth century as it is today, and for the same reason: from the materialist point of view, it ought not to occur. Psychic research, or parapsychology, is still on the outer fringes of institutional science, and has continued to occupy a precarious position "between the scornfully sceptical and the eagerly superstitious," as Myers put it in 1894.[9] Nevertheless, despite all discouragement, and with considerable bravery, psychic researchers have continued to accumulate an enormous body of evidence from case studies and from experimental research that shows that telepathy and other psychic phenomena really do seem to happen, whether or not we can explain them. And because this field of research has been subject to more skepticism than any other branch of science, most psychic researchers have been unusually rigorous in their examination of evidence and in their consideration of alternative explanations.

The foremost objection to the case studies reported in *Phantasms of the Living* was that these were just coincidences. People had hallucinations from time to time, and occasionally these coincided with the death or distress of someone they knew. These meaningful coincidences were so striking that they were remembered, while all the other hallucinations were simply forgotten.

This hypothesis is perfectly reasonable, but like any scientific hypothesis it needs to be tested before we can assess its validity. In order to test it, the Society for Psychical Research organized an enormous Census of Hallucinations, which was summarized in a masterly 400-page report published in 1894, written by two formidable Cambridge academics: Alice Johnson, a biologist, and Eleanor Sidgwick, later to become principal of Newnham College, Cambridge.

The primary task of this survey was to find out how many apparently sane and normal people had had hallucinations when they were awake. With the help of 410 data collectors, 17,000 people throughout Britain were asked, "Have you ever, while believing yourself to be completely awake, had a vivid impression of seeing or being touched by a living being or inanimate object, or of hearing a voice; which impression, so far as you could tell, was not due to any external physical cause?" The outcome of this survey was that 9.9 percent said they had had at least one such hallucination. There did indeed seem to be a tendency for people to forget these experiences, because the greatest number of experiences were said to have happened in the previous year, fewer in the year before, fewer still in the year before that, and so on.

Most of these hallucinations did not coincide with unexpected deaths: in fact, less than 5 percent did so. In other words, just under 0.5 percent of all the people questioned said they had had a hallucination of a person whom they later found had died at the time of their experience, or within twelve hours of that time.

The researchers then carried out a series of calculations to work out the probability of having a chance hallucination of someone at the time of his or her death. To correct for the progressive forgetting of hallucinations that did not coincide with deaths, they boosted the total number of hallucinations occurring per year (by 6.5 times). Then, using statistical death rates for the British population during the period covered by the census, they worked out that, by chance, roughly 1 hallucination in 19,000 would occur within twenty-four hours of the death of the person to whom the hallucination referred. In fact, 1 in 43 did so. In other words, these hallucinations around the time of death occurred about 440 times more frequently than would be expected by chance.[10]

The investigation of spontaneous cases of telepathy continued in the twentieth century, and many case histories have been published over the years.[11] The results generally agree with the pioneering work of the Society for Psychical Research.

DISTANT DISTRESS

The investigations reported in *Phantasms of the Living* and in the Census of Hallucinations made it clear that telepathic influences from people who are dying form a relatively small proportion of telepathic communications in general. They are among the most impressive and most memorable, but there is no evidence to support the idea that "visits" from dying people show that the soul leaves the body at death.

Almost as dramatic and memorable are those cases of telepathy from people who are in distress; for example, as a result of accidents, illness, or suicidal depression. We have already seen several examples in connection with telepathic calls (chapter 3), and in the cases reported in *Phantasms of the Living*—for example, the experience of Arthur Severn's wife, who felt pain in her lip when her husband was struck on the lip in his sailboat (page 70). Perhaps the most fundamental instances are those in which mothers respond telepathically to the needs of their babies (pages 60–65).

Telepathic responses to need or distress are more frequent than responses to deaths. For example, on my own database there are twenty-nine cases of apparent telepathy from people who are dying, compared with fifty from people who are in need, distress, or danger. One reason may be that a given person can be in danger or distress several times, but only die once, so there may be more opportunities for distress to be communicated telepathically.

In biological terms, these telepathic responses to the distress of family members and close friends make good sense: They are not mere curiosities of marginal significance, but are often important for survival. Responding to telepathic intuitions has in some cases actually saved lives, or at least brought comfort and help to those who are suffering, even if it is only in the form of a telephone call. But before the invention of telephones, the most appropriate response was generally for the person who received the impression to go to the person from whom it had come, or at least to look for him or her.

One of the most distinguished of modern psychic researchers, Ian Stevenson, a professor of psychiatry at the University of Virginia, has reviewed some 200 well-authenticated cases of telepathic intuition, and has found some interesting patterns in the data. In his analysis, he concentrated on cases of tele-pathic intuition, rather than those involving visual or auditory hallucinations. In agreement with previous studies, he found that the majority of the agent-percipient pairs were members of the same immediate family (63 percent), most commonly parents and children (34 percent of the total). A further 7 percent of cases were members of the extended families (cousins, in-laws, grandparents, etc.). Friends and acquaintances made up 28 percent of the total, and strangers only 3 percent. As Stevenson pointed out, the relatively high proportion of marital partners and friends gives no support to the idea that blood relationships facilitate telepathy. "Emotional ties seem more impor-tant than biological ones. It happens that we have most opportunity for devel-oping emotional ties with persons with whom we initially have biological relationships. But such emotional ties develop through shared experiences and not from biological relationships as such."[12]

In many of these cases the percipients became aware that a particular per-son they knew well was in distress and needed help. Their reactions often involved feelings appropriate to that awareness, especially anxiety or depres-sion or both, and an impulse toward action to help the distressed person. "In their efforts to reach the agents, the percipients frequently ignored all rational considerations. They often changed plans abruptly, broke off holidays, traveled many miles in discomfort, and put up with or imposed on other persons all kinds of inconveniences in order to get to the places where they felt they should be."[13] We have already seen several example of this kind of behavior. In some cases the percipient felt that something was wrong, and even experi-enced a compulsion to go somewhere without knowing why and without being able to identify the person involved. One example was the mason at Winchester Cathedral in England, who felt the need to go home without knowing why (page 70). As Stevenson commented, "The behavior of some of the percipients as they described it themselves reminds one of marionettes controlled by a puppeteer, or of a subject responding to a posthypnotic sugges-tion while showing complete amnesia for the implanted suggestion which is in fact the origin of the irresistible impulse to his action."[14]

There is often a striking contrast between the responses of people to dis-tant deaths and to people in distress. There is nothing they can do about deaths, and it is often as if the person has come to say good-bye. For example:

Twenty-year-old Willis had been away from his Pennsylvania home for several years, but he returned for frequent visits, especially after his grandfather's stroke. The two had always been close. . . . One night, soon after his return from a visit, Willis struggled awake at his grandfather's call. "Willis, Willis." The room, ordinarily very dark, was lit up brightly and, momentarily, he saw his grandfather smiling at him. Startled, uncomprehending at first, Willis lay motionless for a bit, but he then put on the light. It was 1:10 A.M. He could sleep no more. At 6:00 A.M. a phone call from his brother came, but Willis spoke first: "Grand-pop died last night!"

"Yes, but how did you know?"

"He came to see me — it was about one-ten."

"Yes, that was when he died."[15]

Some people have actually experienced that a "pull" toward someone in distress ceased when the person died. Anita Richards, of Cambridge, England, described to me as follows her changing reactions to her mother, who was ill in the hospital but apparently not in mortal danger. She had been planning to pay her mother a visit, but on the advice of the medical staff she decided to postpone it for a few days.

As I went home I started to feel uneasy about the decision not to go to my mum. I got home, made lunch for my husband, and off he went back to work. As I sat there I had a feeling of my mother pulling me to her. We were not on the telephone in those days at home. Everything in me wanted to go to my mother. On the way back to work, suddenly the feeling left me. I looked at the clock; it was 2:05 P.M. I thought little of this and got back to work. Just after 4:00 P.M. I got a telephone call from the unit telling me my mother had unexpectedly died early in the afternoon. She had died between 2:00 and 2:30 P.M.

In most cases where people felt an urge to take action, the person they were responding to was in serious distress, or in a life-threatening situation. As Stevenson has pointed out, this "marked difference suggests that the need for help on the part of the agent plays an important part in the processes of the experience."[16]

No doubt telepathic experiences of death and distress tend to be remembered more than relatively trivial examples. But some pleasant experiences, such as marriages and winning a lottery, are just as memorable as unpleasant ones, and yet they do not figure in cases of telepathy anywhere near as frequently as unpleasant experiences.

ARE CALLS NECESSARY?

The early psychic researchers had a model of telepathy in which the agent took an active role, and the percipient a passive one. In terms of the radio analogy that later became popular, one was the transmitter and the other the receiver. Or one provided the stimulus, the other the response. This active/passive model seems appropriate for the many cases in which the agent really did call the other person, either by crying, as in the case of babies in distress, or as part of a generic call for help, or specifically by name. It also applies well to many cases of telephone telepathy (see chapter 6): The projection of one person's intention to call another seems to affect that person at a distance. But there are many cases of accidents, illnesses, and deaths in which there is no evidence that the agent consciously called the percipient, either vocally or by focusing thoughts on him or her.

In the cases of telepathic impressions analyzed by Stevenson, in only 32 percent was the agent known to be focusing consciously on the percipient.[17] Stevenson found that in these cases there was a higher chance of the percipient's taking action, such as going to the person or telephoning, than in cases where the agent was not known to have been focusing on the percipient. Even when the percipient did not identify the agent, most still took action. Of course, in some cases, the agent may have been focusing on the percipient without this fact being recorded, and some people in distress may have implicitly or unconsciously been calling for help.

Louisa Rhine, of the Parapsychology Laboratory at Duke University, in North Carolina, suggested a different interpretation of the role of agent and percipient. From the 1930s to the 1970s this laboratory was one of best-known centers of research in parapsychology, and over the years thousands of people wrote in with stories of their own experiences. Eventually a collection of some 10,000 cases built up, and Louisa Rhine undertook the task of analyzing them. Her approach was strongly influenced by ideas about ESP that came out of the laboratory experiments at Duke. The researchers there recognized three kinds of ESP: telepathy, clairvoyance, and precognition. She pointed out that telepathy was the only one that involved two people, rather than just the percipient. In order to produce a unified theory of ESP, she preferred to think of telepathy as involving an activity of the percipient rather than the agent, seeing it as a kind of "thought reading" rather than "thought sending."

Nevertheless, many telepathy cases in the Duke collection seemed to involve an active role of the agent, as in previous collections of cases, especially when the agent was dying or in distress. But Louisa Rhine also found cases in which the agent was making no conscious effort to call the percipient. One concerned a Texas college boy whose roommate had asked to be awakened at a particular time.

When the time approached, he decided to awaken the roommate "in the most devilish manner possible." He would drip one drop of water after another on the sleeper's eyelids until he awakened. He went to the bathroom to get a glass of water, and just as he re-entered, the roommate sat up suddenly, rubbed his eyes, shook his head, and said: "Oh, oh, what a dream I just had! I dreamed I was in a terrible rain storm with water beating down on my face."

She commented that in this case "the process would seem more like thought reading than thought sending, because the message was picked up when the agent had no conscious intent to send it." Nevertheless, the agent was still playing an active role in that he was consciously intending to drop water onto his roommate's eyes, and it was this intention that seems to have been detected telepathically.

Rhine's attempt to play down the role of the agent and play up the active role of the percipient seems misleading. She was motivated by a desire to make telepathy more like clairvoyance, where the percipient plays an active role. She was also strongly influenced by the idea that telepathy was the only kind of ESP involving two people. But this is not true. She had not taken the sense of being stared at into account, because parapsychologists have ignored it until quite recently. The sense of being stared at inevitably involves two people, a percipient and a starer, who plays the role of agent.

In the following chapters I'll continue to discuss how telepathy might work. For the time being, the most important point seems to be that for telepathic calls and for the communication of need or distress, what matters is the relationship between the two people. If two people are linked by a social bond, then this can act as a channel of communication between them (as will be discussed in chapters 7 and 18). If one calls the other, or focuses an intention upon him or her, then this can be transmitted through the channel, resulting in a telepathic influence. Also, if one of the people has a serious accident or dies, this may affect the other, even without any conscious or unconscious intention to communicate. A crude mechanical analogy is provided by an invisible rubber band. Imagine two people are linked by such a connection but cannot see each other. If one shakes the stretched band or lets it go, the other feels a difference. Even if they do not know exactly what is happening to the other person, they know *something* is happening.

As an aspect of the seventh sense, telepathy should behave like other senses in that it depends primarily on changes and differences. The death of one person who is bonded to another undoubtedly causes a major change in the bond between them. From one point of view, this could be regarded as an active sensing by the percipient. From another point of view, the cause of the change can be located in the agent, even without any conscious intention. It is not an either/or situation, but rather depends on the interconnection between the two. It also depends on their states of mind. People are generally more receptive to telepathic influences when they are relaxed or asleep, or at least not otherwise preoccupied.

REACTIONS OF ANIMALS TO DISTANT ACCIDENTS

Not only people but also domestic animals, especially dogs, can react to the distress or death of people to whom they are bonded. Just as some people who sense the need of someone in danger try to reach them, or at least try to do something, so do some dogs. There are thirty-three cases on my database of dogs reacting to distant emergencies in a comparable way, by showing signs of distress or restlessness. In *Dogs That Know When Their Owners Are Coming Home,* I described several cases in detail. Some involved fires; some heart attacks or other medical crises; some attempted suicides; one a woman giving birth in a maternity hospital; and some car or motorcycle accidents. For example, Marguerite Derolet, of Tourcoing, France, told me that one day her dog, a Great Dane, "went crazy. He attacked the entrance door and tore the letter box off. I was very frightened because I couldn't calm him down. I understood everything by what followed because a few minutes later my husband was calling me desperately on the radio asking me to call the police." Her husband, a taxi driver, had had a serious accident about five kilometers from home at the "exact same minute" that the dog began behaving so excitedly.

Although fewer cats than dogs seem to react to accidents and emergencies, the situations in which they do so are similar. For example, Jean Parker, who lives in Peterborough, England, noticed that something unusual was going on when she arrived home from work one afternoon and was surprised to find her cat Timmy waiting for her; he habitually slept on her son's bed all day.

He kept meowing very pitifully and I thought he was in physical pain, but no amount of fussing him would calm him down at all. To cut a long story short, at 8:15 P.M. I learned my son had had a very bad road accident and was in intensive care at Addenbrooke's Hospital in Cambridge and was in danger of losing his life. My son was in that unit for seven weeks in a coma. Timmy would not go into his bedroom. But then one evening Timmy ran straight into my son's room, jumped on the bed, and began purring with deep pleasure. That was the day my son came out of his coma and began to get back to life again.

ANIMALS THAT KNOW WHEN THEIR OWNERS DIE

I have received 106 accounts of the reactions of dogs to the death of an absent person to whom they were attached. In all cases, the animals showed various signs of distress for which there seemed to be no obvious reason, and most made unusual sounds, including howling (in 32 percent of the cases), whimpering, whining, crying, and growling. Typically, the dog's behavior could only be understood in retrospect, usually when a phone call came to break the news.[18]

Some cats also respond to distant deaths by making unusual sounds, such as howls, plaintive meows, or whining, or by showing other signs of distress. With cats, as with dogs and with people, the ability to react to a person's death does not seem to fall off with distance. In some of the cases in my collection the person dying was thousands of miles away, yet his or her cat still seemed to know. For example, a tomcat belonging to the Pulfer family, of Koppingen, Switzerland, was very attached to the son, Frank, who went away to work as a ship's cook. He came home irregularly, and the cat used to wait for him at the door before he arrived. But one day the cat sat at the door meowing and seemed extremely sad. Frank's father, Karl, said, "We could not get him away from the door. Finally we let him into Frank's room, where he sniffed at everything but still continued his wailing. Two days after the cat's strange behavior we were informed that our son had died at exactly that time on his voyage, in Thailand."

HUMAN REACTIONS TO THE DISTANT DEATH
AND DISTRESS OF ANIMALS

If animals can pick up when their owners are in distress or are dying because of the bond between them, then this bond should in principle also allow telepathic influences to travel in the opposite direction, from animal to person. And some people do indeed seem to react at a distance to animals that have had accidents or are dying. Nevertheless, most humans seem less sensitive than their pets. On my database are 211 reports of animals seemingly reacting to the distant death or distress of people, but only 38 vice versa: 16 with cats, 13 with dogs, 6 with horses, 2 with sheep, and 1 with a pet hen. Some of these occurred when the people were awake, others when they were asleep. Some people experienced visual or auditory hallucinations, some an intuitive awareness that something was wrong without any images, and some physical symptoms related to the sufferings of the animal.

Sometimes people knew that an animal needed them, and went to it, as in the cases of sheep, horses, cats, and dogs in distress that seemed to call their owners to them, as discussed in chapter 3. In other cases the people were unable to go to the animal, but nevertheless became aware of its distress. For example, Christine Flood, of Tottington, Lancashire, England, was a staff member on a school trip to France, when one night she woke up shivering and knew that Lester, her cat, had been hit by a car and was bleeding. "He was crying out for me in pain, from the gutter." She told the other members of staff, but did not telephone home because she knew it would upset her, despite the fact that she was certain of the incident. Finally, on the return journey, she called home and discovered that Lester had indeed been run over and had subsequently lost a leg as a result of the accident.

All these episodes involved feelings of worry and distress, but some people experienced physical symptoms as well. For example, Ronita Brown, of McMinnville, Oregon, was out with her husband one day some twenty miles from home: "All of a sudden I got very agitated. My throat felt constricted, and I felt like screaming. I told my husband that we had to leave. When we got home, we found that my dog had tragically strangled."

And sometimes people just knew what had happened, without any images or physical symptoms, as in the case of a Belgian boy and his parrot.

I was ten (or eleven) years old, staying with my grandparents for a week, and the last night I woke up with the sudden idea in my head, "My parrot is dead." All night long this idea kept on banging in my head—"He's dead! He's dead!"—so I couldn't sleep. The next day my parents came to pick me up. They didn't tell me anything particular about my parrot. When we came home I ran to see how he was, and yes, he was lying on the floor of his cage! Of course it was a shock for me, since we were very close friends; he was always sitting on my head or shoulders when I was home, and eating out of my hand. ❖ KOEN VAN DE MOORTEL

More examples of people's seemingly telepathic reactions to the distress or death of their animals are in my book *Dogs That Know When Their Owners Are Coming Home*.

THE BIOLOGICAL BASIS OF TELEPATHY

Research on telepathy has led to a number of important conclusions. First, as we have seen in this chapter, in the early days of psychic research, apparitions of the dying were thought by some people to provide evidence for the soul's leaving the body at death, and hence support the idea of survival. But it soon became clear that these phantasms were particular instances of the much more general phenomenon of telepathy, which was not specifically associated with death and dying, although connections with the dying provided some of the most memorable examples. Rather than being confined to the inside of the body during life and then released at death, the psyche is not confined to the body even during *life*, irrespective of what happens after death. Telepathy is a natural, rather than a supernatural, phenomenon.

Second, telepathic influences can come to consciousness in a variety of ways: in dreams, at the moment of waking, and when fully awake. They can take the form of visual or auditory hallucinations, or bodily symptoms, or intuitions that something is wrong, or emotions, like feeling anxious or depressed, or urges to action for which no reason is apparent.

Third, telepathy generally occurs between people who are closely bonded—especially parents and children, identical twins,[19] husbands and wives, lovers, and best friends.

Fourth, the most striking cases of telepathy involve death, distress, accidents, or other emergencies.

Fifth, in many cases of telepathy, including the telepathic calls discussed in the previous chapter, one person, traditionally called the agent, takes an active role in the communication, either by calling or by focusing thoughts or intentions on the percipient. This is not always the case, however. Since telepathic communications seem to depend on the bond between the two people, a change in one person's circumstances can affect the other through this bond, even in the absence of conscious or unconscious intention to do so.

Finally, telepathy is not confined to human beings. Perhaps as a consequence of its initial preoccupation with spiritual questions, psychic research was for decades almost exclusively human-centered. Its stated goal was "to examine without prejudice or prepossession and in a scientific spirit those faculties of man, real or supposed, which appear to be inexplicable on any generally recognized hypothesis." The study of the psychic powers of nonhuman animals was not specifically excluded; but it was not specifically included, either, and psychic research and parapsychology have (with a few notable exceptions) generally ignored animals. But at least as far as domesticated species like dogs and cats are concerned, telepathy is as much a part of animal nature as of human nature — often more so. As in human-to-human telepathy, human-to-animal and animal-to-human telepathy generally depends on strong social bonds.

Telepathy seems unlikely to have arisen in domesticated species, like dogs, cats, horses, and parrots, simply as a result of domestication, and to be absent from their wild ancestors. It may well occur between members of colonies, flocks, schools, herds, packs, and other animal social groups. But very little is known about telepathy in wild animals, apart from folktales, hunters' stories, and the observations of a few open-minded naturalists (discussed in chapter 7). This is virgin scientific territory.

5 THE EFFECTS OF
INTENTIONS AT A DISTANCE

In *Dogs That Know When Their Owners Are Coming Home*, I discussed many examples of dogs and cats that seem to know when their owners are returning. They usually show their anticipation by going to wait at a window, door, or gate. When they do this only a few minutes before the person returns, they could simply be reacting to the sound of familiar footsteps or hearing a familiar car approaching. But sometimes the animals start waiting half an hour or more before the person arrives home, even when the person comes at an unexpected time in a taxi or other unfamiliar vehicle. No normal sensory information could explain these anticipations. Some react even before the person actually sets off, and seem to anticipate the person's *intention* to return.

Since *Dogs That Know When Their Owners Are Coming Home* was published, I have heard of hundreds of further examples of this behavior. Even Queen Elizabeth has dogs that anticipate her arrival. She is a renowned animal lover, and training her gundogs at Sandringham, her Norfolk estate, is one of her favorite hobbies. The staff at Sandringham do not need to be told when the queen is about to arrive, because the gundogs alert them. "All the dogs in the kennels start barking the moment she reaches the gate—and that is half a mile away," said Bill Meldrum, the head gamekeeper. "We don't know how they can tell, and they don't do that with anyone else."[1]

Sometimes this behavior is just a matter of curiosity for the people at home, but it can have its practical uses. I have received more than fifty reports from women who say that they know from the dog's behavior when their partner is on their way home, and start preparing a meal accordingly. Here is an example from the wife of a forester in Germany:

> Usually I did not know when my husband would be back, but our dog Birko sensed it. About thirty minutes before the car came toward the house he became restless, ran to the door, and lay down there. At first I thought it impossible for the dog to know half an hour beforehand when his owner would arrive. But soon I was not amazed any longer. From then on I was able to prepare a warm meal in time.
>
> ◆ INGEBORG PULLSKEN

These anticipations of arrivals do not occur only when people arrive by car. Dogs also know when their owners are coming home by train, bus, bicycle, ship, airplane, or other means of transport. In some cases the dogs may be responding to a routine pattern, but in many others their reactions occur even when people come at nonroutine times and the people at home do not know when to expect them, and also when people travel by taxi or in unfamiliar cars.

The most spectacular examples occur when people come home unannounced after long absences. This was the case with Alan Cook, an officer in the British Merchant Navy, who was away from home for periods of up to four months. The lengths of his absences varied considerably according to the routes his ships took.

> At no time did I ever inform my wife that I was coming home on leave, as too many things could have caused a delay which might have left her worrying. She didn't ever know what week, day, or hour I was going to arrive. On numerous occasions I used to arrive home to find that she was expecting me. On asking her how she knew I was coming home, she would tell me that my dog had told her. He would always be excited and looking for me well before the time I arrived home.

I have received reports of anticipatory behavior by forty-four distinct breeds of dogs. There is no evidence that some breeds do better than others. Return-anticipating dogs are found in all the main groups, including gundogs, hounds, terriers, working dogs, toy dogs, and mongrels.

Over a period of five years I have carried out numerous videotaped tests with dogs that know when their owners are coming home. The place where the dog usually waited was filmed continuously during the whole of the owner's absence. In some of the experiments, owners came home in taxis or other unfamiliar vehicles, and also came home at randomly selected times, communicated to them by means of a telephone pager.

In *Dogs That Know When Their Owners Are Coming Home,* I described a long series of videotaped experiments with a terrier-cross called Jaytee who lives with his owner, Pam Smart, in Ramsbottom, near Manchester, in northwest England. These experiments were carried when Pam was at least five miles away from home, and in some cases more than forty miles. The results of these tests confirmed that Jaytee waited at the window far more when Pam was on her way home than when she was not. His responses were highly significant statistically. Interestingly, he usually started to wait at the window even before Pam had got into the car to set off home. He generally began to wait when she decided to come home. In other words, he seemed to be responding to her intentions to return, before she had even started walking toward her car or toward a taxi.[2]

I have subsequently investigated a number of other dogs that show similar anticipatory reactions, including a Rhodesian Ridgeback named Kane, belonging to Sarah Hamlett, a veterinary student. Kane anticipated his owner's return by waiting at a window, standing on his rear legs and with his front paws on a table in order to see out. In these tests, during the main period of his owner's absence, Kane was at the window an average of only 1 percent of the time. By contrast, he was there 26 percent of the time when she was actually on the way home. This difference was highly significant statistically.[3]

These videotaped experiments carried out under controlled conditions showed that the dogs' anticipations of their owners' returns did not depend on routine times of return, or on clues from the people at home, or on sounds from familiar cars, or on any other sensory clues. They appeared to depend on their owners' intentions at a distance, and were essentially telepathic.

CATS, HORSES, AND PARROTS THAT ANTICIPATE PEOPLE'S RETURNS

Many cats anticipate the returns of their owners, but fewer do so than dogs. This does not necessarily mean that cats are less sensitive; they may simply be less interested. Some cats ignore their owners' returns when they come home from work or shopping, but are spectacularly successful at anticipating when they are coming back from holidays or long absences, and seem to know many hours in advance. For instance, a couple in Birmingham, England, left on a sailing trip, planning to be away for several months, but with no idea when they would return. Their neighbor fed their cat. When they came home after about three months,

> we found a loaf of bread and a bottle of milk waiting for us in the flat. We were amazed because nobody knew when we were getting back, not even us. When I asked my neighbor how she knew we were coming, she said, "We didn't know, but Thomas did." He never went near the car park at the front of the flats, but that day he sat there, looking up the road the whole day. "So we knew you were arriving today," she concluded. ◇ JACQUI GEATER

Some parrots also anticipate their owners' returns, as do some other members of the parrot family, like cockatiels and parakeets. A few other species of birds are also said to anticipate returns, notably mynah birds. But I have had no reports of return-anticipation in other commonly kept species like canaries and finches.

Some talking parrots signal the arrival of someone either by calling his or her name or by making some other announcement. For example, Deb Whitebread and her husband, Ron, have an African Grey named Rocket that she hand-raised since he was five weeks old.

> He is now eight years old, and although he is bonded to me, he speaks in my husband, Ron's, voice. Ron taught him to say "Hola" when he comes in the door. A couple of months ago I noticed that Rocket would start saying "Hola" about ten minutes before Ron came home. It was not as if he could hear his car or anything like that. Ron works a crazy schedule, and comes home at different times. I used to call him to see when he was coming home, but now I just wait for Rocket to tell me. He does this on a regular basis.

Joanna Berger, a biology professor and the author of The Parrot Who Owns Me, tells how her African Grey, Tiko, was waiting to welcome her home after an exhausting journey, standing on the railing at the foot of the stairs. "I don't know how he knew," her partner said, "but ten minutes before you walked through the door he opened his cage in the dark and flew to the banister, calling softly for you. I looked, but there was no taxi outside." Berger reflected: "How did he know when I was going to arrive? I have spent most of my life devoted to science. But in recent years my relationship to Tiko has begun to give me glimmers into another realm. There is so much yet to grasp about our connection to each other, and Tiko and I are joined in ways I don't begin to understand."[4]

Likewise, some horses anticipate their people's arrivals, either when they come to feed them or visit them in their paddocks, or when they return from absences of weeks or months. In one case this occurred under clinical observation.

We had a mare and her foal in the intensive-care unit at the University of California Veterinary Hospital at Davis. One day when we came to visit, the doctor in charge came up to us and said, "I have never seen a horse more connected to its owners than yours." He went on to explain that the horse's whole attitude would change about ten minutes before we would walk through the door. The entire staff knew when we were coming by seeing the horse change her attitude. Because the unit was specially isolated, had four-inch-thick concrete walls, steel doors, and heavy padding on the walls, this is not a case of supersensitive hearing. Somehow the horse knew when we were there by a sense that has yet to be explained. ❖ BOB GRISWOLD

The common factor in all these cases was that the return-anticipating animals had strong emotional bonds to the people who were coming back. In most cases they reacted to the return of only one particular member of the household. A minority reacted to two members of the household. Very few reacted to three or more.

The species that react to their owners' returns are also those that form the closest bonds with humans. A few members of other species show anticipations of return if they are particularly bonded to the person returning, including geese, hens, hand-reared lambs, rabbits, guinea pigs, and ferrets. But snakes, for example, are essentially solitary and do not even bond to other snakes, and I know of no cases of return-anticipation by snakes. And fish kept as pets literally live in a different element, and do not bond to people in any way comparable to that in which they bond to other fish. I know of no cases of goldfish that know when their owners are on the way, or of any other fish that do so.

It would be surprising indeed if all the very different species that anticipate arrivals had evolved this ability in response to domestication. Perhaps this might be plausible in the case of dogs, which may have been domesticated for some 100,000 years, or even in the case of cats, with 5,000 years of domestication. But many pet parrots were captured in the wild, or have been bred in captivity for only one or two generations, so the ability to anticipate returns could hardly have evolved in so short a time.

Even some wild animals that have been raised by humans show this kind of behavior, like Elsa, a lion cub brought up by Joy Adamson in Kenya. In her book *Born Free*, she describes how, during an absence in Nairobi, Elsa followed her husband around and went for a walk with him each evening, "but on the day of my return, she refused to accompany him and set herself down expectantly in the middle of the drive. Nothing would move her." Later, when Elsa returned to life in the wild, the Adamsons went to visit her every few weeks, and she usually arrived in their camp several hours afterward, "giving us a great welcome and showing more affection than ever."[5] Joy Adamson was convinced that Elsa "sensed our arrival in some mysterious way," even when she was far from the camp when they arrived there.[6]

It seems likely that arrival-anticipation is a part of many species' natural behavior in the wild. Young animals—for example, wolf cubs—may well anticipate the arrival of parents or other elders with food after a hunting trip. But practically nothing is known yet about such anticipations by animals under natural conditions. This would be a fruitful field for research.

PEOPLE WHO KNOW WHEN SOMEONE IS ABOUT TO ARRIVE

Some humans also seem to know in advance when people to whom they are attached are coming home. Several parents have told me that when they go out in the evening leaving their baby with a baby-sitter, quite often the baby wakes up shortly before they arrive home. Some older children actually announce the arrival of a parent. This happened when Sheila Michaels was looking after a three-year-old boy in New York while his mother was hospitalized.

> I did not expect his mother to be released for another day. I was reading a favorite story to him when the boy got off the bed and went to the door, calmly saying "Mommy, Mommy." . . . I tried to get him to come back and read the book with me, but he could not be budged, repeating "Mommy, Mommy" endlessly. I told him she would be back tomorrow, and his father was due in a couple of hours. He was immovable. Then his mother walked in.

Sometimes children at boarding schools know when their parents are coming to visit them. In his autobiography, the English writer Osbert Sitwell related that when he was about ten, and was bullied and extremely unhappy at a boarding school, "I knew beforehand when [my mother], or my brother or sister, was coming to see me. Infallibly, invariably, and without being informed of it, I became aware the previous day, and even when it appeared most unlikely that such a visit was impending, and equally I could tell if suddenly it had to be postponed."[7]

Sometimes parents know when their children are coming home from boarding school without being informed. Vandana Shiva, the environmentalist, was at boarding school in India while her father was an officer in the Indian Forest Service. He was often posted in out-of-the-way places, far from a telephone and difficult to contact by mail. She could not tell her parents in advance when she was going home for the weekend or for a surprise visit, but it did not matter. "My mother would always know which day I was coming and have the special food I liked cooked for me. She did the same for my brother and sister, who were at different schools. She had some uncanny way of knowing what we were up to."

Other examples concern husbands and wives. Here is a husband's story:

When we were living in Yorkshire [England], I took a job at Newcastle-upon-Tyne. One day I so missed my wife I decided on the spur of the moment to get a train and go home. We had no telephone, nor had any of our neighbors. When I arrived at our house, my wife had a meal ready for me and was waiting to greet me. She explained that she had a feeling that I was on my way. ◇ R. H. MOLTON

A particularly impressive return-anticipating husband happens to be a Nobel laureate, Richard Ernst. I learned about his hidden talents in 2000, after speaking about my research on return-anticipating animals in a lecture at the annual conference of the Swiss Academy of Sciences. That evening I was seated at dinner opposite his wife. She said to me enigmatically, "My husband does not believe what you say, but he can do it himself!" Of course I asked her what she meant. She told me that when she was visiting her critically ill mother in Zurich, she did not know in advance when she would be able to return, nor did she telephone to tell her husband which train she would be catching. "When I arrived at the station, my husband was waiting for me. He could not explain how he knew which train I was coming on. He just said he wanted to meet me to make sure I was safe."

In some cases the person's arrival was preceded by a kind of apparition, or phantasm, as the Victorian psychic researchers would have called it. For example, Ann Greenberg, of Silton, Saskatchewan, Canada, was on holiday with her husband in the family cabin by a lake. One night her husband went out in the boat, but a storm blew up and he did not return.

I was alone in the cabin and very worried so I stayed awake until about 2:00 A.M., when I fell asleep on the couch. Some time later I heard my husband walk up from the dock and cross the deck to the front door. He opened the door, walked over to the couch, leaned over, and put both hands on my shoulders. Then I woke up. It was daylight, but my husband wasn't there. I looked at the clock, which read 5:00 A.M. An hour later he pulled into our bay, safe and sound. He described how he had anchored in a sheltered bay and slept in the boat. He had woken up to a calm lake and decided he could make it back. Before setting out, he'd checked his watch, which read 5:00 A.M. The bay where he'd sheltered is about an hour away by boat from our cabin.

This hearing of sounds in advance is well known in northern Scandinavia, as I discussed in *Dogs That Know When Their Owners Are Coming Home*. In Norway there is even a special name for the phenomenon, *vardøger*, which literally means "warning soul." Typically, someone at home hears a person walking or driving up to the house, coming in, and hanging up his coat. Yet nobody is there. Some ten to thirty minutes later the person really arrives to similar sounds. People get used to it. Housewives put the kettle on as the *vardøger* arrives, knowing that their husbands will arrive soon.[8]

Professor Georg Hygen, of Oslo University, investigated dozens of recent cases, and published an entire book on this subject.[9] He concluded that the phenomenon is essentially telepathic rather than precognitive. In other words, the *vardøger* is not so much a pre-echo of what will happen in the future, but is related to a person's intentions. For one thing, the sounds are not always identical to those heard in advance. A person might be heard going up to the bedroom, whereas when he arrives he goes into the kitchen. Moreover, the *vardøger* phenomenon can still occur when a person does not in fact arrive, having changed his mind.

A man arranged to meet his wife in a store. He then changed his mind and decided to pick her up at her office instead. But he was delayed and was unable to do so. So he went to wait for her at the store as originally planned.

She did not arrive. After waiting for about an hour, he went home. She arrived home still later, complaining that he had not come to her office. She had heard his *vardøger*, and from previous experience trusted this so much that she had gone on waiting for him.

In English there is no equivalent word for *vardøger*. Perhaps the closest British parallel is the "second sight" of the Celtic inhabitants of the Scottish Highlands. This faculty includes "visions of 'arrivals' of persons remote at the moment, who later do arrive."[10] But in the Highlands, the primary means of knowing seems to be visual, rather than auditory, as in Scandinavia.

In many parts of Africa, an ability to anticipate arrivals is taken for granted, as it was among the Bushmen of the Kalahari described by Laurens van der Post (see page 95). Also, I have heard several stories about British officers posted in Africa during the colonial period who returned unannounced from long absences to find old houseboys waiting for them, having walked miles from their villages, with no normal means of knowing when their masters would be coming.

When people decide to go home, or are on the way, their intentions are directed homeward. It is those intentions that some people and animals seem able to detect. In this sense the anticipation of arrivals is related to the anticipation of telephone calls (chapter 6), since both are preceded by directed intention.

Although the ability to anticipate arrivals is relatively rare in modern Western societies, it seems to be an important aspect of the natural history of telepathy. The fact that such anticipations occur in babies and also when people are asleep shows that they are not dependent on the higher mental faculties. They work at a more fundamental level. Generally speaking, animals like dogs and cats are more sensitive than people.

On my database there are 46 cases of return-anticipation in humans, and 1,501 cases in animals.

SEXUAL DESIRES AND INFIDELITIES

A variety of emotions seem to be detectable telepathically, sexual feelings among them. The simplest cases involve desire. For example, a young man in New York told me that "my erotic thoughts about my girlfriend stimulated sexual excitement in her at a distance of a hundred miles with no prearrangement." A young man in Holland said, "I was thinking about sex at the same time as my partner twenty kilometers away, without ordinary explanation, and then we sent e-mails to each other about it at the same time."

Of course, separated lovers may often think about having sex with each other, so incidents of this kind could quite easily happen by chance. Simultaneous sexual arousal at a distance cannot be assumed to be telepathic, but on the other hand it cannot be assumed not to be. Only carefully controlled experiments could resolve this issue, and this is not an area where scientific research would be easy to organize.

Less happily, some people seem to pick up telepathically when their partners are engaged in sexual activities with other people. For example, when a student from New Zealand was staying in America, his much-loved girlfriend was still in New Zealand.

I had just got home from work one day when I had a vision of her having sex, not with me. It was late afternoon in New Zealand, so I decided to give her a call. She was shocked to hear from me and didn't want to talk because she had someone in bed with her.

Another example, from an American:

My wife had an affair 2,000 miles from home, and I felt the betrayal in my heart three times, on a long weekend when she was supposed to be with her best girlfriend. She was amazed I told her where, when, and how many times she had sex with that guy. She and he were the only two who knew, she thought.

From a woman in Belgium:

My husband was on a business trip to the United States. He told me that he was going to spend a couple of days hiking with some business colleagues. I felt a sense of panic, and then strong emotions of loneliness and despair. I couldn't sleep that night, and saw images of my husband making love to someone else. I thought I was going mad. I decided to write down what I experienced. The next night the same thing happened. When Paul came home he read what I had written in those sleepless nights and confirmed it all. He met this woman at the hotel where he was having his business meeting, and went on a hike with her, not his colleagues.

Fortunately, the couple overcame this crisis, and are still happily married.

The telepathic detection of infidelities does not generally involve a deliberate attempt to communicate telepathically by the one who is being unfaithful. Probably the opposite is the case. Perhaps the telepathic arousal of jealousy occurs because one member of a couple detects a change in the bond between them. The seventh sense, like the other senses, seems to depend on the detection of changes or differences, whether there is any conscious attempt to communicate these changes.

THINKING OF SOMEONE WHOSE LETTER THEN ARRIVES

Before telegrams and telephones were invented, people could communicate at a distance only by means of human messengers, or by sending letters.

In the second half of the nineteenth century, letter writing had increased enormously, both because of the spread of literacy and because of the establishment of postal services throughout the civilized world. In that period, many people noticed that they would think of a friend or family member for no apparent reason, and then within a few days receive a letter from that person. Or two people's letters to each other would cross in the mail, each having had an impulse to write around the same time.

One person who paid particular attention to this phenomenon was Mark Twain. As he put it in a letter in 1884:

I have reaped an advantage from these years of constant observation. . . . I have been saved the writing of many and many a letter by refusing to obey these strong impulses. I always knew the other fellow was sitting down to write when I got the impulse—so what could be the sense of us both writing the same thing? People are always marvelling that their letters "cross" each other. If they would but squelch the impulse to write, there would not be any crossing because only the other fellow would write. I am politely making an exception in your case.[11]

Such experiences are still quite common. For example, Andreas Roussopoulos, who lives in Athens, found this happened with a close female friend who went to live in Paris for a few months. "On five separate occasions I had very intense feelings of telepathic communication of a strong emotional nature with her. On each occasion I was so impressed that I noted the time, and on each occasion there was a response by post dated on that day! Naturally the letters took three or four days to arrive."

Jack Wilson, of Fareham, Hampshire, England, had a particularly striking experience with a nephew, with whom he had had a close bond when his nephew was a child.

> While traveling as a passenger in a car, I started to think about my nephew whom I had not seen for many years. As far as I was aware, the thoughts were not prompted by or related to anything connected with the surroundings or events. I found myself thinking about episodes in our early relationship. Two days later I received a lengthy letter from him in which he reminisced about the same situations. Later that day, I spoke to his wife on the telephone and asked when he had written the letter. She told me. It was the day and time that I had had my thoughts.

Telepathy seems the most likely explanation in such cases. But another kind of experience with letters is more problematic. Here the person does not think about the other person when the letter is being written, but just before it arrives. For example: "One morning I dreamed of going to the hallway and picking up a letter in a brown envelope from my ex-girlfriend, from whom I had heard nothing for six months. I went downstairs to the hallway and sure enough, there on the mat was the letter in a brown envelope" (Dylan Bates, London).

Perhaps after posting the letter, the sender anticipated when it would arrive, and thought of the recipient at that time. But this argument would depend on the postal service being more predictable than it often is. In cases such as this, precognition seems a more likely explanation than telepathy. We will return to this subject in chapter 16.

6 TELEPHONE TELEPATHY

In his book *The Lost World of the Kalahari*, Sir Laurens van der Post told how Bushmen in the Kalahari Desert, in southern Africa, were in telepathic contact far beyond the range of sensory communication. On one occasion, when he had been out hunting with some Bushmen, he found that people who had stayed behind in the camp knew they had killed an eland fifty miles away, and also knew when they would be returning. They compared their method of communication with the white man's telegraph, or "wire." As they were heading back in Land Rovers laden with meat, van der Post asked one Bushman how the people would react when they learned of their success. He replied, " 'They already know. They know by wire. . . . We bushmen have a wire here' "—he tapped his chest— " 'that brings us news.' " Sure enough, when they approached the camp, the people were singing the "Eland Song" and preparing to give the hunters the greatest of welcomes.[1]

Probably most people in modern societies would have too little confidence in telepathy to try to communicate with others *just* by this means. Telephones provide a more reliable and effective method. Yet, ironically, the very intention of calling someone at a distance by telephone creates favorable conditions for telepathy. The callers think about the people they want to call, maybe look up their numbers, and then dial them. All this time they are focusing their attention on the people they want to call, and their rational minds do not interfere with this focusing because technology has made it possible. Telephones give people permission to call practically anyone they need, whenever they want. Before the invention of telephones, probably the only intellectuals who believed in the possibility of calling someone at a distance were Theosophists or followers of other esoteric movements. Nowadays, even the most die-hard materialists direct their intention toward people with whom they want to get in touch, however far away they are. Whether they like it or not, their intention may be detectable telepathically.

THINKING OF SOMEONE WHO THEN CALLS

Obviously there is nothing strange about anticipating a call from someone expected to ring. But many people have found that for no apparent reason they start thinking about a particular person, then the phone rings and that person is on the line. Here are three representative examples from dozens on my database:

> Often when I think of a friend in Belgium, she calls me five to ten minutes later. The same thing happens with my mother, I think of her and a few minutes later she calls or sends a fax. And that is from Belgium to Sweden!

> I have often anticipated calls from certain patients that I had discharged from psychotherapy. Something made me wonder how they were faring. A short time later they'd call to ask for an appointment or to get some advice.

> I have a friend that I had a strong connection with years ago and although we only talk every few months, I think of him out of the blue just before he calls, almost every time, usually within minutes.

Generally such calls are from people with whom the person is familiar and shares an emotional bond. But occasionally they involve distant acquaintances, or negative emotions, or both, as in the experience of Ersi Hatzimichalis, in Athens, Greece. During the period of military rule in the late 1960s and early 1970s, the security services were looking for his brother Niko, who was in the democratic resistance.

> I was painting one day in my studio when out of the blue there came to my mind the image of a certain Mr. K., an officer of the security services who had collaborated with the Germans during the occupation. I had met him socially before the war, but I always felt very insecure with him; he had a seedy air about him, and was underhanded

and shifty. He seemed just as likely to arrest us as help us. Anyway, I had not thought of him and had no reason to think of him for over twenty-five years. The phone rang and it was him! He was very smooth and asked how I was, but really he wanted to know the where-abouts of Niko. I told him Niko was in Paris.

Quite often, people are not aware of thinking about a particular person beforehand, but while the phone is ringing they know who is on the line. For example: "With my best friend, I would say that about 70 to 80 percent of the time, we know that it's the other calling as soon as the phone rings, and this has continued over a period of about eighteen years" (Dr Eleanor Pryor, Australia). Many people say that the very way the phone rings seems different when a particular person is calling. For example, Ann Murray, of Fife, Scotland, told me, "Some years ago I was in a very close relationship and could always tell by the sound of the phone when my love was ringing. It is difficult to explain, but the phone sounded different when he rang."

ACTIVELY INDUCING PEOPLE TO CALL

If you want someone to call, thinking about him sometimes seems to induce him to do so. I had an experience of this kind myself when I was living in Hyderabad, India, and particularly needed to get in touch with an English friend who lived several miles away and did not have a phone. He rarely called me. I was wondering how I could possibly get a message to him. After about ten minutes the phone rang, and there he was, calling from a public tele-phone, saying he felt he needed to call, but didn't know why.

Alan Cook, of Dungeness, Kent, England, had an experience of this type with a woman friend when she was on vacation in Italy. He had often called her just as she was calling him, but on this occasion he did not know the num-ber of the hotel in which she was staying.

I came home from work one evening while my friend was away, and I remember thinking that I would really like to speak with her. About twenty minutes later my telephone rang, and the first words I heard were "Sorry I'm late." She then went on to explain that she "felt" that I needed to talk with her while she was having dinner in her hotel. She then had to go and buy a telephone card and find a telephone to use, hence the delay. She had absolutely no doubt that I needed to talk with her.

Joann Ertz, of Tacoma, Washington, used to do this with her mother as a kind of game.

It began with her telling me one day that we should both concentrate on each other and have the thought "Call me," and every time it worked. It actually got to be a joke between us, and on several occasions I couldn't think of anything else but that I needed to "call Mom." When I did, she would be laughing, and say, "I just wanted to see if it still worked. How are you?"

Such mental calls at a distance are very similar to the kinds of telepathic call discussed in chapter 3. But before the invention of the telephone and telegraph, there was little that people could do to respond to such calls other than go to the person they felt calling them. Or they could write a letter. Or they could simply try to forget about it. But now telephones are so widespread, it is easy to respond to the impulse to get in touch with a particular person, and probably ever-increasing numbers of people do so. The fact that so many people now have cell phones makes it easier still.

WHO INFLUENCES WHOM?

As we have seen, sometimes people think about a person who then calls, as if he or she were picking up the caller's intention. Sometimes it works the other way around, and someone wants another person to call, who then rings. But quite often the direction of influence is ambiguous: "About six years ago I called a friend long distance whom I hadn't spoken with in months, to find upon her answering that she was in the process of looking up my number to call me when the phone rang. Since then I have experienced this phenomenon many times" (Jai Flicker, Forest Knolls, California).

Sometimes both people call each other at exactly the same time. Jill Andrews, in Wyoming, had this experience repeatedly when she called her mother, a former biology teacher, in Michigan.

On several occasions over the years I have called her only to receive a busy signal. When I hung up the phone, it would suddenly ring immediately. It was my mother calling me at the exact same moment! In other instances I picked up the phone to dial her, and there was no dial tone. "Hello?" I said, to hear if another person in my house was using the phone. My mother responded, "Hello!" I had picked up her phone call without even having heard it ring. Nearly every time I phone home, Mom answers, "Well, Jill! I was just thinking about you!"

HOW COMMON ARE THESE EXPERIENCES?

Seemingly telepathic experiences with telephones are very common. Indeed, they seem to be the commonest kind of telepathic experience in the modern world. Any reader who doubts this can carry out an informal investigation by asking family members, friends, or colleagues if they have had experiences of apparent telepathy in relation to telephone calls. I predict that many, probably most, will say that they have.

As far as I know, there have until now been no attempts to estimate how many people have had seemingly telepathic experiences with telephones. I have also tried to quantify how common they are by three different methods.

First, over a period of five years, I have asked people at lectures, seminars, and conferences in Europe and North and South America whether they have known who was calling before they answered the phone in a way that seemed to be telepathic. On the basis of a show of hands, between 80 and 95 percent claimed to have had this experience. This is, of course, a very crude form of survey, and the audiences I encountered were obviously not a random sample of the population. Nevertheless, by this method I have been able to question large numbers of people, some 6,000 altogether, throughout western Europe and the Americas. At the very least, these preliminary results showed that telepathy in connection with telephone calls is well known in a wide range of countries.

Second, I have asked groups of people attending lectures and seminars in Britain, Germany, the United States, and Argentina to fill out questionnaires about their experiences with telephones. The first question was "Have you ever thought of somebody just as the telephone rang, or just before, and it was indeed the person you had been thinking of? (Exclude anticipations that could have an ordinary explanation and include only those that seemed telepathic.)" In total, 1,562 out of 1,691 people, or 92 percent of those completing the questionnaire, answered in the affirmative.[2]

Third, my research associates and I have carried out formal surveys by telephone of a random selection of households in England and the United States. In these surveys about half of the respondents said they had felt they had known who was calling before they answered the phone: in London, 51 percent; in Bury, in northwest England, 49 percent; and in Santa Cruz, California, 47 percent.[3] An even higher percentage said they had telephoned someone who said they were just thinking about telephoning them. In England the average was 65 percent, and in California 78 percent.[4] In all cases, more women than men claimed to have had these experiences.

These surveys also showed that seemingly telepathic experiences in anticipating telephone calls were commoner than any other kind of telepathic experience.

THE NATURAL HISTORY OF TELEPHONE TELEPATHY

My questionnaires were intended primarily to find out more about the natural history of telephone telepathy, especially how often it seemed to happen and with whom.

The first and most obvious finding was that more women than men had had this experience (see Figure 6.1). This sex difference was apparent in all four countries: Argentina, Britain, Germany, and the United States. This finding confirmed the results from the random household surveys, and supported the widespread belief that women tend to be more intuitive. Among men, the Argentines came out highest and the British lowest.

The people among whom these experiences occurred most were friends, mothers, spouses, partners, and colleagues. They also occurred with other family members, especially sisters, and also with employers and employees (see Figure B.2, page 310). In addition, a small percentage of the respondents reported such experiences with clients, godparents, therapists, patients, and teachers. The same general pattern was found independently in all four countries.

Same-sex friends were more likely to be detected telepathically than opposite-sex friends. This pattern contrasts with reactions to mothers and fathers, where both men and women responded more to mothers than to fathers (see Figure B.3, page 311).

Respondents were also asked, "Have you had any other kinds of telepathic experience?" In total, 68 percent said yes. Again, very significantly more women (72 percent) than men (58 percent) gave a positive answer. These per-

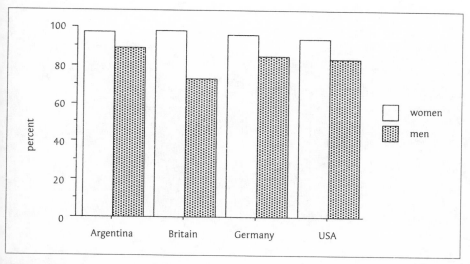

Figure 6.1 *The percentages of men and women in four countries who said they had had seemingly telepathic experiences in relation to telephone calls. Details of this questionnaire survey are given in Appendix B.*

centages are much lower than those for telephone telepathy (Figure 6.2), and provide further evidence that telepathy in connection with telephone calls is the commonest kind in the modern world.

More details of this questionnaire survey are given in Appendix B. In summary, the survey showed that more women than men said that they had had seemingly telepathic experiences with telephone calls. Some people had these experiences quite often, more or less daily (Figure B.1, page 309). Telephone telepathy did not depend on a particular kind of technology, and occurred with cell phones as well as with landlines. In all four countries, most of these experiences happened when very familiar people were calling, especially friends, mothers, spouses, partners, sisters, and colleagues.

RESEARCH ON TELEPHONE TELEPATHY

Even though telephone telepathy seems so common, scientific researchers — even parapsychologists — have surprisingly ignored it. But it is neither difficult nor expensive to do experimental research on this subject.

As always, the first question that needs to be asked is could this apparent telepathy merely be a matter of chance coincidence? Perhaps people often have thoughts about others for no particular reason. By chance, these thoughts

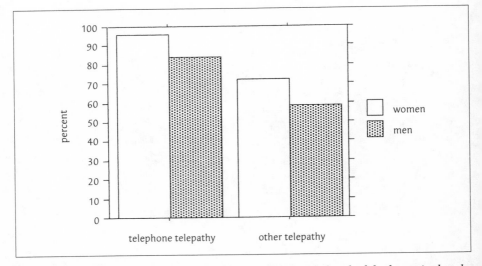

Figure 6.2 *The percentages of men and women who said they had had seemingly telepathic experiences in relation to telephone calls, compared with the percentages who said they had had other kinds of telepathic experience. These figures are the averages from questionnaire surveys carried out in Argentina, Britain, Germany, and the United States, as described in Appendix B.*

may sometimes be followed by a telephone call from that person. If people only remember the times they are right and forget the times they are wrong, then the illusion of telepathy may be created by a combination of chance coincidence and selective memory.

One way that anyone can use to investigate this possibility is to keep a logbook by the telephone, and write down any intuition about who is calling when the phone rings, but before answering. (Of course, for this test, any caller-identifying system should be turned off or covered up.) Then, after the call is over, record the date and time, the name of the actual caller, and whether the call was expected or not. Only unexpected calls are relevant for the investigation of telepathy. From such logbooks it is easy to work out the overall success rate, and also the success rates with individual callers.

Although logbooks are the simplest way to avoid the problem of selective memory, they still leave open another possible "normal" explanation. A person may be expecting a call around a particular time from a particular person, but may be unconscious of this expectation. So when the call comes there is no need to invoke telepathy, because an unconscious expectation could explain it instead. The trouble is that unconscious expectation is an elusive concept. It may well be an untestable hypothesis, which in science is a vice, not a virtue.

For if the expectation of a telephone call is unconscious, how can anyone prove that it is really there? And if it *is* really there, then might this expectation be a *result* of telepathy, rather than an alternative to it?

The best way to resolve these questions is by means of experimental tests that can be evaluated statistically. I have developed an experimental procedure that has given clear, positive, and repeatable results.

EXPERIMENTAL TESTS

In these tests, subjects received a call at a given time from one of four different callers. They knew who the potential callers were, but did not know which one would be calling in any given test, because the caller was picked at random by the experimenter. They had to guess who the caller was before they picked up the phone. By chance they would have been right about one time in four, or 25 percent of the time. Were they right significantly more often than they would be by random guessing?

My colleagues and I recruited subjects who claimed that they sometimes knew, in a way that seemed telepathic, who was calling before they answered the phone. Each subject named four people to whom they thought they might respond telepathically; for example, their mother, their sister, and two friends. They were, of course, asked to do this experiment without any caller-ID system on their phone. (Since all cell phones have built-in caller-ID systems, we used landlines without them.)

The subjects chose a time when they were free to do the experiment, and checked that their four callers would be free to make calls during that period, say between 2:00 and 2:20 P.M. on a Thursday afternoon. They told the experimenter, who then fixed a time for the experimental call, say at 2:15 P.M., and informed the subject when this would be. At the beginning of the experimental period, which began fifteen minutes before the call was due to be made, the experimenter picked a number between 1 and 4 at random by throwing a die. This determined which of the four callers was to make the call. The experimenter then called the caller who had been chosen and asked him or her to phone the subject at the appointed time, 2:15 P.M., and think about that person for about a minute before ringing. By 2:05 P.M. the other three potential callers knew that they had not been chosen because the experimenter had not called them.

When the phone rang at 2:15 P.M., the subject knew that one of these four callers was on the line, and before answering the phone, she had to guess who it was. When answering the phone, she said the name she guessed—for example, "Hello, Ben"—before the caller said anything.

As an additional precaution against possible cheating or inadvertent errors in recording the data, in many of our tests, subjects were filmed throughout the experimental period on time-coded videotape. They said to the camera what their guess was before answering the phone. In some tests, the callers were filmed continuously as well as the subject.

If the subjects had no telepathic abilities and were just guessing, with four potential callers they would be right roughly 25 percent of the time. Some subjects did indeed score at the chance level. But others scored well above chance. By September 2002, we had conducted 854 such tests, with 65 different subjects. The overall success rate was 42 percent, which was astronomically significant statistically, with odds against chance of 10^{26} to 1.[5] Of these trials, 571 were unfilmed, with a success rate of 40 percent, and 237[6] were videotaped, with a success rate of 45 percent.[7] More details of these tests are given in Appendix B.

Many of our filmed investigations were carried out with Sue Hawksley, who lives in Wakefield, Yorkshire, England. In her first 30 tests, which were not filmed, she was right 14 times, a success rate of 47 percent. This result was highly significant statistically, with odds against chance of 2,500 to 1. We then tested her a further 100 times, with all tests videotaped. She was right 49 times. The odds against this result being obtained by chance are more than 100 million to 1. She was much more successful with some people than with others, and with one close friend she was right 75 percent of the time (see Table B.4, page 313).

In a second series of 85 videotaped tests, her overall success rate was 45 percent, again very significantly above the chance levels.[8] But in these tests, only two of the callers were friends; the other two were researchers whom she had not met. With her friends she was right in 66 percent of the trials, and with the researchers in only 18 percent, somewhat below the chance level (see Figure 6.3).

In a further series of trials with Sue, both she and all four callers were filmed continuously by independent cameramen. She was right in 47 percent of the trials. Again she scored well above chance with friends, but at chance levels with a researcher who was not a friend. (For more details, see Table B.5, page 314.)

Several subjects, including Sue, commented that they felt more confident about their guesses at some times than at others. They also thought that they were more often right when they were confident. In order to test this possibility, I asked Sue to record just how confident she felt about her guesses before she answered the phone. She did this in a total of 134 videotaped trials, and registered three grades of confidence: "confident," "not very confident," and "just guessing." She was, in fact, most successful when she felt confident, being right 85 percent of the time. When she was not very confident, her success rate was only 34 percent, and when she said she was just guessing, her success rate of 28 percent was not significantly above the chance level of 25 percent (see Table B.6, page 314).

Since telepathy seems to depend on social bonds, it is not surprising that some caller-subject combinations work better than others. To obtain more comparisons of the success of subjects with familiar and unfamiliar people as callers, we carried out a further series of trials, in which some of the callers were researchers whose names the subjects knew, but whom they had not met, or even computers (in the form of automated alarm calls from British Telecom). The prediction was that the scores would be lower with unfamiliar people and computers than with friends or family members. In a series of trials with 30 different subjects, with friends and family members the success rate was 77 out of 140 trials (56 percent), very significantly above the chance level.[9] With unfamiliar people and alarm calls, there were 27 correct guesses out of 109 trials (24.7 percent), very close to the chance level (see Figure 6.3). This difference between the scores with familiar and unfamiliar people was highly significant statistically.[10]

Experiments on telephone telepathy provide a good opportunity to test for the effect, or lack of effect, of distance. In the experiments conducted within Britain, we have found no indication that callers who are closer are more effective than those who are far away. For example, in experiments with my associate Pam Smart as subject, her success rate with me as her caller, more than 200 miles away, was 67 percent, whereas with a friend 5 miles away, the success rate was 50 percent.

Calls can be made with separations between the caller and the subject up to 12,500 miles, the distance between the antipodes, as far away as anyone can be on the surface of the earth. For these experiments we recruited subjects in London who had recently come to England from Australia and New Zealand, near the antipodes, and also from South Africa and other distant countries. We compared the subjects' success rates with friends and family members overseas with friends in Britain. In a total of 58 trials, involving 7 subjects, the success rate with callers thousands of miles away averaged 61 percent, compared with 36 percent with friends in Britain (Table B.8, page 316). Subjects were *more* successful with callers farther away than with those who were much nearer.

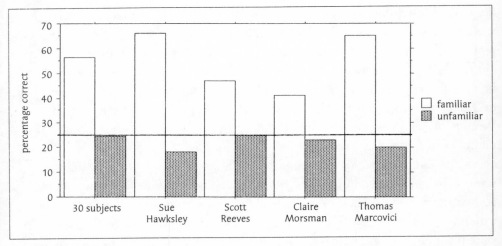

Figure 6.3 *The percentages of correct guesses in telephone telepathy experiments with familiar and unfamiliar callers, comparing the combined results from unfilmed experiments with thirty different subjects, and the results from filmed experiments with four different subjects. The success rate of 25 percent expected on the basis of random guessing is indicated by a horizontal line.*

Why? The most probable explanation is that the majority of the overseas callers were people to whom the subjects were particularly strongly attached, such as mothers and boyfriends, while the callers in Britain were mainly new acquaintances.

The lack of effect of distance on telephone telepathy is in general agreement with previous research on other kinds of telepathy. Telepathic influences did not seem to fall off with distance in experiments either with people[11] or with animals such as dogs, cats, and parrots.[12] These influences seemed to depend on personal closeness and interconnectedness, rather than on spatial proximity.

Experiments with telephones provide a simple and effective way of carrying out research, and further tests of this kind would make excellent student projects. Practical details are given in Appendix A.

PETS THAT KNOW WHO'S CALLING

Some domestic animals also seem to know when a particular person is calling, as I discussed in *Dogs That Know When Their Owners Are Coming Home.* Indeed, it was this ability of dogs and cats to anticipate who was calling that aroused my interest in telephone telepathy in humans. I soon found that this was the only aspect of the seventh sense in which people did better than animals.

One of the first stories I heard about a telephone-answering animal was from the wife of a professor at the University of California at Berkeley. She told me that she always knew when her husband was calling because Whiskins, their silver tabby, would rush to the telephone and paw at the receiver. "Many times he succeeds in taking it off the hook and makes appreciative meows that are clearly audible to my husband at the other end," she said. "If someone else telephones, Whiskins takes no notice." Whiskins did this not only when her husband phoned home from the campus, but also when he called from Africa or South America when he was on field trips.

Some cats, like some people, seem to anticipate calls even before the telephone rings. For example, Sheila Geddes, of Yaxham, Norfolk, England, told me:

Our cat, Mr. Softy, always seemed to know when I was going to phone home, and he would go and sit on the phone seat and purr. Once when I was in Australia, he went up onto the telephone seat one afternoon when it would have been 1:00 A.M. in Canberra. My husband knew how late it was in Canberra, and told Mr. Softy, "It's no good, we won't hear from her now." But I had woken up suddenly, felt very far from home, and realized it would be early evening there, so five minutes later, the phone rang beside him. He was delighted to hear my voice.

The distance between Mrs. Geddes and her cat was about 11,000 miles.

Some dogs likewise seem to know when a particular person is calling, even if they are thousands of miles away. Marie McCurrach, who lives in Ipswich, Suffolk, England, had a Labrador dog that joined the family when her son was ten. Four years later her son left home to attend a naval school and went on to serve in the Merchant Navy, mainly sailing to and from South Africa.

Every time he rang home, the dog would run to the telephone before anyone could answer it. The dog never bothered about any other calls, only our son's, and we had to hold the phone to the dog's ear so that our son could speak to him and the dog would reply. Our son never gave us a time that he would phone, and did not phone at predictable times, so how did the dog know it would be our son on the phone before anyone had lifted the receiver?

As with cats and people, some dogs respond even before the telephone starts ringing. For example, Tansy Ellison, of Hampstead, London, has noticed that her greyhound, Maisie, "senses the phone is going to ring. If she is upstairs, she will run downstairs to stand next to it, or she will start to bark before it rings. She just does this when my mum is calling, never for other people."

Some parrots also react to calls from particular people, and even announce them by name before the phone has been answered. Richard Dalby, of Harrogate, Yorkshire, England, has an African Grey called Kerry who responds to calls from several members of the family, especially his stepdaughters Michele and Jeanine.

> She seems to know instinctively when it is Michele. When she hears the telephone ringing, she shouts "Shell"—we often call Michele "Shell" for short. I don't know how she does it. Michele phones several times a week, not always at the same time, it could be evening or morning. But Kerry will sometimes say "Jeanine" and it is Jeanine on the phone.

As in the case of dogs and cats, some parrots react before the phone starts ringing. For example, Lilla Cabot, of Guilford, Connecticut, found that when her daughter Jane went away to school, their Amazon parrot, Phoenix, took to announcing when she was about to phone home.

> One night around ten, Phoenix suddenly began calling "Jane, Jane." My other daughter said, "Mom, check the clock, Jane's probably going to call!" Ten minutes went by, and still no call came. I was beginning to doubt it when the phone did ring and it was Jane. I asked her about the timing and she told me that at exactly ten she was leaving to make the call when a friend came into the room and delayed her for about ten minutes. Phoenix's announcement must have come when she was first intending to make the call.

On my database are 103 cases of animals that seem to know who is calling: 52 with dogs, 43 with cats, and 8 with parrots, cockatoos, and other members of the parrot family. There is also one recorded example of a call-anticipating monkey, a capuchin called Sunday. Her owner, Richard Savage, left her with a friend in British Columbia while he was away on a filmmaking assignment. "Several minutes before Richard would telephone to talk to me, Sunday would jump up and start chattering. After his call she would settle down for days, ignoring the telephone—until just before Richard called again."[13]

As far as I know, there have not yet been any experimental studies of telephone telepathy in animals. In Appendix A, I suggest how such tests could be carried out.

TELEPATHIC E-MAILS

The evolution of telepathy is still going on. After telephone telepathy comes e-mail telepathy, which generally follows the same patterns. People find that they think of someone they have not thought about for a while, and shortly afterward receive an e-mail from that person. For example: "I think of a friend in Australia or South Africa and receive an e-mail which must have been written at about the time when I was thinking of them," says Christine Steel, of Surrey, England. Sometimes the experience is more or less immediate: "I was about to send someone an e-mail, and they contacted me before I could begin typing" (Nickolai Parker, New York).

Sometimes the e-mails are not ones that people particularly want to receive, but seem to be triggered simply by paying attention to someone. A publishing executive in New York told me that several times when she had been clearing out her files and throwing away material from a would-be author, within a day she received an e-mail from that person, whom she had not heard from for months.

In 2002, I started experimental research on e-mail telepathy, using a modification of the procedure I used in tests for telephone telepathy. Each subject chose four friends or family members to act as e-mailers. At a prearranged time, say at 10:30 A.M., one of these four people, selected at random by the experimenter, e-mailed the subject, sending a copy of this e-mail to the experimenter. One minute before this happened, at 10:29, the subject e-mailed the experimenter to say what her guess was. The times at which these messages were sent were automatically recorded on the e-mails.

As in the telephone telepathy trials, there was a 25 percent chance of being right by random guessing. By September 2002, I had completed 160 trials of this kind, in 67 of which the subject guessed correctly. This 43-percent success rate was very significantly above the chance level.[14]

Experiments on e-mail telepathy are relatively simple and inexpensive to carry out, and would make excellent student projects (see Appendix A for experimental details, and see my website, www.sheldrake.org, for updates on this ongoing research).

7

THE EVOLUTION

OF TELEPATHY

Telepathy occurs in animals of many different species. How widespread is it? And how far back are its evolutionary origins?

A variety of domesticated animals seem to pick up human thoughts and intentions telepathically. Most cases concern dogs, cats, horses, and parrots. There are also scattered reports about telepathy in other species kept as pets, including rabbits, ferrets, hand-reared lambs, cockatiels, parakeets, budgerigars, mynah birds, hens, and geese.[1]

All these animals are either mammals or birds. I am not aware of any strong evidence for pet reptiles picking up human thoughts and intentions. Nor amphibia, nor fish.

Among insects, hives of bees are sometimes said to react to the death of their owners. But the available evidence is not very strong. Through my appeals for information in a variety of beekeepers' journals (including *Scottish Beekeeper* and *L'Abeille de France*) I have received only three firsthand reports of bees swarming soon after the death of their keeper at times of year when swarming would be unusual. But some beekeepers are skeptical about stories of bees reacting to the death of their owners; they also dismiss as superstition the formerly widespread custom of telling the bees that their keeper has died.

Leaving bees aside, and leaving open the question of possible telepathy between people and reptiles, the vast majority of cases of human-animal telepathy involve domesticated mammals and birds. How has human-animal telepathy arisen? Has telepathy in domesticated mammals and birds evolved only because of human influence? Or are animals of these species telepathic with each other in the wild?

Dogs have been domesticated for a very long time, maybe 100,000 years.[2] Cats and horses were domesticated more recently, probably about 5,000 years ago.[3] In these species, telepathy could perhaps have evolved through interactions with humans over many generations. There would have been plenty of scope for natural or even deliberate selection. But this argument does not apply to parrots. Many parrots kept as pets today were captured in the wild when young, and had no domesticated ancestors. The importation of wild-caught African Grey parrots into the United States was banned only in 1993, and birds currently in captivity are, at most, only one or two generations removed from the wild. Many breeders still breed with wild-caught African Greys. Telepathic communications between people and parrots cannot be explained by many generations of genetic selection under domestication.

In addition, some wild animals raised by human beings form strong bonds with their human guardians, and even after being returned to the wild they may retain a telepathic connection, like Joy Adamson's lion cub, Elsa (page 88).

In any case, domesticated animals are unlikely to have picked up their telepathic abilities from people. Cats, dogs, horses, and parrots are generally more sensitive to telepathic influences than their human companions. This asymmetry is clearly apparent on my database, where there are currently 2,731 cases of telepathy from people to animals, as opposed to 251 from animals to people. And in random surveys in Britain and America, more pets were telepathic than their owners, according to the owners themselves.[4]

Thus telepathy in nonhuman animals does not seem to be a special feature of domestication. Perhaps animals of many species are telepathic with other members of their social group under natural conditions. The manifestation of telepathy under domestication seems most likely to be related to telepathic abilities already present in the animals' wild forebears.

ANIMAL-TO-ANIMAL TELEPATHY

There has been very little research on animal-to-animal telepathy either with domesticated or wild animals. Nevertheless, as I described in *Dogs That Know When Their Owners Are Coming Home*, scattered observations suggest that dogs can be influenced telepathically by others to whom they are strongly bonded. Animals of other species also seem capable of communicating tele-pathically with other members of their social group. I know of only three for-mal experiments on animal-to-animal telepathy, and these all point to the same conclusion.

First, in tests with dogs carried out in New York, a mother boxer was kept in a separate room from her son, who was then at particular times "threatened" by an experimenter. He cowered. The mother, in her isolated chamber, cow-ered at exactly the same moment.[5]

Second, the British horse trainer Henry Blake tested horses for telepathy, using pairs of brothers or sisters that were used to living as close companions. In a total of 119 tests, the pairs of horses were separated and kept out of sight and hearing of each other. Blake found that when one was fed or exercised or made a fuss over, in 68 percent of the tests the other horse reacted at the same time. Blake also ran control tests with a pair of horses that were hostile to each other; in only 1 out of 15 tests was there a positive result. Blake con-cluded that horses bonded to each other could communicate telepathically, and suggested that this kind of communication might be vital for their sur-vival in the wild. For example, a herd of horses might be scattered, with some members out of sight and sound of each other. The ability to communicate alarm telepathically might enable some members of the herd to alert others to danger even though they were beyond the range of normal sensory com-munication.[6]

Third, the French scientist René Peoc'h has shown that rabbits seem to communicate telepathically if they are bonded to each other. In his experi-ments, the rabbits were monitored continuously for stress by measuring the blood flow through their ears. Peoc'h compared pairs of rabbits from the same litter that had shared the same cages with control pairs that had been kept in isolation from each other in individual cages. When one of the rabbits experi-enced stress,[7] as measured by decreased blood flow in the ear, there was usu-ally a decreased blood flow in the other rabbit's ear within three seconds. The control pairs showed no such correlation.[8]

TELEPATHY IN HERDS AND PACKS

Naturalists and hunters who have paid attention to herds of wild animals have often seen a whole herd become alarmed and flee after one or more animals has sensed danger. Of course, in many cases this can be explained in terms of alarm signals and normal sensory cues. But sometimes alarm seems to spread silently and rapidly, with no apparent means of sensory communication. The American naturalist William Long observed this phenomenon repeatedly when tracking herds of caribou and elk in Canada, and concluded that whole herds could suddenly feel a silent impulse to flee, and obey it without question, in a way that was essentially telepathic.[9] Perhaps the evolutionary roots of human panics lie in this kind of collective behavior.

Long also studied the behavior of packs of wolves in Canada by tracking them for days on end. He paid particular attention to the way the members of the pack were linked together, even when they were far apart. Wolves separated from the pack seemed to know where the others were: "In the winter time, when timber wolves commonly run in small packs, a solitary or separated wolf always seems to know where his mates are hunting or idly roving or resting in their day-bed. . . . [B]y some bond or attraction or silent communication he can go straight to them at any hour of the day or night, though he may not have seen them for a week, and they have wandered over countless miles of wilderness in the interim."[10] Long found that this behavior could not be explained by following habitual paths, by tracking scent trails, or by hearing howling or other sounds.[11]

These connections at a distance may be a normal feature of animal societies, even though we have hardly begun to study them or understand how they work.

FLOCKS OF BIRDS

Some species of birds, such as starlings, form flocks that fly with a remarkable coordination, changing direction almost simultaneously without the individual birds colliding with each other. How do they do it?

Although there have been surprisingly few studies of the detailed behavior of flocks of birds, there have been several attempts to simulate flock behavior on computers. Craig Reynolds developed the best known of these models, called "boids," in the 1980s.[12] A sample can be seen on the Internet.[13] This model is of course only two-dimensional, but at first sight seems to simulate flock behavior quite impressively.

The boids model is "individual based"; that is to say, it starts from individual boids. These boids are programmed to behave according to three simple rules:

1. Steer to avoid being too close to neighbors.
2. Steer toward the average direction that neighbors are heading in.
3. Steer to move toward the average position of neighbors.

By following these rules, a collection of boids on the computer screen behaves rather like a flock. This simulated "emergent behavior" seems to show that the behavior of the flock as a whole is a product of individuals interacting with their neighbors according to simple rules, with no need for any mysterious organizing principles. But while this may be true of the computer model, it bears little relation to the behavior of real, three-dimensional flocks of birds. Reynolds developed the boids program starting not from data about real birds, but rather from a school of computer programming concerned with "artificial life," typically involving two-dimensional models in which neighboring units "interact" according to simple rules. Special-effects wizards have used these kinds of programs to create animations of flocks or herds in films like *The Lion King* and *Batman Returns*.

Computer models of the boids type are useful for producing two-dimensional animations, but they are biologically naive. Although there has been surprisingly little research into the behavior of real flocks, enough is known to rule out the kind of neighbor-to-neighbor interactions on which the boid-type models depend.[14]

For example, in the 1980s, the biologist Wayne Potts filmed the banking movements of large flocks of dunlins in Puget Sound, Washington, by taking films with very rapid exposures, so they could be slowed down to investigate in detail how the movements of the flocks occurred. (Dunlins are small wading birds that live on seashores.) Potts found that the changes of direction of the flock were not exactly simultaneous, but rather started either from a single individual or from a few birds together. These starting points could come from anywhere within the flock, radiating from them through the flock like a wave. These "maneuver waves" were very rapid, and took on average only fifteen milliseconds (fifteen-thousandths of a second) to pass from neighbor to neighbor.

In the laboratory, Potts tested captive dunlins to find out how rapidly they could react to a sudden stimulus. On average, they showed a startle reaction thirty-eight milliseconds after a sudden flash of light. This means that they could not change direction in response to their neighbors, since this response occurs much quicker than their minimum reaction time.

Potts concluded that birds responded not to their immediate neighbors but rather to the maneuver wave as a whole, adjusting their flight pattern to anticipate the arrival of the wave. He took it for granted that the sensing of the maneuver wave occurred visually. Yet to react to other parts of the flock solely through vision would entail practically continuous, unblinking, 360-degree visual attention. Even assuming total, continuous attention, how could this work when birds were reacting to waves approaching from behind? No birds have 360-degree vision, whether they have their eyes at the front, like owls, or at the side of the head, like geese, dunlins, and starlings.

Canada geese, for example, have a visual field for each eye of 135 degrees, with a 40-degree overlap in front of the head. In other words, they have 40-degree binocular vision. They also have a blind area at the back of the head of 58 degrees.[15] They cannot possibly see anything in this blind zone because the back of the head blocks the view, just as the backs of our heads block our view behind, however much we try to look backward by swiveling our eyes. Geese generally fly in V formations, and the angle of the V is often 30 to 40 degrees.[16] This means that geese are able to see the birds in front of them, but not those in the line behind them, unless they turn their heads by about 45 degrees. Nevertheless, flocks that fly in V formation, as many geese and ducks do, could still be coordinated visually by following the leader.

By contrast, birds like dunlins and starlings do not fly in lines and do not follow leaders. They react to maneuver waves spreading from any direction, including from the back of the flock. This would not be possible if they had to see the other birds behind them. But if they sense changes in the field of the flock directly, then we can begin to understand their behavior.

For decades a number of naturalists have speculated that changes in direction of flying flocks take place so rapidly that they seem to depend on "collective thinking" or telepathy.[17] My own hypothesis is that flocks of birds are indeed organized telepathically through flock fields, the morphic fields of flocks. (I discuss the nature of morphic fields in my books A New Science of Life and The Presence of the Past, and give a summary in chapter 19 of this book.) These fields have two roles.

First, the flock fields enable the individual birds to interpret and respond to seeing the way the other birds in the flock are moving. Different species have different kinds of flock fields: for example, the flocks of geese are V-shaped, while flocks of dunlins or starlings are more amorphous, and the birds do not follow a leader. The birds interpret and respond to the movement of the rest of the flock very differently, according to their species. The forms of these flock fields are inherited. Different species have different kinds of flock fields and different flock dynamics.[18]

Second, the morphic field of the flock directly coordinates the movements of the birds within this field. Of course, visual stimuli may also play an important role, but they cannot in themselves explain the coordination of the flock's movements. There could be a direct influence of the flock field on the individual birds' fields, just as the field of a magnet both depends on and influences the fields of the small magnetic "domains" within it. Magnetic domains are like small magnets within the magnet as a whole.

Significantly, a new generation of computer modelers has tried to overcome the limitations of boids-type models by modeling flocks in terms of fields. Some models are indeed based on an analogy with the way that iron bars become magnetized. If the individual domains are oriented at random, the bar as a whole is not magnetic. As the bar is magnetized, domains tend to line up in a particular direction, others follow suit, and suddenly almost all the domains point in the same direction: The bar becomes a magnet, with a magnetic field within and around it. The field of the magnet as a whole emerges from the fields of the individual domains, and in turn affects and organizes these domains. In a similar way, the field of a flock of birds both depends on and affects the fields of the individuals within it.

Other field models of flocks are based on analogies with the flow of fluids. When physicists model flow, they do not start with individual atoms or molecules, but rather with the fluid as a whole.[19] John Toner, a physicist at the University of Oregon, has combined these two kinds of fields in his models of flock behavior.[20] In these computer models, waves move through the group just like the undulations in flocks of starlings at dusk.

If the flight of flocks of birds is coordinated through morphic fields, this field may well continue to link the birds together when they are engaged in other activities. For example, when a group of birds is foraging, if some members of the group find a good source of food, this discovery could propagate through the field of the scattered flock and alert other members of the group to this discovery.

The naturalist William Long observed that birds do indeed seem to respond in this way to the finding of food. He fed wild birds at irregular intervals, and noticed that when some found the food, others soon appeared. There is no mystery in this, since they could have seen or heard the birds that were feeding. But he also found that when birds were widely dispersed over the countryside, they would rapidly appear when food was available. After making many observations, he came to the conclusion that that the feeding birds sent forth a "silent food call" or that their excitement somehow spread outward in a seemingly telepathic manner. He suggested that this influence was "felt by other starving birds, alert and sensitive, at a distance beyond all possible range of sight and hearing."[21]

SCHOOLS OF FISH

At a distance, a school of fish resembles a large single organism.[22] Its members swim in tight formations, more or less parallel to each other, changing direction and reversing in near unison. Most species, including herring and mackerel, form schools that have no leaders.

When schools are under attack by a predator, they have a number of forms of defensive behavior. The most spectacular is the so-called flash expansion, in which each fish simultaneously darts away from the center of the school as the group is attacked. The entire expansion may occur in as little as twenty milliseconds. The fish can accelerate to a speed of ten to twenty bodylengths per second within that time. Yet they do not collide. "Not only does each fish know in advance where it will swim if attacked, but it must also know where each of its neighbors will swim."[23] This behavior has no simple explanation in terms of sensory information from neighboring fish because it happens far too fast for nerve impulses to move from the eye to the brain and then from the brain to the muscles.

As in the case of flocks of birds, most attempts to model fish schools have started from "artificial life" computer programs, rather than from actual observations on real fish. In these computer models, as in boids models, the virtual fish in a two-dimensional "school" are programmed to respond to the position and movement of their immediate neighbors.[24] In more sophisticated models, individual fish are subject to influences from all other individuals in the school through a field that links them all together.[25]

Most attempts to explain fish schooling assume that individuals respond to sensory information from the other fish through vision, and through detecting pressure changes in the water by pressure-sensitive organs, known as lateral lines, which run along their length. But fish continue swimming in schools at night, so vision is not essential. In laboratory experiments, fish have even been fitted with opaque contact lenses to blind them temporarily. But they were still capable of joining the school and maintaining their position within it.

Perhaps they could judge the position of their neighbors by detecting pressure changes. But this idea has been tested in laboratory experiments by cutting the nerves from the lateral lines at the level of the gills. Such fish still school normally.[26]

I suggest that schools of fish, like flocks of birds, are coordinated by morphic fields, which both shape the way the individual fish respond to sensory information, and also enable them to respond directly to the field around them when their normal senses are disrupted.

SOCIAL INSECTS

Societies of termites, ants, wasps, and bees have often been compared to organisms, or described as superorganisms. Some contain millions of individual insects. These societies build large and elaborate nests, exhibit a complex division of labor, and reproduce themselves.[27]

In *Dogs That Know When Their Owners Are Coming Home*, I suggest that social insects, like other social animals, are bound together in their social groups by morphic fields, which carry the habitual patterns and "programs" of social organization. In the case of social insects that build nests and other structures, these fields coordinate their architectural activity. They contain, as it were, an invisible blueprint for the nest. The morphic field of the colony is not merely inside the individual insects; rather, it is within the morphic field of the group. The field is an extended pattern in space-time, just as the gravitational field of the solar system is not merely inside the Sun and the planets, but contains them all and coordinates their movements.

Social insects have a variety of means of communicating through the known senses; for example, scent trails, touch, and vision, as in the "waggle" dance of honeybees, through which returning foragers convey the direction and distance of food. But all these forms of sensory communication work together with the individuals' connections through the morphic field of the group. It is this field that enables the insects to interpret these scent trails, dance patterns, and so on, and to react appropriately.

Sensory communication by itself would be totally inadequate to explain how termites, for example, could build such prodigious structures, with nests up to ten feet high, filled with galleries and chambers and even equipped with ventilation shafts. These insect cities have an overall plan that far exceeds the experience of any individual insect.[28] There is already evidence that coordination of the insects' activities depends on fieldlike influences that cannot be explained in terms of the normal senses.[29]

TELEPATHY THROUGH SOCIAL FIELDS

I suggest that morphic fields of social groups help coordinate the individual animals' movements and activities, whether they are termites building a mound, fish swimming in schools, birds flying in flocks, herds fleeing from danger, wolves on hunting expeditions, human crowds, football teams, or family groups. The social fields connect together members of the group, and permit forms of communication over and above the regular senses. It is in these morphic fields of social groups that we find the evolutionary basis for telepathy.

Social fields are subject to natural selection, in that successful patterns of social organization tend to survive, and their morphic fields are strengthened through repetition. And, of course, genes associated with these successful patterns are favored, too, and will tend to increase in frequency within the population.

Telepathy is an aspect of the seventh sense that enables members of groups to respond to the movements and activities of others, and respond to their emotions, needs, and intentions. Fear, alarm, excitement, calls for help, calls to go to a particular place, anticipations of arrivals or departures, and distress and dying can all be communicated telepathically. The most spectacular examples of telepathy occur when the members of the group are far apart, beyond the range of the recognized senses, as I discussed in chapters 3 through 6.

When members of the social group are far apart—for example, when a wounded wolf is separated from the rest of the pack—they still remain part of the social group, linked through the morphic field of the group. This field is not broken but stretched. It could be thought of as a kind of invisible thread that continues to connect the separated individuals with the rest of the group, and can act as a channel of communication between them.

Any change or difference in one of the organisms linked through a stretched field of this kind could, through this field, affect another to which it was linked. I suggest that such connections enable people and animals to react to calls at a distance (chapters 3 and 6), to the distress or death of a member of the group to whom they are bonded (chapter 4), and to the intentions of a distant member of the group (chapter 5).

TELEPATHY IN NORMAL COMMUNICATION

Less easy to recognize than telepathic communication at a distance is the role of telepathy in the communication between members of social groups when they are nearby, within the range of normal sensory communication. Communications through normal sensory channels and telepathy are not mutually exclusive. When we hear someone talking, it does not mean that we cannot see that person or smell him or her as well. Just as the known senses generally work together, rather than excluding each other, so the seventh sense can work together with the other senses, rather than being an alternative to them.

Animals may be able to hear the calls of other members of the group, or see visual signals from them, but what these sounds or signals convey may also depend on a telepathic transmission of information. Likewise, fish in a school or birds in a flock may be able to see how other members of the group are moving, but the way they respond depends on the morphic field of the group and on their position within it.

Thus, when individual animals or people are relating to each other through the normal senses, telepathy may play an essential role in the normal communication of intentions, images, and thoughts. For example, when two people are sitting talking to each other, they are not only linked through the words that are said and heard, but through body language and visual contact, through the shared environment, and so on. If they know each other well, then they are also linked by the emotional bonds between them, and by shared memories. These are all favorable conditions for telepathy, and favor the transfer of feelings, images, concepts, and ideas. We saw in chapter 1 how these principles might apply to the transmission of thoughts and intentions from parents to children, between spouses, between therapists and clients, between mathematicians, between riders and horses, and from people to their dogs.

Thus ordinary, normal communication may involve the transfer of information both through the senses in familiar ways and also through telepathy. Although telepathy may be going on continually, unrecognized, it only manifests itself when information through regular sensory channels is reduced or eliminated. It usually operates along with the other senses, enabling the information they convey to be interpreted and assimilated. Telepathy of the thought-transference type, discussed in chapters 1 and 2, is a limiting case of normal communication.

The more attuned the people are, the more easily telepathy occurs. For example, in guessing games, some parents and children almost immediately get what the other is trying to communicate (page 38). In extreme cases, people pick up the other person's thoughts or intentions without any words or gestures at all (pages 30–33). The same goes for picking up tunes in people's minds without any audible humming (pages 29–30). When communication through words and gestures is eliminated altogether, as in experiments where people are placed in separate rooms, then the telepathic aspect of normal communication can be separated from the sensory aspect. But without the sensory connection, which normally helps to maintain the interconnection between the two people, telepathy may be less effective.

◇◆◇

Minds are connected through social fields. They also extend through attention, linking organisms to their environment. Our minds reach out beyond our brains and beyond our bodies every time we see something. As I suggested in the introduction, vision involves a two-way process: an inward movement of light and an outward projection of images. Everything you see around you, including this page, is an image projected outward by your mind. These images are not inside your brain. Rather, they are exactly where they seem to be.

Through these fields of perception, our minds reach out to touch what we are looking at. Thus we should be able to affect things just by looking at them. Is this really so? The best starting point for this discussion is to think about the effects of looking at other people. If I look at someone from behind when she does not know that I am there, and if she cannot tell I am looking by means of any normal sensory information, can she nevertheless sense that I am staring at her? There is in fact a great deal of evidence for a sense of being stared at, as I discuss in the following chapters. This aspect of the seventh sense has many implications for our understanding of human and animal nature.

Part II

THE POWER OF
ATTENTION

8

THE SENSE OF
BEING STARED AT

In the Second World War, RAF fighter pilots were advised not to stare at an enemy pilot when preparing to shoot him down. "The intensity of gaze had been known to make the enemy pilot look straight round at his attacker."[1]

When she was about eight years old, Emma Clarke was walking homeward across an isolated field.

> I cannot remember what I was thinking, just ambling along, when I stopped and looked behind. Then fear struck. I saw a man toward the other end of the field looking at me. He dodged behind a tree. I ran the rest of the way home. I never told my parents because I knew I was not supposed to be so far away from home alone.

In frightening situations such as this, the sense of being stared at is particularly memorable. But most people have experienced it for themselves, usually in less dramatic circumstances. In my own surveys of adults in Europe and in the United States, 70 to 90 percent said they had sensed when they were being looked at from behind.[2] Surveys by other researchers have given similar results.[3] Gerald Winer and his colleagues in the Psychology Department of Ohio State University have found that these experiences are even commoner among children than adults. Ninety-four percent of sixth-grade schoolchildren (aged eleven and twelve) answered yes to the question, "Do you ever feel that someone is staring at you without actually seeing them look at you?" So did 89 percent of college students.[4]

The sense of being stared is often alluded to in short stories and novels. "His eyes bored into the back of her neck" is a cliché of popular fiction. Here is an example from Sir Arthur Conan Doyle, the creator of Sherlock Holmes:

> The man interests me as a psychological study. At breakfast this morning I suddenly had that vague feeling of uneasiness which overcomes some people when closely stared at, and, quickly looking up, I met his eyes bent upon me with an intensity which amounted to ferocity, though their expression instantly softened as he made some conventional remark upon the weather. Curiously enough, Harton says that he had a very similar experience yesterday upon deck.[5]

The phenomenon is also described in the novels of Tolstoy, Dostoyevsky, Anatole France, Victor Hugo, Aldous Huxley, D. H. Lawrence, John Cowper Powys, Thomas Mann, J. B. Priestley, and many other writers.[6]

SENSING THE DIRECTION FROM WHICH THE GAZE IS COMING

The sense of being stared at is often directional. People not only sense they are being looked at, but also detect where the gaze is coming from.

But what if some people unconsciously sense the stare of someone behind them and react with unease, but do not turn around? They might just feel restless without knowing why. Only those who turned and saw someone looking at them would know they had been stared at. The directional aspect of this sense is almost a necessary feature of the phenomenon, at least as it is experienced by the people stared at. To know that they have been stared at from behind, they would have to turn around and identify the starer.

There are exactly 100 case histories in my database in which people describe their experience of being stared at. In 97 of these, the people detected the direction from which the stare was coming. Even the three apparent exceptions were not necessarily exceptions. In one case a schoolboy repeatedly felt classmates sitting behind him stare at the back of his neck to make him blush. He did not turn around because he already knew where the starers were. In another case a woman found that she awoke with a jump if someone stared at her when she was asleep. She did not immediately detect the direction of the gaze precisely because she was sleeping. And in the third case, a woman who felt she was being looked at could not identify the source of the gaze. When Connie Trammel, of St. Charles, Missouri, returned home late one night to her apartment building, it was dark and the man looking at her was hiding.

As soon as I stepped out of my car, I felt someone was watching me. The feeling was sudden and strong. The parking lot was full of parked cars, but there was apparently no one else around. I pretty much dismissed the feeling and walked briskly to the front door. I stopped to get my mail. As I was opening my mailbox, with my back to the front door, I heard the door open suddenly and someone step in. I turned and saw a man standing naked, holding his folded clothes in front of his face. I ran to my apartment and called the police.

In some cases people felt they were being stared at from a particular direction, but could not see anyone there. But the correctness of their intuition became apparent later.

When I was on holiday in rural Wales, I had a strong sensation of being stared at. With a group of friends, I was out walking in hill-pasture land and no one else seemed to be about. The sensation was coming from behind us, and when I looked round I felt it was coming from a clump of shrubs and gorse about 100 yards away up on a hillside. I kept looking round, and when my friends inquired, I said I felt watched by someone. We all stopped and looked back, and at this point a man came from behind the shrubs and walked away over the brow of the hill. We saw him again later; he was a local shepherd.

◈ FIONA RICHARDS

To give some flavor of the variety of cases in my database, here are three more examples, taken from a survey I conducted in Asheville, North Carolina:

I was attending a lecture when fifteen minutes into the program I felt a prickle and uncomfortable. When I turned around, seven rows back I found my husband's ex-wife staring at me.

Recently I felt someone looking at me from behind about fifty feet away and I turned and looked directly at the person without scanning.

In a crowded market in India amid hundreds of people I felt a pull to turn around and saw an old woman staring at me. I felt I knew her and she knew me, but she was a stranger.

Philena Bruce, an Englishwoman who used to live in India, found she experienced exceptionally powerful stares when she was there, especially from beggars. She was convinced that they deliberately used their looks to attract her attention.

I'd find myself looking at a beggar whom I had not consciously chosen to look at, and then of course I'd have to give him some money. I remember training myself to walk and keep my eyes straight ahead and my thoughts on what I felt in my energy body, and when I felt someone hit it very hard, rather than looking at the source of the hit, I'd walk on and then turn my eyes carefully and there would be the beggar. A very clever trick, really. Watch the people who are walking along, and when you see a possible source of money, throw a blast of energy with your eyes at them, which makes them turn and look at you.

In summary, in the vast majority of cases, the sense of being stared at involves detecting the direction of the gaze. The observer and the observed are interconnected directionally.

Not only have most people experienced being looked at from behind; most people have also been lookers, and have noticed how others behave when they look at them. The experience of many lookers confirms that the sense of being stared at is often directional, mirroring the direction of the gaze. But some people react with signs of unease without turning.

MAKING PEOPLE TURN AROUND

Like most people, from time to time I have found that when I look at people from behind they turn and look at me. The most striking instances have occurred when I have looked out of upstairs windows, and people have not only turned but also looked up. In one case, when I was attending a conference in Düsseldorf, Germany, I was looking out of my seventh-floor hotel window at two women walking on a path below when one of them stopped, turned around, and looked straight up at me.

Many other people have had similar experiences. For example, when James Godfrey lived on the ninth floor of a block of flats, "my kitchen window looked out to a busy street. I discovered that if I fixed my gaze on a person below he or she would often look up in the direction of my window. This happened quite often, but not always."

The directional quality of the sense of being stared at is especially clear in such cases. And this sensitivity is not confined to looks by strangers, but also occurs between people who know each other well. For example, Rupert Hitzig, of Los Angeles, told me, "I went to the swimming pool at the gym and down below, a good seventy-five feet away, Karen, my spouse, with goggles and a bathing cap on, was deeply immersed in her laps. I stared, and she stopped swimming, turned back her head, looked up directly, and caught my eye."

In some instances the person looked at did not immediately detect the direction of the person staring, but looked around first. This was Pauline Watson's experience in a disco in Lincolnshire, England.

The chaps all danced together and the girls were left seated to chat. Bored, I went to the balcony above the heaving, strobe-lit dance floor, to look down on them. The music was extremely loud, and although the dancers were quite well lit (in time with the music), the balcony above was not, yet despite this my boyfriend just suddenly stopped, looked around everywhere, and then looked up, directly at me. He left the dance floor to come and join me and said he could feel someone was watching him.

A similar process of looking around before looking up was often observed by Patricia Watts as she traveled home from her job in London by bus. She sat on the top deck.

By the time we reached Selfridges [department store], there were always a lot of passengers embarking and disembarking, so I would take the opportunity to fix my mind and eyes on individuals who were outside the store. They had to have their backs to the bus, and they turned around, scanning the area from side to side — as if with a built-in homing device — starting at ground level and working upward. When they reached the top windows of the bus, I looked away. It's perfectly easy to do, and only requires concentration.

Nevertheless, people reported such scanning behavior in only a minority of the stories on my database. The majority, 83 percent, simply said that the people they stared at turned and looked at them.

However, 13 percent of the people who described the effects of their stares noticed that some people did not turn and look at them, but rather showed signs of discomfort or unease, like scratching the backs of their heads, or fidgeting. In some cases, such as in lectures or church services, this happened when they could have turned and seen the person who was staring at them. But sometimes people also showed symptoms of unease when the person watching them was out of sight, as Delmar Cain found when he worked as a medical librarian for the U.S. Veterans Administration in Boston, Massachusetts. The building has silvered, mirrorlike windows that people cannot see into.

I used to stand by the window observing people walking by on the sidewalk at ground level. There was no possibility of them seeing me. A certain proportion, 10 to 20 percent, could sense me looking at them, turning around, scratching their necks, scratching their backs, showing discomfort at being observed, but unable to tell where the observation was coming from. Many times they were the only person on the block, so they were not experiencing discomfort at someone nearby on the sidewalk observing them.

Several other people have commented that people reacted to their gaze when looked at through windows (as in some of the examples above) or through mirrors. So however the power of the gaze works, it does not seem to be blocked by passing through glass.

In some cases people looked at others to make them turn out of idle curiosity. But often people do it deliberately to attract attention, for a variety of reasons, including sexual attraction, disapproval, or practical necessity, as Gerald Turner found when he worked in a noisy steel factory in the English Midlands: "We couldn't hear each other speak. By accident I discovered that if I wanted someone's attention, by just looking at their heads, and calling out their names in my mind, they would suddenly turn to face me and sign 'What's wrong?' "

Nightclub bouncers, schoolteachers, and college lecturers have told me they deliberately use the power of the gaze to help maintain order. For instance, Donohue, who teaches in Connecticut, said, "I will look at a person who is doing wrong and they usually 'feel' me looking at them and look up. Sometimes it takes longer for the person to realize it, but usually they do."

Several informants have said that they could wake people up by staring at them. Alexander Seferiades, in Athens, Greece, said:

When my sister and I were small and shared a room, I came to realize that when she was sleeping all I needed to do was look at her and she woke up. This would happen almost invariably, so when I didn't want to wake her when leaving or entering the room, I avoided looking at her. This was more difficult in reality than it seems in the telling. When I failed and gazed to see if she was awake, she would immediately awaken.

There are several published accounts of the effects of the gaze. In general they are in good agreement with the reports on my database. Here, for example, are some observations by Renée Haynes, a British researcher, who wrote in 1973:

The impulse to turn is not equally strong in everyone, and there will be instances—as with waiters—when it is probably atrophied, ignored, or directly resisted. A little mild experimentation, though, say at a boring lecture or in a crowded canteen, will show that in the majority of cases to gaze intently at the back of someone's head will produce a fidget and an uneasy turn and glance. This can also be done with sleeping dogs and cats—not to mention children who may be roused thus more humanely than with a cold sponge—and with birds in the garden.[7]

Many other people have noticed that they can wake sleeping animals by looking at them, as I discuss in chapter 10.

SENSITIVITY OF DIFFERENT PARTS OF THE BODY

Most accounts of the effects of staring at people from behind involved looking at the back of the head or neck, or at the back, but several people have commented on the sensitivity of other parts of the body.

When she was about fourteen years old, Martha Fischer, of Bethal, Transvaal, South Africa, had regular opportunities to study the reactions of people's ears.

I used to sit in church of a Sunday morning and "look an ear red." I would settle for an ear about three to five yards in front of me, slightly to my left so that I had a good view of the man's right ear, not just the back edge. After the singing and the prayers, when everybody was sitting still, listening to the sermon, I would stare intently at this ear and after a while it would turn red. For some reason I never tried to get a glimpse of the man's left ear to see if it was also red.

Several young men have commented on the reactions of women to their looking at specific parts of their bodies. Jeffrey Darlington, of Richmond, Surrey, concentrates on breasts.

I am a man without a sexual partner, and when I notice an attractive woman, I look at her. This seems to be a largely automatic process. I look first at her face, then my gaze drops to her breasts and then quickly moves away. Amazingly often, without looking at me, the women instantly gazes down at her breasts, perhaps to check that she is properly dressed. The "conventional" explanation of this would have to run something like this: A woman is walking alone, looking straight ahead, when her peripheral vision picks up a slight movement. Without turning her central vision on the source, she visually perceives the direction of a man's gaze so accurately that she knows exactly where he is looking! At a distance of perhaps fifty meters and sometimes through a car windshield, this would require fantastic precision, even for central vision. I find this explanation unconvincing. The idea that a woman can sense without visual cues that she is being stared at seems a better explanation. This mysterious "sense" could tell that sexual interest is present, which would explain how she knows not to return the look.

John Pasic, of Los Angeles, told me of several examples of women's reactions to his looks. Here are two of them:

As a student intern working at a clinic, I'm walking about twenty feet behind a particular female coworker, outside, within a loosely packed group of other coworkers and patients. I notice how attractive her rear is in her tight pants, and *instantly* she turns around and finds my eyes with hers and smiles while touching her rear with her hand in a smoothing-the-fabric motion. We had been attracted to each other over the weeks previously, but we had not had any personal interaction beyond hello. Another instance: I'm in the lobby of a crowded Las Vegas hotel, the Luxor, in March 1997. I'm walking perhaps twelve feet behind a young lady, among many other people walking the same direction. I notice how beautiful her long, thick, shiny blond hair is, and *instantly* she turns around quickly, and finds my eyes with hers and smiles slightly.

I know of no systematic studies on the sensitivity of different parts of the body, and most people have no reason or opportunity to investigate this subject. Exceptions are artists who draw or paint nude models. Several have noticed that the models react to their concentrating on some parts of the body more than others. Ann Holms, of Canterbury, Kent, England, who had drawn models in life classes ever since she was an art student, found that many models were particularly sensitive in their hands and feet. "This occurs whether or not they are facing you (the artist) while they are posing. With some models, their hands or feet respond in these instances when I am concentrating on them as if they have been tickled, sometimes with involuntarily twitching."

Of course, in most situations when people are looked at by others, they are wearing clothes. The fact that so many people react when their covered backs are looked at shows that bare skin is not necessary for feeling looks. Nor is bare skin necessary for feeling that someone is looking at the back of the head or neck. This sensitivity is not confined to people who are bald or have short hair. The fact that people with long hair react, as do people with clothes on, shows that neither hair nor clothing blocks the influence of the gaze.

THE DETAILS OF PEOPLE'S EXPERIENCES

To obtain a more detailed understanding of the sense of being stared at, I have carried out a systematic survey of by means of a questionnaire (for details, see Appendix B). More than 320 people took part in Britain, Sweden, and the United States. Ages of participants ranged from under eighteen to over seventy, and there were similar numbers of men and women.

In all locations, a higher proportion of women than men said they had experienced being looked at from behind, and turned around to find someone was in fact looking at them. The overall averages were 81 percent for women and 74 percent for men. Of course, the people attending my lectures and seminars are not a random sample of the population; nevertheless, these levels of response are similar to those in surveys by other researchers, including random surveys.[8] The main point of this questionnaire was not, however, to establish how many people had had the experience of being stared at, but to find out in more detail about the natural history of their experiences.

The experience of being stared at seemed to be fairly frequent, and about half the people surveyed said it happened at least once a month.

With whom did it happen? Most of all with strangers, especially male strangers (Figure 8.1), then with friends and colleagues, spouses and partners, and then with parents, children, and siblings. There were also some striking sex differences in people's responses: Women reacted more to male strangers than to female strangers, whereas men reacted to males and females to a similar extent (Table B.9, page 318).

Where did it happen? Most commonly in the street, for both men and

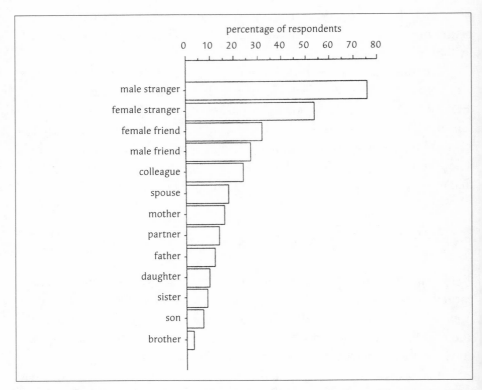

Figure 8.1 *Comparisons of the categories of people to whose stare respondents said they had reacted. Details of this questionnaire survey are given in Appendix B.*

women. Next most frequently in bars or clubs. Then at theaters and similar public places; on trains and buses; in cars; in the home; and also in other place, such as offices and airports (Figure 8.2).

When asked about their experience in the active role, significantly more women (88 percent) than men (71 percent) said they had found they could stare at others and make them turn around.[9] At first sight this seems to conflict with the finding that the commonest experiences of being stared at were with male strangers. But maybe women tend to stare less at people they do not know and more at people they do know, while men may tend to do the opposite. Both women and men had noticed being looked at more by female friends than by male friends, more by mothers than by fathers, more by daughters than by sons, and more by sisters than by brothers. So although male strangers produced more reactions than female strangers did, more women caused people they knew to turn around (Table B.9).

I also asked people what emotions or intentions they found affected other people when they were staring at them. The results are shown in Figure 8.3. For both men and women, curiosity was the commonest motive, followed by

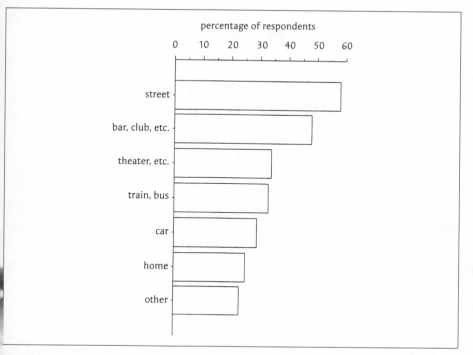

Figure 8.2 *Comparisons of the places in which people said they had had the experience of feeling they were being stared at. Details of this questionnaire survey are given in Appendix B.*

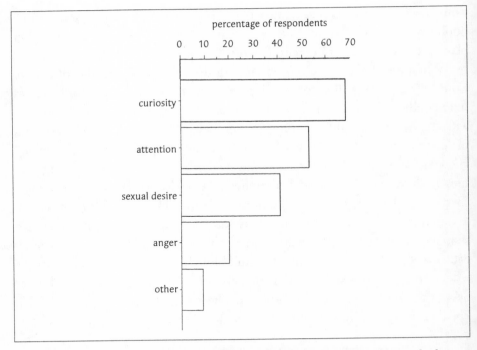

Figure 8.3 *The emotions and intentions that people have found affect the people they are staring at. Details of this questionnaire survey are given in Appendix B.*

the wish to attract the person's attention. Desire came next, followed by anger. Other emotions included wishes for well-being, affection, recognition, and distress. These findings illustrate the wide range of circumstances and emotions associated with the sense of being stared at. There were no significant differences between men and women in their responses to this question.

Most people take these experiences for granted, and remember them in a rather casual way. But some people spend a lot of time observing others, especially professionals involved in surveillance work. This is the subject of the next chapter. Before going any further, it is important to consider the arguments *against* the existence of the sense of being stared at. Even though so many people claim to have experienced it, could it be an illusion?

OBJECTIONS

If the sense of being stared at is real, it implies a sensitivity that goes beyond hearing, sight, touch, taste, and smell—beyond the known senses. It could be thought of as a sixth sense, or a seventh sense; or as a form of perception beyond the known senses—in other words, "extrasensory perception," or ESP; or it could be regarded as a "psychic" ability. It can also be seen as an aspect of the extended mind. But whatever we choose call it, this ability would imply the need for a larger, more inclusive map of reality. Science as we know it would seem seriously incomplete.

This is a potentially dangerous thought. It would be much less disturbing to dismiss the sense of being stared at as an illusion—or even as a form of paranoia.

There are three standard arguments against the reality of the sense of being stared at. The first is not really an argument but an assertion: Belief in a mysterious power of looks is nothing but a superstition, and should not be taken seriously by educated people. This is enough to shut most people up, since no one likes to be thought stupid.

Second, people are not really reacting to some mysterious power of the gaze, but rather to sounds, to movements in their peripheral field of vision, or to other subtle sensory clues, perceived subliminally.

Third, if sounds and other sensory clues cannot provide a plausible explanation, then the feeling of being stared at depends on a combination of blind chance and selective memory. People may often turn around but only remember the occasions when someone was staring at them, and forget all the times they turned and no one was looking. This illusion would be enhanced by the tendency for our visual systems to detect movement. As we turn around to look behind us, if someone behind us sees us moving, we are likely to attract their attention, and our eyes will meet.[10]

These speculations are attractive. They seem to provide scientific-sounding reasons for paying little further attention to the sense of being stared at, and for leaving it beyond the pale of science. But where is the empirical evidence that the sense of being stared at depends on sensory clues, or on coincidence and selective memory? There is almost none.

The taboo against taking this phenomenon seriously was so effective that until the late 1980s there were almost no scientific investigations. I have been able to find only four papers on this subject in scientific journals between 1890 and 1990, plus two unpublished student projects, one in 1978 and the other in 1983.

The earliest reports were by skeptical American professors of psychology, E. B. Titchener (1898) and J. E. Coover (1913), who dismissed this sense as an illusion (pages 168–169). The apparent authority of their conclusions gave the standard skeptical position a seemingly scientific underpinning, and helped to inhibit research for decades.

Almost all subsequent experimental studies have gone against the skeptical hypothesis.[11] In chapter 11, I summarize the results of recent experiments that provide powerful evidence for the reality of the sense of being stared at. In Appendix A, I will show how anyone can carry out these tests for themselves.

9 SURVEILLANCE AND WARINESS

Some people watch others as part of their job. If the sense of being stared at really exists, surveillance professionals are likely to have encountered it. In order to find out what they have noticed about this sense, I and my research associates Jane Turney, in England, and David Brown, in California, have interviewed police officers, sheriffs, prison guards, criminals, military surveillance officers, customs officers, security guards, and private detectives. We also interviewed people skilled in a variety of martial arts.

But first I discuss what people have noticed when they observe others through telescopes or binoculars. Can people tell when they are being watched at a distance?

EFFECTS OF LOOKING THROUGH TELESCOPES OR BINOCULARS

The sense of being stared at seems to occur at a considerable distance when the person is observed through telescopes or binoculars. Here many non-professionals, as well as professionals, have noticed that some people seem to know when they are being focused on by a hidden observer at a distance.

Bernadette Wainwright discovered this for herself when she used a telescope to look out of a window in her parents' house over the Ribble Valley in Yorkshire, England.

One day, I noticed some tents in a field on the far bank of the river. I focused the telescope and watched the campers, some young lads, wandering about. I had been watching one for a minute or two when suddenly he turned around and looked toward me. His gaze seemed to be scanning in my general direction. He was too far away to be able to see me with the naked eye. I looked away quickly, rather unnerved. I focused on some of the other boys, and after a short time the same thing happened. One in particular seemed very sensitive and would turn to look in my direction each time, almost as soon as I focused on him.

Several other people have told me similar stories. A lady who lived on the south coast of England said she liked looking out of a window through powerful binoculars at sailors on yachts. They were far away, and could not have seen her with the naked eye; but often, she said, the sailors would turn and look straight toward her, and seem uneasy. She was sure they were feeling her looking. She enjoyed doing this, and said it happened again and again.

Dianne Arcangel, who lives by the San Jacinto River in Texas, kept a pair of pet ducks that one day went missing. Her husband suggested that they might be nesting on a nearby island, which they scanned with a telescope. They failed to locate the ducks. However, they did see their neighbors' boat on the island.

With the telescope aimed at the distant side of the island, I could see what appeared to be two human images, but they were so out of focus that I could only assume they were the neighbors since we could identify their boat. Later my husband and I went outside and walked along the shore trying to find the ducks there. Much to my surprise the couple raced up and the woman yelled out, "What were you doing watching us through binoculars? I could tell you were watching us from inside your house while we were on the island sunbathing in the nude."

In these cases the intentions were harmless, but this sensitivity can manifest itself more dramatically in literally life-threatening situations. In 1995, Sergeant Robert Hendrickson was a sniper in the U.S. Marine Corps, serving in Bosnia. It was one of his tasks to shoot "bandits," or "known terrorists." While he was aiming through the telescopic sight of his rifle, "within one second prior to actual termination, a target would somehow seem to make eye contact with me. I am convinced that these people somehow sensed my presence at distances over one mile. They did so with uncanny accuracy, in effect to stare down my own scope."

Long-lens celebrity photographers often look at people from a distance through telescopic lenses. We interviewed the leading practitioners in Britain to ask if they had noticed whether their subjects seemed aware of their focusing on them, even though they were at a distance, and concealed.

There was a general consensus that some people seem unaware of being watched, while others seem to have an uncanny ability to know when they are about to be photographed, such as Princess Diana, who, over the years, seemed to become increasingly sensitive. One photographer commented: "She was possibly the most extreme example of somebody being constantly aware that there was a possibility of being photographed. Because she was so against being photographed, she honed that awareness down to such a fine degree that it was almost impossible to catch her unawares. She claimed that she had a sixth sense, and said she could smell a photographer a mile away."

One long-lens photographer who worked for the *Sun*, the most popular tabloid newspaper in Britain, said that he was amazed by how many times people whose picture he was taking would "turn around and look right down the lens," even if they were looking in the opposite direction to start with. He did not think they could see him or detect his movements. "I am talking about taking pictures at distances of up to half a mile away in situations where it is quite impossible for people to see me, although I can see them. They are so aware it is uncanny."

The ability of people to detect when they are being stared at through telescopic lenses shows that telescopes not only focus light into the eye of the observer, but also focus the looker's attention onto the subject.

PROFESSIONAL SURVEILLANCE

Much modern surveillance work involves the use of closed-circuit television, which I discuss in the following section. Here I concentrate on direct surveillance carried out by observing people unobtrusively, or watching them through one-way mirrors, or by trailing them.

Among surveillance personnel, it is generally agreed that when people are being watched or followed, it is important to look directly at them as little as possible. A senior officer in the Customs Investigation Unit at Heathrow Airport told us:

A good surveillance officer should not stare at anybody. An officer should be looking to one side, or staring past or looking in any other direction. The main thing is to avoid eye-to-eye contact. You are always far more conscious of someone you have seen looking at you. That will then trigger a very human response of "Why is that person looking at me?" and people become conscious of that person. They might check subsequently to see if that person is still looking at them.

All the surveillance officers we interviewed agreed that some people were unusually "surveillance conscious," especially criminals and other people with something to hide. As one British police officer expressed it, "A lot of our clients, as it were, are professional and professionally try to avoid any form of surveillance and are constantly looking for it. We have to devise ways to be there without being seen." Moreover, the "clients" are known to be more vigilant at some times than at others:

They are at a very heightened state of awareness at the start of their day, because they want to be sure that they are not being watched. The second state of heightened awareness comes just before the bit of work that they are going to do. They want to reinforce the fact that they are not being watched and that they are going to get away with the enterprise. We recognize those two stages and our state of awareness rises with theirs.

When it came to the question of whether people had a "sixth sense" about being watched, we found a divergence of opinion. One private security officer, a former policeman, told us that he was sure that most criminals had no such ability: "If you have a good covert observation going and there is no outside influence that interferes with that, they haven't got a clue. They just get on and do it. There's blatant stuff going on and they do not know they are being watched."

A senior police officer in the Surveillance Unit at New Scotland Yard in London (the headquarters of the Metropolitan Police) asserted categorically that there was no such thing as a "sixth sense." He recognized that some people did in fact detect when they were being watched, but he explained it in terms of the operator having made a mistake, like allowing eye-to-eye contact to occur.

Others experienced in surveillance work have a different opinion. Rick Dickson, a narcotics officer in Plains, Texas, said, "I've noticed that a lot of times the crook will just get a feeling that things aren't right, that he's being watched. We often have somebody look right in our direction even though he can't see us. A lot of times we're inside a vehicle." A sheriff from the Midwest told me she was convinced that some people could tell when she was watching them through binoculars, even when she was well hidden.

Some officers simply say that some people know when they are being watched. The chief security officer at a leading department store in London summarized his experience as follows: "Definitely when you are on the job on the shop floor you can see that people will turn and stare at you. You can be hidden out of the way watching somebody and they will turn around and look at you. Any in-store detective who says he has never been caught out watching somebody is a liar."

Everyone agreed that some people under surveillance seem to know when they are being watched, and detect the people watching them. Everyone agreed that there is an increased chance of the watcher being noticed if he or she looks directly at the person under observation. But if the detective is detected, did his looking cause the client to look at him because of the sense of being stared at? Or did the client know he was being watched simply because he was alert and saw someone looking? As we have seen, some surveillance officers take the sense of being stared at for granted, while others deny its existence.

These questions are easier to answer when people are being watched through closed-circuit television (CCTV). Especially when the cameras are hidden, it is impossible for someone to know by normal sensory means when he or she is being watched on a TV monitor in a distant room. Can some people tell when they are being watched through CCTV surveillance systems?

SURVEILLANCE THROUGH CLOSED-CIRCUIT TELEVISION

Closed-circuit television surveillance systems are installed in many office blocks, hospitals, shopping malls, airports, car parks, and other public places. Several different kinds of cameras are used: overt cameras, often deliberately placed so that people can notice them, with the intention of deterring undesirable activities; adjustable cameras concealed within dark or mirrored covers so they can be rotated and zoomed without the movements of the camera being seen; and covert cameras, disguised or hidden from view.

Surveillance by CCTV is a substantial industry, which grew dramatically throughout the 1990s. In Britain alone there are several trade journals covering this field, such as *Security Surveyor* and *CCTV Today*, filled with articles reviewing new products, trade statistics, and debates about the efficacy of different surveillance systems. For example, do open-street systems, the installation of which is encouraged by the British government, lead to a reduction of crime? Or do they simply cause criminals to move elsewhere?

In many cases, CCTV cameras are used to record videotapes, so that if an incident occurs, the tape can later be examined to try to identify the perpetrators. Many cameras are also linked to TV monitors that can be watched by security officers. In practice, most monitors are not watched most of the time. When I have visited security control rooms containing banks of monitors, I have often found that the security officers were reading newspapers, giving only an occasional glance at the TV screens.

There is general agreement among surveillance professionals that most people do not notice when they are being observed through CCTV. Some people commit crimes right in front of the cameras. But others do seem able to detect when they are being observed.

We interviewed ten CCTV surveillance officers, and found that two were inclined to a skeptical view. Barry Thorne, head of security at Harrods department store, in London, said, "People who are looking at the cameras are the exception and are often the ones hoping to commit a crime. Security officers will obviously look at these people, particularly if they are looking around in a suspicious manner. Therefore it is hard to tease out whether looking at someone makes them look at the camera, or whether these people were looking at the camera in the first place because they sensed they were being watched."

Nevertheless, most of the officers were convinced that some people could indeed sense they were being observed. For example, Charles Sibert, head of security at a large restaurant complex in Lakewood, Colorado, said that even when hidden cameras were used, "some people know they're being watched, mostly crooks. They look at the camera. They get fidgety; they walk back and forth. They try to get out of the eye of the camera. They look up. It's kind of comical sometimes." Tony Coopland, the security manager for Sheffield City Council, in Yorkshire, had had similar experiences: "It is amazing how many people do look back at the camera when you are looking at the monitor. It is like an extra sense, or whatever."

A former SAS officer engaged in antiterrorist surveillance in Northern Ireland told us that the men they were watching often seemed to know when they were being observed. On one occasion they were watching suspected terrorists going in and out of a betting shop through a hidden camera in the roof of a shop opposite. "We removed a slate and drilled a small hole in the roof and put a lens through it to look down the street and watch. After a couple of days we got the feeling they knew we were there. The third day they did a raid on the shop. They ran a van into the bottom of the shop to burn it out."

Les Lay, who works as security manager in a large firm in London, has no doubt that some people have a sixth sense. "They can have their backs to the cameras, or be scanned using hidden devices, yet they still become agitated when the camera is trained on them. Some move on, some look around for the camera."[1] When he worked for an international bank in the City of London, some of the staff were suspected of dishonesty, and in an attempt to find the culprits, he said, "we set up covert surveillance cameras targeting one area for a few days and then moved to different areas. People definitely got a sense they were being watched. We even had guys go up to sprinklers and smoke detectors to see if there was a camera there."

Sometimes store detectives find that when shoplifters detect that they have been watched, they return the goods that they were about to steal. Here is an example from London:

> The incident that sticks in my mind the most was when two women were shoplifting in the shoe department. They had a shopping trolley, and they had taken quite a few pairs of shoes off the shelf and put them in this trolley. There were no staff around, but we were watching them on a discreet camera when they suddenly took them all out and put them back and left the store. There was no reason at all why we could see they had changed their mind. The camera was hidden behind a half-black dome on the ceiling so you could not see when the camera was pointing at you. They were looking at the camera as they put the shoes back on the shelf. They made it very purposeful, as if they were saying, "We are not going to steal these; we do not want to be arrested."

One store detective told me that he used to be a shoplifter himself, specializing in bookshops.

> The prickle of a nearby camera would pop me out of my fear, indecision, and consumer choice. I have a stark memory of selecting a corner hidden from store detectives and selecting the book I wished to steal, when my eye unerringly swerved and located a high-mounted camera. It is rare in a shop for the eye level to drift above the shelf of

wares. I can only attribute this sudden shift of perspective to an intangible feeling of being watched.

We encountered only one amateur who had carried out a surveillance exercise, Denis Williams, who lives in Sussex. A drug dealer rented a flat in a block near his house, and the coming and going of his customers caused much distress to local residents. The police were reluctant to take any action, so Mr. Williams, the organizer of the local neighborhood watch, decided to film people visiting the dealer, using a video camera on a tripod at the rear of his front bedroom.

At times I would simply leave the camera running on auto-record. I later edited the tape showing dates and time on the footage covering people going to the flat. What was interesting was that while I was actually in the room operating the camera, a fair number of people who were simply walking along the road seemed to look up at the bedroom window. Yet when I was not present and the camera was running on auto, few seemed to look!

Although observations such as these are very suggestive, only controlled experiments can reveal whether people really can detect when they are being watched through CCTV. I discuss such experiments in chapter 12.

MARTIAL ARTS

Some schools of Asian martial arts place a strong emphasis on the role of intentions. They generally think of the sense of being stared at in this wider context.

Intentions are closely related to the direction of "life energy," usually transliterated as *ch'i*, *chi*, or *qi* from Chinese, or *ki* from Japanese. In one of the tai chi classics, this is expressed in the saying "The intention directs the ch'i. The ch'i directs the body."[2] A British practitioner expressed it as follows: "This subtle, delicate level of the intention can be sensitive and flexible, finding out the right angle for a throw or a punch, sensing the weak spots in an opponent's defense, exploring the line of least resistance. Here the will is like a soft mental feeler or antenna, which goes out sensitively and explores the terrain, as if, before the actual execution of the technique, one were to perform it in imagination first."

The other side of the coin is the awareness of these intentions by the person toward whom they are directed. An opponent's intentions are detected not only by observing body movements and other sensory clues, but also by being aware of the flow of chi. In several schools of Chinese and Japanese martial arts, students carry out exercises in which they are blindfolded and try to feel when and where an opponent is about to hit them. In the following exercise, the blindfolded person was placed within a circle of classmates.

At some time a preselected member in the circle would begin to think hostile thoughts at the person in the middle. They would slowly raise one arm, the hand held as if holding a handgun, and attempt to "shoot" the blindfolded person. If that person sensed something, he was told to shout out "stop," and point in the direction he perceived the threat to be coming from. At first we weren't too successful, but after a couple of months we did get better and better. Our teacher said that there was nothing magical about any of it, and that in man's early history our senses would have been far sharper than they are now. All he was teaching us was a way of trying to get back some of the lost abilities. ◇ ROGER AINSWORTH

Since 1990 there has been an upsurge of interest in Japan in research on martial arts, and laboratory studies have now been carried out with both Japanese and Chinese practitioners.[3] Of particular interest are a series of investigations of to-ate, an ancient martial arts technique of attacking an opponent without physical contact. Mikio Yamamoto and his colleagues carried out these studies at the National Institute of Radiological Sciences, in Chiba, Japan.

In order to rule out the possibility that the person attacked was responding to visual or other sensory clues, or to suggestion, the researchers kept an "attacker" and a "receiver" in sensory-shielded rooms, three floors apart. The "attacker" was a Chinese *qigong* master. They videotaped the receiver, and measured his skin resistance and his brain waves, by means of an electroencephalograph (EEG). In a series of trials, the *qigong* master directed to-ate at the receiver at times randomly chosen by the experimenters. In many of these trial periods the receiver visibly recoiled and showed alterations in EEG and skin resistance. The results of these randomized, double-blind trials were highly significant statistically, indicating that the to-ate involved an "unknown transmission"; that is to say, a form of transmission currently unknown to science. From the point of view of the *qigong* master, what was being transmitted was *ki* or *chi*.[4]

In the context of the theory that *chi* flows out of a person, directed by intention, and can affect the person to whom the intention is directed, the influence of the power of the gaze is one example of a more general process. Terry Ezra, who teaches aikido and has practiced for more than thirty years, said, "One of the things I am always telling my students is you are always projecting awareness and consciousness through your eyes." But this influence can be projected in other ways, too: "Not only out of my eyes; it feels as though it comes out from everywhere but especially my hands, lower belly, and forehead. When I do this there is definitely something like electricity flowing through me."

A practitioner of the Korean martial art *Jung Do*, Andy Macarthy, emphasized that the projection of energy through the eyes could be practiced deliberately in order to intimidate opponents:

In a sparring situation you can just put on "the look" and as soon as you get the other person to look down you know you have won. If you imagine looking at a lion, you don't want to do it for very long because all of a sudden you feel its immense strength. You must imagine your opponent as subordinate to you. You can never allow thoughts of failure to slip into the mind, because what you perceive is what is going to happen.

This analogy with the intimidating look of a lion draws attention to the fact that the principles of martial arts may not be limited to human beings. Indeed, several systems of martial arts have been based on careful observation of animals' fighting. Tai chi is said to have originated when its founder, Chang San-feng, saw a crane fighting with a snake. The tiger, the monkey, the leopard, and the praying mantis have all been the inspiration for various styles of kung fu.[5]

In the following chapter I discuss the sensitivity of animals to being looked at by people or by other animals. I also discuss people's ability to detect the stares of animals.

10 ANIMAL SENSITIVITY

Is the sense of being stared at confined to human beings? Or is it widespread in the animal kingdom? In this chapter I discuss evidence for the sensitivity of animals to human looks, and humans to animal looks, and animals to the looks of other animals. The ability to detect looks seems to exist in many species.

Why might animals be sensitive to looks? How might this ability have evolved? The most obvious possibility is in predator-prey relationships. A prey animal that can detect when a predator is looking at it would probably stand a better chance of escaping than an animal without this ability. Natural selection would favor animals able to sense looks and dangerous intentions.

PREDATORS AND PREY

The three main ways that animals hunt their prey are by lying in wait, by stalking, and by searching for relatively immobile prey.

Obviously, natural selection strongly favors animals that can avoid being killed by predators. The first line of defense against predators is the animals' appearance or habits of life. These are called primary defenses because they operate all the time. They continuously reduce the probability that a predator will find the prey animal or attack it. For example, some animals habitually lead hidden lives, like moles in holes. Some are camouflaged and thus hard for predators to see, like stick insects that resemble twigs. Some are poisonous, or have unpleasant features such as stings. They often warn off potential predators by prominent colors or markings, as some wasps do with their yellow and black stripes, or give sound signals, like rattlesnakes with their rattle. Others increase their chances of survival by copying dangerous or poisonous species; they are mimics.

By contrast, so-called secondary defenses only operate after the animal has detected a predator. Scientists who study animal behavior distinguish six basic categories of defensive behavior.[1] Most of us can probably recognize parallels in our own responses when under threat.

1. **Withdrawal.** For example, rabbits run into burrows when they sense danger, or tortoises withdraw into their protective shells.

2. **Flight,** by running, jumping, swimming, or flying away.

3. **Freezing.** Most predators are less likely to notice an animal if it stays still, and many predators only chase and attack moving prey. Many kinds of animals freeze temporarily, like pheasants, and then suddenly attempt to escape, taking the predator by surprise. But some go so far as to pretend to be dead, like opossums.

4. **Deflecting attacks.** Most predators prefer to attack the prey at the head end, where their victims are generally most vulnerable. Some animals escape by causing the predator to attack less vulnerable parts of the body. Some fish, like butterfly fish (Figure 10.1), have prominent eyespots at the rear end of their body. In addition, some species swim slowly backward at the first sign of trouble, making their prominent false eyes seem even more real. When the predator moves in for the kill, at the last moment the fish dashes rapidly forward, leaving the would-be killer snapping at empty water.[2]

5. **Startle displays.** Some animals try to defend themselves by frightening their attacker. Even if this fails to cause the would-be killer to panic and flee, it may buy time, giving a chance to escape. As the directors of horror films are well aware, suddenness is essential for producing an instinctive fright reaction: a sudden sound, like a gunshot, or a strange shape darting close to the hero's face, causes the audience to jump and gasp.

Animals use either sudden sounds or suddenly displayed fright patterns. For example, some animals, especially those that hide in dark dens or crevices, like wildcats, respond to the approach of a predator with an explosive spit and hiss, resembling that of a venomous snake. Many species have an instinctive fear of snakes, and usually the attacker jumps smartly backward.

Figure 10.1 *Eyespots in a variety of animals.*
Upper row, left: eyespots on the back of the head of an African owl, *Glaucidium perlatuim*. Upper row, center: the defensive posture of the caterpillar *Dicranura vinula*, whose real head is below the bug-eyed monster face. Upper row, right: eyelike marks on the shell of the Burmese turtle *Trionyx hurum*.
Lower row, left: the eyespots on the emperor moth *Pavonia pavonia*. As in many other butterflies and moths, these spots on the wings may help to misdirect the attention of predators from the more vulnerable parts of its body, as shown by many specimens with beak marks around the eyespots that escaped with their lives. Lower row, right: the eyespots on the butterfly fish *Chaetodon sp.* may serve a similar purpose by attracting predators to the wrong end, while the fish darts off in the opposite direction. (After Huxley, 1990, and Plant, 1993.)

Interestingly, in the context of the sense of being stared at, many of the suddenly displayed fright patterns used by animals resemble eyes, making it seem as if the attacker itself is being confronted by a predator. These scary, fright-inducing "eyes" differ from the eyespots used for deflecting attack, like those on butterfly fish, in that they appear suddenly. For example, the eyed hawk moth normally spends its days resting on leaf litter, with wings folded back, making the insect look like a dead leaf. But if a bird comes too close, the moth suddenly "opens its eyes" by raising its forewings, exposing its large eyespots.[3] The potential attacker is challenged by a pair of staring blue eyes on a pink and yellow background (Figure 10.2). Forward-facing eyes are characteristic of predators like owls and hawks, and when an insect-eating bird has the impression that it is face to face with a killer, it backs away, maybe giving the moth time to escape.[4]

6. **Retaliation.** The final defense of many species when attacked is to fight back, using whatever weapons they have, such as teeth, horns, and claws.

Animals vulnerable to attack by potential killers are at an advantage if they can detect the presence of the predator as soon as possible. Of course, animals use their "normal" senses for this purpose, some relying primarily on the sense of smell, others on sight and body language, others mainly on hearing, or on a combination of different senses. They may also have a seventh sense that enables them to detect threatening intentions. They may be able to sense when a would-be killer is looking at them, even if they have not yet detected the predator through sight, smell, or hearing. This sense of impending danger might primarily arouse the emotion of fear.

This is a subject that has not yet been investigated by scientists, largely because of the taboo against anything that seems inexplicable in terms of standard physical principles. Nevertheless, much information is already available.

Figure 10.2
Left: an eyed hawk moth (*Smerinthus ocellata*) at rest on leaf litter on the ground, well camouflaged, with its forewings folded back over its hind wings. Right: when alarmed, the moth raises its forewings, suddenly exposing the eyespots on the hind wings, with a startling effect on potential predators. (From Willmer, 1999.)

The people who have most experience are not academics in laboratories, but hunters. Many hunters have observed that animals can detect when they are being looked at by the hunter, and also that potential prey react differently according to a person's intentions.

HUMAN PREDATORS

For millions of years our ancestors, particularly our male ancestors, were part-time predators.

Hunter-gatherer societies long preceded all agricultural societies and civilizations. Many people still hunt today, some as part of a traditional way of life, some as a profession, and some as a sport.

Everyone agrees that if potential victims hear, see, or smell a human hunter, they are likely to take flight. But there also seems to be a widespread belief among hunters that some animals can detect their intentions from a distance, and also that some can sense when they are being looked at.

Among both traditional hunters and people who hunt for sport, many are convinced that some animals can pick up their predatory intentions at a distance. For example, describing the ambushing of tapirs when they came down to the river to drink, a proficient young hunter from the Tukano group in the Amazon rain forest in Colombia said, "If we think of her [the tapir], then she will see us in her thoughts. If we think of her she will become aware of our intentions and then she won't go down to the water; she will have a foreboding and will know. If we want to kill her we must think of other things. I tell you, should we not think of something else but only of her, we won't be able to kill her. But otherwise, we will make a kill."[5]

Many hunters in Europe and North America are also convinced that their intentions reach out ahead of them. For example, if they go to a place where they have often seen animals with the intention of shooting them, the animals are nowhere to be found.

Here is a dramatic story by J. Allen Boone, author of *Kinship with All Life*, of an experience he had in an Asian jungle where he had spent several hours watching monkeys playing in a clearing. They paid little attention to him. But suddenly everything changed:

With startling abruptness, every monkey quit whatever he happened to be doing and then looked in the same southerly direction. And then, motivated by obvious fear and panic, they went stampeding out of the clearing in a northerly direction. . . . What had caused this sudden exodus I couldn't remotely imagine. I decided to remain where I was . . . and see what was going to happen next. . . . Three puzzling hours went ticking by. Then into the clearing from the south came five men walking in single file. The first two were carrying rifles, the other three were attendants. They were as surprised to see me there as I was to see them. We introduced ourselves. . . . In the midst of this a most illuminating fact was revealed. At the precise moment those two hunters had picked up their rifles and headed for the clearing, three hours' walking distance away, every monkey in the clearing had fled from the place.[6]

My associates and I have been told over and over again by hunters and fishermen that they are less successful when they have a strong intention to kill. For example, David Boston, from Northumberland, England, has been fishing and shooting small game for fifty years. He told me:

I often wondered why when my mind wandered I would hook a salmon after hours of fruitless fishing. Then I read about an American Indian belief that animals were receptive to the hunter's thoughts, and your mind therefore should be free of all inimical thoughts. I decided to try this approach and started to practice letting my mind "freewheel," so to speak. My catch and kill rate increased considerably. If I stalked rabbits, deer, or, on one occasion, a fox, and then just thought about shooting them, although I was unarmed, they became very agitated, uneasy, and quickly went to cover.

Some animals seem able to detect the general intentions of predators from far away, but when those intentions are focused directly through the hunter's looks with intent to kill, the effect is more intense. Peter Bailey, of Hampshire, England, who has also been hunting and fishing since the 1940s, attributes this effect to his emotions.

It is the excitement you generate when you see the fish that is transmitted to them, I am convinced of that. The first time a friend of mine ever fished, he caught a twenty-five-pound sea trout. The following three years he never caught a fish, because he was so expectant, so excited. My pulse rate goes up when I suddenly see a ten-pound sea trout swimming toward me. The most success I have had is when I have drunk some whiskey and am absolutely relaxed.

When hunting deer, he found that the animals seemed to detect his intention, especially if he delayed shooting when he had them in his sights. "You have dwelt on the shot too long, with full concentration, holding the rifle, and you have got the deer beautifully in the scope, but if you just wait a fraction too long, it will just take off. It'll sense you."

Jack Jones, who lives in Staffordshire, England, is another experienced stalker who has noticed the sensitivity of deer to his intentions.

I get a real kick out of getting within a few yards of deer and apparently being unobserved. However, I can spot one 200 yards away with the intention of stalking and killing it, and it can become uneasy. Which of its many self-protection senses have I alerted? It stops feeding, checks its progress, shifts its feet, turns its head left, right, rear, front with sharp movements, blows through its nostrils, moves sideways or backwards, but does not see me. I am downwind and it has not scented me. Have I made a sound, which is of a frequency I cannot hear, but the animal can? Has it sensed a vibration I have unknowingly caused? Can it "feel" my killer intent? I have observed many times that if I cannot get a clean shot (for example, a twig which would deflect a bullet), I will relax and decide not to shoot and the animal will relax! However, this is very short-lived, unless I give up or move away. Its survival depends on being alert.

Like detectives, many experienced animal stalkers try to avoid looking directly at their quarry, because they have found that a direct gaze is more likely to alert it to their presence, even if it could not see them. John Frankcom, who worked for many years as a gamekeeper on the Beaulieu estate, in Hampshire, England, found that whether he was stalking deer or stalking poachers, the same principles applied. "You don't want to look directly at a deer—and it is the same with the human being, if you are trying to catch a human being. I think there is a certain ray or something that tells them that you are about."

Some people have specifically noticed the sensitivity of animals to their looks. One day as Dr. Hans-Heinrich Hatlapa, of Grossenaspe, Germany, was sitting in an elevated blind, a herd of red deer was grazing peacefully and gradually moving toward him.

The wind was very favorable, which excludes an olfactory influence. I didn't look out, but turned my eyes down. When the animals had approached within about 20 meters, I looked at them through the opening and they stopped immediately. Each animal raised its head staring toward me. Then they turned around and went back in the direction from which they had come.

Some species are better at detecting when they are being looked at than others. Several people have told me that among birds, members of the crow family, including ravens and magpies, seem especially sensitive. This sensitivity is definitely of survival value when they are in the vicinity of Tony Butler, of High Wycombe, Buckinghamshire, England: "I have an abhorrence of magpies. I sometimes try to stalk and shoot them with an air rifle. In all the time I have been doing this I have only ever managed to 'bag' one bird. They seem to have an uncanny sense of being observed, and even about when I am going to pull the trigger."

Probably a systematic survey of the experiences of hunters in different parts of the world would reveal a wealth of information about the reactions of animals to human looks and intentions. Such a survey has yet to be made.

WILDLIFE PHOTOGRAPHERS

Like hunters, wildlife photographers have to find the animals they want to "shoot" and try to get close to them. Like hunters, too, many have found that their intentions affect their chance of success. Some of the British photographers that we interviewed saw this effect as an example of "Sod's law," whereby things perversely happen at the wrong times. They would come across the animal they wanted to photograph only when they had left their camera behind, or run out of film.

Geoff Trinder, who, as well as being a photographer, works for the Lincolnshire (England) Trust for Nature Conservation, said:

If you want to go out and photograph something, the best thing is to leave your camera home and you will see it. I look after a couple of nature reserves and a couple of blinds, and if I go out with my camera thinking, "There might be a sparrowhawk bathing this morning," there never is. On the other hand, if I go for a casual walk to stretch my legs and go into the blind, I open the flap and there right in front of me is the sparrowhawk bathing, and it is totally oblivious to everything I do.

Several underwater photographers have had similar experiences. Here is just one example:

I have set my sights on photographing particular animals which I know are in a certain area and I haven't been able to find one, and then I have switched off or have got to the end of my film, and there are a hundred of them. I am certain marine creatures have this ability to know when your film is finished! ◇ LAWSON WOOD, BERWICK-SHIRE, SCOTLAND

Like hunters and detectives, most photographers have found that they are more successful if they avoid looking directly at the animals they are stalking. Even if the animals are aware of their presence, they are much less alarmed when they are not being looked at. As Roger Wilmshurst, a professional wildlife photographer in Sussex, England, put it:

If you're photographing birds, when you are not using a blind you try to get closer and closer to them. There is no doubt, in my experience, that if each time you move up a little bit, you don't look at the bird, you look somewhere else altogether and then settle down and gradually look at it, there is a fair chance you won't frighten it away. They definitely have an awareness that you are looking at them.

Several photographers commented that they found it best to approach animals indirectly or obliquely, while avoiding staring at them. The worst method is to walk straight toward them, looking hard.

Several bird photographers said that when they were in blinds, and invisible to the birds they were watching, the birds still seemed to know when they were being looked at. Russell Hartwell from Buckinghamshire has noticed this with herons.

I spend a lot of time in blinds, and it is uncanny how birds can just seem to sense you are there, become agitated, even though you know you haven't moved. With herons you can tell instantly that they are alert to danger. They go about their business with their heads down, and if they become frightened, their head goes up like a periscope. Very often the lens is completely still and they suddenly seem to realize that there is something looking at them, and their heads go up and they go very stiff and wait to see if they can see anything else. If you were then to move the lens, they would be off like a flash.

The experiences of wildlife photographers, like those of hunters, suggest that a wide range of species seem able to detect human intentions. They also seem to sense when they are being looked at even when they cannot see the person watching them.

LOOKING AT PETS

Many pet owners have noticed that their animals respond to their looks, even when the animal cannot see them looking.

In surveys that Gerald Winer and his colleagues carried out at Ohio State University, they asked both adults and children, "Do you think an animal like a dog or cat could feel you staring at it without seeing your eyes, or that it couldn't?" Fifty-three percent of the children and 50 percent of the adults said they thought it could.

In my own surveys of adults in Europe and the United States, an average of 55 percent answered yes to the question "Have you ever found that you could stare at an animal from behind and make it turn around?" More women than men said they had had this experience. The species this happened with most frequently were dogs and cats, in roughly equal numbers, but some people said they had made horses turn by looking at them, and some said the same of birds.

Here is a representative sample of comments from people in the American surveys:

My cat almost always responds when I look at her and think of her— she turns around.

My dog reacted while he was lying asleep in the yard and I was watching him through the windows of the house—he would lift his head and look.

If I stare at my dogs and cats while sleeping, they wake up and look at me.

Our dog is almost completely deaf. Many times she turns around when I stare at her. She couldn't have heard me.

Clearly, in such situations the animals were not under threat; they were simply the focus of their owners' attention, and some seem to have detected this attention even when they were asleep. Fiona Richards, who lives in Reading, Berkshire, England, noticed a similar sensitivity in two pet hens that she had hand-reared, and that followed her around.

Sometimes I would sit at a table facing through the window and the hens would perch on the windowsill, or on a ladder propped outside. After a while they would usually get drowsy and close their eyes, with their heads up, or roost with their heads turned around and buried in their back feathers. I noticed they would become alert and open their eyes if my attention shifted to watching them. I was fascinated by this, and experimented by trying to eliminate possible signals such as noise and movement. I found that if I was absorbed in reading, then shifted just my eyes and my attention, they would respond. I tried also just physically looking at them, trying to keep my mind on something else, or a blank, then moving my attention to them. This didn't work so well; they would roost, but uneasily. They seemed again to respond immediately when my full attention was on them.

From an evolutionary point of view, it is not surprising that animals wake in response to being stared at while asleep. This sensitivity would enable them to react to the unwelcome attention of predators, and would be of major survival value.

HUMANS AS POTENTIAL PREY

For at least 4 million years our human and hominid ancestors lived as hunter-gatherers — and as scavengers on the kills of stronger and more accomplished predators, like lions. We are familiar with the image of Man the Hunter from museum dioramas. We can easily forget that for the vast majority of human history, it was also man the hunted. Some of the bones of early hominids excavated in Africa and elsewhere show signs of the toothmarks of leopards and other large cats.[7] Even as recently as the nineteenth century, tigers were taking thousands of lives a year in parts of India. According to British government records, between 1800 and 1900 approximately 300,000 people were killed by tigers in India, along with 6 to 10 million farm animals.[8]

Most young children are fascinated by fairy tales about child-eating predators. The villains include tigers, wolves, monsters, ogres, and wicked witches. Some are not only exposed to stories of such predators; they also encounter adults who say to them, "You're so cute I could eat you up!" When they are older, many are fascinated by dinosaurs, especially huge flesh-eaters like *Tyrannosaurus rex*, which have the advantage of being both terrifying and extinct.

In 1933, a survey in the United States about the fears of urban children found that the majority's greatest fear was of animals and monsters. That was before television had brought monsters into living rooms. A further study in 1965 found that American schoolchildren were relatively unconcerned about actual threats like traffic, nuclear war, and germs. In response to the question "What are things to be afraid of?" 80 percent of five- and six-year-old children mentioned snakes, lions, tigers, bears, and other wild animals.[9] The author concluded, "The strange truth is that they fear an unrealistic source of danger in our urban civilization: wild animals."

These fears of children may well be rooted in our ancestors' experiences of predators. The fear of predators persists as children grow up, but becomes more focused on other humans. While children fear wild animals, grown-ups fear robbers, murderers, kidnappers, terrorists, and armies. Much of our entertainment concerns predators, as in murder mysteries, thrillers, and war stories.

In real wars, entire nations turn into predators. The insignia of many nations are predatory animals: the eagle for the United States, Mexico, Germany, Austria, and Spain; the lion for England, Finland, Holland, and Norway; the hawk for Egypt; and so on.

THE SENSE OF DANGER

The fear of predators is not only inherited culturally. Most kinds of animals, including ourselves, have an innate fear of potential predators. And this fear is associated with a variety of instinctive responses that can often enable individuals or even whole groups to escape.

Jim Corbett, a noted hunter in India in the 1920s and 1930s, was convinced that the "sense of imminent danger" had saved his life on many occasions. He was the savior of many people in remote villages in the Himalayan foothills through his shooting of man-eating tigers and leopards. In his book *Man-Eaters of Kumaon* (1944), he describes how he was in the jungle searching for a particularly dangerous tigress, when, after fourteen unsuccessful days, as he approached a pile of rocks, "I suddenly felt there was danger ahead. . . . I had been along this track many times, and this was the first time on which I hesitated to pass." But it would soon be dark, and he decided he had no choice but to continue. He passed a deer grazing, which took no notice of him, although soon after he had passed it, it ran off in alarm. He knew it must have seen the tigress, and went back to investigate. Where he had just walked, he saw his own footprints in the damp clay. "Over these footprints I now found the splayed-out pug marks of the tigress where she had jumped down from the rocks and followed me."

Corbett was sure that the "sense of danger" was real. "I do not know, and therefore cannot explain, what brings it into operation. On this occasion I had neither heard nor seen the tigress . . . yet I knew, without any shadow of doubt, that she was lying up for me among the rocks. I had been out for many hours that day and had covered many miles of jungle with unflagging caution, but without one moment's unease, and then, on cresting the ridge, and coming in sight of the rocks, I knew they held danger for me."[10] Corbett was convinced that as well as this general awareness of imminent danger, he could tell when a hidden tiger was looking at him.

Jeremy Stafford-Dietsch, an experienced underwater photographer, has found that the "sense of danger" operates both on land and underwater.

There are occasions when diving or working in the mangroves that I am just plain spooked. Once I was walking along a riverbank in the Northern Territory [in Australia], sneaking up on crocodiles that were basking on the mud below. There was an obvious route along the bank to creep up on them, but for some reason I found myself making a seemingly unnecessary detour through the grass on the top of the bank. When I looked back at the area I had avoided, I saw a crocodile sunning himself there. The sense of being spooked, the feeling that there is something very dangerous nearby, is readily admitted to by colleagues in the field; I don't think any of them try to ignore it!

On another occasion he was underwater off the coast of South Australia, photographing a great white shark from a protective cage.

There was a gap in the cage for operating the camera, and I had my arms well out of it, with the camera held in front of me, to try to get a picture of the beast. I was looking toward it and with a jolt had the urge to look the opposite way. Sure enough, another great white had turned up and was about a meter from me, swimming straight for my arms.

SENSING THE LOOKS OF WILD ANIMALS

When Jane Goodall first went to Africa, before beginning her studies of wild chimpanzees, she was helping to excavate fossils in Olduvai Gorge. On one occasion when she was with a companion among some thornbushes, "I had that prickling sensation that one sometimes feels if one is being watched. I turned to find a young male lion about forty feet away. He gazed at us with great interest." Luckily, she and her companion walked away slowly and escaped. If they had run, the lion would probably have given chase.[11]

When Ken Pole was thirteen, he was with a Boy Scout group in the interior of Vancouver Island, Canada. They were camping by a remote lake.

> I awoke about dawn, needing to pee. I walked down to a rocky shelf jutting out into the lake and was quietly tending to my business when I felt my hackles stand up in a very atavistic fashion. I had a powerful feeling someone was watching, but there had been no noise from my tentmates or from the other tents. Hoping to catch the prankster by surprise, I didn't move for a few seconds before lifting my head very slowly, and I found myself staring into the eyes of a large cougar or mountain lion. It was standing on an outcropping about fifteen yards away.

Many people have sensed the looks of other species even when they are not potentially dangerous. I have heard from dozens of people about finding themselves being looked at by hawks, blackbirds, crows, deer, coyotes, dingoes, badgers, bears, opossums, weasels, raccoons, cattle, and lizards. Sometimes these were frightening experiences, sometimes not. But most were surprising.

Dame Miriam Rothschild, the naturalist, told me that during the Second World War one winter evening she had gone out at dusk to shoot a pheasant for dinner.

> I went into a thick cover to wait among the bushes for birds coming in to roost. I began to feel I was being watched and I spent several minutes looking nervously but very quietly (scarcely moving my head) for another human being in the area. I thought there was probably a poacher somewhere in the area immediately ahead of me. There was no one to be seen, but the feeling grew. I told myself I was just being hysterical. Then suddenly I looked up and there was a barn owl about

three feet above me, sitting on a branch and staring at me with two golden eyes!

Sometimes people have felt they were being stared at even when indoors. Anna Michailides, of Athens, Greece, went to her room to change one summer afternoon. "As usual the French window leading to a large balcony was wide open. No one can see in. I undressed completely and standing naked in front of the mirror. I was trying to decide what to wear. I had an intense feeling that someone was peeping at me. There was nothing threatening or negative about it, just an awareness of being looked at. I turned around to see an Egyptian dove standing at the French window, staring straight at me. It even entered the room. Not frightened by my movements, it calmly watched me dress."

Camille Einoder, of Chicago, Illinois, had a more alarming indoor encounter at the school where she teaches. "I came in early one day and was in the supply room kneeling for a bottom shelf when I felt the hairs on the back of my neck rise like hackles. I slowly turned upward and saw a huge boa that had escaped from the biology room coiled atop the overhead projector above my back, staring down at me."

Usually such experiences occur quite unexpectedly, but some people deliberately pay attention to them as a way of finding animals that would otherwise be hard to locate. When Dr. Russell Hanley wanted to photograph the elusive mangrove monitor lizard in an Australian mangrove swamp, he could not find any of these well-camouflaged creatures despite hours of searching. Then "I just had a feeling: 'Well, there is one here.' And in a tree there was one of them looking at me."

SENSING THE LOOKS OF PETS

In their surveys in Columbus, Ohio, Gerald Winer and his colleagues found that not only did about half the adults and children think that animals could feel their looks (page 158), but many said that they themselves could feel the looks of animals: 34 percent of the adults and 41 percent of the children.

In my own surveys of adults in England, Sweden, and the United States, an average of 54 percent said they had sensed when they were being stared at from behind by an animal. Significantly more women (62 percent) than men (44 percent) said they had had this experience. The animals to which they had reacted were mainly cats and dogs. Other species to which people said they had reacted included horses, pigs, cows, goats, squirrels, bears, a monkey, mice, birds, iguanas, snakes, and fish.

Here are some examples of people's experiences, from the United States and Britain:

> My dog wakes me up at night by staring at me. I've had more than one dog who has done this. It's usually when they need to go out. They don't make a sound, just stare intensely. I wake up and know immediately what's going on.

> On several occasions whilst out walking with my Alsatian bitch I felt I was being told to stop. When I looked back she had stopped to urinate, and was staring at me most intently, her expression plainly saying "Wait for me."

> I was out at the front of my house, bending down and clearing weeds from under a tree. I felt I was being stared at and glanced behind me but saw nobody. I turned back to my task, but the feeling was so strong that I stood up and turned around to look properly. There was my neighbor's spaniel, staring hard at me as if to say, "Why don't you turn around and speak to me?" So I did and after a little petting he turned around and went home.

Jack London, a keen literary observer of canine behavior, described in his book *The Call of the Wild* a particularly intimate situation involving the dog Buck: "He would lie by the hour, eager, alert, at Thornton's feet. . . . Or, as chance might have it, he would lie farther away, to the side or rear. . . . And often, such was the communion in which they lived, the strength of Buck's gaze would draw John Thornton's head around, and he would return the gaze, without speech, his heart shining out of his eyes as Buck's heart shone out."[12]

ANIMALS SENSING THE LOOKS OF OTHER ANIMALS

Presumably, just as people can detect when animals are looking at them, and animals can detect when they are being looked at by people, so can animals detect the looks of other animals. But unfortunately there has been no systematic research on this subject, and very little is known about the sense of being stared at in the wild.

As the experiences of people with nonhuman animals show so clearly, the sense of being stared at plays an important role in detecting the attention of potential predators, but it also works in more intimate situations in which the gaze conveys no threat. Observations on both captive and wild animals support the idea that both hostile and nonhostile looks are detectable.

For example, among bonobos (pygmy chimpanzees), looks play an important part in social interactions, as observed by Betty Walsh, the senior keeper at Twycross Zoo, in England.

> I have seen some apes glare at others from behind, and the ones in front will turn around as if they have felt the glare. Usually this happens with food. If one ape has got something, another will stare hard at it, and they will try not to look because if they catch their eye they will have to share it, but they always do in the end.

When he was observing foxes in the wild, the American naturalist William Long was impressed by the way that vixens maintained discipline among their cubs without uttering a sound:

> For hours at a stretch the cubs romp lustily in the afternoon sunshine. . . . [T]he old vixen, who lies apart where she can overlook the play and the neighborhood, seems to have the family under control at every instant, though never a word is uttered. Now and then when a cub's capers lead him too far from the den, the vixen lifts up her head to look at him intently; and somehow that look . . . stops the cub as if she had sent a cry or a messenger after him. If that happened once, you might overlook it as a matter of mere chance; but it happens again and again, and always in the same challenging way. The eager cub suddenly checks himself, turns as if he had heard a command, catches the vixen's look, and back he comes like a trained dog to the whistle.[13]

THE EVOLUTIONARY ORIGINS OF THE SENSE OF BEING STARED AT

Clearly, the sensitivity to being stared at is not a feature specific only to human beings, but is shared with many other members of the animal kingdom. All the above accounts of animal sensitivity to human looks, or of human sensitivity to animal looks, concern mammals, birds, reptiles, or fish.

Can invertebrates like worms, insects, scorpions, spiders, and mollusks tell when they are being looked at? And can higher animals tell when invertebrates are looking them at? I know of no evidence one way or the other. A particularly interesting subject for research would be the octopus, which has eyes not unlike our own but is a mollusk, related to snails and clams. Can people tell when an octopus is watching them? Can the fish and other creatures on which octopuses prey tell when they are being looked at? And can octopuses themselves tell when they are being watched by other octopuses, or by other animal species?

At present, too little is known to answer these questions, but there is no reason why they should not be investigated by naturalists, and also in laboratory experiments. Only when we have a better idea about which groups of organisms seem to possess a sense of being stared at can we trace in detail the evolutionary origins of this ability.

A sensitivity to looks could not have evolved before there were eyes to see, but eyes go back a long way in evolutionary history. The first multicellular animals probably arose some 570 million years ago, and by 530 million years ago a wide variety of animals already possessed eyes, as revealed by the fossil deposits in the Burgess Shale, in the Canadian Rockies.[14] Perhaps the sense of being stared at evolved along with eyes themselves. It could be very old indeed.

11

EXPERIMENTS ON
THE SENSE OF
BEING STARED AT

As we have seen in the previous chapters, most people have, at times, sensed they were being stared at, or made others turn around by staring at them. Also, many kinds of animals seem to be sensitive to human looks, and humans to animal looks.

In spite of all this evidence, a powerful taboo has inhibited scientific research on this subject for generations. Between 1890 and 1990, only four papers on this subject were published in scientific journals, as far as I know. In the following two chapters I discuss the reasons for this taboo and the historical circumstances that gave rise to it. In this chapter I continue to approach the subject in an open-minded way, and describe experiments that have been done to test this phenomenon.

The sense of being stared at can be investigated easily and inexpensively in experimental tests. Since around 1990, many such tests have been carried out. There is now strong evidence that people really can tell when they are being looked at from behind in a way that cannot be explained in terms of the known senses. Three kinds of experiments have been done.

First, a subject sits with his or her back to a person who either stares at the back of the subject's neck, or looks away and thinks of something else. The staring and not-staring trials take place in a random sequence. In each trial the subject guesses whether he or she is being stared at. These guesses are either right or wrong. Do the subjects make more correct guesses than would be expected on the basis of chance?

Second, in tests under more real-life conditions, hidden observers either look or do not look at people who are unaware of their presence. The observers may, for example, be looking out of a darkened room or through a one-way mirror at people in a foyer or shopping mall. Do more people turn around and look toward the hidden observers when they are being looked at than when they are not? In order to find this out, a video camera is placed near the hidden observers. The unwitting subjects are filmed continuously, so that both the periods when they are being looked at and when they are not being looked at are recorded. The video is later analyzed by a person who does not know which periods were which.

Third, the subject is viewed through closed-circuit television by observers in another room, who either look or do not look at the subjects on the TV monitor. In these CCTV experiments, the subjects are not asked to guess whether they are being looked at. Instead their skin resistance is monitored (as in a lie-detector test) so that changes in their emotions can be registered automatically. Do these unconscious responses change when they are being looked at?

THE PIONEERS OF EXPERIMENTAL RESEARCH

Scientific research on this subject was both initiated and set back for decades by two American psychologists, E. B. Titchener and J. Edgar Coover. Both claimed to have shown that the sense of being stared at was illusory.

Titchener was one of the founding fathers of experimental psychology in the United States. In the 1890s he found that many of his students at Cornell University firmly believed they could feel when they were being stared at from behind, or make others turn around by gazing at the backs of their necks. He was certain that no mysterious influences could possibly be involved, and he assumed that there must be a "rational explanation." He speculated that people tend to turn around anyway and, by their movement, might attract the attention of someone behind them, so that they would catch each other's eyes. "These accidents evidently play into the hands of a theory of personal attraction and telepathic influence."[1]

In a paper published in *Science* in 1898, Titchener announced that he had carried out laboratory experiments on this phenomenon "which have invariably given a negative result; in other words the interpretation offered has been confirmed." He gave no experimental details, and published no data. But he felt the need to justify doing the tests in the first place:

If the scientific reader object that this result might have been fore-seen, and that the experiments were, therefore, a waste of time, I can only reply that they seem to me to have their justification in the breaking-down of a superstition which has deep and widespread roots in the popular consciousness. No scientifically-minded psychologist believes in telepathy. At the same time, the disproof of it in a particular case may start a student upon the straight scientific path, and the time spent may thus be repaid to science a hundredfold.[2]

Titchener's paper was very influential, and was widely cited by skeptics for more than 100 years, even though he said nothing about the actual experiments except that they were negative.

By contrast, Coover described an elegantly simple experiment, and published his data. The subject sat with his back to the looker, who either looked or did not look in a series of trials, in which the decision whether to look or not was random, determined by throwing dice. The subjects were Coover's own students at Stanford University. He claimed that there was no significant ability to detect looks, and concluded that popular belief in the sense of being stared at was "groundless."[3] By reinforcing Titchener's negative conclusions, Coover's work seemed to put an end to the matter from a scientific point of view. His paper was published in 1913.

The next report in the scientific literature was in 1939, in Dutch, by a professor in the Netherlands, J. J. Poortman.[4] Only in 1959 was a summary of his paper published in English.[5] Poortman became interested in the subject both as a result of his own experiences of being stared at and through finding that many other people seemed to have experienced it, too. Using a modified version of Coover's method, he carried out a series of trials with himself as the subject and a woman friend as the looker. She was a city councillor in The Hague, and she was accustomed to attracting the attention of other council members by the power of her gaze. Poortman was right significantly more often than wrong in guessing when she looked at him.[6]

After Poortman's experiment, there was apparently no further research on this subject until 1978, when Donald Peterson carried out an experiment as a student project at the University of Edinburgh. In Peterson's experiment, the looker sat in a closed booth separated from the subject by a one-way mirror, and was invisible to the subject. The results were positive and statistically significant.[7]

In 1983, Linda Williams, a student at the University of Adelaide, Australia, pioneered the use of closed-circuit television in staring research, and found a statistically significant effect when the subject was looked at through CCTV by a person in a different room.[8]

MY OWN RESEARCH

My interest in the sense of being stared at was aroused in the 1980s when I realized that it had enormous theoretical implications. As I was developing my ideas about morphic fields, I realized that when a predator looks at a prey, it would be linked to it by a field that could in principle affect the prey animal, even if it could not see the predator.[9]

I then realized that this idea could be extended to visual perception in general. When we look at anything, fields of perception link us to what we see. Hence we might affect things or people just by looking at them. The sense of being stared at seemed to provide evidence for just such an effect, and suggested a way of testing it experimentally.

In 1986 I developed a simple experimental procedure and began doing tests with my family and friends. I later discovered I had reinvented the method used by Coover. People worked in pairs, with one person, the starer, sitting behind the other, the subject. The starer tossed a coin to decide whether to look or not: heads meant "look at the back of the subject's neck"; tails meant "look away and think of something else." The looker indicated when the trial was beginning by giving a sound signal, and the subject after ten seconds or so guessed "looking" or "not looking." The looker recorded whether it was a looking or not-looking trial and whether the subject was right or wrong, and then told the subject whether the guess was correct or not.

This simple procedure worked well, and the results were positive. I then tried the experiments with groups of volunteers at lectures, seminars, and conferences in Britain, Germany, Sweden, and the United States. The positive effect proved remarkably repeatable, even though the participants were so varied. The simplicity of the procedure and the fact that it cost nothing meant that students could carry it out. The first of many student projects on the sense of being stared at was carried out in 1991 in California.[10]

In 1994 I described this procedure in my book *Seven Experiments That Could Change the World*, and encouraged readers to try it for themselves. Many did so. I continued my own experimental program with the help of teachers and children in schools in London, as well as with groups of adult volunteers. In addition, through South Connecticut State University, I helped to organize an extensive series of experiments in schools in Connecticut, starting in 1996, carried out by science teachers and their pupils.[11]

In 1997, *New Scientist* magazine wrote an article about this research, and published my experimental procedure on its website. This further widened the scale of participation in this research. A program about these experiments on the Discovery Channel in 1997 encouraged further research. In the following years, many more people took part in this research, downloading the instructions from my own website. Dozens of school and university students carried out projects based on these methods. Several won prizes in science fairs. Many thousands of trials have now been carried out, and the evidence for the reality of the sense of being stared at is very strong indeed.

In these experiments, if people had no ability to detect when they were being stared at and were guessing at random, they would be right, on average, 50 percent of the time. In fact, on average they were correct about 55 percent of the time. Although this is not very much above the chance level, when repeated over and over again it became extremely significant statistically. By 1999 the combined results from a total of 13,900 trials were astronomically significant, with the odds against the results being due to chance more than 10^{20} to 1 (10 with 20 zeros after it).[12] The combined results to date are yet more significant.

If people really can tell when they are being looked at, why is the effect detected in these experiments so small, only 5 percent above the chance level? There could be several reasons.

First, under the artificial conditions of experiments, people are being asked to do consciously what they usually do unconsciously. Thinking and self-consciousness may interfere with their sensitivity.

Second, some of the subjects and lookers may have become bored or distracted during the experimental sessions, reducing the rate of success.

Third, some people are better as lookers or as subjects than others, and the inclusion of ineffective lookers and insensitive subjects in the trials may have diluted the effect. In a series of trials with selected lookers and subjects in a school in Freiburg, Germany, up to 90 percent of the guesses were correct.[13] And in experiments with schoolchildren in Ireland, when twins worked in pairs as starer and subject, they did much better than nontwin siblings or unrelated children.[14] But most of the experiments described above were carried out with unrelated people, with no selection for sensitive subjects or good starers.

THE PATTERN OF RESULTS

In *Seven Experiments That Could Change the World*, I summarized the results of preliminary experiments carried out by myself and others in terms of the overall success rates. Only after that book was published did I realize that the detailed results showed a remarkably consistent pattern, a pattern that has now been repeated over and over again. The scores in looking trials were positive and staggeringly significant statistically, while they were at chance levels in the not-looking trials (Figure 11.1). In the looking trials the success rate was generally around 60 percent, while in the not-looking trials the score was around the chance level of 50 percent. Dozens of independent investigators all over the world have obtained very similar patterns of results.[15]

Could these results be due to a small number of people scoring very well, while most of the others showed no sensitivity at all? Looking at average scores in terms of percentages cannot tell us the answer to this question. A better way of analyzing the results is to give equal weight to each subject, on a one-subject-one-vote system.[16] If a person's guesses were more often right than wrong, this was represented by a plus (+) sign, if more often wrong than right by a minus (−) sign, and if an equal number of guesses were right and wrong, by an equal (=) sign. For example, if a person did 10 looking trials, and guessed 6 or more right, she would be scored +. If she got 4 or fewer right, she would be scored −. If she got 5 right and 5 wrong, she would score =.

If people were just guessing at random, there should have been approximately equal numbers of people with plus and minus scores. But in the looking trials this was not the case; there were far more pluses than minuses. The contrasting patterns of results in looking and not-looking trials were very clear (Figure 11.1).

Even the supposedly negative results of Coover published in 1913 showed a similar pattern when analyzed in this way (Figure 11.2).[17] Ironically, this experiment has been taken to support the skeptical position for more than ninety years, but in fact it shows the very same pattern of positive results as my own experiments, and those of many other independent experimenters.

These results show that the better performance of subjects in looking trials did not depend on a minority of particularly sensitive subjects, but rather represented a general tendency for subjects to score better when they were being looked at than when they were not. This is shown in more detail by the exact distributions of people's scores (Figure 11.3). In the control trials, the distribution curve centered on a score of 5 out of 10, the level expected by chance. In

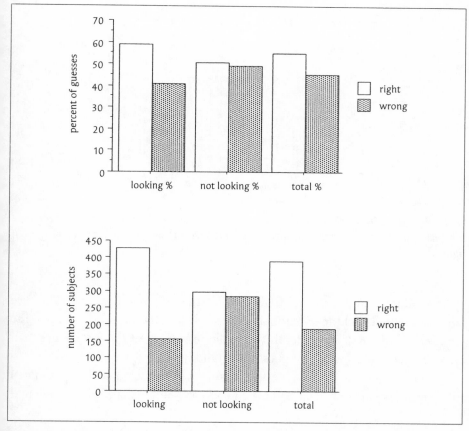

Figure 11.1 *Combined results of experiments on the sense of being stared at, carried out in Britain, Germany, and the United States, with a total of 661 subjects (data from Shel-drake, 1999b, Table 5).*

In the upper chart, the data are shown as percentages of correct and incorrect guesses in looking trials, not-looking trials, and total scores. The lower chart shows the data in a different way, in terms of the number of subjects who were more right than wrong compared with the number who were more wrong than right. For the purpose of this comparison, the number of subjects who made equal numbers of right and wrong guesses were ignored. The subjects were novices, being tested for the first time.

the looking trials, the entire curve was shifted to the right, with its peak at a score of 6 out of 10.

Why should there be such a striking difference between the looking and the not-looking trials?

If there really is a tendency for people to know when they are being looked at, they would indeed tend to be right when they are being looked at.

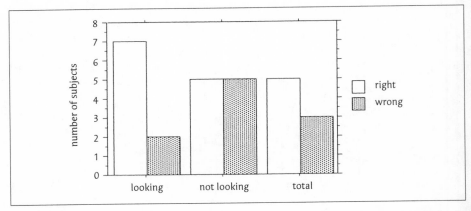

Figure 11.2 *Results from the staring experiments of Coover (1913), showing the number of subjects who were more right than wrong compared with those who were more wrong than right.*

By contrast, in the control trials people are not being looked at. They are being asked to detect the *absence* of an effect, which has no parallel in real-life conditions. And, indeed, under those conditions the results were no better than chance; the subjects were just guessing at random.

Interestingly, the highly positive results with selected and experienced subjects show not only that some people score better than others, but that

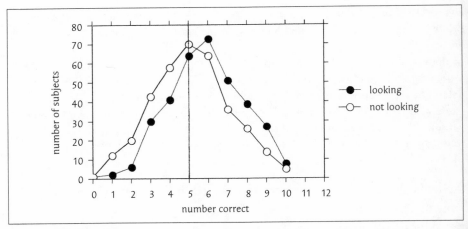

Figure 11.3 *The distribution of scores in looking and not-looking trials in schools in Connecticut (data from Sheldrake, 1999b).*
The vertical axis shows the number of subjects who had a given score, and the horizontal axis the number of correct guesses out of 10. The vertical line shows the average score expected on the basis of random guessing, namely, 5 out of 10.

people can improve their scores with practice, both in looking and in not-looking trials. Although novices tend to score best in looking trials, and at chance levels in not-looking trials (Figure 11.1), those who are tested repeatedly and given feedback tend to improve in both kinds of trials. It seems possible to *learn* to detect the difference between being looked at and not being looked at.

CAN THE RESULTS BE EXPLAINED AS ARTIFACTS?

These simple experiments seem too good to be true. They give repeatable positive effects. They cost practically nothing. They are so simple that a child can do them, and indeed many children already have done them.

When I first realized that these experiments were giving consistently positive results, of course I expected dogmatic skeptics to be skeptical about them. I soon found that parapsychologists were skeptical, too. Some were so convinced that psychic phenomena were weak, unpredictable, and elusive that they could not believe that an experiment as simple as this could give consistent positive results. Indeed, I was skeptical myself. Perhaps there was some fatal flaw that I had not spotted. Could these results be explained in terms of subtle sensory cues? Or could they be artifacts that arose from errors in the procedures?

First, consider the possibility that subjects tended to say "looking" in most of the trials because of some inherent bias in favor of saying "looking." This would make subjects seem successful in looking trials. But at the same time it would make them equally unsuccessful in not-looking trials, and the effects would cancel out. To take an extreme example, if a subject said "looking" in all 20 trials, she would be right 10 times out of 10 in the looking trials, and wrong 10 times out of 10 in the not-looking trials. The overall score would be 10 right out of 20, or 50 percent, the result expected by chance. In fact, the positive scores in the looking trials were not offset by negative scores in the not-looking trials. Rather, in the not-looking trials the scores were at chance levels, and the overall scores, combining looking and not-looking trials, were positive (Figure 11.1).

Second, perhaps some subjects were picking up unconscious sensory cues from the looker, such as hearing or feeling the looker breathing differently in the looking and not-looking trials. Or some subjects may even have been cheating by peeking to see what the looker was doing. Or some lookers may have been signaling secretly to the subject, telling them whether they were looking.

These are all reasonable possibilities, and might conceivably explain the highly significant success in the looking trials. But they cannot explain why cheating or subtle cues should have failed to let the subjects know when they were *not* being looked at. Cheating, for example, should have raised the scores to a similar extent in looking and in not-looking trials. This pattern of results argues strongly against these possibilities. Nevertheless, to be yet surer, these possibilities needed to be tested as rigorously as possible.[18]

I carried out a new series of experiments in which the subjects were blindfolded, using the kind of blindfold supplied by airlines to help passengers sleep on planes. Such blindfolds prevent peeking and eliminate cues from peripheral vision. Blindfolding the subjects made no significant difference.[19] Nevertheless, just to be sure, from 1997 onward I used blindfolds as a matter of course in my experiments, and incorporated the use of blindfolds into the standard procedures described on my website.

To prevent the possibility of subjects' learning how to pick up subtle sensory cues of any nature, no feedback was given, so that subjects had no way of knowing whether their guesses were right or wrong until they had completed all twenty trials. Without feedback the results were still positive and highly significant statistically.[20]

To block any possible clues from sounds or smells, the experiments were carried out through closed windows. The lookers were indoors, and the blindfolded subjects were outdoors, up to 100 yards away, with their backs to the windows. In addition, the subjects were given no feedback. The results were still positive and highly significant statistically.[21]

My own positive results with blindfolds, without feedback, and with lookers and subjects separated by closed windows have now been independently replicated by other investigators in Europe and the United States.[22] These results strengthen yet further the evidence for the reality of the sense of being stared at.

Skeptical researchers who carried out staring experiments following my own procedures obtained positive, statistically significant results in close agreement with my own (Figure 11.4). I discuss their results in detail in Appendix B.

THE AMSTERDAM EXPERIMENT

The largest experiment ever conducted on the sense of being stared at has been going on in Amsterdam, Holland, since 1995. More than 18,700 looker-subject pairs have taken part, and the statistical significance of the positive

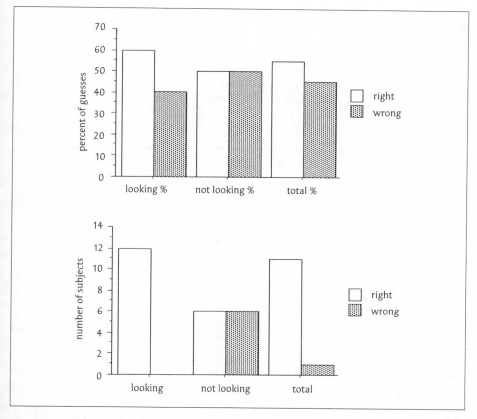

Figure 11.4 *The results of staring experiments by John Colwell and his colleagues at Middlesex University, plotted in the same way as in Figure 11.1.*
The upper chart shows the percentages of right and wrong guesses, and the lower chart shows the number of subjects who were more right than wrong and more wrong than right. (Data from Table 1 of Colwell et. al., 2000, for trials in which subjects were given feedback.)

results is astronomical: the odds against chance are 10^{376} to 1. Such a figure defies all imagination.

Based on my suggestions, Diana Issidorides and her colleagues at the New Metropolis Center, a science museum in Amsterdam, developed an ingenious computerized procedure that made the experiment seem like a game, with moving graphics and instructions. They employed a sophisticated but user-friendly statistical methodology[23] that gave immediate feedback on how the subject was doing.

In the Amsterdam experiment, the looker sits behind the subject and is instructed whether or not to look by a signal on the computer screen. For each trial, the subject guesses out loud and the looker entered the guess into the

Table 11.1 *Percentage of people who had "eyes in the back of the head" in the Amsterdam staring experiment.*
The percentage expected by chance as a result of random guessing was 20. By March 2002 the total number of participants was 18,793.

	Aged under 8	Aged 9–16	Aged over 17
Male	41	37	35
Female	38	32	33

computer. Depending on the number of correct or incorrect guesses, after a maximum of thirty trials, the computer announces whether the subject "has eyes in the back of the head" or not.

The statistical program was designed in such a way that if everyone were just guessing by chance, 20 percent of the participants would be classified as having eyes in the back of their head. Against this chance expectation of 20 percent, in fact between 32 and 41 percent of the subjects "had eyes in the back of their heads."[24] The most successful subjects were boys under the age of eight and, surprisingly, the least sensitive were girls from nine to sixteen (Table 11.1).

EXPERIMENTS ON THE EFFECTS OF STARING THROUGH MIRRORS

Many people have noticed that if they stare at someone through a mirror (for example, in a bar), the person may turn and look at them—through the mirror. This implies that the sense of being stared at depends on the direction from which the gaze is coming, even if it has been reflected.

My associates and I have carried out preliminary research on the effects of staring though mirrors. In the first series of tests, the procedure was similar to the usual staring experiments described above, but the starer and the subject sat in adjacent rooms rather than in the same room. They could not see each other directly. But the connecting door was open and a mirror was placed at the side of the doorway in such a way that the starer could see the subject's back through it (Figure 11.5). The subject wore a blindfold. As usual, in a randomized series of twenty trials, the starer either looked at the subject or not. The results were very similar to those of normal staring trials, showing that subjects could indeed tell when they were being looked at through mirrors.[25]

I then did another experiment with mirrors to test whether subjects could detect from which direction the gaze was coming. The starer sat behind the blindfolded subject in the same room, and two mirrors were placed symmetri-

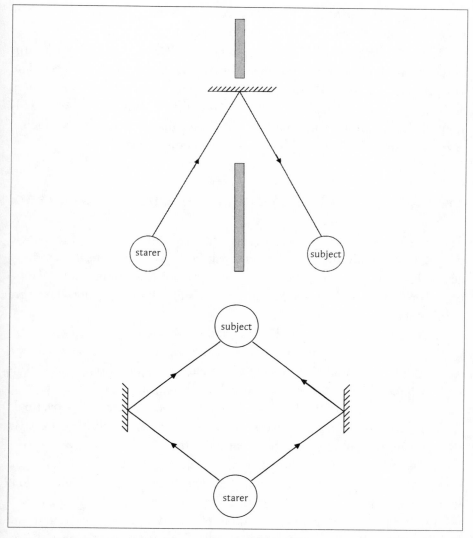

Figure 11.5 *Diagrams showing the positions of starers and subjects in experiments involving mirrors.*
Above: the starer looks at the subject through a mirror in a doorway. Below: the starer either looks at the subject through a mirror on the left or on the right. The subject has to guess which side the look is coming from.

cally, on either side of the room (Figure 11.5). In every test, the starer looked at the subject, but did so either through the mirror on the left or the one on the right, in a randomized sequence of twenty trials. This meant that either the right or the left side of the subject's head was looked at. The subject had to guess from which side he was being looked at, and indicated the guess by raising his right or left arm. The guesses were either right or wrong, and by chance the success rate would have been 50 percent.

In tests I carried out with my sons, then aged ten and eight, we took turns as starers and subjects. A significant majority of the guesses were correct.[26] The same experiment, carried out at my request in a German prison for women, again gave significant positive results.[27] Thus these preliminary experiments support the observation that people can detect the direction from which a gaze is coming (see chapter 8), even after reflection through a mirror.

STARING EXPERIMENTS WITH HIDDEN OBSERVERS

The experiments I have discussed so far are very artificial. In real life, people do not know in advance that someone will be looking at them from behind according to a randomized schedule. To carry out tests under more natural conditions, the observers were hidden and the subjects did not know they were being observed.

I carried an experiment of this kind at the BBC Television Centre in London, for a television program on unexplained phenomena.[28] The subjects were an audience waiting to go into a studio for a quiz show. The lookers included myself; the presenter, Carol Vorderman; and four other people, including a member of the BBC Karate Club. We were in an office overlooking the area where the people were waiting on a staircase with their backs to us. We were invisible to the subjects because the office window was of darkened glass and the lights in the office were switched off.[29] A video camera was running continuously, and in a randomized sequence of one-minute periods we either stared at the backs of people in the crowd, or did not look at all.

During the staring periods, we quite often saw people turn around and look straight at the darkened glass through which we were staring at them. Interestingly, when we interviewed them afterward, none of those we questioned were conscious of having turned around, or feeling they were being looked at. Of course, if we had not been hidden and they had made eye contact, they would immediately have become conscious of our looking at them.

The video was analyzed by an independent judge who did not know which one-minute periods were staring periods and which were not. During the nonstaring periods, some people did turn around to look behind, or to talk to somebody behind them. But more people turned during the staring periods than during the not-staring periods: 27 as opposed to 12. This difference was statistically significant, and supports the idea that some of the subjects were indeed responding to the gaze of the hidden observers.

The same experimental method can be used with nonhuman subjects. Two experiments of this kind have already been carried out with birds. The first was carried out by five art students in a bird park called La Selva, near Rome, Italy, as part of a conference on science and art. The students hid in bushes near a lake, from which they could watch geese on the shore through binoculars. The geese were filmed continuously. The experiment took place during a period when the birds were resting. During the three-minute watching periods, each of the five students observed a different goose, and in the three-minute nonwatching periods they did not. An analysis of the video revealed that during the looking periods, on 10 occasions geese woke up and looked toward the hidden observers, whereas in the not-looking periods this happened only 3 times.[30]

Another bird experiment was less successful. Several bird-watchers had told me that members of the crow family, and especially ravens, were exceptionally sensitive to being stared at. With the help of Dr. Tony Cross, an experienced naturalist, I set up a series of tests with ravens in order to investigate this observation experimentally.

We placed a blind on the edge of a large rubbish heap in central Wales where hundreds of ravens gathered in the early mornings and evenings to feed on the rich pickings. We left the blind in place for a couple of weeks so that the birds could get used to it. Then, braving the mud and strong smells, we installed ourselves in the blind before dawn or in the afternoon before the ravens came for their evening feed. After the birds had arrived and started feeding, we looked intensely at the ravens in a given area of the rubbish tip for one-minute periods, and did not look during control one-minute periods, filming the birds continuously on video throughout. Unfortunately, there were so many ravens and so much frenzied activity that it was impossible to detect any differences that could have been due to our looking; the experiment was inconclusive. In future tests of this type it would be important to find situations in which the birds under observation are calm, rather than busy and excited.

EXPERIMENTS USING CLOSED-CIRCUIT TELEVISION

Since the late 1980s there has been a growing interest in the sense of being stared at among parapsychologists, who have adopted a sophisticated experimental procedure using CCTV, with the subjects and lookers in separate rooms. The subjects were not asked to guess whether they were being looked at. Instead, they could relax while their galvanic skin response was recorded automatically, as in lie-detector tests. The procedure was similar to that in experiments on the effects of intention, discussed in chapter 2 (page 53), except that in these tests the agents looked at the subjects on TV monitors, while in the intention experiments the agents focused their intention on the subjects without seeing their image.[31]

One advantage of these CCTV experiments is that they depended on an unconscious physiological response rather than on conscious guessing. Another is that they ruled out conclusively the possibility of the subjects' responses being caused by subtle sensory clues from the looker. No such clues are possible when the looker is in a distant room.

Most of these experiments have been successful, with statistically significant positive results.[32] People's skin resistance changed significantly when they were being looked at, even though they were unconscious of it. I discuss this CCTV research in more detail in Appendix B.

CONCLUSIONS

The reality of the sense of being stared at is strongly supported by experimental research. The gaze still works when it has passed through windows and been reflected by mirrors. People can detect from which direction they are being stared at, in agreement with real-life experience. Looking at people affects them even through closed-circuit television, and even when they are unconscious of being looked at.

Much remains to be discovered in this field of research. For example, can most people get better with practice? What kinds of people are most effective as lookers, or most sensitive as subjects? Do several starers have more effect than one? Does the distance between the starer and the subject make much difference? Can people tell when they are being looked at on television broadcasts? Most of these experiments could be done very inexpensively, and some would make ideal student projects. (For details, see Appendix A.)

That so little is yet known about the sense of being stared at is not because research on this subject is particularly difficult or expensive, but because of powerful taboos that have inhibited thought and inquiry. These taboos arose for two main reasons.

First, the power of the gaze is taken for granted in many traditional societies, and is often connected to a belief in the evil eye. This belief is classified by rationalists as a superstition, and hence by definition lies beyond the pale of rational discourse.

Second, the theory of vision taken for granted in Western science for nearly 400 years rules out the possibility that looks can affect what is being looked at. So the sense of being stared at is theoretically impossible.

If the sense of being stared at is real, as it seems to be, it throws into question some of the fundamental doctrines of rationalism, as I discuss in the following chapter. It also casts grave doubt on the standard scientific theory of vision, as I will show in Chapter 13. It points toward a new understanding of the nature of the mind.

12

THE EVIL EYE AND THE
RISE OF RATIONALISM

The belief that influences are transmitted through the eyes by looks is found in many traditional societies. The negative effects of looks are attributed to the evil eye, the eye of envy. It blights what it looks upon, causing ill health and misfortune. "He that hasteth to be rich hath an evil eye," warns the biblical Book of Proverbs (28:22). Young children, cattle, crops, houses, cars, and indeed anything capable of being envied are supposed to be affected by the evil eye.

The positive effects of looks, especially loving looks, are also widely acknowledged. In India, many people visit holy men and women for their *darshan*, literally their look, which is believed to confer great blessings.

The evil eye used to be thought of as a kind of "fascination," the casting of a spell through the eyes, from the Latin *fascinum*, meaning a magical spell. This original usage still survives in relation to the legendary power of snakes to immobilize birds by their gaze. In the mythology of ancient Greece, the glare of the snake-haired Medusa turned men to stone. The mask of the Medusa, also known as the Gorgon's head, was on the shield of the goddess Athena, and signified her terrifying power.

Here are some reflections on the evil eye by one of founding fathers of modern science, Sir Francis Bacon. This passage is from his essay "On Envy," published in 1625, the year before he died.

There be none of those affections which have been noticed to fascinate or bewitch, but love and envy; they both have vehement wishes, they frame themselves readily into imaginations and suggestions, and they come easily into the eye, especially upon the presence of the objects which are the points that conduce to fascination, if any such there be. We see likewise that Scripture calleth envy an evil eye. . . . [T]here seemeth to be acknowledged, in the act of envy, an ejaculation, or irradiation of the eye. Nay some have been so curious as to note, that the times when the stroke, or percussion, of an envious eye doth most hurt, are, when the party envied is beheld in glory; for that sets an edge upon envy.

The word *envy* itself is from the Latin *invidia,* from the verb *invidere,* "to see intensively." But although envy is the emotion most frequently associated with the evil eye, other negative emotions like jealousy and anger are also believed to affect people through the eyes, as in the familiar phrase "she looked daggers at him."

Some scholars regard belief in the evil eye as practically universal. The Egyptologist Sir Wallis Budge wrote: "[I]n no part of the world is it doubted that its influence exists and the belief in it is beyond all doubt primeval and universal. Moreover, every language, both ancient and modern, contains a word or expression which is the equivalent of 'Evil Eye.'"

There are some modern societies, however, in which this belief has more or less died out, as in England. And, contrary to Budge's opinion, there are parts of the world where it is not as predominant as he thought. Some scholars claim that it is almost absent from the indigenous cultures of the Americas,[1] and also that it is rare in sub-Saharan Africa, in aboriginal Australia, and in Oceania.[2]

But even if a belief in the evil eye is not universal, it is very widespread and very ancient. Allusions to the power of fascination are found in Sumerian sources from the third millennium B.C., and there are many references to it in Assyrian documents, and in ancient Greece and Rome. The evil eye is referred to repeatedly in the Bible, and even more so in the Talmudic and Midrashic literature of the Jews. It features in Nordic epics, Irish and Scottish myths, and in many other European literatures.

Belief in the evil eye is also very common in the Islamic world. The prophet Muhammad sanctioned the use of talismans against it.[3] Several verses from the Koran are believed to have a protective effect, particularly the prayer for protection in Surah 113: "I seek refuge in the Lord of Daybreak . . . from the evil of malignant witchcraft, and from the evil of the envier when he envieth." In the Greek Orthodox church, there are several officially sanctioned prayers for defense against the evil eye and for the protection of the angels against it. A belief in the evil eye and in the destructive power of envy is still very common in southern Europe, throughout the Islamic world, in India, and in many other countries.

Those who believe in the evil eye generally accept that some people have the evil eye more than others, and also that some of those who have the evil eye may be unconscious of the power they exert. But even though there are individual differences in the power of the look, envy makes all looks more dangerous. Because envy is closely linked to praise and admiration, these are also feared.

I discovered something of the power of these beliefs for myself when I lived in southern India, working in an international agricultural research institute near Hyderabad.[4] A few weeks after I arrived, I was invited to dinner at the house of a senior government officer, a Muslim. While we were drinking whiskey and soda, I made some complimentary comments about one of the pictures hanging on the wall, and to my astonishment my host immediately plucked it from its hook and presented it to me. Only with great difficulty did I manage to give it back.

A week or two later, at another social gathering, I made a favorable comment about the tie an Indian acquaintance was wearing. He took it off and gave it to me, saying graciously but implausibly, "I bought it for you." It was difficult to avoid accepting it. Through these and other experiences, I realized that praising or admiring something often led to socially embarrassing consequences. At first I assumed that this must be because of an exaggerated sense of hospitality, or exaggerated modesty; but I soon learned that there was more to it than that.

The English word *admire* comes from the Latin roots *ad* = to + *miriari* = to wonder, meaning "to wonder at." To praise or admire something is to imply that you want it, or envy it, and hence you can bring ill fortune through fascination or the evil eye.

One of the best antidotes to praise is generosity. Giving people that which they have admired defuses their envy. But this only works in limited circumstances. For example, it does not work for children, who cannot generally be given to those who praise them.

Worst of all is the admiration of babies. The Roman writer Pliny tells how a nurse tending a baby would spit three times in its face to protect it if a stranger saw the baby, especially when it was sleeping.[5] In Turkey, babies are spat on if they are looked at admiringly. "Abusive and false epithets are employed by Turkish women under all circumstances worthy of inviting praise or admiration, in order to counteract the supposition of ill-feeling or malice underlying the honeyed words of the speaker."[6] Similar behavior is found in many other places. It was common in Scotland as recently as the nineteenth century.

I found for myself that these beliefs are still very strong in India. I once took an American woman to visit a family I knew in a village in Tamil Nadu. There was a baby in the house, and my companion lavished effusive praise on his cuteness and his beauty, quite unconscious of the alarm she was causing. The baby was quickly whisked away. I later learned that the family had felt obliged to carry out a special ritual, with special mantras, within a circle of salt, to protect him against dire consequences of this admiration. The most dreaded praise is that from childless women, since they are thought to be most prone to envying other women's children.

Crops are also thought to be vulnerable. In the fields in Tamil Nadu, the farmers often place upside-down pots on sticks in the fields. The pots are painted with large, eyelike spots for protection against the evil eye.

On a bus journey from Tiruchirapalli to Tanjore, in Tamil Nadu, I first began to think of an experimental test of the efficacy of such traditional practices. I was sitting next to a young Indian scientist with whom I was engaged in conversation. I commented on the painted pots in the fields we were passing, and he replied, "This is all just superstition. Uneducated people believe it."

I wondered how he could be so sure that these practices were completely ineffectual. There had been no controlled experiments on the subject. Do painted pots help protect fields, or not? No data existed. Instead, it became clear in our conversation, there were two conflicting belief systems, the traditional and the rationalist. My companion was himself divided between them. At work, he was a professional scientist and a rationalist. At home, in his Hindu family setting, he was a traditionalist.

We thought about how to test whether these painted pots had any measurable effect, and came up with a possible experiment. If half the fields along the roadside had the standard protective eyespot-painted pots, and the other half did not, would there be any difference in yield per acre, or in the incidence of pests and diseases? The fields in each sample would, of course, be selected at random; the experiment would have a randomized design that could be analyzed by standard statistical methods.

In practice, such an experiment would be difficult to organize. Randomly selected farmers would probably be unwilling to forgo the traditional protection of their fields against the evil eye for the sake of scientific research that offered them no benefit. But perhaps they might agree to take part if they were paid well enough to do so.

The scientific method could, in principle, help us move beyond a mere conflict of beliefs. It should be possible to find out by experiment if negative intentions can indeed affect that which they are focused upon, and in particular if eyespots on pots offer any measurable protection to crops, even if only by frightening wild animals. As far as I know, no such research has ever been done.

PROTECTIVE AMULETS

There are a variety of other ways in which people take practical precautions against the evil eye, through prayers and protective amulets, talismans, and charms. An amulet "is an object which is endowed with magical powers, and which of its own accord uses those powers ceaselessly on behalf of the person who carries it, or causes it to be laid up in his house, or attaches it to some one of his possessions, to protect him and his belongings from the attacks of evil spirits or from the Evil Eye."[7] The word *talisman* is often used interchangeably with *amulet*, but, strictly speaking, talismans have a more specific and more limited role: for example, a talisman may be buried with hidden treasure to protect it, and have no other function.

Many different kinds of amulets have been, and still are, employed against the evil eye. In Greece, one of the commonest is a blue eye, probably descended from the eye amulets of ancient Egypt, with both the eye of Osiris and the eye of Horus. The Phoenicians, the Etruscans, and other ancient peoples also used eye amulets. They are common in modern Turkey. And the radiant eye of Horus looks out from every dollar bill, on the Great Seal of the United States. This use of false eyes to protect against the predatory looks of real eyes recalls the protective role of eyespots in butterflies, fish, and other animals (see Figure 10.1).[8]

In some parts of the world, models of phalluses or of clenched fists with a phalluslike protruding thumb are used, as are crescents and horns, Gorgon's heads, grotesque figures, crosses, rings, gems, coral beads, cowrie shells, dried sheeps' eyes, pieces of deerskin, onions, garlic, and written prayers or spells. At the Pitt-Rivers Museum in Oxford, there is a large collection of such objects, both in the open display cases and in an intriguing series of drawers beneath them. The diversity is bewildering. But they all are supposed to serve a similar purpose. What do they have in common?

The Greek author Plutarch (c. A.D. 46–120) advanced the theory that objects used to ward off witchcraft and fascination worked by attracting mischief-working eyes to themselves through the strangeness or ridiculousness of their forms.[9] A modern scholar has similarly concluded that amulets act as a kind of "lightning conductor," drawing attention to themselves, and hence away from that which they are designed to protect.[10] The same would apply to larger objects used to protect crops, like the inverted pots covered with eyespots in farmers' fields in southern India.

WITCHCRAFT AND THE RISE OF SKEPTICISM

In classical antiquity, belief in the evil eye was very widespread. There were also skeptics who rejected it. One of the dialogues in Plutarch's book *Table Talk* opens as follows: "Once at dinner a discussion arose about people who are said to cast a spell and to have an evil eye. While everybody else pronounced the matter completely silly and scoffed at it, Mestrius Florus, our host, declared that actual facts lend astonishing support to the common belief."[11] In the fourth century, St. Basil discussed the belief that "envious persons bring bad luck merely by a glance," and dismissed it: "For my part, I reject these tales as popular fancies and old wives' gossip."[12]

In northern Europe and North America, such skepticism about the evil eye is now taken for granted. So is skepticism about the sense of being stared at. Staring in itself is not normally believed to bring about enchantments or ill fortune, and hence differs from the evil eye. But it is related to the evil eye in that both imply a mental influence that extends outward from the looker to affect that which is looked upon.

How did this growth of skepticism occur? I will confine the discussion of this process to one particular country, namely, England. I do so partly because I am English myself; partly because this history has been well studied by historians, in particular by Keith Thomas in his remarkable book *Religion and the Decline of Magic: Studies of Popular Beliefs in Sixteenth- and Seventeenth-Century England*; and also partly because attitudes in England have had a strong historical influence on the culture of North America, and on the international culture of science.

In medieval England, as elsewhere in Europe, belief in the evil eye was widespread, and people took precautions against "overlooking" or "fascination" through prayers and amulets. But the very possibility of such malign influences started to be questioned in the sixteenth century, when many traditional beliefs were attacked by the Protestant reformers as superstitions. These religious revolutionaries campaigned against the survival of pagan practices that the Roman Catholic Church had assimilated. Skepticism was an essential ingredient in the Protestant Reformation, which in England began in the 1530s under King Henry VIII. Skepticism developed further as a result of controversies about witchcraft.

In the seventeenth century, the English Puritans took to an extreme the attempt to eliminate all ceremonies and observances with pagan, superstitious, or magical connections. Some even condemned the drinking of healths as a heathen oblation. In its most extreme forms, this anti-pagan zeal became a skeptical rationalism that turned against the practices of the Reformed Church itself. During the English Commonwealth, from 1645 to 1660, some of the more zealous nonconformists denounced the Prayer Book of the Church of England as "witchcraft," and fanatics interrupted services, calling on the minister to "leave off his witchery, conjuration and sorcery."[13]

In sixteenth- and seventeenth-century England there was an upsurge of trials for witchcraft. In some parts of continental Europe, the persecution of witches began on a large scale in the fifteenth century. It began in England only after the Protestant Reformation, in the sixteenth century.

In medieval England there was a general belief that some witches used magic for malicious purposes, while others used it to help and to heal. But these occult powers do not seem to have provoked much serious concern or indignation. Historians have so far found fewer than a dozen cases of supposed witches being executed in England between the Norman Conquest in 1066 and the Reformation; and most of those condemned had been involved in plots against the king or his friends.[14] The first specific laws against witchcraft were passed in 1542, in the reign of Henry VIII. New statutes were introduced under Elizabeth I in 1563, and laws against witchcraft remained in force until 1736. During this period, including the worst excesses of the witch-hunts during the Commonwealth, fewer than 1,000 people were executed for witchcraft in England.[15] The last execution was in 1685, and the last trial in 1717.

The theological arguments put forward by Roman Catholics in continental Europe against witchcraft mainly concerned its supposed dependence on a contract with the Devil. But these arguments had little influence in England, where almost all the allegations against witches were about damage to lives and property through magic, curses, and "overlooking."[16] These were the traditional reasons why people feared witches, and they had little to do with theology. "The people's hatred of witches was not a form of religious intolerance; it sprang from fear of their hostile acts towards their neighbours, not from outrage at their supposed association with the Devil."[17]

However, while increasing numbers of people were being tried in the courts for witchcraft, skepticism about the very possibility of witchcraft was growing. Some Protestant theologians denied that witches and devils could possibly have the powers attributed to them by the Roman Catholics, finding no biblical authority for such opinions. Instead, they asserted that diabolical spirits were all in the mind.

The standard skeptical position was defined as early as 1584 by Reginald Scot in his book *The Discoverie of Witchcraft*. He identified four categories of witches. The first kind were not witches at all, but had merely been accused out of malice. The second category believed themselves to be in contact with devils, but were suffering from delusions. The third group were genuinely malicious and secretly injured their neighbors, but not by supernatural powers; rather, they used natural means such as poison. And finally, some were charlatans and impostors who defrauded country people by pretending to be able to heal diseases, tell fortunes, or find lost goods.[18]

The English laws against witchcraft were repealed in 1736. They were replaced by a new Witchcraft Act that prohibited *accusations* of witchcraft or sorcery. The new law also made it an offense to claim to be able to use magic, tell fortunes, or find lost goods. The previous situation was reversed. It was no longer an offense to *be* a witch; instead, it was an offense to *pretend* to be a witch, or to accuse someone of witchcraft.[19] This official skepticism reflected educated opinion. Nevertheless, beliefs in the power of the evil eye and malicious spells persisted among the less educated. Such popular beliefs were classified as superstitions. From the eighteenth century on, educated opinion became increasingly rationalistic.

There is an important distinction between being rational—that is to say, using reason—and rationalism. Rationalism is both a belief system and a social movement. Some of its roots were in classical antiquity and in medieval Scholasticism, but in its modern form it was shaped first by the Protestant Reformation and then by the mechanistic revolution in science in the seventeenth century. It became the predominant spirit of the Enlightenment in the late eighteenth century, and has been the characteristic belief system of intellectuals ever since, whether capitalist, socialist, or communist. Rationalists rejected both popular folklore and many religious beliefs on the grounds that they had no rational foundation.

Rationalist attitudes have had a deep and enduring influence on the culture of science, and rationalist assumptions are usually treated as if they were self-evident scientific truths. They have, in effect, become rather like religious dogmas. Although many people equate science with the rationalist ideology, others, including myself, do not. Science is not a dogmatic belief system or an ideology; it is a method of inquiry. In this spirit of inquiry, we can investigate whether phenomena like the sense of being stared at actually exist, using the experimental method. If they do, we can expand our scientific understanding of the world. If they do not, we have good reason to dismiss them.

But such an investigation is inherently controversial. The sense of being stared at was long ago classified as a superstition, and surrounded by an intellectual taboo, a boundary that should not be crossed. No educated person wants to be thought superstitious, precisely because this undermines his or her claim to be educated. To go against this taboo involves a serious loss of intellectual standing, a relegation to the ranks of the uneducated, the childish, and the superstitious.

In England, skepticism about anything historically associated with witchcraft, including psychic powers, has dominated the scientific and academic worlds for generations. Whatever intellectuals may think in private, skepticism is usually an integral part of their public image.

A similar attitude is now found among intellectuals practically everywhere. The rationalist attitudes that grew up in northern Europe have been disseminated through educational systems all over the world. They were propagated with crusading zeal by communist governments in the Soviet Union, China, and other places. In most countries, rationalist beliefs are found in their strongest form in universities, within institutional science, and among technocrats.

Each country has a different intellectual history, and although skeptical rationalism goes back several centuries in England and in other parts of northern Europe and North America, it is relatively recent in most parts of the world, and usually confined to a small urban elite. Even within such elites, it often seems like a thin veneer superimposed upon more traditional beliefs, as, for example, in modern Greece.

THE EVIL EYE IN MODERN GREECE

In modern Greece, belief in the evil eye is still all-pervasive. Greece underwent none of the intellectual upheavals associated with the Protestant Reformation. And the Greek Orthodox Church has a very different kind of theology from the Roman Catholic and Protestant churches: more mystical and less intellectual.

Most of Greece was under Turkish rule until the 1820s, and had been so since the fall of Constantinople, the capital of the Byzantine Empire, in 1453. Among the Turks, then as now, belief in the evil eye was very common. In Greece in the sixteenth and seventeenth centuries, there were no intellectual forces encouraging the growth of skepticism comparable to those in England. In the nineteenth and twentieth centuries, Greek intellectuals were exposed to the same kind of rationalism as intellectuals elsewhere, but until quite recently Greece remained a predominantly rural society, and intellectuals a small urban minority.

I first became aware of the pervasiveness of beliefs in the evil eye in Greece when traveling there on holiday. Having noticed the protective amulets against it even in modern cars and air-conditioned buses, I raised the subject with a young Greek engineer, whom I met through family connections. As a modern, scientifically educated person he immediately dismissed the evil eye as superstition. But as the conversation continued, he talked first about his pious grandmother and her beliefs, with a mixture of mockery and respect, and then said he had himself experienced some things that he could not explain. In particular, one day he was with a friend who was reputed to have the "eye" when they visited someone who kept pigeons. The birds took off and were flying around when his friend looked up at them admiringly. One of them fell out of the sky dead.

In 2000, at my request, Socrates Seferiades, an architect living in Athens, carried out a survey about beliefs in the evil eye in urban and rural Greece. At first his attempts to find out about people's attitudes and experiences met with considerable reticence. He told me:

Perhaps, in part, it stemmed from my own somewhat skeptical attitude. Also, the manner of posing the question, "Do you believe in the evil eye?" elicited rational responses conforming to a supposedly acceptable social image for our times. However, the question "Have you ever had an experience that could possibly be attributed to the evil eye?" generally brought an affirmative responses even from those who professed *not* to believe in it. I soon came to realize that ostensible belief or no, the evil eye is deeply embedded in Greek culture at many levels, coloring experience and the manner of response to the world. Ill luck or misfortune can be ascribed to the evil eye, hence to other people's sinful and envious natures, rather than fate.

Socrates found that it is generally believed that the evil eye can be cast unconsciously, and people with envious or jealous personalities are those most feared. Many people take precautions to protect anything or anybody that is admired, usually by spitting three times: "Ftou, ftou, ftou." A common expression throughout the Greek world, uttered immediately after expressing admiration, is "Ftou, may the evil eye not be cast upon him [or her]." People often touch wood as well.

Even Greek skeptics did not deny that people suffer from symptoms they attribute to the evil eye. For example, the poet Spyro Harbouri said he does not believe in the evil eye himself, but those who do can be affected because of their beliefs: "People believe in it because they believe in witchcraft, which they consider as evil. Therefore they believe they can be exorcised. It's all in the mind, autosuggestion. If they believe in voodoo, then it exists."

Even though rationalists consider themselves immune because they do not believe in the evil eye, some conceded that they might still be susceptible to the negative effects of other people's emotions. Yet because of their rationalist beliefs, they deny themselves the possibility of being helped by traditional methods of healing.

Some people thought that their own emotions could affect others adversely, like Anna Barry, who lives in Athens.

I believe in the evil eye absolutely, or at any rate the projection of our negative emotions influencing others. I feel very bad about it, but I think I sometimes do this. If someone annoys me intensely I sometimes wish something bad will happen to them out of anger, and unfortunately it sometimes does.

Others were not so sure, but felt they might have cast the eye unwittingly. For example:

I don't think I believe in the evil eye, but once I was sitting at McDonald's drinking a milk shake, when a very handsome young man was coming up the stairs and I said to myself, "What a devastatingly handsome young man!" and immediately he tripped on the last step and fell, dropping all the potatoes he was carrying. ◇ MONIKA KALINOWSKA

If all the supposed effects of the evil eye were on people, they could perhaps be explained purely psychologically, as skeptics suggest. But some of these effects are said to be on animals, such as horses, or on plants, or on inanimate objects. For example, Despina Perimeni tells how the looks of a family friend devastated her mother's three favorite plants.

He visited us on three different occasions in the same year and admired my mother's ten-year-old geranium, her gardenia, and her fir tree. The day after his visits, the plant he had admired was dead. I specifically remember that the fir tree looked as if it had been burnt by fire. My mother has the reputation of having green fingers, but she did not manage to revive her plants.

All sorts of objects are supposed to be affected. For example:

A young woman reputed to have the ability to cast the evil eye visited us one day. Upon entering the living room she admired one of our paintings, saying, "What a lovely painting that is." Unbelievably, it fell off its hook there and then! ◈ DR. MICHAEL STAVROPOULOS

Anna Michailides, a potter, believes in the evil eye herself, but her mother, also a potter, took a rationalist attitude and often mocked people's belief in it. Nevertheless,

whenever a particular friend visited my mother's workshop while she was firing her ceramics in the kiln, a high percentage would inevitably break. She would try to keep her friend away on such occasions. It seems to me a part of my mother did somehow believe in the evil eye after all.

Dimitri Yiatsouzaki is another partial skeptic.

I don't believe in the evil eye. But I fear it. When I'm on my motorcycle and see someone who I think is in some way admiring me, I immediately pray to the Virgin Mary, in whom I don't believe, either, except at the moment of fear!

Even modern machinery is believed to be susceptible. Poppy Stavropoulos relates how she was visited by a woman friend who had returned from eastern Europe in poverty, making her living by selling books from door to door.

We talked of the good old times. We had a meal together and I gave her some of my clothes, as I could see she was in need. I drove her to the station. All the way, she kept on saying how lucky I was, what a lovely house I had, how well I lived, and so on. After saying good-bye, I tried to start the car and it made horrible noises and smoke came out of the engine. It was almost brand-new then. The mechanic said the starter had caught fire and could have set the whole car alight. He had never seen anything like it before. I think it was the evil eye of envy, even unwittingly.

As well as amulets and charms, people use a variety of other methods to cast off the evil eye and gain relief from its spell. The Orthodox Church has a number of officially approved prayers for protection against it and for driving away its effects. Father Ioannis, the parish priest of Erithrea, explained it as follows:

The Orthodox Church absolutely accepts the existence of the evil eye. I consider it to be a projection of bad and negative thoughts that can affect people very strongly. These thoughts or intense feelings stem from envy and jealousy. . . . Parishioners come to me quite often to be exorcised. I always start by making the sign of the cross three times with a cross held in my hand. A gold cross is best. At the same time I sprinkle them with holy water. The devil abhors the purifying and healing powers of holy water. I then recite one of the prayers of exorcism against the evil eye.

In addition, all over Greece, many people are reputed to have the power of curing physical illnesses that could be due to the effects of the evil eye. They often use special incantations or secret prayers that are passed on from mother to daughter or from father to son, and perform a ritual. One method involves a glass of water with a hair of the patient placed in the water or under the glass. The water is blessed with a thrice-repeated sign of the cross. A small amount of ash, often from a burned carnation clove, is dropped on the water. If it floats, the disease cannot be attributed to the evil eye. If it sinks, it can. The water is used to form a cross on the brow of the patient while the healer murmurs the secret prayer under his or her breath. The procedure ends with the patient drinking a little of the water.

The commonest method involves the use of oil and water, as described here by Mario Georgakopoulos, a lawyer in Athens:

My grandmother can cast out the evil eye. She learned it from her mother, and her mother from her mother in turn. She has often exorcised me, and I have watched her do it to friends and relatives. On rare occasions she will exorcise over the phone, using the secret prescribed formula. This must never be said to another person, at the peril of losing its efficacy and therefore one's power to cast the spell out. With her finger dipped in oil, my grandmother places a few drops in a cup full of water. If the oil spreads evenly over the surface, the presence of the evil eye is indicated. If the oil remains contained in a drop floating, then the evil eye is not indicated. The prayer is repeated continuously like a mantra throughout the whole procedure. She continues to place drops of oil in the water until there is a definite separate blob of oil, indicating that the process is complete and the evil eye has been cast out. She yawns throughout and feels exhausted at the end. Granny requires about ten minutes to recover, though now that she is getting older it takes her even longer and she tires more easily. She can't do more than two a day anymore.

Some patients also yawn repeatedly during the ritual, but apparently this is less common than yawning by the healers. Dr. Hero Thomopoulos thinks this is part of the process whereby the healer removes the harmful influence.

As the healer begins to feel the effect of the spell, his eyes may start running and he yawns repeatedly. He can feel so bad that on occasion he is physically sick, but recovers quickly, usually within ten minutes. In effect, the evil is taken away through the healer. One begins to feel better almost immediately after this, traditionally described as "your eyes being opened." Certainly there is always a feeling of lightness and relief, as if a weight has been lifted off you.

The traditionalists cite many examples that seem to support their beliefs. Some, like Monica Diamantopoulos, in Athens, even argue that it is a helpful belief, and that the cures can bring genuine relief.

Believing in the evil eye is a very useful psychological trait. People are helped enormously to face the daily problems of life if they can blame someone or something for untoward misfortunes. It is a great relief to feel that a health problem can be solved. It is a way of resolution, a fix, a way around a problem, perhaps, but nevertheless a resolution. A poor man's psychology. It helps me from being crushed by the weight of adverse events or circumstances and the stress of life. It's a pity people don't believe in it in contemporary Western society—in America, for example. Here in Greece, a surprising number of people do, many university graduates and sophisticated people. It's a good thing.

Skeptics argue that both the afflictions and the cures are all in the mind. But even if the cures are a kind of placebo effect, placebos actually work, and have genuinely beneficial effects, although no one knows how.

On the other hand, the skepticism that predominates in countries like England liberates people from fears of envy and malice. It frees people from chronic paranoia about the looks and intentions of others. Disbelief in the evil eye is reassuring, and it can be empowering.

Beliefs in the evil eye, and rejections of these beliefs, influenced the evolution of theories of vision, and hence theories about the nature of the mind, as we see in the following chapter.

Whatever the psychological advantages and disadvantages of belief in the evil eye, the fact is that people do seem able to influence others by their looks. The sense of being stared at exists in both humans and other animal species. If this sense evolved in the context of predator-prey relationships, as I suggested in chapter 10, it is not surprising that fear is one of the emotions aroused by staring.

13

ARE IMAGES IN THE BRAIN, OR ARE THEY WHERE THEY SEEM TO BE?

The sense of being stared at raises fundamental questions about the nature of vision, which is why it is so controversial. A debate about the nature of vision was going on in ancient Greece at least 2,500 years ago. It was taken up in the Roman Empire and in the Islamic world, and continued in Europe throughout the Middle Ages and Renaissance. This debate played an important part in the birth of mechanistic science in the early seventeenth century, and is still alive today. It is one of the main themes of this book.

There have been four main theories of how we see. The first is the idea that vision involves an outward projection of invisible rays through the eyes. This is often called the "extramission" theory, which literally means "sending out." This theory agrees with people's experience of vision as an active process. We look *at* things, and can decide where to direct our attention. Vision is not merely passive. This active theory of seeing was supported by the Greek philosopher Plato, and was worked out in mathematical detail by Euclid, famous for his works on geometry. The extramission theory also accorded with the general belief in fascination and the evil eye, and explained the sense of being stared at.

The second is the idea of a "sending in" of images through light into the eyes, the "intromission" theory. Early versions of this theory also date back to ancient Greece. Since the early seventeenth century this has been the orthodox scientific view, largely thanks to the work of Johannes Kepler (1571–1630), best known for his discoveries in astronomy.

The third theory, a combination of the other two, states that there is both an outward movement of attention and an inward movement of light. The fourth is the theory that vision depends on alterations in the transparent medium between the object and the eye. This theory was put forward by the philosopher Aristotle, and was often combined with one of the preceding theories.

Some of the questions that preoccupied thinkers more than 2,000 years ago have been resolved, but some are very much alive today. In Appendix C, I trace the history of theories of vision up to the beginning of the seventeenth century, when Kepler proposed his theory of the retinal image.

Kepler was influenced by medieval theories of vision, and also by four major technical advances in the preceding centuries: first, the development of linear perspective by artists; second, by an improved understanding of the anatomy of the eye, and especially the recognition that the lens was lens-shaped, not spherical; third, the discovery of the camera obscura, a dark room into which light entered through a small hole, producing an inverted image on the opposite wall; and, fourth, by the making of spectacle lenses, and the recognition that double convex lenses cause rays of light to converge.[1]

KEPLER'S THEORY OF THE RETINAL IMAGE

Kepler realized that light entering the eye though the pupil behaved like light entering a camera obscura. The lens focused the light, and produced an inverted image on the retina. He published his theory of the retinal image in 1604. Although he did not himself provide a diagram of this process, René Descartes published one thirty-three years later (Figure 13.1), and Kepler's theory has been accepted without serious dispute ever since.

Kepler's theory of the retinal image provided one of the foundations of mechanistic science. The intromission theory appeared to have triumphed. But at the same time it presented a new problem that Kepler admitted he could not solve, and raised questions still unanswered today. The problem was that the image on the retina was inverted and reversed; in other words, it was upside down and the left side was right, and the right left. Yet we do not see everything inverted and reversed.

The Renaissance artist and polymath Leonardo da Vinci (1452–1519) anticipated Kepler in comparing the eye to a camera obscura, and confronted the same problem of the inversion of the image. He tried to solve it by proposing a second inversion within the eye so that the image became upright again.

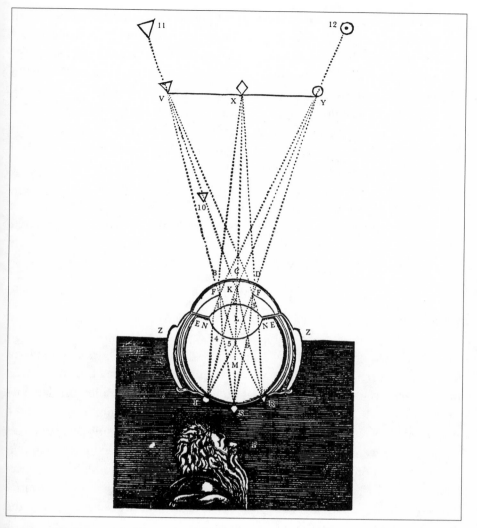

Figure 13.1 *Descartes's illustration of the theory of the retinal image, first published in 1637.*

Kepler likewise did his best to find a way to make the images the right way up. He confessed that he "dutifully tortured" himself to show that there was a second inversion within the eyeball, but failed. He concluded, "Geometrical laws leave no choice in the matter."[2]

The only way Kepler could deal with this problem was by excluding it from optics. Once the image had been formed on the retina, it was someone else's business to explain how we actually see it.

How the image or picture is composed by the visual spirits that reside within the retina and the [optic] nerve, and whether it is made to appear before the soul or the tribunal of the visual faculty by a spirit within the hollows of the brain, or whether the visual faculty, like a magistrate sent by the soul, goes forth from the administrative chamber of the brain into the optic nerve and the retina to meet this image, as though descending to a lower court—[all] this I leave to be disputed by the physicists. For the armament of opticians does not take them beyond this first opaque wall encountered within the eye.[3]

Vision itself was "mysterious." Ironically, the triumph of the intromission theory was achieved by leaving the experience of perception unexplained. The mystery was relegated to the interior of the brain. This problem has continued to haunt science ever since.

THE GHOST IN THE MACHINE

Kepler's contemporary Galileo Galilei (1564–1642) also withdrew perceptions from the external world and squeezed them into the brain, but in an even more radical way. He made a distinction between what he called primary and secondary qualities of objects. The primary qualities were those that could be measured and treated mathematically, such as length, width, weight, and shape. These were the concern of objective science. The secondary qualities, such as color, taste, texture, and smell, were not within matter itself; they were subjective rather than objective. And "subjective" meant "within the brain." Thus our direct experience of the world was split into two separate poles: the objective, out there, and the subjective, within the brain.

René Descartes (1596–1650) went yet further. In his mechanistic theory of nature, originally called the "mechanical philosophy," the entire universe was literally inanimate or soulless, and so was everything within it, except for the human intellect. Animals and plants became soulless machines, as did the human body. By contrast, the realm of spirit was nonmaterial and hence nonspatial, outside space altogether.[4] Descartes was, of course, the prototypical Cartesian dualist ("Cartesian" is the adjective from the second part of his name). In this dualism there is an unbridgeable split between the realms of mind and matter.[5] Yet the mind, according to Descartes, nevertheless interacted with the machinery of the body in the pineal gland, a small region of the brain.[6] Descartes could not explain how this interaction occurred.

Cartesian dualism raises a host of insoluble logical and philosophical questions. One of these concerns the fact that we see things all around us, in the space outside our bodies. What has become of the world we experience? It is all contracted into particular regions of the brain, yet the experience itself is supposed to be nonspatial.

Educated people have been brought up to believe that their minds are located inside their heads, and that all their perceptions and experiences are somehow concentrated in their brains. Since the time of Descartes, however, the supposed seat of the mind has shifted a couple of inches from the pineal gland into the cerebral cortex.

The theory that the mind is in the brain is a dogma accepted on the authority of science, and most people never think of questioning it. Few are even aware that it is a theory at all, and accept it as the scientific truth. The developmental psychologist Jean Piaget found that the average European schoolchild had assimilated this theory by the age of about ten or eleven (see page 206).

But if our minds are in our heads, how do we become consciously aware? The usual assumption is that there must be a conscious self inside the brain, a "ghost in the machine," to use a phrase coined by a twentieth-century philosopher, Gilbert Ryle. This conscious self is often represented as a little person. But, of course, this leads to an infinite regress, for presumably inside that little person's head there is a yet tinier person, and so on.

In spite of all these paradoxes, and in spite of the fact that it contradicts our experience of seeing things outside our bodies, this view is still widely regarded as "scientific." In a current exhibit at the Natural History Museum in London, called "Controlling Your Actions," you look through a Plexiglas window in the forehead of a model man to see what goes on inside the head. Inside is the cockpit of a modern jet plane, with banks of dials and computerized flight controls. And there are two empty seats, presumably for you, the ghostly pilot, and your copilot in the other hemisphere.[7]

MECHANICAL MINDS

The usual way in which modern scientists and philosophers try to overcome the problems of dualism is to deny that the mind has any independent existence at all. There is only the activity of the brain. Either consciousness is an epiphenomenon of this physical activity—rather like a shadow that does not do anything—or it is just another way of talking about brain activity. These points of view are all varieties of the philosophy of materialism or physicalism, the doctrine that the only kind of reality is material or physical.

In the twentieth century, academic psychology in the English-speaking world was dominated for decades by a school of thought called behaviorism. In 1913 the American behaviorist John B. Watson wrote that "the time has come when psychology must discard all reference to consciousness." He attributed belief in its existence to superstition and magic. He later declared that the scientific vocabulary should be purged of "all subjective terms such as sensation, perception, image, desire, purpose, and even thinking and emotion as they are subjectively defined." Behaviorists duly followed this policy, and in 1953 the influential American psychologist B. F. Skinner proclaimed that mind and consciousness are nonexistent entities "invented for the sole purpose of providing spurious explanations. . . . Since mental or psychic events are asserted to lack the dimensions of physical science, we have an additional reason for rejecting them."[8]

A similar denial of conscious experience is still to be found among contemporary philosophers of the school known as eliminative materialism. One of these is Paul Churchland, who argues that subjectively experienced mental states should be regarded as nonexistent because descriptions of such states cannot be reduced to the language of neuroscience.[9]

By the 1980s, behaviorism was going out of fashion within academic psychology, and was largely replaced by cognitive psychology, a school of thought dominated by the metaphor of the computer. Its theoretical framework is based on three fundamental tenets: first, people behave by virtue of possessing knowledge; second, knowledge consists of mental representations; and, third, cognitive activity consists in the application of computational operations to these representations.[10] All these representations and computations are supposed to be located within the machinery of the brain.

The philosopher who has most enthusiastically adopted the computer metaphor is Daniel Dennett. He is a materialist who regards our subjective experience as an illusion: "We are organic robots created by a research-and-development process called natural selection."[11] In his book *Consciousness Explained*, he summarizes the theory predominant within institutional science as follows:

The prevailing wisdom, variously expressed and argued for, is *materialism*: there is only one sort of stuff, namely *matter* — the physical stuff of chemistry, physics and physiology — and the mind is somehow nothing but a physical phenomenon. In short, the mind is the brain.

According to the materialists, we can (in principle!) account for every mental phenomenon using the same physical principles, laws and raw materials that suffice to explain radioactivity, continental drift, photosynthesis, reproduction, nutrition and growth.[12]

This is what Francis Cricke called "The Astonishing Hypothesis" (pages 13–14). In 1995, during the "Decade of the Brain," *Time* magazine ran a cover story called "Glimpses of the Mind: What Is Consciousness? Memory? Emotion? Science Unravels the Best-Kept Secrets of the Human Brain." The author quoted several eminent scientists, and summarized their view as follows: "After more than a century of looking for it, brain researchers have long since concluded that there is no conceivable place for such a self to be located in the physical brain, and that it simply doesn't exist."[13] Susan Greenfield, a British brain scientist, expressed the same ideas more graphically in her description of seeing a brain exposed during an operation: "This was all there was to Sarah, or indeed to any of us." She reflected that "we are but sludgy brains, and . . . somehow a character and a mind are generated in this soupy mess." In the case of another patient with a degenerative brain disease, she commented that the disappearance of his abilities was "a tragic testament to the stark truth that we are nothing but brains."[14]

Yet in spite of the commitment of many scientists and academic philosophers to the materialist philosophy, most people remain unconvinced that they themselves are mere automata whose decisions and opinions are determined solely by physical causes in their brains. The commonsense idea is that our conscious selves are more than our brains. This view prevails in everyday life, including courts of law, where individual choice and responsibility are taken for granted, except in cases of mental impairment or insanity.

The main arguments in favor of dualism depend on the weaknesses of materialism. The materialist theory goes against our own most immediate experience of ourselves and of others. Whatever they might say in the context of intellectual arguments, most materialists behave as if they themselves had a conscious self, capable of making free choices—including the choice to believe in materialism. Fortunately for their friends and families, in practice few materialists seem to regard themselves and their loved ones as unconscious automata.

Conversely, the main arguments in favor of materialism depend on the weaknesses of dualism. If we have an immaterial conscious self somewhere inside the brain, then where is it? What is it? And how does it interact with the activity of the nervous system?

For generations, Western intellectuals have been caught in this materialist-dualist dilemma, forced to choose between unacceptable alternatives. This dilemma is rooted in the mind-matter dualism of Descartes. But Descartes was not the first to withdraw the mind from the extended world in which we live. His system depended on Kepler's intromission theory of vision, and on Galileo's distinction between primary and secondary qualities. Kepler and Galileo had already laid the foundations for the theory that everything we experience about the world around us is inside the brain, and not outside us where it seems to be.

SPONTANEOUS THEORIES OF VISION

Whatever academic scientists and philosophers may believe, most people do not accept that all their experience is located inside their heads. In a pioneering series of studies, Gerald Winer and his colleagues in the psychology department at Ohio State University have found that most American adults and children they questioned took for granted the outward projection of images.

Their studies were prompted by the observation of Jean Piaget[15] that children believe that something goes out of the eyes when they are looking. They called this as a "striking instance of a scientific misconception,"[16] and investigated it through a series of questionnaires and tests. But the very fact that they carried out this study was controversial in the academic world. Many of their colleagues simply could not believe that anyone could think that something passed out of the eyes in vision.[17]

Winer and his coworkers were themselves surprised to find that extra-mission beliefs were common among children, and were "shocked" when they discovered that they were also widespread among college students, even among psychology students who had been taught the "correct" theory of vision.[18] However, few children and college students believed that vision was a matter of extramission alone. In common with Plato, Galen, and other ancient theorists, most thought that both extramission and intromission were involved. Among schoolchildren from grades five to eight, more than 70 percent believed in a combined intromission-extramission theory; among college students, 59 percent.[19] By contrast, fewer than 30 percent of the children and only 41 percent of the college students believed the "scientifically correct" intromission theory.[20]

Winer's group also carried out surveys on people's beliefs about being able to feel the stares of another person without seeing that person looking. As we have already seen (pages 125–126), they found that 89 percent of college students said they could feel stares, and so did more than 90 percent of schoolchildren in the sixth grade. Younger children gave a lower percentage of positive answers, but this percentage increased as the children got older.[21] Winer and his colleagues commented that the belief in the ability to feel stares "seems, if anything, to increase with age, as if irrationality were increasing rather than declining between childhood and adulthood!"[22] Belief may, however, have increased not because of irrationality but because of experience, given that the sense of being stared at seems really to exist. Is it more irrational to believe in one's own experience, or uncritically to accept a theory that goes against experience?

Nevertheless, the teaching of the orthodox doctrine did have some effect, and Winer and his colleagues drew some comfort from the fact that more college students than schoolchildren believed in the intromission theory.[23] But they recognized that the educational system had been unsuccessful in converting most of the students to the "correct" belief: "Given that extramissionists in our studies affirm extramission even though they have been taught about vision, our attention is now directed to understanding whether education can eradicate these odd, but seemingly powerful, intuitions about perception."[24]

No doubt these intuitions about perception persist because they are closer to experience than to the official doctrine, which leaves so much unexplained—including the existence of consciousness itself.

THE EXTENDED MIND

The only way out of this conflict between experience and the standard theory of materialism is to question the idea that all our experiences, all our perceptions and intentions, are indeed confined to the insides of our heads.

In agreement with the widespread intuition about perception, I propose that vision involves a two-way process, an inward movement of light, and an outward projection of images. The images of the things we see around us are just where they seem to be: outside our heads. This outward projection occurs within mental fields, which I call perceptual fields. These fields are a kind of morphic field, discussed in more detail in chapter 19. Perceptual fields are rooted in our brains, and affected by the patterns of activity within brains, but project outward to link us to the world we perceive around us.

Trying to understand minds without recognizing the extended fields on which they depend is like trying to understand the effects of magnets without acknowledging that they are surrounded by magnetic fields. No amount of chemical analysis of melted-down magnets could explain the way magnets affect things at a distance. Magnetic effects only make sense when magnetic fields are taken into account. The fields exist both within and around magnets.

Michael Faraday introduced the field concept into science in the 1840s. Fields are defined as "regions of influence." They connect things together across apparently empty space, and are responsible for many kinds of interconnection within the natural world. For example, the gravitational field of Earth stretches out far beyond the limits of our planet's atmosphere, and holds the Moon in its orbit. It is inside Earth, and also all around it.

The electromagnetic field of the Sun affects all life on Earth, even though the Sun is 93 million miles away. The light and other radiations from the Sun are vibratory patterns of activity within the Sun's field, reaching out over literally astronomical distances.

Many modern technologies also depend on invisible fields. Cell phones, for instance, would make no sense at all if they were simply material structures whose activities were confined to electronic circuitry inside them. They take in and give out information through the electromagnetic field. There is both an intromission and an extramission of invisible influences.

Unfortunately, modern thinking about the nature of the mind was shaped in the seventeenth and eighteenth centuries, when the only concepts available were those of matter in space, and spirit outside space. Most mechanistic scientists simply ignored consciousness, and consequently there was practically no progress in scientific thinking about the nature of the mind. And to this day the materialist-dualist debate has stayed stuck within the narrow limits of an outmoded way of thinking about matter. It is like a living fossil of an earlier mode of thought. An unquestioning faith in the intromission theory of vision has meant that all perceptions still have to be crammed inside the head, just as Kepler supposed them to be.

Nevertheless, over the years a minority of philosophers and psychologists have recognized that our perceptions may be just where they seem to be, rather than inside our heads.[25] Alfred North Whitehead, for example, wrote in 1925 of sensations being "projected by the mind so as to clothe appropriate bodies in external nature."[26] The most recent, and also the most persuasive, recognition of the extended mind is by the British psychologist Max Velmans. In his book *Understanding Consciousness*, as well as in a series of technical papers, he proposes what he calls a "reflexive model" of the mind. He illustrates this model by a picture of a subject looking at a cat (Figure 13.2) and explains it as follows: "[T]he initiating stimulus (the observed) is an entity located in space beyond the body surface that interacts with the visual system of the observer to produce an experienced entity out in space beyond the body surface."[27]

But Velmans is ambiguous about how this projection might take place. He calls it "psychological" rather than "physical" and, in the end, says he does not

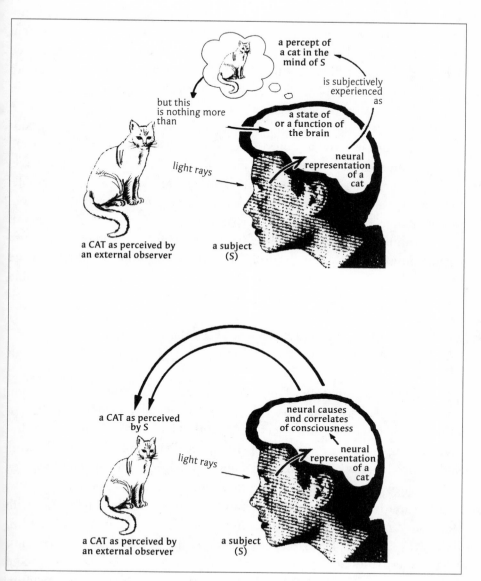

Figure 13.2 *Above: a diagrammatic representation of the materialist theory of perception. Below: a reflexive model of perception, as advocated by Max Velmans. (From Velmans, 2000.)*

know how it happens.[28] But he adds that "not fully understanding *how* it happens does not alter the fact *that* it happens."

I propose that the outward projection of visual images occurs through perceptual fields. These are both psychological, in the sense that they underlie our conscious perceptions, and also in some sense physical, in that they actually exist outside the brain and have detectable effects, as in the sense of being stared at. Human perception is not unique in being extended, and neither are human minds. Of course, the kinds of minds and perceptions in different species differ, but what they have in common is that they depend on extended fields and are not confined to the inside of the body. I propose that all animals capable of vision see things through fields projected beyond the surfaces of their bodies.

Moreover, eyes are not static. They move as we look at things, our heads move, and our entire bodies move around in the environment. As we do so, our perceptual fields change. And these perceptual fields are not separate from our own bodies, but include them. We can see ourselves—for example, the side of our nose, or our hands and feet. We are inside our fields of vision. Our awareness of three-dimensional space includes an awareness of our own bodies within it, and an awareness of their movements. Like other animals, we are not just perceivers but behavers, and our perceptions and behavior are closely linked.[29]

HOW DOES THE SENSE OF BEING STARED AT WORK?

Fields of vision are only one of the ways in which our awareness of the environment is projected out around us. We are also embedded in fields of hearing and of smell. Although we can project our attention farthest and with the greatest focus through seeing, our peripheral vision, together with the senses of hearing and smell, give us a background awareness of the environment around us.

When we focus our visual attention on something at a distance (or by focusing our hearing), it is as if our mind extends outward to connect us with this distant object (see chapter 18). But although our attention is focused in this way, we retain a background awareness of the environment all around us to a greater or lesser degree. This general sense of the environment is also projected in a perceptual field all around us. We experience our bodies as embedded in three-dimensional space, and moving around within it. This experience is not confined to the insides of our heads. It is not an internal model somewhere inside our brains. Rather, it depends on an extended field within and around our bodies.

When someone stares at another person from behind, the projection of the starer's attention means that his field of vision extends out to touch the person he is staring at. His image of that person is projected onto that person through his perceptual field. Meanwhile, the person stared at also has a field all around herself. I suggest that the starer's field of vision interacts with the field surrounding the person stared at. One field is influenced by another field. This field interaction is detected through a change or difference in the field around the body. Just as the field around a magnet is changed when another magnet is placed nearby, this field interaction is directional. The interaction may be weak, and need not be experienced consciously by the person stared at. But if the interaction is strong enough, the person stared at may respond by turning around, without thinking and without knowing why.[30]

Some people may prefer not to use the word *field*,[31] but instead talk in terms of vibrations, energy flow, *chi*, or nonlocal quantum effects that link observers to what they observe. But whatever theory is preferred, the sense of being stared at must depend on an influence at a distance of the looker on the person looked at, a projection of influences outward. This sense reveals that through the power of attention the mind is connected to the world beyond the body.

Part III

REMOTE VIEWING
AND FORESHADOWINGS
OF THE FUTURE

14 REMOTE VIEWING

"Remote viewing" means seeing things at a distance, beyond the range of the normal senses. Clairvoyance, a French word meaning "clear seeing," means more or less the same thing. And so does the "second sight" of the Celtic inhabitants of the Scottish Highlands and islands.

Sometimes the word *clairvoyance* is also taken to mean seeing into the future. But that is more a matter of precognition or premonition, discussed in the following chapters. In this discussion I take remote viewing, clairvoyance, and second sight to mean seeing things in the present in other places, rather than in the future.

Remote viewing is a kind of natural television. In fact, *television* literally means the same thing: distant vision. Through the electromagnetic field, we can all see at a distance on television, and witness what is happening right now in London or Dallas or New Delhi or anywhere else, however remote. Television enables everyone to be clairvoyant. We take it for granted. In a sense, television democratizes what was once a special gift of shamans, seers, and visionaries.

Although telepathy is common both among people and among nonhuman animals, clairvoyance seems relatively rare. On my database, for example, there are currently 39 cases of clairvoyance or remote viewing, compared with 827 cases of human telepathy. And of these 39 cases, most might have involved telepathy instead of, or in addition to, direct remote viewing. Here is an example that shows how hard it is to distinguish between them. The narrator is a young man from Switzerland.

In 1992, I was studying in southern California. My girlfriend, Katarina, had gone to northern Australia for a few weeks to visit a friend. One evening before falling asleep on the patio, I closed my eyes and relaxed. With my mind I wanted to go and visit Katarina in Australia. I imagined myself being there and let everything happen naturally. As I did so, suddenly I saw images appear before my closed eyes, as in a dream. I saw Katarina standing by a horse. She had a hose in her hand and was cooling the horse with the splashing water. When she finished doing that, she walked over to a bench, sat down, and began talking to people sitting around a table beside a trailer. When we figured out the time of the day in southern California and northern Australia, we realized that my out-of-body-experience had been identical to her actual physical experience.

Was this just a coincidence? Or was it an informed guess based on what he knew about Katarina's movements and activities? These theories might be plausible if this were an isolated case. Yet, as I discuss below, numerous experiments on remote viewing have refuted the coincidence and informed-guessing theories. That leaves open the possibility of telepathy or some form of clairvoyance.

Then could this have been a case of telepathy, arising from the young man's emotional bond with his girlfriend and his desire to be with her? Did he pick up on her experiences telepathically, and then dramatize them as an out-of-the-body visit to Australia, as if in a kind of dream? We know from our own dreams that minds are amazingly creative. We are surprised by some of our dreams precisely because we do not make them up consciously. This combination of telepathy and imagination seems to provide a plausible explanation.

Or was it direct clairvoyance, seeing at a distance? Clairvoyance is much more mysterious than telepathy. Either it implies that a person's center of consciousness can move out of the body to another place and "see" what is going on, as if with disembodied eyes, or it implies that a person can project a part of his or her mind to a distant place and "see" what is happening through a direct contact of the mind with that place.

Although nowadays we can all see at a distance through television, until recently remote viewing was one of the traditional attributes of shamans and seers. Some of the Old Testament prophets were said to have this power, and the New Testament relates several examples of second sight by Jesus (e.g., John 1:48–50). In Europe, too, over the centuries there were many reports of visionaries seeing at a distance. In the fifteenth century, Joan of Arc's clairvoyant abilities helped to make her a legend in her own lifetime. In the eighteenth century the Swedish seer Emanuel Swedenborg was at a reception in Gothenburg, attended by local notables, when he went into a trance and "saw" a disastrous fire sweeping Stockholm, 300 miles away. He gave a running commentary on its progress. Later, when a courier arrived from Stockholm, it turned out that his descriptions had been correct, and there were plenty of witnesses to vouch for the accuracy of this story.[1] Was this a matter of direct seeing at a distance, or was it a kind of telepathy from people in Stockholm who were seeing the fire?

Richard St. Barbe Baker, a British government officer in Kenya during the colonial period, described how on several occasions local chiefs or spirit mediums told him about events in distant places, which they said they "saw." For example:

As my boy placed the coffee on the table, he remarked: "Did you see that Bwana Katchiku is dead?" "Where did you get that from?" I asked. "Chief N'degwa has just seen it," he answered simply. "Send N'degwa to me," I told him. N'degwa came immediately. . . . He wore the usual kaross made of hyrax skins, and he stood before me and made his customary salute. I took his head and welcomed him. "What is this?" I asked. "Bwana Katchiku dead, do you say? How did you learn this?" "I see it," was his astonishing answer. "When?" I demanded. "Now," he said. Somehow I knew he was speaking the truth, nor was there any reason for him to do otherwise. . . . Seven days later a runner arrived at my camp with the news that Bwana Katchiku had died, at a distance of 250 miles from my camp. I recorded the incident and calculated that he must had passed away a few minutes before I got the message from N'degwa.[2]

In this case, too, it would be hard to distinguish between clairvoyance and telepathy, either from the dying man himself or from other people who were present with him. The same ambiguity applies to most of the experimental tests of remote viewing described below. But although these experiments do not reveal how remote viewing works, they show beyond reasonable doubt that it actually happens

EXPERIMENTS ON REMOTE VIEWING

Modern research on remote viewing began in the 1970s, largely funded by the CIA and other U.S. government agencies, which were primarily interested in the possibility of psychic spying. Two physicists, Hal Puthoff and Russell Targ, developed the basic experimental procedure at the Stanford Research Institute (SRI).[3] In these tests the subject had to try to describe a place where an agent, or "beacon person," was located.

The researchers usually worked with a small number of preselected subjects with good remote-viewing abilities. During the test the subject was closeted with one of the experimenters, and isolated from any possible information about the beacon person's movements. Meanwhile, the beacon person went with another experimenter to a randomly chosen place several miles away, called the target site. After they had arrived there, at a prearranged time the subject tried to describe and draw what the beacon person was seeing, while being tape-recorded. Independent judges later evaluated the recording and drawings.

These tests involved a double-blind procedure to avoid any possible cheating or unconscious passing on of clues from experimenters to the subjects. After the subject and his companion experimenter had been closeted together, the second experimenter picked a target site at random from a pool of potential targets specified in sealed envelopes. He and the beacon person then drove to this site and stayed there for a prearranged period. The subject did not know which target site had been chosen, nor did the experimenter who was with him.

After a series of tests had been completed, independent judges evaluated the subject's descriptions and drawings "blind." The judges were taken to each of the target sites and given a set of packets containing the subject's descriptions and drawings, one packet from each trial. Each judge independently ranked the subject's descriptions, comparing them with each actual place.[4] Using these blind methods, it turned out that the subjects' descriptions corresponded to the target sites far better than would have been expected by coincidence. A review of 26,000 separate trials conducted at SRI between 1973 and 1988 showed that the overall results were very significant statistically, with odds against chance of a billion billion to one.[5]

Other groups of researchers independently replicated these experiments, with similarly positive results.[6] For example, in one series of tests, the agent and subject were research scientists, and also friends. The subject, Marilyn Schlitz, was in Detroit, Michigan, while the agent, or beacon person, Elmar Gruber, was 5,000 miles away, in Rome, Italy. In Rome, an Italian colleague prepared a pool of forty potential target sites, including the view from the roof of St. Peter's cathedral, the Spanish Steps, and the ruins of the Caracalla Baths. Ten of the target sites were selected at random, and on ten successive days Elmar visited one of them at a prearranged time. At the same time, Marilyn sat quietly in Detroit trying to think about Elmar and his surroundings. She wrote down her impressions and also made sketches. After the series of trials was over, five independent judges went separately to each of the ten sites in Rome and ranked each of the subject's responses.

The results were positive. The overall statistical significance of the results showed the scores exceeded the chance level, with odds against this result being due to chance of 200,000 to 1.[7] In some tests the correspondences were remarkably close. In one, Marilyn wrote, "Flight path? Red lights. Strong depth of field. Elmar seems detached, cold. A hole in the ground . . ." After the fifteen-minute experimental period, she added: "He was standing away from the main structure, although he could see it. He might have been in a parking lot or field connected to the structure that identifies the place. I want to say an airport but that just seems too specific. There was activity and people but no one real close to Elmar."[8] In fact, the target site was Rome International Airport, near which Elmar had been standing on a little hill. Near the hill were some holes in the ground, where clandestine diggers were searching for Roman coins.

Following the success of the SRI remote-viewing experiments from 1973 to 1988, the U.S. government funded a further series of rigorously controlled trials at a think tank called the Science Applications International Corporation (SAIC), which ran from 1989 to 1993. Again the results were positive and highly significant statistically.[9] In 1995 the CIA commissioned a review of the results by an expert panel that included an eminent statistician, Jessica Utts, a professor at the University of California, Davis, and also a well-known skeptic, Ray Hyman, a professor of psychology at the University of Oregon. Both ended up agreeing that the results were "far beyond what is expected by chance." In addition, despite all attempts to do so, neither could identify any faults in the experimental procedure. Hyman finally conceded that "the SAIC experiments are well designed and the investigators have taken pains to eliminate the known weaknesses in previous parapsychological research. In addition, I cannot provide suitable candidates for what flaws, if any, might be present."[10] He suggested that further experiments should be done to see if the results could be replicated independently.

The results were independently replicated in an extensive series of remote-viewing experiments at Princeton University, with a very positive overall result, with statistical odds against chance of 100 billion to 1.[11]

As well as establishing that remote viewing works, the experiments revealed that it did not fall off with distance, and also that it was not affected by electro-magnetic shielding. Another conclusion was that most people were not very good at remote viewing. Only a minority of the unselected volunteers proved to be consistently successful. Remote-viewing ability, like mathematical ability or musical talent, is not shared to an equal degree by everyone, but is relatively rare.

FINDING ANIMALS AND LOST OBJECTS

All the cases of remote viewing I have discussed so far might have been examples of telepathy rather than clairvoyance. To describe what the agent is seeing in a distant place is similar to describing a video that the agent is watching in a ganzfeld experiment (discussed in chapter 2), which would normally be classified as a form of telepathy. The general procedure was also rather similar to that used in the Maimonides dream telepathy research (chapter 2).

The phenomenon that most strongly calls for an explanation in terms of clairvoyance is finding things. If no one knows where they are, then they cannot be located by means of person-to-person telepathy.

Finding game animals was a traditional role fulfilled by shamans in hunter-gatherer societies. Even today some hunters and wildlife photographers have experiences in which they seem to know where they will find an animal they are looking for. For example, Peter Bailey, who lives in Hampshire, England, and who has stalked and hunted deer for many years, observed that "I have this uncanny knack of knowing where there is a deer. It seems that I can detect their presence. Before I pick the binoculars up, or look through the scope, something tells me there's a deer there and I just look, and I am spot on, even at phenomenal distances."

Barry Blackwell worked for ten years as a wildlife ranger with the British Forestry Commission, and one of his duties was to control the deer population in coniferous plantations. He walked up and down the different trails, looking for deer to shoot. The deer had to come to these trails to feed, as there was no food inside the plantation.

I could come to an intersection and I would not even take the rifle from my shoulder, but before I arrived at the next intersection, some strange feeling told me that there would be deer there. Carefully looking around the corner, I would see deer grazing on the trail. This peculiar sensation proved correct again. I would not get this feeling all the time, maybe once or twice a week. And it was not just a matter of knowing where deer were likely to be. I have had this feeling in areas where I would not normally expect to find a deer.

Jeremy Stafford-Dietsch, the underwater photographer, described finding a tawny shark when exploring a reef in the Pacific:

I have seen one or two in thousands of dives, so it is not as if you bump into them every day. On that instance I was swimming along a large area of coral heads. It wasn't a particularly interesting dive, and I was bored. There was one coral head way off in silhouette in the distance, and I saw in my mind's eye the tail of a tawny shark protruding from underneath the coral head, though from the position I was in, it was impossible to see it. There were thirty coral heads between me and that one. And yet I had seen it so vividly. I thought, "This is ridiculous, I am not going to yield to this superstition and zoom over and check," so I puttered along looking at every other coral head. Then I thought, "Well, there's nothing else to do," so I went over to that coral head, and sure enough, there was the tail of the shark protruding just as I had imagined it.

Finding lost objects was also a traditional role played by shamans, psychics, and professional clairvoyants. People still consult psychics to find lost objects, and ask "animal communicators" to find lost pets. Sometimes they are successful.[12] There is even a saint reputed to help find lost objects, Saint Anthony of Padua. In many Roman Catholic churches, people burn candles before his image and pray to invoke his aid.

The most famous European clairvoyant in recent times was the Dutchman Gerard Croiset, who often helped the Dutch police. He was particularly in demand for finding people who had vanished without a trace, and often had to tell anxious relatives that the person was dead, because he had "seen" the corpse. Sometimes he successfully directed the police to where it was. He obtained his information through visual images that appeared to him like clips of film, showing what was happening or had happened at a distance. And on some occasions when it appeared that he was wrong, he turned out to be right after all. When consulted about the kidnapped wife of a London newspaper executive, he rightly said she was dead, and gave details of the route the kidnappers had taken, saying that at one point there was an airplane that was "prewar" or "not of this decade." No such aircraft was found, casting doubt on his story. Only later did it turn out that a cinema along the route had been showing a film on the Battle of Britain, with a full-size mock-up of a Spitfire fighter plane on the roof.[13]

PSYCHIC SPYING

Most of the remote-viewing experiments funded by the CIA and other U.S. government agencies involved a beacon person who went to the target site. These tests could therefore have worked telepathically. But in some of the tests, the subjects were asked to describe a place for which they had only been given a map reference, without even seeing the map. In one particularly striking example, an SRI researcher asked one of their most gifted subjects to describe what was present at a map reference written in binary digits. Unknown to the subject, Hella Hammid, the target site was a particle accelerator, the Berkeley Bevatron, a large circular structure with four beam tubes coming out of it to the research labs. She closed her eyes, paused, and then said: "I see some kind of round structure. It looks like a belly-button-shaped energy expander." She then sketched what she "saw" and also made a clay model of it, showing a circular structure with four rays coming out of it.[14]

Yet even in this case, telepathy cannot be excluded because the experimenters knew what the target was, and hence the subject could have picked it up from them. But sometimes subjects were asked to describe places in the Soviet Union when the researchers themselves did not know what was there. For example, in one of the tests at SRI, the target site was a map reference provided by the CIA, which simply said it was a "Soviet site of great interest to the analysts." The remote viewer was Pat Price. After a few minutes he began his description: "I am lying on my back on the roof of a two- or three-story brick building. . . . There's the most amazing thing. There's a giant gantry crane moving back and forth over my head. . . . As I drift up in the air and look down, it seems to be riding on a track with one rail on either side of the building." He then made a sketch of the layout of the buildings and the crane on wheels.

In fact the site was a secret nuclear weapons factory at Semipalatinsk, Kazakhstan, and CIA photographs from spy satellites showed a complex of buildings with a giant crane on rails very similar to the one drawn by Price. One of the most interesting things about Price's description was that he "saw" inside one of the buildings and reported something that no one in the U.S.

government knew at the time. He said people were assembling a giant metal sphere about sixty feet in diameter, making it out of gores (tapering pieces of metal), but were having trouble welding the pieces together. Only three years later was this observation confirmed. According to a report about this site in *Aviation Week* magazine:

> In a nearby building, huge, extremely thick steel gores were manufactured. The steel segments were parts of a large sphere estimated to be about 18 meters (57.8 feet) in diameter. U.S. officials believe that the spheres are needed to capture and store energy from nuclear driven explosives or pulse power generators. Initially, some U.S. physicists believed there was no method the Soviets could use to weld together the steel gores of the spheres . . . especially when the steel to be welded was extremely thick.[15]

Although Price could not have picked up this information from anyone in the United States when he "saw" this installation, could he have picked it up telepathically from the people working at this site in the Soviet Union? If his mind somehow reached out to link him to this weapons factory, did the focusing of his attention there somehow enable him to see the place directly? Or did it somehow enable him to connect with the minds of people in that place? We cannot know the answer to these questions. Nevertheless, in many laboratory experiments on clairvoyance, the targets were unknown to anyone at all when the subject guessed them. Hence, telepathy would not have been possible. And yet the results were still positive.

CLAIRVOYANCE IN THE LABORATORY

In chapter 2, I described the card-guessing ESP experiments that dominated research in parapsychology from the 1920s to the 1950s. In J. B. Rhine's parapsychology laboratory at Duke University, and also in other laboratories, many of the tests were carried out under clairvoyant rather than telepathic conditions. That is, the subject guessed the order of cards in a shuffled pack before anyone had looked at them. Or he guessed what cards were present in sealed envelopes before anyone opened the envelopes to find out whether the guess was right or wrong. Or he guessed what cards were present in shuffled packs behind opaque screens, or in different rooms or different buildings, before anyone had looked at them.

Hundreds of thousands of these trials were carried out at Duke and elsewhere. In a pack of twenty-five Zener cards with five different symbols, by random guessing a subject would get about one in five right, or about five per pack. In other words, the score should be around 20 percent. Some of Rhine's best subjects fairly consistently guessed around eight to ten cards correctly per pack, giving a success rate of 30 to 40 percent.[16] Most people did not do so well, but when all the results were taken together, the success rates were still more than the 20 percent expected by chance. For example, in half a million trials with the cards placed behind opaque screens, the overall score was 21.8 percent. Although this is not a very impressive figure, with such large numbers of trials, the odds against this result being obtained by chance were astronomical.

At first sight these results appeared to provide overwhelming evidence for clairvoyance, and ruled out an explanation in terms of telepathy. Rhine and most other parapsychologists were quite happy with this conclusion, and saw them both as different aspects of the more general phenomenon of ESP. But they had no idea how ESP worked, except to suggest that it depended on a nonphysical mind that was somehow free from the limitations of time and space.[17]

The situation was further complicated by the fact that another kind of ESP, precognition, seemed to work as well as clairvoyance in card tests and in remote-viewing tests. Subjects could guess what card or what remote-viewing target would be selected in the future! I discuss this evidence in chapter 17.

Some researchers go so far as to suggest that pure clairvoyance with inanimate targets does not happen at all. All apparent clairvoyance, they suggest, depends on interactions between living organisms. Either clairvoyance is an aspect of telepathy, as in remote-viewing tests with a beacon person, or it depends on the subject making contact with future thoughts about the target, after the answer is known.[18]

Trying to explain clairvoyance in terms of influences from the future seems to plunge us deeper into obscurity. But precognition really does seem to happen, however we might eventually explain it.

15 ANIMAL PREMONITIONS

A premonition is literally a warning in advance (from Latin *pre* = before + *monitio* = warned). Many animals seem to sense when a disaster or catastrophe is about to occur. The most striking examples concern earthquakes.

Some kinds of premonitions may depend on detecting subtle physical changes in the environment. For example, some animals may sense changes in Earth's electrical field or slight tremors before earthquakes. And some apparent premonitions may be telepathic, like dogs anticipating the arrivals of their owners by picking up their intentions at a distance, or people anticipating telephone calls while someone is intending to call them.

Other kinds of premonition are more mysterious. They seem to involve precognition (knowing in advance) or presentiment (feeling in advance). They imply that influences travel "backward" in time, from the future to the present. Thus they appear to defy our ordinary ideas of causation, where the cause comes before the effect. They also seem to create a host of philosophical problems. Does precognition mean the future is determined in advance? Does it mean free will is impossible? Does it lead to paradoxes whereby knowledge of the future affects the present, which in turn can change the future?

Given such thorny theoretical problems, it is simpler to ignore the evidence for precognition, and avoid thinking about it. The traditional way of doing this was to assume that if it occurred at all, it was very rare and confined to prophets, seers, oracles, and psychics. Anyway, their prophecies were often vague and ambiguous. But if some did turn out to be correct, then the foreknowledge must have been supernatural rather than natural, and hence beyond the scope of scientific thought.

This approach is no longer plausible. First, premonitions occur among many species of animals. They are natural, not supernatural. In general, animals better able to anticipate disasters and catastrophes might have a better chance of avoiding them and hence surviving. An ability to detect impending dangers would probably be favored by natural selection.

Second, twentieth-century research on human experiences has established that premonitions and precognitions are widespread, and not confined to a tiny minority of abnormal individuals.

Third, parapsychologists have obtained strong evidence for precognition in several different kinds of controlled experiment (chapter 17).

In this chapter we'll look at evidence for premonitions and anticipations by animals, and discuss how they might be understood.

PREMONITIONS OF EARTHQUAKES BY ANIMALS

In *Dogs That Know When Their Owners Are Coming Home*, I summarized a large body of evidence for unusual animal behavior before earthquakes, including historical accounts from ancient Greece onward. I gave examples from recent earthquakes in California, including the Loma Prieta earthquake in 1987 and Northridge in 1994, from the 1995 Kobe earthquake in Japan, and from the 1997 earthquake in Assisi, Italy. In all those cases there were many reports of both wild and domesticated animals behaving in fearful, anxious, or unusual ways hours or even days before the earthquakes struck.

With very few exceptions, Western seismologists have ignored such stories of unusual animal behavior, dismissing them as anecdotal or even superstitious. By contrast, in China since the 1970s, the authorities have encouraged people to report unusual animal behavior, and they have an impressive track record in predicting earthquakes, in some cases evacuating cities hours before devastating earthquakes struck, saving tens of thousands of lives.

I suggested that paying attention to unusual animal behavior, as the Chinese do, rather than ignoring it, might make earthquake warning systems feasible in California, Greece, Turkey, Japan, and elsewhere by enlisting the help of thousands or even millions of volunteers, using modern communication technologies.

Unusual behavior by a *single* animal could be due to an unsuspected illness or a number of other causes, and could not be trusted to mean that an earthquake was coming soon. But unusual behavior by many animals independently in a particular area would show there was an external cause, which could be an impending earthquake. In the past, people could not find out about the behavior of animals in other places until it was too late. For an effective earthquake warning system based on unusual animal behavior, rapid communication would have been essential, as would a rapid analysis of the data. This is now possible, thanks to telephones, the Internet, and computers. And this is a very good time to start paying attention to unusual animal behavior.

Through the media, millions of pet owners and farmers in earthquake-prone areas could be asked to take part in this project. They could be told what kinds of behavior their pets and other animals might show if an earthquake were imminent—in general, signs of anxiety or fear. If people noticed these signs or any other unusual behavior, as soon as possible they would call a telephone hot line with a memorable number—in California, say, 1-800-PET QUAKE. Or they could send a message on the Internet. A computer system would then analyze the places of origin of the incoming calls, and sound an alarm and display on a map any places from which there was an unusual surge of calls.

There would probably be a background of false alarms from people whose pets were sick, for example, and there might also be scattered hoax calls. If there was a sudden surge of calls from a particular region, however, this could indicate that an earthquake was imminent. But other factors could also affect the behavior of animals in that region, including approaching storms or hurricanes, forest fires, an influx of predators, and fireworks displays. If a surge occurred all over California on the evening of July 4, for example, it would probably mean that a lot of people were celebrating Independence Day, rather than that earthquakes were about to strike simultaneously around all the fault lines.

To do research on such an earthquake warning system would cost only a small fraction of current earthquake research budgets. It could even be sponsored privately if governments were not willing to pay for it. By doing this research we would learn something. By doing no research we will learn nothing, and earthquakes will continue to strike without warning.

Since *Dogs That Know When Their Owners Are Coming Home* was published in 1999, I have continued to monitor major earthquakes to see if they were preceded by unusual animal behavior. They were.

On August 17, 1999, a devastating earthquake (magnitude 7.4) struck Turkey, with its epicenter near Izmit. Newspaper reports mentioned that dogs had been howling for hours before the earthquake struck, and there were a variety of other reports of unusual behavior by dogs, cats, and birds.

The following month, on September 7, a serious earthquake of magnitude 5.9 afflicted Greece, with its epicenter near Athens. At my request, Katarina Plassara and Socrates Seferiades carried out surveys in and around Athens to find out whether people had noticed unusual animal behavior before the earthquake. Some had, and some had not. Several people commented that there had been more unusual animal behavior before the last big earthquake, in January 1981. But that earthquake was much more destructive and of a greater magnitude, at 6.7.

Of the dozens of reports of unusual behavior before the 1999 quake, most concerned dogs and cats. Stray cats "disappeared," and domestic cats hid, or ran out of houses, up to several hours before. Some dogs were howling inexplicably for hours before the quake struck, others were agitated and tried to get out of the house, and others seem terrified and would not leave their owners. In a riding school near Athens, the horses became "nervous" and "jumpy" and, a few minutes before the earthquake, tried to get out of their stalls by kicking the doors. Pigeons were said to have fluttered around in their lofts in an unusual way, and other birds behaved abnormally. Dimitris Kalomenidis, in the village of Aghios Mercurios, observed:

> Nearly all our birds—chickens, pheasants, partridges, ducks, and geese—showed enough nervousness a couple of hours before the earthquake of September 7 for me to wonder what was disturbing them. Especially the geese made a lot of noise and ran hither and thither seemingly aimlessly and individually rather than in their usual unified manner. I thought there must be a fox about. This behavior became progressively more intense and by the time of the quake they were quite panic-stricken, running about their enclosure as if they wanted to escape. About five minutes before the earthquake, my dogs began to howl in a way that I had never heard before.

Several people said that huge numbers of ants came out of their nests a day or two beforehand. Others said that mice came out of their holes and ran around strangely.

On February 28, 2001, a 6.8-magnitude quake struck the Seattle area, and once again animals behaved unusually beforehand. Some cats were said to be hiding for no apparent reason up to twelve hours before the earthquake; others were behaving in an anxious way or "freaking out" an hour or two before; some dogs were barking "frantically" shortly before the earthquake struck; and other animals were behaving unusually.

Laurie Hall, who keeps goats and lives twenty miles south of the epicenter, told me that the female goats were normally shut in a barn around 11:00 P.M., but the night before the quake they fought going in, and then "bleated and bleated" in a very unusual way. The following day, about eight minutes before the earthquake struck, the outdoor dog was barking, and the goats "were running in circles out in the pen. One goat was simply running in a circle as tightly as he could, which I have never seen before in a goat. Then our indoor dog began barreling up and down the stairs and barking wildly. As I stood to go out and see what was going on, the earthquake hit."

No one knows how some animals seem to sense earthquakes coming. The three main theories are that they somehow pick up subtle sounds, vibrations, or movements of the earth; that they respond to subterranean gases released prior to earthquakes; or that they respond to changes in Earth's electrical field preceding earthquakes. As well, or instead, animals may somehow "sense" in advance what is about to happen in a way that lies beyond current scientific understanding. In other words, they may be presentient—that is, having a feeling that something is about to happen—or precognitive. This hypothesis would be unnecessary if all the facts could be explained satisfactorily by more conventional theories. At present the electrical theory seems sufficiently promising to justify ignoring this more radical possibility.[1] But several other kinds of animal premonition cannot be explained electrically.

ANTICIPATING AVALANCHES

On February 23, 1999, an avalanche devastated the Austrian village of Galtur in the Tyrol, killing dozens of people. It was the worst avalanche disaster in Austria since 1954. The previous day, the chamois (small goatlike antelopes) came down from the mountains into the valleys, something they don't usually do. As reported in the *Sunday Times*, "The mood in the village became distinctly uneasy. That evening, the assistant manageress of his hotel started talking about avalanches in the village, including one thirteen years before that had destroyed a house. The following day, when the first really big avalanche hit, she lost three members of her family."[2]

Albert Ernest worked for nearly fifty years as an avalanche protection officer in the Swiss Alps, mostly in the Enns Valley. He is also a dedicated wildlife photographer and well acquainted with the habits of mountain animals. He told me: "Again and again I observed that the chamois were not staying in the danger zone of avalanche breakoffs. Based on my observations, I hold the opinion that wild mountain animals have a presentiment of unsteady situations in the snow cover through an inborn instinct and behave accordingly."

Through surveys in villages in the Austrian and Swiss Alps, kindly conducted on my behalf by Theodore Itten, I have found that the animals most often said to anticipate avalanches are chamois and ibex, and also dogs. Some dogs are said to have barked persistently for no apparent reason for hours before an avalanche struck; and some refused to go outside. For example, Josef Flollriol, who lived in Stuben, in the Tyrol, had a trained avalanche search dog. One morning in March 1988 the dog simply refused to leave the house for his usual morning walk. "We tried several times to get him out, and after thirty minutes a huge avalanche came down beside our house. We would have been dead if we had been outside."

As in the case of earthquakes, it is not clear how these animals anticipated the coming disasters. Perhaps they reacted to electrical or other physical changes. But if so, no one knows what these changes are. Or perhaps they have a more mysterious presentiment of danger.

However they do it, an ability to anticipate avalanches would be of obvious survival value in mountain animals, and would be favored by natural selection. But many animals also anticipate man-made catastrophes that would not have occurred in the natural world, such as air raids.

ANTICIPATING MAN-MADE CATASTOPHES

In Dogs That Know When Their Owners Are Coming Home, I described how dogs, cats, and other animals during the Second World War anticipated air raids. Many families in Britain and Germany relied on their pets' behavior to warn them of impending attacks, before any official warnings were given. These warnings occurred when enemy planes were still hundreds of miles away, long before the animals could have heard them coming. Some dogs in London even anticipated the explosion of German V-2 rockets, even though these missiles were supersonic and hence could not have been heard in advance.[3] If animals were not anticipating air raids by hearing approaching bombers or rockets, how did they sense the attacks were coming? Precognition or presentiment seems the only possibility.

Mountain-dwelling animals like chamois that are capable of anticipating when and where they would be endangered by an avalanche have, no doubt, been favored by natural selection over many generations. This sensitivity is of obvious survival value, however it might work. Perhaps animals living in earthquake-prone areas have likewise evolved a special sensitivity to physical signs preceding earthquakes. And perhaps animals of many kinds have benefited by being able to anticipate storms and hurricanes.

But no animals have been subject to natural selection over many generations for an ability to anticipate air raids, which were unknown until the twentieth century. Nor have animals been selected over many generations for their ability to react to other kinds of catastrophes brought about by human agency. Unlike air raids, some of these man-made disasters are entirely accidental.

During the night of October 9, 1963, a huge landslide plunged into the lake above the newly built Vajont Dam in the Italian Alps. As the lake filled up and submerged its lower slopes, the mountainside had become unstable. As a result of the landslide, a 100-meter wave overtopped the dam, and vast volumes of water surged down the valley, wiping out most of the small town of Longarone, just downstream. More than 2,000 people perished.

I asked Professor Giaochino Bratti, a historian of the disaster who lives in Longarone, if anyone had noticed unusual behavior by animals just before the tragedy. He summarized the stories of survivors as follows: "They talked about dogs that did not want to remain chained that evening, and kept barking so badly that they had to be taken indoors. There are testimonies of birds that killed themselves trying to escape their cages, foxes running fast through the woods, and animals that were very nervous and unable to sleep."

If these animals had a presentiment of danger, this would all make sense. It does not make sense to suppose that they were somehow reacting to subtle physical changes in a mountainside miles away.

Some animals seem to sense impeding danger in particular places, and either try to leave those places or avoid going into them. For example, Deidre Griffin was living in Lesotho, in southern Africa, and often used to go riding on her horse. One day they were rushing back home, trying to get there before a storm hit.

We had to go past the house, past a large wattle tree and then to her paddock. She suddenly stopped and stood rooted to the spot on the path. I could not move her. I know she was afraid of something, but I couldn't see anything in our way. Then the rain and wind hit us and we had a tug-of-war, and she finally relented and shot past the tree and into her paddock. As I was closing the gate, I saw her actually jumping up and down on the same spot, something I have never seen before or since. I ran to my kitchen door, and just as I closed it, the wattle tree snapped and fell over. It missed me by about five seconds. Somehow she "sensed" danger. I am absolutely convinced about this. I really believe that by stopping and refusing to go on, she was trying to prevent us from having to go past the tree.

On my database are dozens of other accounts of animals that tried to prevent their owners from going ahead when unexpected danger was imminent. Some dogs refused to walk along paths when shortly afterward branches or trees fell where the person and the dog would have been. Other dogs, horses, and cats delayed or prevented their owners from setting off on a journey when road accidents happened soon afterward, in which they might well have been injured or killed. One dog prevented its owner from getting onto a boat that exploded shortly afterward. Another dog pulled its owner away from the roadside just before a van hurtled around the corner and crashed into the place they would have been.

In some cases it is just possible, though implausible, that the animals heard something unusual that caused their alarm, but I have found it hard to avoid the conclusion that some of these forebodings must indeed have involved precognition or presentiment.[4]

As well as giving warnings of external dangers like air raids, falling trees, and road accidents, some animals, especially dogs, warn their owners of impending medical problems, especially epileptic seizures.

ANIMALS THAT GIVE WARNINGS OF FITS AND COMAS

Jackie Evans, who lives in Mansfield, Nottinghamshire, England, suffers from epilepsy. She says her miniature schnauzer, Sam, has changed her life. "I can suffer up to four seizures a day, sometimes in clusters. I was black and blue with bruises on my knees from falling unconscious so many times. After I had a fit on a main road, I became terrified of collapsing in heavy traffic. Having to be so cautious made me feel trapped and depressed." But now Sam lets her know when a seizure is coming about twenty minutes in advance. "If we're in the house, he warns me by barking. If we're in public, Sam will sit in front of me and stare, remaining rigid like a stuffed animal. His gaze is so insistent it's as though he's drilling holes in my head. If I ignore this, he gets annoyed because I haven't responded, and he'll jump up and down when the seizure is imminent. That twenty minutes allows me to find a safe place to have a seizure. He has helped take the stress and anxiety out of suffering seizures."[5]

Sam is not unique. Many other dogs give their epileptic owners warnings of seizures, and have changed their lives. Some, like Sam, have been specially trained,[6] but most do it spontaneously. A British veterinarian, Andrew Edney, carried out the first systematic survey of this warning behavior by dogs in the early 1990s. He studied in detail twenty-one dogs that seemed able to predict attacks. There was no particular breed that predominated; the sample included working dogs, gundogs, terriers, toy dogs, and mongrels. Male and female dogs and young and old ones did it.

Before a seizure began, the dogs all looked anxious, apprehensive, or restless. Most barked or whined, and some jumped up and nuzzled their owners. They sat nearby or "herded" the person to safety, and encouraged him or her to lie down. While the seizure was taking place, they either stayed beside the person, some licking the face or hands, or went to seek assistance. Above all, they were remarkably reliable. As Edney commented, "No dog seemed to get it wrong—one even ignored 'fake' seizure attempts."

None of the animals in Edney's sample had been trained; all had shown their warning behavior spontaneously. And most of the epileptics had to discover their animals' behavior for themselves. Some commented that it took some time before they realized the significance of their dog's signals.[7]

No one knows how dogs predict epileptic fits, and there has been very little research on this subject. The three most common speculations are that the animal notices subtle changes in behavior or muscular tremors of which the person is unaware; that it senses electrical disturbances within the brain associated with an impending seizure; or that it smells distinctive odors that might be given off by the person before an attack. All three possibilities would require the dog to be quite close to the person. The detection of electrical changes in the nervous system, if possible at all, would require them to be very close indeed. Dogs would not be expected to react if they are out of range of sight or smell. But, as I discuss in *Dogs That Know When Their Owners Are Coming Home*, some dogs can still give warnings of fits if they are in another room.

Could telepathy play a part? This seems unlikely because the person has no knowledge of an impending fit when the dog gives its warning. Presentiment seems more likely.

Some dogs also give warnings of other impending crises, such as heart attacks and diabetic comas.[8] Just as there are no effective technological alarm systems for epileptic seizures, so there are no reliable and effective alarm systems for patients whose blood sugar levels are too low, despite intensive research on the subject. Here, too, dogs can come to the rescue, as a recent paper in the *British Medical Journal* pointed out.[9] In one case, for example, a thirty-four-year-old woman had about two hypoglycemic attacks per week, and did not wake up when they happened at night. But her three-year-old golden retriever, Natt, gave her reliable warnings: "During the day, he paces up and down and puts his head on her lap; during nocturnal episodes, he barks and scrabbles against the bedroom door. Natt only settles once her hypoglycemia has been corrected." (The paper in which these findings were reported was titled "Non-invasive detection of hypoglycaemia using a novel, fully biocompatible and patient friendly alarm system.") No one knows how the dogs do it.

There are many other examples of forebodings by dogs and cats about medical emergencies and sudden deaths. But like all premonitions, their significance is apparent only after the event.

Premonitions of various kinds are widespread in the animal kingdom, among both wild and domesticated animals. They also occur in people. Although most modern people are probably less sensitive than species like dogs and cats, unlike nonhuman animals they can say what they see or feel.

16 HUMAN FOREBODINGS

Like many nonhuman animals, some people seem to sense danger in advance. This kind of premonition or intuition is of obvious survival value. Many people have lived to tell the tale about it because they have paid attention to premonitions.

Sixteen-year-old Carole Davies was about to leave a video arcade in London that she had been visiting with some friends when heavy rain began. The entrance was crowded as people came in from the street to shelter.

While standing there looking out into the night, I had a sense of danger. Then I saw what looked like a picture in front of me showing people on the floor and with tiles and metal girders on them. I looked around and up and realized this was to happen here. I began to shout at people to get out. No one listened. I ran through the rain, with my friends following, to a nearby café. After a while we heard sirens that stopped outside the arcade building. We all ran down the road to find out what had happened. It was just as I had seen. A man I had shouted at to get out was being pulled from under the debris.

During wars, people tend to be more alert to danger, and of course there is in fact more danger. Dramatic premonitions are more common in wartime than in relatively uneventful peacetime, and the most impressive stories on my database concern life-threatening dangers in wars.

During the Second World War, Terry Miller had been evacuated from

London with her young children. She was living in Babbacombe in Devon, while London was being bombed during the German Blitz. Even though Babbacombe was bombed once or twice, she felt safer there than she would have been in London.

Quite suddenly I had a feeling that I must leave Devon and return home. At first I dismissed the idea; why leave when I was so happy and contented despite the war going on around me. But the feeling increased. The walls of my room seemed to speak to me (or so I thought), "Go home to London." I still resisted the call for about four months. Then one day, like a flash of light, I knew that I must leave and take the children back to London. I made arrangements to join my mother and brother (who had survived the Blitz) in London. On a Saturday in late 1942 we traveled back to London. A few days after our departure from Devon, I received a letter from a mutual friend in Babbacombe who wrote the following: "Thank God you took the children back on Saturday. Early Sunday morning the Germans dropped three bombs and one fell on the house where you were living, demolishing it and killing all the neighbors on either side."

Charles Bernuth, in the U.S. Seventh Army in the Second World War, experienced a sense of danger several times. He took part in the invasion of Germany, and soon after crossing the Rhine, he was driving along an autobahn at night with two fellow officers.

All of a sudden, I got the still, small voice. Something was wrong with the road. I just knew it. I stopped, amid the groans and jeers of the other two. I started walking along the road. About fifty yards from where I had left the jeep, I found out what was wrong. We were about to go over a bridge—only the bridge wasn't there. It had been blown up and there was a sheer drop of about seventy-five feet.

Sometimes premonitions are heeded at once, with no delay. Catherine Curtis, of Santa Monica, California, had such an experience when driving.

I was commuting to work with a girlfriend when I suddenly "felt" an accident in the making. This may have been due to subtle visual cues, but I cannot recall or imagine any. In any event, we were in fast but crowded freeway traffic when I reached across my friend to protect her and began to pump my brakes. A second later, the car just ahead of me in the lane to the right drifted into a concrete curb, and spun out of control into our lane. Only my advance braking and the driver's Herculean efforts to pull his car back into his own lane (albeit facing the wrong way) prevented us from a head-on collision. When my girl-friend recovered from the initial shock, she became quite perturbed by my apparent precognition and has never gotten over it.

People who had these premonitions, or people close to them, survived because they heeded the sense of danger. People lacking these premonitions, or people who paid no heed to them, would have had a lower chance of sur-vival.

If the ability to feel premonitions is part of our biological heritage, favored by natural selection over innumerable generations, this is because premoni-tions are of practical value. The most effective premonitions are those that seem most urgent and "irrational," precisely because the cause is not yet appar-ent. Less urgent anticipations are generally less effective.

ANTICIPATIONS OF DEATHS AND DISASTERS

On my database there are 312 cases of human premonitions, precognitions, or presentiments. Of these, 76 percent are about dangers, disasters, or deaths; 21 percent are about neutral events; and only 3 percent are of happy events, like meeting a future spouse, or being saved or delivered from danger. Dangers, deaths, and catastrophes predominate.

In a survey of well-authenticated cases of precognition collected by the Society for Psychical Research between the 1880s and the 1930s, H. F. Salt-marsh found that 174 out of 290 cases, or 60 percent, concerned deaths or acci-dents. Very few were of happy events. Most of the others were trivial or neutral, although some were very unusual.[1] In one such case, the wife of the bishop of Hereford dreamed that she was reading the morning prayers in the hall of the Bishop's Palace. After doing so, on entering the dining room, she saw an enor-mous pig standing beside the table. This dream amused her, and she told it to her children and their governess before she actually read the morning prayers in the hall. She then went into the dining room and saw a pig standing in the exact spot where she had seen it in her dream. It had escaped from its sty.[2]

No doubt people tend to remember such unusual events and premoni-tions of disasters because they are dramatic, and more interesting to relate.

This may well bias samples toward deaths and dangers. But anticipations of happy events, like winning the lottery, also make good stories, and yet are rare. So are anticipations of unusual events like seeing pigs in dining rooms.

It is unlikely that selective memory alone can account for this predominance of dangers, deaths, and disasters in reported cases of premonition. There are strong evolutionary reasons for this bias. In people, as in animals, natural selection must have favored the ability to sense impending dangers.

In the modern world, many people feel they ought to disregard these "irrational" feelings. Here are two very different examples. The first is from a young mother about her baby.

I was half asleep one evening when I suddenly found myself composing a letter to my mother telling her that my three-month-old baby had died. He was well at the time, and I went into a sort of denial telling myself to stop being stupid and so on. One week later my baby got diarrhea and vomiting and died within twenty-four hours.
◇ JO LEWIS

The second example is from a young man in Athens.

One day I needed to go to the center of Athens, and had the choice of car or motorcycle. That day it seemed a terrible dilemma. My feelings were against using the bike, but my logic insisted that it would be easier to park and to stop being silly. When I went to take the bike, I had a bad feeling and was sure that my peculiar emotions meant that someone had cast the evil eye on me. My premonition of danger persisted. On the way to the center of Athens, a car suddenly changed lane and hit me. My ankle was badly twisted and I was taken to the hospital. I often have premonitions of danger, which in the past I took little notice of, since I didn't consider them to be logical. Now I listen more to my inner feelings. ◇ MERLIN KAROLOS

And sometimes people have forebodings that they cannot do much about, even if they want to. One day Shawn Tinder, of Beloit, Wisconsin, woke up with "the most discomforting feeling." He "just knew" that something bad was going to happen, but he had to continue with his work schedule.

Later that day I actually "heard" a voice, in my right ear only, that said to me, "You're going to get busted," three times. I have never had anything like that happen before or since. Later that evening I was turning a corner in my car, when another automobile swerved into my lane, and I had to drive off the road into some grass to avoid being struck by the vehicle. As I recovered, a police officer pulled me over for reckless driving. The officer did not see the car that almost hit me, but he saw me swerving off the road.

In the case of spectacular disasters, it often turns out that many people say they had forebodings beforehand. On October 21, 1966, at 9:15 A.M., a huge coal pile, rendered unstable by underground water, slid down a mountainside onto the Welsh mining village of Aberfan. The sludge engulfed the local primary school and a nearby street, burying children alive in their classrooms and people in their houses. One hundred forty-four people were killed, including 128 children. A psychiatrist, J. C. Barker, who worked in the village after the disaster, found that many people had had premonitions. Altogether he investigated seventy-six cases. Of these, thirty-six concerned dreams, some so vivid and horrific that the dreamers woke screaming. One woman had a waking vision the night before of an avalanche of coal hurtling down a mountainside onto a terrified child. Other people felt intense anxiety. One ten-year-old girl, Eryl Jones, who was killed in the disaster, had told her mother two weeks beforehand, "Mummy, I am not afraid to die." She said she would be with her friends. Her mother wondered why she was talking like this. Then the day before, Eryl told her mother, "I dreamt I went to school and there was no school there. Something black had come down over it!" At her mother's request, she was buried next to her friends.[3]

One of the most famous disasters of the twentieth century was the sinking of the *Titanic* on her maiden voyage from Southampton to New York. She went down on the night of April 14–15, 1912, after striking an iceberg. More than 1,500 lives were lost. She was at the time the largest ship in the world, and was constructed in such a way that she was supposed to be unsinkable. Premonitions of this particular disaster were particularly striking because practically no one believed it was possible. Even when the *Titanic* was actually sinking, some passengers were so convinced she was unsinkable that they refused to get into lifeboats when asked to do so by the crew.

Some people canceled their journeys on the *Titanic* as a result of their own forebodings or because people close to them persuaded them not to go.[4] One of those fortunate people was Harry Burroughs, who lived in Southampton with his mother and worked on ocean liners. He had waited a month to sign on for this maiden voyage, and left on April 10 to board the ship. Soon afterward he came home again, and told his mother he had changed his mind because "some sort of feeling" had come over him.[5] Others who decided not to sail included Frank Adelman, a violinist from Seattle, and his wife. Shortly before they were due to embark, Mrs. Adelman had a sudden premonition of danger and said she wanted to postpone their journey. "After discussing the matter with his wife, Mr. Adelman consented to flip a coin to decide whether they should still sail as planned, or take another ship." Mrs. Adelman won the toss, and they canceled their booking on the *Titanic*.[6]

Dozens of other people had forebodings or were warned by others not to sail, but decided to travel anyway. Some of them were among the survivors; some were not.

Some people with no plans to sail on the boat likewise feared the worst. One of them was Blanche Marshall, who lived near Southampton and, together with her family and friends, watched the *Titanic* set out. Suddenly she clutched her husband's arm and said, "That ship is going to sink before it reaches America." The people present tried to persuade her that this was impossible, but she got angry and said, "Don't stand there staring at me! Do something! You fools, I can see hundreds of people struggling in the icy water!"[7]

Of course, in this case as in all others, we have to trust in the testimony of the people who told these stories and those who corroborated them. But even in true stories about premonitions, the validity of the premonitions becomes apparent only in retrospect. Perhaps many people have forebodings before ships sail or flights take off that are not followed by disasters. No doubt such false alarms tend to be forgotten. On the other hand, perhaps some people may not be conscious of premonitions, but nevertheless avoid dangers without knowing why.

One way of investigating these possibilities quantitatively is to study the numbers of passengers on ships, trains, or planes when accidents occurred. Were there fewer passengers than there might otherwise have been? Were there more cancellations or no-shows compared with the numbers on preceding days, or in preceding weeks, when accidents did not happen?

If fewer people booked, or if more people canceled, this would provide a way of measuring possible premonitions, even if these were not experienced consciously. As far as I know, this kind of investigation has been carried out only once, when W. E. Cox analyzed railroad accidents in the United States between 1950 and 1954. He obtained passenger figures for the day of the accident itself, for the same train on the preceding seven days, and also for the same train on the same day of the week over the preceding four weeks. Sure enough, he found that significantly fewer people traveled on the trains that had accidents than on comparable trains that did not.[8] As Cox himself pointed out in 1956, this kind of analysis could be even more revealing if air disasters were studied.

THE WORLD TRADE CENTER, SEPTEMBER 11, 2001

The terrorist outrage that destroyed the twin towers of the World Trade Center in New York was seen on television by hundreds of millions of people. It must have been one of the most vivid and appalling images in history. Thousands lost their lives, both in the planes themselves and in the towers.

Soon afterward, I appealed for information about dreams and premonitions that might have been related to this disaster both through posters in Union Square, New York, where there were meetings and memorials to the victims, and also through advertisements in a New York newspaper, the *Village Voice*. I received 57 seemingly relevant accounts. (A further 11 were too vague or too unspecific to be analyzable.) Of these, 38 involved possibly precognitive dreams, and 15 premonitions or presentiments. In many cases the people told others about their dreams or fears before the terrorist attack took place. I have no doubt that an appeal on a larger scale would have brought many more cases to light.

About one-third of the dreams happened on the night before the disaster, and another third in the preceding five or six days. In some, the dreamers were on planes, like Mike Cherni, a forensic scientist who lives in Manhattan, and works about 300 yards from the World Trade Center.

Some five days to prior to the disaster, I had an unusually vivid dream. I dreamt that I was a passenger on a commercial jet, seated at a window seat on the left-hand side. The cabin was filled with sunlight, and outside visibility was excellent. I don't remember the beginning of the dream, but I remember a pervasive sense of dread. The passengers and I were deeply concerned about the flight path we were taking; we were flying very low over Manhattan's buildings. I have flown into New York City's three major airports many times and am familiar with the normal approach routes, and this approach was quite out of the ordinary. I also love flying and have had no bad experiences as a passenger or any bad dreams about flying. Yet in this dream I was very frightened about how close we were to the buildings. Many of the passengers were very vocal and shared my concern. I recognized buildings as we flew over them, and it was clear that we were flying directly south over the southern tip of the island. Then there was a tremendous impact and I woke up. This dream disturbed me for days afterward, enough that I described the dream to my wife.

Some plane journeys were not specifically localized in New York, nor were they exactly like the situation in the doomed flights, but had a number of striking similarities. For example, on the morning of September 10, Leora Giacoi dreamed she was on a commercial flight,

sweating, nervous, almost as if I was afraid we may hit something. There was a man sitting across from me. I could not see his face, only his dark skin tone, long thin nose, and shoulder-length black hair. I was facing forward and I saw all of the controls of the plane. It was as if I was in the backseat of a car, only a lot bigger, and there were people behind me. I could see the windshield and outside the sky was clear and blue. I saw this light gray building. We crashed into the building. Flames shot out of the glass windows and the plane caught on fire. I heard voices screaming and sirens. Then the building began to fall. . . . I amazingly was still in my seat alive and well. There were flames everywhere around me.

Some dreams were not about planes, but about being in terrifying situations inside skyscrapers. A number specifically concerned the World Trade Center, as in the case of Steven Brown, who lives in Manhattan. On the morning of September 11 he dreamed that he was "in the stairwell of the World Trade Center with a lot of people trying to get out." That same morning, around 6:00 A.M., Audry Parrish also dreamed she was in the World Trade Center. "I was in World Trade 1 and it caught on fire. I escaped by crawling across a glass bridge about halfway up into the second building when it too caught fire and burned."

By contrast, Keith Vass dreamed that he was high up in a prominent skyscraper, not in New York but in Philadelphia, at the Mellon Bank Center, where he used to work.

Across the way from me was an identical building to the Mellon Bank Center. In reality there is no such building, but this one was identical in every way. It was dusk, and there was a major storm whirling. My building was shaking, as was the one across the street. I did not know whether to vacate or not. Then I noticed the building across the way began to break and crumble at the top. Chunks of the gray granite facing started to break away and fall to the street. Then the entire building imploded and went down, visually appearing much like the WTC when it went down. I was horrified and hurried to the exit staircase and walked briskly about thirty floors to the first floor and exited the building. When I got outside, I notice that it was not a hurricane or storm at all. It was a war and there were bombs falling everywhere.

Several people dreamed of explosions in New York, or planes crashing into buildings, or buildings collapsing, or people running in panic. Gina Vigo dreamed on the morning of September 11 that "Manhattan was hit by an incredible blizzard. People were running for cover from the fierce gusts of snow and everything was white. Later on, when I saw footage of the falling ash, it was strangely reminiscent of my dream that morning."

People who had premonitions spoke of "a sense of dread," "eerie feelings," "intense panic and pain," "a strong sense something was wrong," and "feeling something bad was going to happen." Amanda Bernsohn said that the night before,

I could not stop crying, and couldn't explain it at all. The next morning I slept through my alarm clock (a first for me during my eight months at my job) because I was having an extremely vivid and involving dream. I was woken out of my dream that morning by a friend who called to tell me about the first plane hitting WTC 1. Had I woken in time, I would have gone to my office, about three blocks from the World Trade Center.

Although her dream was not at all like the WTC disaster, it was one of horror in Manhattan. "I was walking down a street that was covered in swastikas that were spray painted on the building walls. The Nazis had invaded New York, but I wasn't able to find any people at all."

Many other people did not go to work on time that morning, including people who worked in the World Trade Center and who would have been killed or severely endangered if they had gone to work as usual. An article in the *Chicago Tribune*, published on September 17, 2001, titled "Lucky to Be Alive," told the stories of fifteen people who escaped. One did so by oversleeping after drinking too much at a party the night before; another because of a delayed train; another by his car breaking down; another by suddenly deciding to stop for a coffee on the way to work; another by thinking it was a beautiful day and deciding to walk to work, hence arriving late. Good luck indeed. And perhaps unconscious premonitions also played a part in some of these cases. Who knows? And how can we tell?

No doubt every day some people fail to go to work for all sorts of reasons, and no doubt every day some people have fears or forebodings that are not followed by disasters. No doubt every night some people have nightmares about planes crashing or buildings falling down or other disasters. The fears or nightmares followed by disasters will tend to be remembered more than those that are not. But can these general principles explain all the facts? Similar arguments have been used for years by skeptics to try to dismiss telepathy as an illusion due to coincidence and selective memory. Only through detailed research and quantitative data can we hope to find answers to these questions.

Cox's quantitative research on train crashes in the 1950s (pages 240–241) set a precedent. And for the doomed flights on September 11, 2001, quantitative data actually exist. In the computer systems of American and United Airlines are the passenger numbers of the four flights that crashed, and also figures for cancellations and no-shows. Were there fewer passengers than usual, or more cancellations and no-shows? To find this out, the figures for that day could be compared with those for previous days and weeks. They could also be compared with unaffected flights on the same morning. If there were fewer passengers, more cancellations, and more no-shows on the planes that crashed than would have been expected by chance, this would provide statistical evidence for the efficacy of premonitions, whether people were conscious of them or not.

I tried to obtain such figures from American Airlines, and asked a high-ranking executive if I could have access to the relevant data. He was friendly and open-minded, but unfortunately could not help. He told me that all the data for the September 11 flights had been impounded by the FBI, who were investigating in minute detail every booking, cancellation, and no-show. Perhaps the FBI could be persuaded to do an analysis comparing the data for these flights with those for the same flights on previous days, and with other comparable flights.

PRECOGNITIONS IN RETROSPECT

The term *precognition*, literally meaning "knowing in advance," is inherently paradoxical, because we cannot know that precognitions are in fact precognitions until after the events to which they refer have taken place. Before the event, they are mere possibilities, even if they seem unusually urgent and convincing. Usually they are too vague to serve as detailed predictions.

Imagine that there was a telephone hot line or a website to which anyone could report a premonition or potentially precognitive dream as soon as it happened. Probably some days there would be more reports than others, and before the morning of September 11, 2001, there could well have been a big surge of reports. If so, this might have indicated that something bad was going to happen. But what?

Assume for the sake of argument that all the people who had unusual and disturbing dreams before the disasters in New York and Washington, D.C., called the hot line or e-mailed the website to report them. Even had they done so, it would probably have been difficult if not impossible to make a specific prediction of planes crashing into the World Trade Center and the Pentagon. A predominance of dreams about plane crashes and buildings collapsing might have indicated the general kind of disaster that might occur. But the details would probably have been too varied to predict exactly where or when the planes would strike. Some dreams were indeed about the World Trade Center, but some were of other buildings in New York, such as the Empire State Building, or in other cities, like Philadelphia. Only afterward could the significance of these dreams have been recognized.

Precognitions may tend be overestimated because of selective memory for two reasons. First, most potential precognitions not followed by any related event may be forgotten. Second, people may falsely remember precognitions after the event, by inflating the significance of dreams or images they only vaguely remember. For these reasons, they are most convincing if they are recorded in advance, or at least told to another person before the event takes place. If someone recorded many possible precognitions, and most did not come true, or were too vague to identify, this would strengthen the coincidence theory, and weaken the case for genuine precognition. On the other hand, if a person only rarely recorded possible precognitions, and these did turn out to happen, this would strengthen the case for precognition. The most impressive anticipations of the World Trade Center disaster were those that people told to others, and from people who rarely had such forebodings.

On the other hand, selective memory may also cause the power of precognition to be seriously underestimated. In particular, many precognitive dreams may be forgotten because they seem trivial, or simply because most dreams are forgotten anyway. And as we see in the following chapter, many people may have precognitive dreams without knowing it.

17

EXPLORING
PRECOGNITION

In the early twentieth century, a British aeronautical engineer, J. W. Dunne, made an astonishing discovery about dreams, summarized in his remarkable book *An Experiment with Time*, published in 1927. He found that he often dreamed about events that were about to happen, but easily forgot these dreams. Only by keeping careful records of his dreams, writing them down as soon as he awoke, did this phenomenon become clear. Dunne persuaded friends and acquaintances to do the same, and found that they, too, were having precognitive dreams without having been aware of it. He described a simple method by which anyone could do his experiment. I tried it, and to my surprise it worked, as I describe below.

Dunne made his key discovery when he was a young man serving in the British army in South Africa. In a particularly vivid nightmare, he found himself on an island that he knew was in imminent peril from a volcano. He was desperately trying to persuade the French authorities to evacuate 4,000 people whose lives were threatened.

He told several people about this dream the next day. Soon afterward he received a copy of the *Daily Telegraph* from England, containing the headline "Volcano Disaster in Martinique." The article described how the capital of this French island in the Caribbean had been swept away, and how more than 40,000 people had been killed.

The article was written before Dunne's dream, and many thousands of people had already read it, so telepathy rather than precognition was one possible explanation. But although Dunne dreamed that 4,000 were endangered, and thought the paper mentioned this figure, he later discovered that he had in his haste misread the paper, which in fact gave a figure of 40,000. He then realized that the dream referred not to what the paper actually stated, nor to what really happened, because later reports gave more accurate figures that were neither 4,000 nor 40,000. Instead, the dream was related to what he *thought* he had read. As he pointed out, this would have seemed normal enough if the dream had occurred the night *after* he had read the paper, as a memory of the experience of reading it. What was surprising was that it was like a memory of an experience, but it happened in advance! It was as if the dream had happened on the wrong night.

Dunne carefully recorded his dreams and studied what happened before and after them, and came to the conclusion that some referred, in the normal way, to things that had happened in the previous day or two. But others referred to things that were about to happen in the next day or two, and sometimes farther in advance. Without the written records he would never have realized this.

He also found that sometimes he had experiences that seemed familiar, and later found that they corresponded to dreams he had already had, but forgotten. Such uncannily familiar experiences are often described as déjà vu, French for "already seen." Dunne suggested that some of these déjà vu experiences happened because they had been foreshadowed in dreams.

He tried to calculate what proportion of his dreams related to past experiences compared with those that related to the future. He confined the timescale for this analysis to the near future and the near past, because otherwise the comparison would be misleading—memories from the distant past could be recognized and counted, but anticipations of the distant future could not be recognized and counted because they had not yet happened. He came to the amazing conclusion that "images which relate indisputably to the nearby future are about equal in number to those which pertain similarly indisputably to the nearby past."[1]

Dunne gave instructions for recording details of dreams immediately on waking, and emphasized the importance of writing down the actual images seen, rather than any interpretation that might be given to them. Then the records are read on subsequent days to find out if any of the details correspond to experiences that happened after the dream. He pointed out that the experiment is best carried out when traveling or in other nonroutine periods, because in normal everyday life it is hard to identify familiar images in dreams as belonging to the past or the future. Also, the more unusual the images, the better the evidence for precognition.

When I tried out Dunne's experiment for myself, at first I found it hard to remember my dreams at all, and even harder to summon up the effort to write them down as soon as I awoke. With practice it became easier. I soon found that I did indeed seem to have dreams that foreshadowed experiences that happened later. For example, in one disturbing dream I was at a gathering in which a man was chasing people around, brandishing what looked like a metal syringe — a shiny cylindrical object with a needle sticking out at one end. I recorded the image itself, as Dunne suggested, as distinct from my interpretation of the image, which was that he was trying to inject people with heroin. The following day I was at a lively party in London, where I saw someone chasing others around holding a shiny metal object with a needle sticking out. It was an ear-piercer. He was not trying to inject them, but threatening to pierce their ears, as a kind of joke. If I had concentrated on my *interpretation* of the dream image, rather than the image itself, I would probably not have recognized the similarity.

If you want to experience precognitive dreams yourself, then try following Dunne's instructions. The idea that we often dream of things that have not yet happened is so contrary to our usual assumptions that it can easily seem impossible, or something we would rather dismiss — until it becomes a matter of personal experience. But even personal experiences of precognition are still hard to assimilate because they conflict with our usual ideas about time.

Nevertheless, the reality of precognition is strongly supported both by spontaneous experiences and by experimental tests.

THINKING OF SOMEONE AND THEN MEETING

In the course of my research on the seventh sense, I received dozens of accounts from people about a phenomenon that I had never before seen mentioned or discussed, and which I found difficult to classify. Many people have had the experience of thinking about a friend or acquaintance, for no particular reason, and then shortly afterward meeting that person. No one thinks this strange if he meets someone he was expecting to meet, or someone he encounters frequently. It is with unexpected meetings that the phenomenon is so striking. For example, Andreas Thomopoulos, a film director from Athens, was recently visiting Paris with his wife. "Walking through the streets, we thought of a close student friend of mine in London. We wondered how he was nowadays since I hadn't seen him for over twenty years. Shortly after, on going around a corner, we bumped straight into him!" Mary Flanagan, of Hoboken, New Jersey, is one of many other people who have had a similar experience: "Walking down the street, I was thinking of someone I had not seen or spoken to for three years and who lives in a different city. I met her on the street about ten minutes after I started thinking about her."

In most cases the people thought about were met soon afterward, seconds or minutes later. A variant form of this experience occurs when people mistakenly think they have seen someone they know, realize it is not that person, and then meet the person they thought it was soon afterward. Anne Knowles, who lives in Devon, England, says she has had this experience quite often.

> I would walk along the road and see somebody and think, "Oh, there is Mrs. So-and-So," and when I came up to her it wasn't that person. But then I would go around the corner and there would be the person that I thought that first figure was. It happened so often I reached the stage where I would think, "Oh, they are going to be around the corner" — and they were. They might be five or ten minutes farther on, but I would see them. It was as if I was picking up an imprint from the second person and putting it on to the first person.

Anticipations of meetings even seem to occur with vehicles, rather than specific people. David Campbell had a job during the school holidays working on a construction project in County Durham, in the north of England.

> We traveled to the site in the company's van, and for no good reason I memorized the registration number of the van, I can still remember it—BRO 868B. Anyway, the job finished and I went back to school. A couple of years later I was out with the local cycling club one Sunday morning when for some inexplicable reason I started thinking about this builder's van and its number plate. About half a minute later the van passed me going in the opposite direction!

Some people also anticipate encounters with animals. In chapter 14 I discussed how some hunters and wildlife photographers seem to anticipate meetings with animals they are trying to hunt or to photograph, and suggested these might be examples of remote viewing. But they could also be interpreted as examples of precognition. Some anglers have had similar experiences, and here precognition might be more plausible than clairvoyance, since the fish are not "seen" in the water; rather, there is an anticipation of catching them. Paul Hicks, for example, who used to be an avid angler, would sometimes camp out by the water's edge for days on end. "There were instances I knew for a fact that within a minute or two I was going to catch a fish. It was uncanny when that happened. It wasn't just because the weather was good, or the time of day was right or whatever, it was just a knowledge that something was going to happen."

Are all these cases just coincidence and selective memory? Perhaps. But perhaps there is more to them, and only further research will be able to settle this question. For a start, people who have such anticipations quite frequently could make a note of them, and then see how many were followed by actual meetings. A statistical analysis should be able to reveal whether their anticipations could in fact be explained by the coincidence hypothesis.

At first I thought that anticipating meetings might be essentially telepathic, analogous to the anticipation of telephone calls (see chapter 6). But there is an essential difference between the two situations. In the case of telephone calls, one person thinks about the other and forms an intention to call. This intention is directed toward the other person, creating appropriate conditions for telepathy. By contrast, in the case of unexpected meetings, the person thought about is not usually intending to meet the other person, or thinking about him or her. The anticipation of meetings therefore seems more precognitive than telepathic.

In addition, the anticipation of phone calls usually happens with people to whom a person is closely bonded, favoring the telepathic explanation. By contrast, the anticipation of meetings happens with mere acquaintances, or even with vehicles, or with wild animals.

PRECOGNITION IN THE LABORATORY

Since the 1930s, parapsychologists have done numerous experiments on precognition, with generally successful results.

The first methods involved guessing cards, and followed procedures similar to other ESP tests (pages 46–49). The difference was that subjects were asked to guess the order of cards in a pack *before* the pack had been shuffled. On average, they did much better than would have been expected by chance.[2] To avoid the possibility that any human bias could have entered into the shuffling of the pack, automatic shuffling machines were used, and packs were cut according to random numbers. But subjects were still somehow able to guess what had not yet happened. In later experiments, packs of cards were replaced by fully automated tests on computers, with the symbols presented in a random order that was determined only after the subjects had made their choices. On average, the results were still positive.

Altogether, between 1935 and 1987, some 50,000 subjects were tested for precognition in a total of nearly 2 million individual trials. Precognition effects were replicated by dozens of different investigators. These studies were reported in a total of 113 scientific articles. The combined results of these studies produced odds against chance of 10^{24} to 1.[3] Something was clearly going on.

An important feature of these results was that the subjects performed very differently according to whether they were given feedback. When they were not told what the target was, and never knew if their guess was right or wrong, the results were no better than chance. Precognition occurred only when they were given feedback. Moreover, the sooner after their guess that they were shown the target (which, of course, was selected at random only after they had guessed what it was) the better they did.[4]

All these experiments involved "forced choices" among a limited number of symbols, such as the five patterns on Zener cards. But, in addition, several researchers carried out precognitive remote-viewing experiments. In standard remote-viewing tests, a sender, or beacon person, went to a place chosen at random from a pool of possible locations, and when the sender was there, the subject tried to describe what the sender was experiencing (see pages 217–220). In the precognitive version of these tests, the subject was asked to describe the scene *before* the sender had arrived there. The subjects were given feedback about the target location after they had described it, and in some cases were actually taken there. Experiments of this kind carried out at the Stanford Research Institute, Princeton, and elsewhere were remarkably successful. The most comprehensive experiments were those at Princeton, where the researchers conducted 227 such tests. Their positive results had odds against chance of 100 billion to 1.[5]

What all these experiments showed was that precognition was related to the subjects' future experiences, not to some future state they never knew about. They confirm Dunne's discovery that precognitive dreams were related to the future *experience* of the dreamer, rather than to objective facts. For example, his dream, recounted at the beginning of this chapter, that 4,000 lives were threatened by the volcanic eruption in Martinique corresponded not to the actual report he later read in the newspaper, but to his *misreading* of it.

DETECTING FUTURE FEELINGS

A presentiment is a *feeling* that something is about to happen, but without any conscious awareness what it is. Some of the most innovative research in modern parapsychology has shown that presentiments can be detected in the laboratory, even though the person having the presentiments is quite unconscious of them.

In the mid-1990s, Dean Radin and his colleagues at the University of Nevada at Las Vegas devised an experiment to test for presentiment in which a subject's emotional arousal could be monitored automatically by measuring changes in skin resistance with electrodes attached to the fingers, as in a lie detector test. As people's emotional states change, so does the activity of the sweat glands, resulting in changes in electrodermal activity registered in a computerized recording device.

In the laboratory it is relatively easy to produce measurable emotional changes in subjects by exposing them to noxious smells, mild electric shocks, emotive words, or provocative photographs. Radin's experiments used photographs. Most were pictures of emotionally calm subjects like landscapes, but some were shocking, like pictures of corpses that had been cut open for autopsies, and others were pornographic. A large pool of these "calm" and "emotional" images was stored within the computer.

In Radin's experiments, two of the fingers on a subject's left hand were wired up so that electrodermal activity could be monitored, and the subject sat in front of a computer screen. When she was ready to begin, she clicked on the computer's mouse button. This caused the computer to select one of the photographs at random from the pool within the computer. The screen remained blank for five seconds, and then the randomly selected image was displayed for three seconds before the screen went blank again. After a rest period of five seconds, a message on the computer screen told the subject she could press the mouse button for the next trial whenever she felt ready.

As expected, when calm pictures appeared on the screen, the subjects' emotions remained calm, and when emotional images were displayed, the subjects were emotionally aroused, as shown by an increase in their electrodermal activity. The interesting thing was that when emotional images were about to appear, the increase in electrodermal activity began *before* the picture appeared on the screen. The subjects' emotional arousal began three to four seconds in advance (Figure 17.1). But when they were later asked if they had been conscious of what kind of pictures were about to appear, almost all said they were not. Their presentiments were largely unconscious.

Dick Bierman, a professor of psychology at the University of Amsterdam, has independently replicated Radin's experiments in Holland. As in Radin's experiments, subjects showed significantly more emotional arousal before

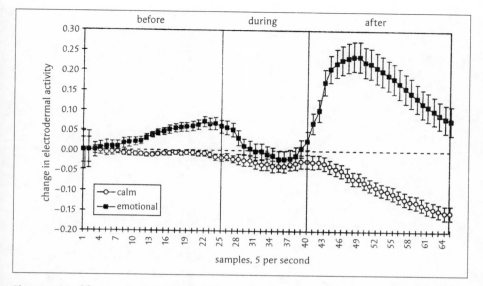

Figure 17.1 *Changes in participants' electrodermal activity before, during, and after the display of target pictures on a computer screen.*
Not surprisingly, there was a big change in the participants' electrodermal activity after being shown emotionally arousing pictures. But there was also a significant change before these pictures were shown. There were no such changes in the control trials with calm pictures. These results are averages from a total of 900 trials involving 24 participants. The bars show standard errors. (Data from Radin, 1997.)

emotional images appeared on the screen than before calm images appeared. Bierman also found that the erotic pictures tended to be more arousing before they appeared than did the violent ones.[6]

In February 2001, I myself served as a subject in one of Bierman's tests, with the results shown in Figure 17.2. I showed a strong emotional arousal before the erotic images appeared, even though I was quite unconscious of it. The dramatic rise in my electrodermal activity began five seconds before the pornographic pictures came up on the screen. No such arousal occurred before the calm images appeared, or even before the violent ones.

I had already read about Radin's and Bierman's experiments when I did this test, and had been impressed by the remarkable effect they had discovered. But I was amazed to find how well the test worked when I was a subject myself, and to see such clear-cut results from an experiment that lasted only about fifteen minutes. Since the randomization was automatic and took place inside the computer, there was no way I could have detected by any "normal"

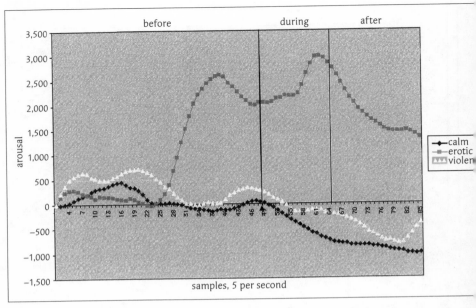

Figure 17.2 *Changes in Rupert Sheldrake's electrodermal activity before, during, and after the showing of calm, erotic, or violent images.*
In the case of the erotic images, there was a large response *before* the images appeared. (The effect was statistically significant at the *p* = 0.03 level.) This experiment was carried out by Dick Bierman in his laboratory at Starlab, in Brussels, Belgium.

means what kind of picture would come up next, nor could I have picked up any clues from Bierman. He himself did not know which images would appear, and in any case he was not in the room when I did the tests. I was alone with the computer, the images, and my emotions.

WAKING UP BEFORE ALARMS GO OFF

Finally, I want to discuss a common but little-understood phenomenon, namely, waking up just before alarm clocks go off. This is not usually thought of as precognitive, but I suspect that it might turn out to be. At present the question is entirely open, and this is a field of research almost completely unexplored.

Like many other people, I have quite often had the experience of setting an alarm clock and then waking just before it went off. At first, when I used old-style, windup alarm clocks, I assumed that this was because I heard the click that such clocks often make shortly before they go off. But then I found that the same thing happened with electronic alarm clocks, with no preliminary mechanical sound.

Without thinking about it very much, I then assumed that the phenomenon must depend on an intrinsic time sense or "biological clock." Human beings, like many other organisms, have intrinsic daily rhythms, often called circadian rhythms, which underlie daily cycles such as waking and sleeping. The biological clock seemed likely to provide an explanation for this ability to wake at a particular time, although the details as to how this might happen were vague. For years I took this idea for granted, and found that most other people I talked to assumed there must be some explanation of this kind.

But when I began to think about the biological-clock theory in detail, I began to have serious doubts about it, for two main reasons.

First, this theory did not make much sense in terms of evolution. There is undoubtedly a strong evolutionary basis for biological clocks that underlie daily rhythms. Circadian rhythms help organisms adapt their activities to the natural cycles of day and night, and are found in many kinds of animals, including insects, and also in plants. But nothing in our evolutionary history would set a precedent for waking precisely at, say, 4:45 A.M., in order to catch an early flight. Mechanical clocks themselves were invented less than a thousand years ago, and until the invention of chronometers in the eighteenth century, they were not particularly accurate.

Precisely standardized clocks first became important in the determination of longitude, for navigation at sea, starting in the late eighteenth century.[7] Only with the building of railways and the invention of the telegraph in the nineteenth century were clocks precisely synchronized on land, because of the need to operate railways according to fixed timetables. Synchronization is now continually maintained through time signals on the radio and through telephones.

We take all this for granted, but it is a surprisingly new phenomenon. So is the wearing of watches by the majority of the population. Industrialized societies depend on precise timing and punctuality. Traditional, preindustrial societies are far less obsessed with exact timing, and have a more relaxed and approximate attitude, as any one who has lived or traveled in a predominantly rural society will know.

Thus, for the vast majority of human evolutionary history, there would have been no need for people to be able to wake in the night at unusual times with a precision of a few minutes. How could this ability have evolved so rapidly on the basis of an approximate biological clock? The very word *circadian* expresses the essentially approximate nature of these rhythms (in Latin, *circa* = approximate, *dies* = day).

Second, I realized that my own time sense was not particularly well developed in the daytime. I could often guess the time with an accuracy of about ten minutes, but I was sometimes off by more than half an hour. For many years I did not wear a watch, and as a result developed a better time sense than most people I know, but still my daytime performance was far poorer than my accuracy at night. Why?

I was unable to find any answers to these questions in the scientific literature,[8] so I tried to find out more by asking friends and acquaintances about what they had noticed themselves. I soon found that most people had had similar experiences to my own. And some dogs also seem to have similar abilities. For example, David Klein, who lives in California, has noticed that his German shepherd "shows up beside our bed just seconds before our battery-operated clock goes off. It's as if she doesn't want us to be late for work. At first I thought she must hear something actually working inside the clock, but it makes no noise. It doesn't matter what time we set it for, she's there. I have actually tried to screw up her usual waking times and have lain in bed waiting, and sure enough she shows up."

An opportunity for a more detailed inquiry arose in July 2000, when I was a visiting scholar at the Woods Hole Oceanographic Institution on Cape Cod, Massachusetts. With the help of a very bright group of graduate students, I explored in more detail how the time sense seemed to work when people were awake and asleep. In this group of forty-nine people, to my surprise, every single one had experienced waking up just before an alarm went off. Some commented that they could also program themselves to wake at particular times even without an alarm clock.

Was this just a matter of routine? No, because thirty-four people (79 percent) had found that they still woke up before the alarm when it was set for a nonroutine time. Most of the others could not remember if this had happened or not.

How soon before the alarm was due to go off did they usually wake? Seventeen said within two minutes, and fourteen within five. That is to say, a total of thirty-one people (63 percent) woke within the five minutes before the time the alarm was set for. By contrast, when it came to guessing the time during the day, most said they were often wrong by half an hour or more. This was indeed the case, as I found by suddenly asking everyone to guess the time without looking at clocks or watches. Some were wrong by as much as forty-five minutes!

And most of those who were reasonably accurate said they had recently looked at their watches.

Try it with your family or friends. Without warning, ask them to guess what the time is. Under most circumstances I expect you will find most people's guesses are quite inaccurate. Yet the same people will probably say they have woken a few minutes before an alarm goes off at night.

In the autumn of 2000, I carried out further surveys by means of questionnaires at lectures and seminars I gave in London and also in the United States, in Chicago, and in Santa Rosa and Santa Cruz, California. Altogether I questioned 377 people. The pattern of results was almost the same in all these places. Overall, 96 percent said that they had woken just before an alarm went off. Only 1 percent said they had not; 3 percent were not sure. Eighty-eight percent said this had happened even at nonroutine times; 2 percent said it had not; 10 percent were not sure. Most people said that they also woke up shortly before telephone wake-up calls, just as they did before alarm clocks went off. (But a few people said that when they had to get up early, they were so worried about oversleeping that they kept waking up all through the night or couldn't sleep at all!)

In addition, most people (73 percent) said that they could program themselves to wake at a particular nonroutine time even *without* an alarm clock. Here are two typical comments: "I can tell myself what time to wake up in the morning before I go to sleep and will wake up within five minutes of that time. I am self-employed and don't wake up at the same time every day." "I can program myself to wake up at any time I wish, no matter how tired I am. I am always within five minutes." Some people were so confident of this ability that they did not need an alarm clock at all. For example: "I never use an alarm clock, as I can always wake up before the necessary time." Others were less confident and used an alarm "just in case."

These surveys confirmed that most people have a much more accurate time sense when asleep than when awake. Why should this be so? The more I thought about it, the more surprising it seemed. During the day we receive all sorts of external clues, like hearing clocks chime, looking at watches, and hearing the time on the radio, as well as natural clues like the position of the Sun. This should make it easier for us to know what time it is. At night we receive very few clues for hours on end, and yet we are far more accurate. Also, we have twice as great a chance of guessing accurately during the day because errors could go both ways: the guess can be late, or it can be early. By contrast, at night only waking *before* the alarm goes off can count, because after it goes off people are awake anyway.

Why should the sensing of clock time work so much better when we are asleep than when we are awake? The most obvious possibility is that biological clocks work better during sleep, for some unknown reason. But then, if the phenomenon is based on an internal clock synchronized with the daily rhythms of day and night, and waking and sleeping, it should be severely disrupted when people go to bed at irregular hours, or when they are suffering from jet lag. Yet several people have explicitly told me that they can still wake before alarms go off when they are traveling and moving from one time zone to another. I have no idea how common this experience is. I would like to find out more about the effects of jet lag on the ability to wake at predetermined times, either with alarm clocks or without.

Perhaps an approximate internal "clock" plays a part when people know in advance when they need to wake. But the precision with which people can awaken raises the possibility that precognition, or presentience, may play a part as well. At first I was reluctant to take this idea seriously, but the more I thought about it, the more plausible it seemed. There is already much evidence for premonitions and precognitions, and also good experimental evidence for presentiment in the form of unconscious emotional arousal. An alarm going off in the night is literally arousing. This could well be preceded by a physiological arousal, as in the presentiment experiments discussed above (Figures 17.1 and 17.2). If this is the case, then more alarming alarms should have more effect than less alarming ones. A few people have spontaneously commented on this. For example: "I very often wake up one or two minutes before my alarm goes off. This happens frequently when I use a very loud, unpleasant-sounding alarm, but rarely when I use a quieter, less unpleasant alarm." I do not know how many other people have had this kind of experience.

It should be possible on the basis of evidence to decide between the clock-only hypothesis and the precognition hypothesis. What would happen if people were woken in the night by alarms that they did not know about in advance, such as fire alarms, or unexpected loud noises? On the precognition hypothesis, waking in advance should still occur, but on the biological-clock hypothesis, it should not. To find out if anyone had noticed that they woke before unexpected alarms, in my surveys I asked, "Have you ever found that you have woken up just before an unexpected alarm or event?" To my astonishment, a majority (53 percent) answered yes; 16 percent said no, and 31 percent were not sure.

In this context, it is interesting to recall that many nursing mothers say they often wake up just before their baby starts crying, even when the child is in a different room (see chapter 3). In such cases it is hard to tease apart telepathy and precognition, and both may play a part. The same goes for people who wake just before they receive a telephone call.

But not all awakenings before alarm clocks are followed by alarms or loud sounds or other causes of arousal. Many people wake up before the time for which the alarm is set, and then turn the alarm off before it sounds. And many wake at a predetermined time without using an alarm clock at all. In both of these situations, waking cannot be a result of a precognition of the alarm actually going off. So, of what could it be a precognition? It must be of the time the clock is showing when we look at it after we wake. Even people who can wake without an alarm must look at a clock or watch after they have done so. Otherwise they would not know that they had woken at the right time.

Significantly, a dreamlike image of his watch telling a particular time was the very experience that first started J. W. Dunne on his inquiry about precognitive dreams. The image was not of his watch as it actually was while he saw the image. It was a foreshadowing of the way he looked at his watch when he woke up.[9]

The precognitive hypothesis of waking at predetermined times may seem far-fetched at first sight. Nevertheless, the available evidence makes it plausible. The next stage is to test it experimentally, as I discuss in Appendix A.

An alarm clock gives a great shock to the system. It is indeed an alarm. The Italian root of this word expresses the idea clearly: *all'arme* means "To arms!" By dictionary definition, an alarm is "a call to action," "news of approaching hostility," or "a sound to warn of danger."[10] Any animal or human that could wake before danger or approaching hostility would have a better chance of surviving than one that did not. Precognitive waking before alarms makes good evolutionary sense. All animals are vulnerable when asleep. Animals that can anticipate danger and wake up in advance are likely to be favored by natural selection.

Part IV

HOW DOES THE SEVENTH SENSE WORK?

18 EXTENDED MINDS AND MODERN PHYSICS

In this book I have suggested that minds are not confined to the insides of heads, but stretch out beyond them. The images we experience as we look around us are just where they seem to be.

Our intentions likewise extend beyond the brain. They are generally directed toward people, things, and places in the outer world, in accordance with our needs, appetites, desires, loves, hates, duties, ambitions, and, sometimes, ideals.

Through attention and intention, our minds stretch out into the world beyond our bodies. In this book I have suggested that these extensions of the mind take place through morphic fields. I suggested that these extended fields of the mind help to account for the sense of being stared at and for telepathy.

A metaphor that helps in thinking about the extended mind is provided by one of the simplest forms of animal life, the single-celled amoeba. Some species of amoeba live in ponds and feed by engulfing bacteria. The prototypical amoeba of biology textbooks is *Amoeba proteus*, named after the classical sea god Proteus, a shape-shifter (Figure 18.1).

Amoebas move around by sending out projections into the world around them. These are called pseudopodia, literally meaning "false feet." (The singular of this Greek word is *pseudopodium*.) The pseudopodia project out in any direction (Figure 18.1). Some projections can be retracted while others form, stretching out in a different direction.

Although amoebas are very primitive animals, amoebalike, or "amoeboid,"

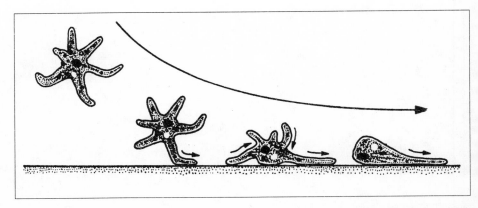

Figure 18.1 *On the left, a floating amoeba sends out pseudopodia in different directions. When one of them makes contact with a solid surface, it grows along it, and the other pseudopodia are retracted. (After Jennings, 1906.)*

cells are part of our own cellular makeup. As in all other complex animals, amoeboid cells are vital for our survival.[1] For example, some of the white blood cells, the macrophages, are amoeboid and send out pseudopodia that engulf bacteria and other foreign bodies, just as free-living amoebas in ponds gobble up bacteria by engulfing them. The most extreme examples of amoeboid cells are the nerves.[2] Some nerve cells have enormously elongated pseudopod-like projections, which serve as the nerve fibers that conduct nerve impulses. These pseudopodia, called axons, can be several feet in length, such as those in the sciatic nerve linking your toes, feet, and legs to the sacral plexus, at the base of the spinal column. As axons grow, they send out many thin, hairlike projections (called filopodia) that explore the area around the tip of the growing axon.

Nerve cells have many axons, some of which project out toward the surface of other nerve cells, forming a network of interconnections. Some stretch out from the brain or spinal cord into the sense organs; and some stretch out make contact with the muscles and glands, whose activity they can trigger.

It is no coincidence that the mind is rooted in networks of nerve cells, with pseudopod-like axons stretching out far beyond the main part of the cell body. The mind in turn is capable of sending out mental pseudopodia into the world beyond the body, and is forming networks of interconnections with other minds.

In visual attention, the mind is focused on a particular person, animal, plant, machine, place, object, or field of view. A visual pseudopodium reaches out from the body to touch the object of attention and, by doing so, affects it. Of course, visual pseudopodia shoot out very fast, in the twinkling of an eye. Other people and animals may detect this attention through their own extended fields, and sense that they are being stared at.

Through social fields, the pseudopodia of attention and intention link one person to another. The bonds between people serve as channels of thought transference. They are the medium of telepathic calls (chapters 3 and 6), telepathic detection of intention (chapter 5), and telepathic sensing of distant distress and death (chapter 4).

Through a combination of attention and intention, the pseudopodia of the mind may also reach out to distant places and objects, and make contact with them, beyond the range of the senses. One result may be clairvoyance, or remote viewing. Another may be psychokinesis, the influence of mind over matter at a distance.

In this book I have not discussed the evidence for mind-over-matter effects, because my focus is on the seventh sense. Suffice it to say that there is much evidence from well-controlled experiments that people can influence physical events, like the activity of random-event generators, at a distance through their intentions.[3] Exactly how these intentions bring about their effects is obscure; but, in general terms, psychokinesis is consistent with the idea of the extended mind focused on physical systems at a distance, and linked to them through pseudopodia of intention.

In addition to the experimental evidence for psychokinesis, there is a growing body of evidence for the beneficial effects of prayer at a distance. In several independent series of experiments, some people were prayed for while others were not. These experiments were conducted according to standard double-blind procedures, as in clinical trials. The patients themselves did not know they were being prayed for, nor did their physicians. Nevertheless, those who were prayed for without their knowing it tended to survive better or heal more quickly than those who were not prayed for.[4] But the healing effects of prayer may involve more than psychokinesis, or even telepathic hypnotic suggestion. Those who pray do not think that the healing power comes from themselves, but from God. But most would probably agree that the focusing of their intention provides a channel for healing grace or divine power.

Finally, one of the most intriguing fields of contemporary research is the study of the possible effects of shared experience on the patterns of activity in random-event generators. Such devices produce random "noise" as a result of quantum processes. On several occasions these "random" patterns have shown large, statistically significant changes all over the world at times when billions of people's minds were focused on the same events at the same time, such as the verdict of the O. J. Simpson trial (in which he was unexpectedly found not guilty of murder), and the cataclysmic events in New York and Washington on September 11, 2001.[5]

INTENTIONS PROJECTING INTO THE FUTURE

Precognition is the most puzzling of all psychic phenomena. Insofar as it implies that future events reach backward in time to influence minds in the present, it seems to defy all our normal ideas about causality, in which causes precede effects. How could we possibly sense something that has not yet occurred?

We could do so either if an influence worked backward in time, or if our minds in some way extended forward in time, connected to their own future states. Could our minds in the present in fact be connected to themselves in the future? We already know that minds are connected to themselves in the past, through memory. But perhaps these two alternatives, a working backward in time or a projection forward of the mind, are not really alternatives, but different aspects of the same process.

Our minds project forward into the future through our intentions, which extend outward not only in space, but also in time, toward future aims. By their very nature, intentions extend into the future. Say, for example, that I form an intention to take the train with my family from London to Edinburgh to attend a friend's wedding next month. I make plans, buy a ticket, and so on. My intention stretches out both in space, from London to Edinburgh, via the Great Northern Eastern Railway, and also in time, from now to the time and place of the ceremony. I also have many other future plans. Some, like my plan to go to Edinburgh, are formal arrangements entered in my diary; others are more vague ambitions and hopes, and others more implicit and habitual, like my intentions to sleep tonight, get up tomorrow at a normal time, have breakfast, work, have lunch, and so on. All these pseudopodia of intention stretch out from my mind now into the future, toward various places, times, and events.

Say that one or more of these intentions is interrupted, for example, by a disaster. If the disaster affects my intentions, perhaps it can in some way be sensed by the mental pseudopodia that it interrupts, even though these are in the future from the point of view of the present moment. This change in the future may be detected through my fields of intention. It may affect me first of all physiologically and emotionally. I may remain unaware of it, or I may become aware of this impending change either through a vague feeling of unease or foreboding, or through a more specific intuition, or through a dream. The connection from the future event to me now takes place through my intentions, extended outward in space and time, like mental filaments in the future—more in the near future, and fewer in the remote future.

FREEDOM AND DETERMINISM

Precognition inevitably raises deep questions about freedom and determinism. If we know that something is going to happen, does that mean the future is fixed? And if the future is fixed, does that mean that free will is an illusion?

These problems are not as bad as they seem. First, precognition is not definite. Any premonition or precognition can be recognized only in retrospect (chapters 15 and 16). Hence, before the event to which it refers, it has an indeterminate status, at best a probability.

Second, the usual theoretical contrast between a future that is entirely determined or entirely undetermined is unrealistic and artificial. The view of an entirely determined future admits no freedom or choice, or even chance. By contrast, the view of an entirely undetermined future implies that in the present there is a sudden collapse of all undetermined possibilities into determined facts the instant they enter the present, a vertical drop from total indeterminism to total determinism (Figure 18.2A). As the mathematician Ralph Abraham has pointed out, a more plausible view is that there are intermediates between those extremes. One simple model is that there is a gradient of determination (Figure 18.2B). The immediate future is more determined than the remote future.

Immediately, much is indeed more or less fixed. For example, for straightforward physical reasons like inertia and acceleration due to gravity, the Moon will continue in its orbit, and a stone dropped a second ago from the top of a cliff will continue to fall until it reaches the ground. Animals and people will continue to act in accordance with their already formed intentions. The closer the future is to the present, the more determined it seems, and the more predictable—except for unexpected disasters or accidents, or surprising decisions, or creative acts. The farther away the future is from the present, the less determined and the less predictable.

Even the relatively determined near future is predictable only in terms of probabilities. We are used to this kind of probabilistic prediction from everyday life—for example, in weather forecasts, or in economic forecasts, or in the life-expectancy calculations of insurers. Indeed, actuaries in insurance compa-

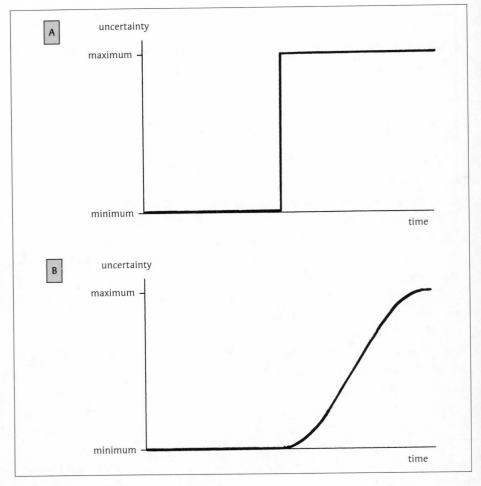

Figure 18.2 *Two models of the nature of time.*
A: a "step-time" model in which in the present there is an abrupt transition from a completely undetermined future to a completely determined past. B: a "slope-time" model. Instead of the instant passage of the knife of the present there is an "extended-now" window in which the future gradually freezes into the past. (After Abraham, 1999.)

nies were among the first people in the world of business to use mathematical theories of probability, starting in the late seventeenth century. These theories of probability originated in a correspondence between the mathematician and philosopher Blaise Pascal (1623–1662) and the mathematician Pierre de Fermat (1601–1665) about the mathematics of games of chance, the throwing of dice, and the value of bets.

At the beginning of the twentieth century, most scientists believed that messy and inexact predictions in terms of probabilities were simply a result of limited human knowledge and limited capacities to carry out calculations. All events in the physical world were fully determined. The future was *in principle* entirely predictable, although in practice most things could not be predicted with any accuracy. Nevertheless, it was believed that everything would be predictable if there were a mathematical intelligence vastly superior to our own. In the early nineteenth century, the French physicist Pierre-Simon Laplace epitomized this ideal in a kind of thought experiment.

Consider an intelligence which, at any instant, could have a knowledge of all forces controlling nature together with the momentary conditions of all the entities of which all nature consists. If this intelligence were powerful enough to submit all these data to analysis, it would be able to embrace in a single formula the movements of the largest bodies in the universe and those of the lightest atoms; for it nothing would be uncertain; the future and the past would be equally present before its eyes.[6]

Physicists have now abandoned this fantasy. Indeterminism lies at the heart of quantum physics. Predictions are possible only in terms of probability, even in principle. In addition, through the rise of chaos and complexity theories, many natural processes are now modeled in terms of chaotic dynamics.

Old-style determinism is no longer a fundamental principle of physics, though it may be useful as a mathematical abstraction in technologies like rocket science. Mechanistic determinism works best when it is applied to machines, which are specifically made and designed to act in a predictable way, such as computers. The last thing we want to happen is for our machines to work capriciously, subject to random errors or fluctuating probabilities. But they go wrong anyway, and break down unpredictably.

The pseudopodia of intention that project into the future from people, and from other animals, are projected into a realm not of complete determinism or of complete indeterminism, but of probability. They themselves contribute to the probabilities of what will happen. My intentions affect the future. Other people's intentions, and what is probably going to happen, also affect my intentions.

Can pseudopodia of intention themselves interact in the future? For example, because of my intention to take the train from London to Edinburgh, I need to be at Kings Cross Station on a particular day at a particular time. Someone I know may be planning to take a different train from Kings Cross, and our plans mean that we are likely to meet at the station. Our intentions overlap or intersect. Shortly before we actually meet, I may start thinking about this other person, or that person may start thinking of me. And then we actually meet. Such anticipations of meetings are quite common (see chapter 17).

The idea of pseudopodia of intention reaching into the realm of future probabilities is not a full and complete theory of precognition, or of other aspects of the seventh sense; rather, it is a preliminary attempt to think about the seventh sense in terms of the extended mind, using a biological metaphor. We can see the "sense organs" of the seventh sense as the pseudopodia of the mind stretching out into the external world, and into the future.

THEORIES OF PSYCHIC PHENOMENA

Before discussing in more detail my own ideas about the extended mind, I will briefly survey a variety of other theories of psychic phenomena, to give an idea of the alternatives.[7]

1. First of all, there is the standard viewpoint of dogmatic skeptics, who claim that there is nothing to explain. All apparent "paranormal" phenomena are illusions, errors, coincidences, the products of subtle sensory cues, or even the result of fraud and deceit. All the evidence, without exception, can be denied, dismissed, or ignored. The mind is nothing but the activity of the brain, and there are no new fields or kinds of information transfer that are not already recognized by orthodox physics.

2. For many decades, some psychic researchers have adopted dualistic theories of mind and matter, following the extreme dualism of René Descartes. The world of matter is entirely separate from the world of consciousness or spirit, which is nonmaterial and exists outside space and time. Descartes himself thought of the mind as essentially spiritual, and thought that humans were the only mortal beings to have this spiritual nature. They were also the only spiritual beings to have a bodily nature. All other kinds of spiritual beings were nonmaterial, like angels and God.

A nonmaterial consciousness unlimited by space and time, or rather outside space and time, might help explain how psychic phenomena take place at a distance. But unfortunately no one has been able to suggest exactly how it might interact with brains or anything else material, given that it is essentially outside space.[8] Another problem is that much of the mind is unconscious, not conscious. And where is the unconscious located? Is it material and inside space, or spiritual and outside space?

Last but not least, Cartesian dualism limits consciousness to human beings, and denies it to nonhuman animals. Hence, it cannot explain the biological nature of the seventh sense.

A form of disembodied consciousness outside space and time might be ideal for understanding eternal abstract ideas and mathematical equations. It would be entirely rational and impersonal. But these kinds of disembodied rational thoughts would not be much help to a mother in picking up her baby's needs telepathically, or to a dog in knowing when its owner is coming home.

3. A variety of theorists have proposed that in addition to the familiar three dimensions of space and one of time, there are extra dimensions that might help to explain psychic phenomena. In the 1920s, when researchers like J. W. Dunne suggested the existence of a single extra dimension, it seemed extremely daring.[9] In the 1970s, Gertrude Schmeidler suggested that the universe contains an extra dimension that permits "topological folding," so that two regions that appear to be widely separated might be in immediate contact through this extra dimension.[10] A few years later an eight-dimensional model of space-time was proposed to explain ESP.[11]

Within mainstream physics, extra dimensions now come cheap. The equations of quantum physics involve numerous extra dimensions. So does the branch of mathematics called dynamics. In modern dynamics, processes of change are modeled in "phase spaces" in which the system moves toward a goal, called an attractor. Such attractors are an essential aspect of chaos theory, which, in the 1980s, revolutionized scientific thinking about complex systems. Complex systems may have dozens of dimensions, or even hundreds or thousands, in their phase spaces.[12]

In superstring theory, a branch of physics that combines cosmology and fundamental particle physics, the universe is supposed to be embedded in eleven dimensions, ten of space and one of time.[13] Brane theory, as advocated by Stephen Hawking in his book *The Universe in a Nutshell*,[14] has ten or eleven dimensions.

In this context, it is not surprising that some researchers have suggested that extra dimensions might help explain psi phenomena. Some have also proposed that numerous independent space-time systems may coexist and interact with each other.[15] The problem is that such suggestions are very vague. They do not make it clear how these extra dimensions might help explain telepathy, for example, or precognition.

4. Jon Taylor has recently proposed a theory of ESP in which information transfer occurs between living brains by a kind of resonance between simi-

lar patterns of nervous activity. He accounts for precognition by supposing, first, that future events already exist and, second, that resonance can occur through time. His theory is based on the special theory of relativity. "Einstein's special theory of relativity combines the three coordinates of space with one of time, to create a frozen-block universe of four-dimensional space-time. The model implies that all events, future as well as past, already exist on the space-time continuum."[16] One problem with this theory is that even within physics itself, the Einstein block-universe seems incompatible with quantum physics, in which the future is not fixed. Another problem is that the block-universe seems to be incompatible with any form of free will.[17]

5. In the 1970s, the parapsychologist Rex Stanford put forward a general theory of psi phenomena that he called "conformance behavior." Although this theory was vague, it focused attention on two essential features of psychic phenomena: first, that psi effects occur in accordance with the goals or needs of living organisms, and, second, that organisms, through their goals and needs, affect random processes.[18] One of the strengths of Stanford's theory was that it did not require conscious intention, in good agreement with the observation that psi phenomena often occur unconsciously.

6. The parapsychologist William Braud has made an important contribution to theories about psi, even though it is not a theory in itself. He contrasted conditions of "lability" and "inertia." Lability is the ready capacity for change, "the ease with which a system can move from one state to another, the amount of 'free variability' in the system."[19] Inertia is the opposite, the tendency to resist change.[20] Braud proposed that psychokinesis should be related directly to the amount of randomness in the target system: the more lability, the more the capacity for psi effects; conversely, the more the inertia, the lower the capacity for psi effects. In relation to telepathy and other aspects of ESP, labile minds should be more receptive than minds with a strong inertia. In dreaming, meditation, and relaxation, the mind is more labile; it can flit quickly from one idea or image to another, and in such states, minds do indeed seem more open to psychic influences. Novelty also facilitates receptivity to psi; by definition, it involves a change from an old pattern. By contrast, when attention is focused on the external physical and social worlds, their stability and inertia usually make the mind less labile, and less receptive to subtle psychic influences.[21]

7. For more than forty years, some researchers have suggested that quantum physics may help provide an explanation for psychic phenomena.

Among quantum physicists there is a long-standing controversy about what constitutes a "measurement" or "observation." Some physicists argue that consciousness plays an essential role, interrelating the observer and the observed. A few, most notably Evan Harris Walker, have gone further and proposed that consciousness interacts with quantum processes not only in the external world, leading to psychokinesis, but also within the brain itself.[22] According to this theory, consciousness imposes coherence, meaning, order, or information on what would otherwise be random noise within the brain and in the external world.[23]

Another aspect of quantum theory is quantum "nonlocality," also known as "nonseparability" or "entanglement." According to quantum theory, when a quantum system (such as an atom) breaks up into parts, these parts remain "entangled" with each other in such a way that a change in one is instantaneously coupled to a change in another, even though they may be many miles apart. For example, when a pair of photons are emitted from the same atom, their polarization is undetermined, although one is obliged to have a polarization opposite to the other. As soon as the polarization of one is measured, the other has the opposite polarization instantaneously. Albert Einstein was deeply unhappy about this aspect of quantum theory precisely because it appeared to allow a "spooky action at a distance." But experiments have shown that quantum nonlocality is indeed a fundamental feature of reality.[24]

Several quantum physicists have suggested that phenomena like telepathy and psychokinesis involve quantum nonlocality. Through quantum physics, there really may be a spooky action at a distance, by which minds affect other minds or physical systems on which they are focused.

Brian Josephson and his colleague Fotini Pallikari-Viras, in a paper entitled "Biological utilization of quantum nonlocality," have proposed that focusing in relation to goals may change quantum probability distributions, and that this focusing would become more effective as learning took place.

The kind of focussing process involved can be illustrated with a simple example. This consists of a coil attached by a length of wire to an ammeter a short distance away. The meter needle can be caused to deflect by moving a magnet in the vicinity of the coil. A person who does not understand the facts of magnetism and attempting to produce a meter deflection in a particular direction will at first move the magnet randomly and hence produce deflections in a random direction. But he may in time discover the principle that is involved and utilise the magnet in a non-random way, and gain the ability to produce deflection in the prescribed direction at will. In exemplification of the processes described above, his learning process changes an initially random distribution of magnet movements into one focussed with regard to the goal, the principles referred to above. The proposal being made here is that mechanisms of a similar kind may be operative at a *microscopic* level in biosystems.[25]

This is not a complete review of all the various theories of psi, but it illustrates the main ideas in this field. It also shows how far we are from understanding these unexplained phenomena. My own hypothesis resembles some of the ideas proposed above, but it starts neither from quantum physics nor from theories of human consciousness, but from biology. As a biologist, I see psychic phenomena as rooted in our biological nature. I suggest they arise from fields of a kind that are fundamental to all living organisms—namely, morphic fields.

19 MENTAL FIELDS

I first became convinced that living organisms were organized by fields when I was doing research at Cambridge University on the development of plants. How do plants grow from simple embryos inside seeds into foxgloves, sequoias, or bamboos? How do leaves, flowers, and fruits take up their characteristic forms? These questions are about what biologists call *morphogenesis*, the coming into being of form (from Greek *morphe* = form + *genesis* = coming into being). The same problems arise in understanding how fertilized egg cells in animals give rise to fruit flies, goldfish, or elephants.

The naive answer is to say that everything is genetically programmed. Somehow each developing plant or animal follows the instructions coded in its genes. The problem with this theory is that we actually know what genes do: they code for the sequence of building blocks, called amino acids, that make up protein molecules. Also, some genes are concerned with the control of protein synthesis. This is a very different matter from "programming" morphogenesis or instinctive behavior.

Genes enable cells to make the right proteins at the right times as the organism develops. But how does having the right proteins explain the shape of a flower, or the structure of a mouse? No one knows. This is one of the major unsolved problems of biology. Sydney Brenner, one of the most perceptive of molecular biologists, summarized the situation in 2001 as follows:

> If you simply say, "Development is just a matter of turning on the right genes in the right place at the right time and that's the answer,"

that's absolutely true. But it's absolutely useless, because somewhere deep down what we'd really like to do is to actually go on and make a mouse. . . . Of course no one will build a real mouse, but we'd like to be able to make a *gedanken* (imaginary) mouse.[1]

Over the last forty years an enormous effort has gone into studying genes and the control of gene activity. A vast amount of detailed information is now available, but as Brenner points out, this does not amount to understanding the development of a mouse or any other organism. Turning on genes and making the right proteins in the right cells and at the right times is only the first of many steps.

To say that cells, tissues, and organs simply assemble themselves automatically is like saying that if all the materials were delivered to a building site at the right times, the building would automatically assemble itself in the right shape as a result of blind physical forces. Obviously this is not the case. Buildings do not construct themselves, and they are built to a plan. Moreover, the plan is not contained in the building materials. It is more like a spatial idea, a pattern of information. Nevertheless it has real effects, and determines where the building materials are put, and what form the building takes.

Since the 1920s, many biologists who have studied the development of plants and animals have been convinced that in addition to the genes, there must be organizing fields within the developing organism, called morphogenetic fields. These fields contain, as it were, invisible plans or blueprints for the various organs and for the organism as a whole. In mathematical models of morphogenetic fields, the goals of morphogenetic process are represented as *attractors*. These attractors lie within "basins of attraction" in a multidimensional phase space, and draw the developing organism toward developmental aims or goals.[2] The development of a mouse is shaped by mouse fields, and the development of a pine tree by pine fields.

These fields not only help to explain normal development, but also regeneration. If you cut a willow tree or a flatworm into pieces, each piece can regenerate to form an entire new organism (Figure 19.1). Like other kinds of field, morphogenetic fields are intrinsically holistic. The isolated parts retain the capacity to re-form a whole organism, because each part is still associated with the field of the whole organism.

If you cut a magnet up into parts, each part is a complete magnet, with a complete magnetic field. Systems organized by fields are very different from purely mechanistic systems, such as computers. Computers do not assemble

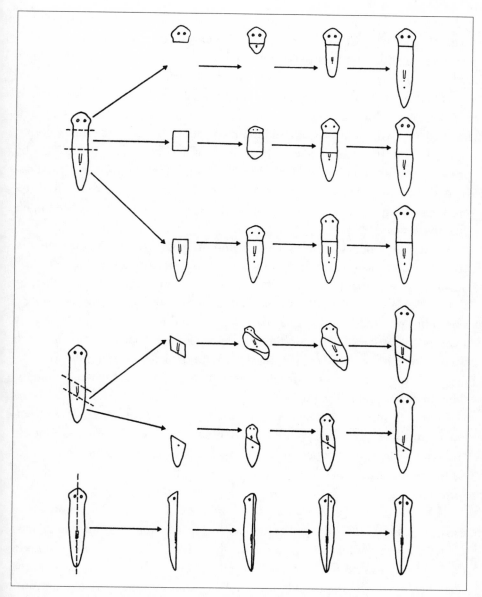

Figure 19.1 *The regeneration of complete flatworms (of the genus* Planaria) *from pieces of worm, cut as indicated on the left. (After Morgan, 1901.)*

themselves; they are put together in factories according to external designs. If you cut a computer up into parts, all you get is a broken computer.

In systems organized by fields, the parts all interact through the field of the whole system. For example, the planets and the Sun all interact through the gravitational field of the solar system. Magnetic fields are within and around magnets, and interact with other magnetic fields nearby, and also with electrical currents. Likewise, morphogenetic fields are within and around the plants and animals they organize, and interrelate their parts.[3]

The trouble is that no one knows exactly what morphogenetic fields are, or how they work. Most biologists assume that they will eventually be explained in terms of conventional physics and chemistry. For a variety of reasons, I do not agree. I think they are a new kind of field, of a kind not yet recognized by physics. In my two books on this subject, A New Science of Life and The Presence of the Past, I discuss the nature of these fields in detail, and also the supporting experimental evidence.[4] Here I will only summarize three of their main characteristics.

First, morphogenetic fields work by imposing patterns or structures on otherwise random or indeterminate processes in the systems under their control. Second, they contain attractors, which draw systems under their influence toward future goals. Third, they evolve, along with living organisms themselves. The morphic fields of all species have history, and contain inherent memory given by the process I call morphic resonance. This resonance occurs between patterns of activity in self-organizing systems on the basis of similarity, irrespective of their distance apart. Morphic resonance works across space and across time, from the past to the present.

Through morphic resonance, each member of a species both draws upon and contributes to a collective memory of the species. For example, as a mouse embryo develops, it is shaped by mouse morphogenetic fields containing a spatial memory of countless previous mice, and of the organs, tissues, and cells within them.

Morphogenetic fields not only shape cells, tissues, organs and living organisms, but also work at the molecular level. For example, the morphogenetic fields of protein molecules shape the way that chains of amino acids fold up in the right way to give the proteins their characteristic form. Genes specify the sequence in which amino acids are strung together, but they do not determine how these chains of amino acids fold up. A given chain could potentially fold up into an astronomical number of different forms. A typical chain of 100 amino acids has trillions of possible three-dimensional forms. If it folded up by "exploring" these at random until it found the most energetically stable form, it could take longer than the entire age of the universe to do so.[5] (This is sometimes called the Levinthal paradox, after the molecular biologist Cyrus Levinthal.)[6] In fact, the folding process may take only a few seconds, or at most a matter of minutes. Worse still, proteins do not have only a single possible form with a minimum energy; many alternative minimum-energy forms are possible, according to calculations. In the literature on protein folding, this is called the "multiple minimum problem."[7] Despite thirty-five years of intensive research, the folding of proteins is still one of the major unsolved problems in molecular biology.[8]

The most successful mathematical models of the folding process take the final form of the protein as an attractor, or "basin of attraction."[9] These models are consistent with the idea that folding is determined by a morphogenetic field that greatly restricts otherwise random or indeterminate processes.[10]

Morphogenetic fields are part of a larger class of fields, called morphic fields, all of which contain inherent memory given by morphic resonance. Other kinds of morphic fields include the behavioral fields that underlie the behavior and instincts of animals. As a kitten grows up, its instincts and behavior are shaped by morphic resonance from countless cats in the past. Its morphic fields contain a collective memory of the species. These fields interact with nervous systems and brains by imposing pattern and order on otherwise indeterminate or chaotic processes within them, as I discuss below.

In addition, the morphic fields of social groups, or social fields, coordinate the behavior of animal groups, such as termite colonies, flocks of birds, schools of fish, and packs of wolves (see chapter 7).

Morphic fields also underlie our perceptions, thoughts, and other mental processes. The morphic fields of mental activities are called mental fields. Through mental fields, the extended mind reaches out into the environment through attention and intention, and connects with other members of social groups. These fields help explain telepathy, the sense of being stared at, clairvoyance, and psychokinesis. They may also help in the understanding of premonitions and precognitions through intentions projecting into the future.

MENTAL FIELDS AND BRAINS

The morphic fields of perception, behavior, and mental activity are rooted in the activity of brains, but they are far more extensive than brains. A crude analogy is provided by a cell phone. The transmissions it sends out are rooted in the electrical activity in its circuits and electronic components. Yet the radio transmissions travel in electromagnetic fields that extend far beyond the material structure and electrical circuitry of the phone. Analogously, I suggest that mental fields of perception and behavior are intimately related to the activity of the brain, but they extend beyond it, through attention and intention.

A few decades ago, scientists thought of brains as like telephone exchanges, with nerves linked to sense organs transmitting signals to the central switchboard, where switches connected them to other neurons that stored memories, or that triggered muscular or glandular activity. Old-style telephone exchanges have now been replaced by the computer metaphor: Brains are like computers, and nerve cells work like transistors in an electronic network. But research on brain activity does not support these computer models, with their hardwired circuits.

Instead, there are complex patterns of activity in large populations of neurons. These patterns of activity can be detected either through brain imaging techniques, where different parts of the brain "light up" as a result of the increased activity within them, or by measuring patterns of electrical activity through electrodes placed over the surface of the brain.

The neuroscientist Walter Freeman, at the University of California at Berkeley, has spent many years investigating these patterns of activity, especially in relation to the perception of smells. He and his colleagues have found that these patterns are not fixed, but change in accordance with the animal's experience: "[B]rain activity patterns are constantly dissolving, reforming, and changing, particularly in relation to one another. When an animal learns to respond to a new odour, there is a shift in all other patterns, even if they are not directly involved with the learning. There are no fixed representations, as there are in computers; there are only meanings."

Freeman argues that these meanings depend on intentions, which are often unconscious. He models the interpretation of meaning in terms of attractors, using the language of dynamics.[11] He proposes that the activity of the brain is modified by meanings and intentions, precisely because it is chaotic, in the sense of chaos theory: "[B]rains are drenched in chaos."[12]

My suggestion is that morphic fields help impose order and pattern on this sensitive chaos, and interact with the brain through their ordering activity. They contain an inherent memory, through morphic resonance. They also project out far beyond the brain through attention and intention.

BODY IMAGES AND PHANTOM LIMBS

Just as our images of the things around us are located where they seem to be, outside the brain, so is our image of our body.

The conventional theory is that your body image is inside your brain. If you feel the pressure of your bottom on a chair, or a pain in your knee, these sensations are not located where they seem to be, but are actually inside your head. By contrast, I suggest that these feelings are just where they seem to be. They are not all crammed into the brain.

The contrast between the brain theory and the field theory is clearest in the case of phantom limbs. When people lose a limb as a result of an accident or amputation, usually they feel as if the limb is still there. It is a phantom, but it feels real.

These phantoms persist indefinitely. People who lost limbs in the Second World War more than fifty years ago told me that their phantoms are as vivid as ever. Leo Unger, for example, had both feet badly damaged by a land mine when fighting in Norway in 1944. Both his legs had to be amputated below the knees. "From the very first day, I have always had the feeling that my legs and feet were still in place. Early on I had severe phantom pains that felt like balls of fire going down my limbs and off my toes. After twenty years I seldom got that feeling, but I do often feel the bones in my feet were just broken, just as they were when I was wounded."

Many people with phantoms can move them around, just as if they were real. For example, people who have recently had an arm amputated find themselves trying to pick up the telephone with it, before they remember that their arm is no longer made of flesh and blood.

Some phantoms tend to shrink with time. But this does not usually happen when people wear artificial arms or legs. The phantom fills the artificial limb and it "usually fits the prosthesis as a hand fits a glove."[13] If someone whose phantom has shrunk starts wearing a prosthesis, the phantom tends to grow again to fit it.[14] In fact, phantoms play a important part in people's adaptation to artificial limbs, and make it much easier for them to use them. In the medical literature, it is usually said that the phantom "animates" the prosthesis. As one researcher expressed it, "the lifeless appendage is animated by the living phantom."[15]

I suggest that the phantoms are the fields of the missing limbs. They are just where they seem to be.[16]

The conventional view is that phantoms are in the brain, just as all other experiences are supposed to be. Yet medical attempts to track down phantoms within the nervous system have shown them to be remarkably elusive.

At first, the predominant hypothesis was that phantoms were produced in the brain because of impulses from nerves in the remaining limb stump, particularly in nerve nodules at the cut ends of the nerves, called neuromas.

Impulses from the neuromas were supposed to travel up the spinal cord into the brain, generating sensations in the sensory regions of the cerebral cortex that were then "referred" to the missing limb. This theory was tested repeatedly in surgical attempts to relieve pain in the phantoms, by cutting off neuromas, or severing the nerves from the stump at the roots, next to the spinal cord. Unfortunately for most of these patients, the phantoms persisted, and the pain was not cured.[17]

The stump hypothesis faced another serious problem. It could not explain how some people born without limbs experience phantoms of their missing limbs, when there is no injury to the nerves.[18]

Another hypothesis was that the phantoms arose from excessive nerve activity within the spinal cord because the nerves were missing their normal input from the limb. So surgeons cut various nerve pathways within the spinal cord to try to relieve phantom pain. But again these treatments did not work. The phantoms and the pain persisted.[19]

In addition, the experience of paraplegics does not support the theory that phantoms arise from excessive nervous activity in the spinal cord. Paraplegics are partially paralyzed because they have a broken spinal cord, with no feeling or control of the body below the break. They often experience phantom legs and even phantom genital organs. They may also experience phantom pain in the legs or groin, even though no nerve impulses from these lower parts of the body can cross the break in their spinal cord.[20]

The source of phantoms had to be pushed back into the brain itself. Hopeful surgeons removed areas of the thalamus and sensory cortex that would have received nerve impulses from the missing limb in further valiant attempts to relieve phantom pain, but the pain generally persisted, and so did the phantom.[21]

The source of phantoms was therefore sought even deeper in the brain. One hypothesis proposed that the body image was generated by a complex nerve network within the brain, called a neuromatrix, supposedly hardwired in the nerves. This neuromatrix "generates patterns, processes information that flows through it, and ultimately produces the pattern that is felt as the whole body."[22] The trouble with this theory is that it is virtually untestable. To try to remove a phantom by destroying the neuromatrix "would mean destruction of almost the whole brain."[23]

Another hypothesis locates the source of phantoms in the "remapping" process in areas of the brain that previously received nerve impulses from the amputated organs and now no longer do so.[24] The sprouting of new nervous connections within the brain may shed light on some aspects of phantoms, but it cannot explain their existence in the first place, because they appear immediately after amputation, long before any remapping has had time to occur.

Most of us could potentially experience a phantom arm if we wanted to, without suffering from any amputation or nerve damage at all, and certainly without remapping. Anesthesia can produce phantoms in less than an hour. This commonly happens in patients who are about to undergo surgery on their arms, after being given local anesthetics in the spinal cord. About 90 percent of patients experience a phantom arm within twenty to forty minutes of the injection of the anesthetic into the brachial plexus, causing anesthesia of the nerves running to the arm. When they close their eyes, they can move their arm around and lift it up, and also flex their hand and move their fingers. The arm feels completely real. Yet when they open their eyes they are usually amazed to see that their actual arm is lying immobile on the bed, while the phantom arm they experience is in a different position. Typically, when they realize the discrepancy, the phantom rapidly moves back into the real limb, fusing with it.[25] The patient's perception of the limb adjusts to reflect reality. As the anesthetic wears off, the phantom disappears. Likewise, many patients whose legs have been anesthetized experience phantom legs. When a patients is lying on his back, the phantom leg usually rises in the air above the actual leg.[26]

In trying to account for phantoms, medical researchers have returned again and again to concepts such as the "body schema" or "body image" somewhere inside the brain.[27] But the theory that the body image is all in the brain is no more than an assumption. Attempts to find it there have been remarkably unsuccessful. The brain theory also goes against people's own direct experience. It is far simpler to suppose that the body image and phantom limbs are located exactly where they seem to be.

The existence of phantom limbs has breathtaking implications for out-of-body experiences. Several surveys have shown that about one person in five has experienced being out of the body, especially in moments of crisis.[28] Typically, people find themselves separated from their physical body, as if they are in another body. For example, a man who had undergone an operation after general anesthesia said, "I myself, freely hovering and looking downward from above, saw my physical body, lying on the operating table."[29] Rather than simply having a phantom limb, he had an entire phantom body, detached from his physical body. Such out-of-body experiences are common when people nearly die, as part of the "near-death" experience.[30] The neurologist Ronald Melzack concluded, after many years of studying phantoms, "It is evident that our experience of a body can occur without a body at all. We don't need a body to feel a body."[31]

I suggest that a phantom limb is the morphic field of the limb experienced from within. A phantom body is the morphic field of the body experienced from within. A really big question is whether the phantom body can survive the death of the physical body. I do not know the answer.

EXTENDED MINDS AND PERSONAL EXPERIENCE

In this book I have suggested that our minds extend beyond our brains. They do so even in the simplest act of perception. Images are where they seem to be. Subjects and objects are not radically separated, with subjects inside heads and objects in the external world. They are interlinked.

Through vision, the external world is brought into the mind through the eyes, and the subjective world of experience is projected outward into the external world through fields of perception and intention.

Our intentions stretch out into the world around us, and also extend into the future. We are linked to our environment and to each other.

Likewise, our minds pervade our bodies, and our body images are where we experience them, in our bodies, not just in our heads.

At first it may seem shocking to take our most direct and immediate experience seriously. We are used to the theory that all our thoughts, images, and feelings are in the brain, and not where they seem to be. Most of us picked up this idea by the time we were ten or eleven. Although Francis Crick called this theory the Astonishing Hypothesis, it is not usually treated as a testable scientific hypothesis. Within institutional science and medicine, it is generally taken for granted, and most educated people accept it as the "scientifically correct" view. Yet the mind-equals-brain theory turns out to have very little evidence in its favor. It contradicts immediate experience. And it rules out the possibility of the seventh sense, forcing believers in the brain theory to deny or ignore all the evidence that goes against it.

The idea of the extended mind enables us to take seriously the evidence for the seventh sense in people and in animals. It helps us recognize that the seventh sense is part of our biological nature. And it opens up vast new areas of the natural world for research and exploration. In Appendix A, I suggest how anyone interested can take part in this new research program.

Above all, the recognition that our minds extend beyond our brains liberates us. We are no longer imprisoned within the narrow compass of our skulls, our minds separated and isolated from each other. We are no longer alienated from our bodies, alienated from our environment, and alienated from other species. We are interconnected.

APPENDIXES

Appendix A
How to Take Part in Research

Most of the areas of research discussed in this book are remarkably undeveloped, and there is an enormous potential for exploration and discovery. Anyone sufficiently interested can take part. In particular there are great opportunities for student projects.

Please tell me about your observations and results, either by e-mail through my website (www.sheldrake.org), or by regular mail through one of the addresses listed at the end of this appendix.

Keeping Notes About Spontaneous Experiences

Many people have personal experiences of telepathy, the sense of being stared at, or premonitions, or they observe such behavior with their families and friends, or they notice it in their companion animals. But all too often this is simply forgotten, or remembered only vaguely. The best way to make sure it is recorded as accurately as possible is to make notes soon afterward, preferably in a special notebook or computer file.

Evidence from personal experience is even more valuable if there are witnesses, so it is also worth recording if any other people were present, and who they were. For example, if someone has an unusual dream that later seems to have been precognitive, the evidence is stronger if the dream is recorded soon after waking, and better still if other people were told about it before the events happened that it seemed to refer to.

For experiences that happen repeatedly, it is very valuable to keep a logbook. For example, if you often know who is calling before answering the phone, note these intuitions in a book kept next to the phone before answering it. Afterward, record whether you were right or wrong, and note the date and time. Also note whether the call was expected or not.

Mothers and Babies

For nursing mothers who find that their milk sometimes lets down when away from their babies, it is helpful to have two notebooks, as described in chapter 3. The mother carries one with her, and leaves the other with her partner or baby-sitter. When the mother's milk lets down, she makes a note of the time and circumstances. The person with the baby notes the times at which the baby cries or seems distressed. Comparing the two notebooks later reveals how often the mother's milk letdown coincides with the baby's need, and how often it does not.

For mothers who find they often wake up in the night just before their baby starts crying, it should be possible to monitor both mother and baby on videotape, so that the exact sequence of events can be studied in more detail. If mother and baby were in the same room, it would be hard to rule out normal sensory clues such as sounds, so these observations are of more significance if they are in different rooms. If both mother and baby are filmed during the night by separate cameras on time-coded videotape, a later examination of the video recordings should enable a number of questions to be answered. Does the baby show signs of waking first, and then somehow alert the mother? Does the mother wake before the baby shows any signs of doing so? Do both start to stir at the same time? And what happens if either mother or baby wakes at an unusual time, or as a result of emergency or crisis?

Cats, Dogs, and Parrots That Know When Their Owners Are Coming Home

If any animals seem to anticipate the return of a member of the household, the easiest way to start research is for a person at home to write down in a notebook the times at which the animal shows signs of anticipation. Then the time at which the person arrives home should also be recorded, as well as the means of travel and the time at which he or she set off. To rule out the possibility that the animal is responding to routines or, for example, familiar car sounds, the person should come home at unusual times, unknown to the people at home, and travel by unusual means—for example, by taxi.

For more precise observations, it is important to use a video camera that runs continuously during the person's absence, pointing at the place where the animal usually waits or shows its anticipatory reactions. The time code should be recorded on the videotape. The videotapes are later to be analyzed "blind" by a third party who does not know the details of the person's movements. This person notes when the animal shows signs of anticipation—for example, by waiting by a door or window—and records the exact times at which the animal is in that place. In this way an objective record of the animal's behavior can be obtained and compared with the person's movements.

In formal experiments, an experimenter instructs the person when to return home by means of a pager or a cell phone. These return times are randomly chosen by the experimenter, and are not known in advance to the person who is away from home, or to the people at home with the animal.

Pam Smart and I have carried out many experiments of this kind with dogs,[1] but as far as I know, no videotaped experiments have been done with cats, parrots, or other return-anticipating animals.

Telepathic Calls to Cats and Dogs

As I discussed in chapter 3, some cat and dog owners have noticed that they can call their cat or dog silently and apparently telepathically when the animal is in another room, or even outdoors. It should be relatively simple to investigate such calls experimentally, although as far as I know, no one has yet tried to do this.

The person would be separated from the animal in such a way that he or she could not be seen or heard by the animal. The animal would be outdoors or in another room. A video camera would be set up to film the room in which the person was sitting continuously, and the time code would be recorded on the tape. Then, at randomly chosen times, the person would try to call the animal telepathically. If, in a series of such tests, the animal usually appeared soon after the calls, yet did so significantly less at other times, this would provide evidence for the telepathic nature of these calls.

Telephone Telepathy

In the simplest version of this experiment, the subject nominates four people to whom a telepathic response seems likely. The subject gives the experimenter the names and telephone numbers of these people, and also identifies times at which all concerned will be free to take part in tests. Obviously this experiment needs to be conducted with a telephone that does not have a caller-identification display. For this reason the experiment cannot be done with a cell phone, since all available models have a caller-ID display.

Fifteen minutes before the time chosen for a trial, the subject sits quietly reading, or engaged in some other relaxing activity (but not watching TV or a video, which can be too distracting). In videotaped trials, the subject should remain on camera for the whole of this period. For example, if the test tele-phone call is scheduled for 11:15 A.M., the subject sits down, within the field of view of the camera, at 11:00 A.M. Shortly afterward—say, at 11:02—the experimenter throws a die to pick one of the four potential callers, each of whom has been assigned a number from 1 to 4. (If the die shows 5 or 6, it is thrown again until 1, 2, 3, or 4 comes up.) The experimenter calls this person, and asks him or her to call the subject at 11:15. If the other potential callers have not heard from the experimenter by 11:05, they know they are not taking part in this particular trial.

At the prespecified time, the chosen caller telephones the subject, having thought about the subject for a couple of minutes beforehand. When the phone rings at 11:15, the subject knows it is one of the four potential callers, and has to guess which one it is before picking up the phone. The subject says this guess to the camera, and then picks up the phone, saying "X," or "Hi, X," or "Hello, X," before the other person says anything.

There is a 25 percent chance of being right by chance. If the subject's guesses are more than 25 percent correct, the data need to be analyzed statisti-cally to assess their significance. The most appropriate statistical method is the binomial test. According to this test, in a series of 10 trials with four potential callers, if 6 or more are correct, the result is statistically significant at the con-ventional threshold level of $p = 0.05$; in other words, with odds against chance of 20 to 1. In a series of 15 trials, scores of 9 or more correct guesses are signifi-cant. In a series of 20 trials, again 9 or more are significant. In 25 trials, 10 or more correct guesses are significant.

Another way in which this experiment can be done is to have all four callers in the same place, together with the experimenter. Then all of them can be videotaped continuously by a single camera, while the subject, in a dif-ferent place, is filmed continuously on another camera with a synchronized time code. As before, the experimenter picks one of the four callers at random for each trial, and the person calls at the prespecified time. Having all the callers in a single place makes it possible to control the experiment more tightly, and to record every aspect of it on videotape.

Experiments could also be carried out with call-anticipating animals. One simple experimental design would be to videotape the animal during a series of test periods in which four different people made phone calls, in a random sequence and at randomized times. One of these people would be someone to whose calls the animal usually responded. The others would be strangers. If the animal showed its usual reactions when the person it knew rang, but ignored calls from the other three people, then this would provide strong evidence for telephone telepathy in the animal.

E-mail Telepathy

Experiments to test for telepathy in connection with e-mails follow a similar design to the telephone experiments. Out of four potential e-mailers, nominated by the subject, one is selected at random by the experimenter to send an e-mail to the subject at a prespecified time, say 10:30 A.M. At 10:17 the experimenter e-mails this person with a request to send the subject an e-mail at 10:30. The others receive no e-mail from the experimenter, and by 10:20 they know they have not been chosen. The chosen e-mailer thinks about the subject for a couple of minutes before 10:30 and writes him or her a message, and then at exactly 10:30 sends it to the subject, with a copy to the experimenter.

At 10:29 the subject guesses which of the four potential e-mailers is going to send the message a minute later, and e-mails this guess to the experimenter.

The subject's e-mail with the guess on it automatically shows the time at which it was sent, as does the e-mail from the chosen e-mailer to the subject. Thus there is clear objective evidence that the guess was made before the e-mail was sent.

The subject can be filmed throughout the fifteen-minute period prior to the guess to show that he or she has not been cheating by receiving e-mails or phone calls from any of the e-mailers. The experiment can also be conducted with all four e-mailers in the same room (but in a different room from the subject, and preferably miles away), on camera continuously, to be even surer that there was no possibility of cheating.

The expected success rate by chance is around 25 percent. Scores above this level can be tested for statistical significance by the binomial test in the same way as in the telephone experiments.

The Sense of Being Stared At

In the basic experiment to test for the sense of being stared at (see chapter 11), people work in pairs. One is the subject, the other the looker. The subject sits with his or her back to the looker, and wears a blindfold of the type provided by airlines to passengers to help them sleep. These blindfolds both eliminate the possibility of peripheral vision by the subject and make most subjects feel more relaxed, by reducing distraction and creating a mild form of sensory deprivation.

The looker sits behind the subject and, in a series of twenty trials, either looks at the back of the subject's neck, or looks away and thinks of something else. The sequence of trials is randomized. The simplest way to do this is for the looker to toss a coin before each trial. Heads means "look," tails means "don't look." Random-number tables, or a random-number generator, can be used instead, taking odd numbers to mean "look," even numbers to mean "don't look." Or ready-made randomized instruction sheets can be downloaded from my website (www.sheldrake.org).

Just before each trial the looker signals to the subject, by means of a mechanical click or beep, that the trial is beginning. Within about ten seconds the subject guesses "looking" or "not looking." These guesses are either

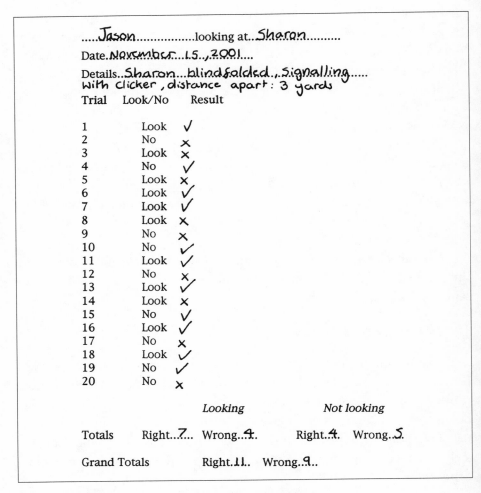

.....Jason................looking at..Sharon..........
Date.November...15.,.2001....
Details..Sharon...blindfolded.,.Signalling.....
with clicker, distance apart: 3 yards

Trial	Look/No	Result
1	Look	✓
2	No	✗
3	Look	✗
4	No	✓
5	Look	✗
6	Look	✓
7	Look	✓
8	Look	✗
9	No	✗
10	No	✓
11	Look	✓
12	No	✗
13	Look	✓
14	Look	✗
15	No	✓
16	Look	✓
17	No	✗
18	Look	✓
19	No	✓
20	No	✗

	Looking		*Not looking*	
Totals	Right...7...	Wrong..4.	Right.4.	Wrong..5.
Grand Totals		Right.11..	Wrong..9..	

Figure A.1 *A specimen score sheet from a staring experiment.*

right or wrong, and are recorded on the score sheet. A specimen score sheet is shown in Figure A.1.

This experiment can be done with feedback, or without. Either the looker tells the subject immediately after each guess whether it is right or wrong, or the looker does not tell the subject. Both methods generally give significant positive results, but subjects tend to perform better when given feedback, if only because the experiment is more interesting to do.

The total numbers of right and wrong guesses are added up for the looking and the not-looking trials separately, as are the overall totals (Figure A.1). Then the results from a series of subjects are tabulated, as in Table A.1, which shows actual data from an experiment conducted at a school in London.

Table A.1 *A specimen tally of scores from a staring experiment.*
Each looker-subject pair carried out 20 trials. The numbers of correct and incorrect guesses are shown for the looking and not-looking trials (NL) and also for the totals. In addition, the subjects were scored + if they made more correct than incorrect guesses, – if they made more incorrect than correct guesses, and = if the number of correct and incorrect guesses was the same. This experiment was conducted at St. James' School for Senior Girls, London, with girls in year 11 (ages 15–16) on November 20, 2001.

Looker/ Subject	Look Right	Look +/–/=	Look Wrong	NL Right	NL +/–/=	NL Wrong	Total Right	Total +/–/=	Total Wrong
Mimi/Emma	7	+	3	4	–	6	11	+	9
Emma/Mimi	12	+	2	4	+	2	16	+	4
Jayvanti/Rajvee	6	+	3	4	–	7	10	=	10
Rajvee/Jayvanti	6	=	6	5	+	3	11	+	9
Neela/Grace	10	+	2	4	=	4	14	+	6
Grace/Neela	9	+	5	2	–	4	11	+	9
Sam/Jessica	8	+	1	4	–	7	12	+	8
Jessica/Sam	5	=	5	6	+	4	11	+	9
Lucy/Alix	5	+	3	9	+	3	14	+	6
Alix/Lucy	3	–	5	5	–	7	8	–	12
Anna/Clare	6	+	4	3	–	7	9	–	11
Clare/Anna	7	+	4	4	–	5	11	+	9
Holly/Stella	7	+	3	7	+	3	14	+	6
Stella/Holly	5	=	5	4	–	6	9	–	11
Totals	96		51	65		68	161		119
Right (%)	65			49			58		
Totals +/–/=	10+	1–	3=	5+	8–	1=	10+	3–	1=

There are two ways of adding up and analyzing the data. The first is simply to add up the total numbers in each column. The second (suggested to me by Professor Nicholas Humphrey) is to assign a score to each subject depending on whether there are more right than wrong guesses (+), more wrong than right guesses (–) or equal numbers of right and wrong guesses (=). The advantage of this method is that it gives an equal weight to every subject, whereas with the first method a minority of subjects who score either very positively or very negatively can have a disproportionate influence on the totals. The total scores using both of these methods are shown in Table A.1.

For statistical analysis, the scores for right and wrong guesses in the looking, not-looking, and totals columns can be compared using standard statistical tests, such as the chi-squared test. The null hypothesis is that the number of correct and incorrect guesses will be the same. In other words, if people just guess at random, the average scores in all cases should be 50 percent correct and 50 percent incorrect. Using the +, –, and = method, the null hypothesis is that the number of + scores will equal the number of – scores. (For this method, the = scores are ignored.)

Over and over again, these tests have shown a characteristic pattern of results, whereby subjects score above chance levels in the looking trials and at levels close to chance in the not-looking trials (see chapter 11).

There have so far been very few tests in which subjects have been tested repeatedly while being given feedback to see how much they can improve through practice. People's potential for improvement with practice would be well worth exploring.

As discussed in chapter 11, staring experiments can be carried out through closed-circuit television. In the CCTV tests conducted so far, the subjects have not been asked to guess whether they are being looked at or not; rather, their unconscious responses have been monitored through recordings of their skin resistance, as measured by means of electrodes placed on the fingers. The skin-resistance method obviously requires a more sophisticated setup than the guessing method, but is still relatively inexpensive, and is quite feasible for a student project at the college level.

If people's skin resistance changes when they are being looked at through CCTV, it might well change when they are being looked at through the Internet. This opens up the possibility of online experiments, with the subject on a webcam.

In addition, the experiment might even work through live television. There could, for example, be four subjects, all continuously on camera in different rooms in the TV studio. In a series of trials, they would be shown one at a time, in a random sequence, to a live audience of millions. They would not themselves know by any normal means in which trials their images were being seen by millions of people, or by no one. Would the skin resistance of the subjects change when they were being seen live by millions, and could they guess correctly when they were being seen and when they were not?

If such experiments do in fact work on television, they would have immediate implications for people who are in the public eye. Not only would their image be transmitted to millions of viewers, but also an influence from viewers might in turn affect those who appear on television.

Effects of Looking at People's Photographs

Can people tell when someone is looking at their photograph and thinking about them, even though they are far away?

I have begun to explore this question experimentally, using a procedure like that used in the basic staring experiment described above. The difference is that in the photograph experiment, instead of staring at the subject directly, the looker stares at her photograph. The subject is meanwhile in another room, or in another building. The looker signals the beginning of each trial by means of a call signal on a wireless intercom. As in the staring experiments, the sequence of looking and not-looking trials is random, and in each trial the subject has to guess whether she is being looked at or not. She is either right or wrong, and if she guesses at random, her score will be around 50 percent correct. The same kind of score sheets and statistical analysis can be used as in the staring experiments.

If people can tell when someone is looking at their photograph, would this be a case of the sense of being stared at? Or would it be a case of telepathy? It would resemble the sense of being stared at in that the looker would be concentrating on a visual image of the subject. But it would be like telepathy in that the visual image might serve to focus the looker's thoughts on the subject, and it might be those thoughts that affect the subject at a distance.

One way in which the sense of being stared at differs from telepathy is that telepathy works best between people who know each other well, rather than between strangers. By contrast, the sense of being stared at works with strangers.

In my preliminary photograph experiments with lookers and subjects who were close friends or family members, the results were positive and statistically significant, and showed the same pattern as straightforward staring experiments. In the looking trials, the proportion of correct guesses was above the chance level, at 58 percent; whereas in the not-looking trials, 50 percent of guesses were correct, exactly at the level expected by chance.

By contrast, when my associates and I carried out photograph experiments in schools in Britain, the United States, and Germany, the results were at chance levels in both looking and not-looking trials. In these tests, looker-subject pairs were selected more or less at random, and most did not know each other well. In the same schools, straightforward staring tests gave the usual pattern of results, with highly significant positive scores in the looking trials, and nonsignificant results in not-looking trials.

Thus these preliminary photograph experiments bear out the idea that they depend on telepathy rather than on the sense of being stared at.

If looking at photographs of friends and family members helps in establishing a telepathic connection with them, this has immediate implications for the common practice of displaying photographs of loved ones on mantelpieces and in living rooms, or carrying their photographs around in wallets.

Experiments on Waking Before Alarms

In chapter 17, I discussed the possibility that the phenomenon of waking shortly before alarms go off may be more a matter of precognition than of a time sense. How could this idea be tested?

My first idea was to ask subjects to go to sleep knowing they would be woken by an alarm clock, but not knowing what time it was set for. Then, during the night, an experimenter would tiptoe into the subject's bedroom and place an alarm clock beside the bed. The clock would have been set at a randomly chosen time, say between 4:00 and 6:00 A.M.

The subject would then note at what time he awoke, and he could also be filmed throughout the night by means of a surveillance video camera installed in the bedroom to see when he showed signs of restlessness. In a series of such tests, would the volunteers wake up soon before the alarm was due to go off more often than would be expected by chance?

The obvious drawback to this idea was that most people would not want to have experimenters tiptoeing around their houses during the night. I then realized that this problem could be overcome by having the person awakened by telephone, using computerized wake-up calls at randomly selected times. The experimenter could order these calls in advance from the telephone company, and no one would need to tiptoe into anyone's bedroom.

At the time of writing, no one has yet carried out such tests. Obviously, subjects would need to be highly motivated to submit themselves to this ordeal—for example, by being well paid.

If it turns out that people do indeed wake up before alarm calls when they could not possibly have known by conventional means when the calls would happen, this would strongly favor the precognition hypothesis.

Addresses

Please let me know what you find out, either by e-mail through my website, www.sheldrake.org, or by mail at one of the following addresses:

Rupert Sheldrake
BM Experiments
London WC1N 3XX
UK

Rupert Sheldrake
Institute of Noetic Sciences
P.O. Box 6007
Petaluma, CA 94955-6007
USA

Appendix B

Details of Experiments and Surveys

CHAPTER 1

Testing a Perceptive Parrot

I summarized the experimental procedure for testing for telepathy between Aimée Morgana and her parrot, N'kisi, in chapter 1. During the tests, Aimée and N'kisi were in separate rooms on different floors and were filmed continuously throughout the test sessions by two synchronized cameras on time-coded videotape. N'kisi was also recorded continuously on audiotape.

There were twenty-nine test sessions, in each of which there were five two-minute-long trials. At the beginning of each trial, Aimée opened a sealed envelope containing a photograph, which she then looked at for the rest of the trial period. The end of the two-minute period was signaled automatically by a timer.

Another person, unconnected with the experiment in any other way, had selected the photographs on the basis of a list of thirty key words that were part of N'kisi's vocabulary and could be represented by visual images. He sealed these images in opaque envelopes, one image per envelope, and randomized their order before numbering the envelopes for use. Thus neither this person nor Aimée nor I had any way of knowing in advance what photograph she would be looking at in any given trial.

Three people independently transcribed the audiotapes for each test session, two of them in the United States and one in England. These transcripts were done "blind," in the sense that the scorers did not know what pictures Aimée was looking at, or when each trial period began and ended. The division of the transcripts into portions corresponding to the two-minute trial periods was carried out later, based on the videotaped record of the tests.

There was a remarkably good agreement between the three "blind" scorers. An example of these transcripts for one of the trials is shown in Table B.1. The image in this trial was of a couple on a beach in skimpy swimwear.

Table B.1. *The independent transcripts for trial 25/3 by Anna Yamamoto, Betty Killa, and Pam Smart.*
For comparison, Aimée Morgana's transcript is also included. The key word "naked body" (underlined) is present in all the transcripts.

Anna Yamamoto	Betty Killa	Pam Smart	Aimée Morgana
	tones, whistles, creaks	whistles and beeps	(beeps and whistles)
Look at my pretty naked body	Look at my pretty naked body	Look at my pretty naked body	Look at my pretty naked body
	whistle, creaks	whistles and beeps ?	(beeps and whistles)
Look at the little . . . (?)	Look at the little . . .	whistles and beeps	Look at the little pict . . . (-ure)
	tones, whistles, beeps		(beeps and squeaks)
Look at my pretty naked butt	Look at my pretty naked body		Look at my pretty naked body
	tones, creaks, whistles		(beeps)

In a few cases, one or more of the scorers missed some words, or heard them differently. This was most often the case with the English scorer, Pam Smart, who was not familiar with the American accent in which N'kisi speaks. These differences between scorers had relatively small effects on the overall conclusions. To find out just much difference this made, the data were analyzed in three ways: first by using the figures in which all scorers were in agreement; second by taking a majority verdict; and third by including words that were recorded by only one out of the three scorers. In addition, Aimée herself transcribed the audiotapes, but her transcripts were not used in the scoring process because they were not carried out blind. Nevertheless her transcripts were in excellent agreement with those of the blind scorers.

The data were analyzed statistically on the basis of the key words specified in advance, such as "doctor," "flower," "naked body," and "phone." Out of the initial list of 30 key words, photographs corresponding to 20 of these words were included in the test. The person who selected the photographs could not find appropriate images corresponding to the remaining key words, so the experiment was based on the 20 key words for which images were available. In addition, one further key word, "camera," had to be eliminated because N'kisi frequently said "camera" when he saw Aimée switching on the cameras prior to a test session and while the cameras were in use during the tests. Consequently the high degree of "noise" associated with this word meant that any possible "signal" would be swamped. This left a total of 19 key words for the analysis.

Altogether there were 142 trials out of a maximum possible of 145. Three had to be abandoned because of interruptions by callers in the test sessions. Three more had to be eliminated because the test image was a camera. This left a total of 139 trials for analysis.

In 71 trials, N'kisi said one or more of the 19 key words, and these are the tests on which the analysis is based. In the remaining 68 trials, N'kisi either remained entirely silent, or said none of the 19 key words corresponding to the test images. Thus, in these trials, neither a "hit" nor a "miss" was possible, and they were irrelevant to the analysis. Nonscorable comments made by N'kisi during these sessions were generally attempts to contact Aimée, or unrelated chatter about events of the day.

Using a majority verdict, in which at least two out of the three blind scorers agreed on key words, N'kisi said 117 key words. Hits occurred when N'kisi said a key word corresponding to the image that Aimée was looking at during that particular trial. By chance, assuming that N'kisi had been saying these words at random, there would have been 7.4 hits. In fact he scored 23 hits (Table B.2). This result was highly significant statistically.

When all three blind scorers were in complete agreement, N'kisi said 105 key words, of which 19 were hits. If N'kisi had been speaking at random, he would have been right 7.6 times. And when only one out of the three scorers picked up a key word, N'kisi said 136 key words, of which 26 were hits, when only 7.4 hits would have been expected by chance. (In every case where only one of the scorers picked up a key word, Aimée's transcripts showed the same word, so these were unlikely to have been idiosyncratic scorings. Aimée is, of course, more familiar with N'kisi's speech than anyone else.)

By all these methods, and by three different statistical tests, N'kisi obtained very significantly more hits than would have been expected by chance (Table B.3.I). Fuller details of N'kisi's scores and of the statistical analyses can be found in our technical paper on this experiment.[1]

Our selection of key words was derived from an unedited list of his entire vocabulary, and included some words that N'kisi had used only rarely, and in fact did not utter at all during this series of trials. These words were "cards," "CD," "computer," "fire," "keys," "teeth," and "TV." There were 18 trials involving the corresponding images, in which N'kisi could not have scored

Table B.2. *Results of the N'kisi telepathy trials based on key words, as scored by a majority of the independent scorers.*

This table includes data from all trials in which N'kisi said a key word at least once. Column E shows the probability of N'kisi saying a given key word by chance on any particular occasion, calculated by dividing the number of trials in which the word was said (column C) by the total number of words said (117). Column F shows the probability (p) of N'kisi achieving a hit by chance, calculated by multiplying the probabilities in column E by the number of images, as shown in column B.

A. Image	B. No. of Images	C. Times Word Said	D. No. of Hits	E. p word = C/117	F. p hit = E × B
1 Book	4	3	1	0.026	0.103
2 Bottle	5	3	0	0.026	0.128
3 Car	4	8	1	0.068	0.273
4 Cards	1	0	0	—	—
5 CD	7	0	0	—	—
6 Computer	4	0	0	—	—
7 Doctor	2	16	0	0.136	0.274
8 Feather	1	4	0	0.034	0.034
9 Fire	3	0	0	—	—
10 Flower	17	23	10	0.197	3.341
11 Glasses	7	10	1	0.085	0.598
12 Hug	7	5	1	0.043	0.299
13 Keys	3	0	0	—	—
14 Medicine	4	16	3	0.137	0.547
15 Naked body	4	11	3	0.094	0.376
16 Phone	6	6	1	0.051	0.308
17 Teeth	1	0	0	—	—
18 TV	1	0	0	—	—
19 Water	10	12	2	0.103	1.128
TOTALS	**90**	**117**	**23**	**—**	**7.409**

either a hit or a miss, since he never said these words. Thus a fairer way of analyzing the results was to exclude the trials involving these images. The results of this analysis are shown in Table B.3.II. This method reduced the number of misses, and so the proportion of N'kisi's hits increased. For example, by the majority scoring method (B), 23 words out of 82 were hits (28 percent). Nevertheless, using this method made little difference to the statistical significance of the results, as a comparison of parts I and II of Table B.3 shows.

In at least two other ways, this test procedure was not "fair" to N'kisi. First, since he was not a human subject, we could not explain to him that he was

Table B.3. *Statistical significance of N'kisi's hits in the telepathy experiment, using data from the three blind scorers.*

For the data in row A, all three scorers were in agreement; in row B, two were in agreement; and row C includes key words that were detected by only one out of three. The statistical significance is given in terms of the probability *(p)* that the observed results would have arisen by chance. The odds against the results arising by chance are given by the inverse of the probability: for example, a probability of $p = 0.0001$ is equivalent to odds against chance of 10,000 to one. The upper table (I) includes trials with images corresponding to all 19 key words; the lower table (II) includes only those trials with images corresponding to the 12 key words that N'kisi actually said in one or more of the trials. Jan van Bolhuis, a statistician at the Free University in Amsterdam, carried out the statistical analyses using three different methods. In the Randomized Permutation Analysis (RPA), the key words uttered by N'kisi during the series of trials were combined with the images used in these trials in 20,000 different random permutations. The probability of the observed number of hits arising by chance was calculated on the basis of how many times out of 20,000 there were as many or more "hits" as N'kisi actually obtained. In the second method, the Monte Carlo Procedure (MC), the probablility of N'kisi saying a given word in a given trial was calculated by dividing the number of times the key word was said by the total number of key words said, as in Table B.2. Then, for each trial, random "responses" were generated by the computer in accordance with the probabilities that any given key word would be said. This random generation of responses was repeated 20,000 times. The probability that N'kisi would have obtained the actual number of hits by chance was calculated from the number of random "trials" out of 20,000 in which there were as many "hits" as those actually observed, or more. This MC procedure resembles the RPA procedure, but it is much quicker to carry out, taking only minutes on the computer, rather than the days needed for the RPA. The third procedure simply compares the overall number of hits with the number of hits expected by chance on the basis of the probability of a given word being said in a given trial, as shown in Table B.2. This analysis used the binomial test (bn), and is cruder and less reliable than the RPA and MC methods.

I. Including All 19 Key Words

Scorers	Hits	Misses	p (RPA)	p (MC)	p (bn)
A. Three	19	86	0.004	0.004	0.0002
B. Two	23	94	0.0003	0.0002	0.000001
C. One	26	110	0.0002	0.0002	0.0000006

II. Including Only the 12 Key Words Actually Said

Scorers	Hits	Misses	p (RPA)	p (MC)	p (bn)
A. Three	19	55	0.005	0.004	0.0002
B. Two	23	59	0.0005	0.0003	0.000001
C. One	26	73	0.0003	0.0003	0.0000001

being tested for telepathy and that he was supposed to say the key word only in the two-minute trial period. On 13 occasions he either went on saying a key word that had been a hit in one trial after the next trial had begun, or else he said the word corresponding to the previous image only during the subsequent trial. These words were therefore counted as misses, but perhaps they were not really misses, but rather repetitions of hits, or delayed hits.

Second, N'kisi could not have known that we were confining our analysis to a list of prespecified key words. In some cases he said words or phrases that could well have been telepathic hits, but we could not count them as such in our formal analysis because of the prespecified scoring procedure. For example, in one trial Aimée was looking at a photograph of a car whose driver had his head out of the window. As she was looking at this protruding head, N'kisi said, "Oh, oh, careful, you put your head out."

For our own interest, Aimée and I scored the number of hits including examples such as the "head out" comment that did not involve prespecified key words. By this more flexible method, the total number of hits was 32, as opposed to the 23 hits in the method based on key words, as recorded by a majority of the independent scorers, and the 26 key-word hits recorded by at least one of the scorers. The formal analysis underestimated the number of hits because of the inflexible rules specified in advance. But in such a controversial area of research, rigidly defined criteria that eliminate as far as possible any subjective judgments are necessary, however unfair they may be to the parrot. Even with these rigid criteria, N'kisi's scores were far higher than chance, and highly significant statistically. The results therefore point to the conclusion that N'kisi really was picking up what was in Aimée's mind telepathically.

CHAPTER 3

A Study of the Milk Letdown Reflex in Nursing Mothers When Away from Their Babies

As described in chapter 3, Katy Barber, an experienced midwife, carried out this study for me. The nineteen women who took part were each given two sets of notebooks that they undertook to fill in for a period of eight weeks, during the period they were breast-feeding. The mother carried around one of the notebooks when she was away from her baby, and in it recorded the times at which her milk let down, and any other comments about her feelings. The baby's caregiver kept the other notebook and noted down the times at which the baby cried, seemed hungry, or showed other signs of distress. By comparing the two sets of notebooks, we could then determine whether the letdown occurred when the baby was distressed or not.

Out of the nineteen participants, seven never left their babies, or had no milk letdown when away from them. Three of the others had milk letdowns when their babies needed them, but the records were not kept well enough to analyze the results statistically.

That left nine mothers for whom the data could be analyzed in detail. I divided up the time the mothers were away from their babies into 10-minute periods, and calculated the number of 10-minute periods in which the babies showed signs of distress. On average, the babies showed distress in 9.4 percent of the 10-minute periods while their mothers were away. In total, these mothers had 88 milk letdowns when they were away from their babies. If these had happened at random, by chance 9 of them would have occurred when the babies were distressed. In fact, 35 did so. The odds against this result being due to chance are more than a billion to one.

Nevertheless, although the milk letdown occurred much more often when the babies were distressed than would be expected by chance, 53 out of 88 of the letdowns happened when there was no record of the babies being distressed. Why were there so many false alarms? Some of these may not in fact have been false alarms, because in 11 out of these 53 cases, the caregivers had written nothing in the notebook, which could mean that they simply forgot to do so, and the babies could in fact have been distressed. And a further 17 out of these 53 letdowns occurred with one particular mother during her lunch hour at work, when she habitually expressed breast milk, and the letdown often occurred as she was preparing to relieve the pressure in her breasts. Nevertheless, even excluding these from the total number of false alarms, there were still 25 unaccounted for, showing that the mother's letdown reflex was not a very reliable index of the baby's needs. In some of these cases the mothers commented that the letdowns may have reflected their own anxieties about leaving the baby, for example because it had just had an injection or was teething, or simply because they had rarely done so before.

Only one of the mothers returned to work on a full-time basis during the period of this study and had relatively frequent letdowns, permitting a possible examination of the synchronized-rhythm theory. Apart from the letdowns in her lunch break, when she was about to express milk or thinking of doing so, most occurred between 3:30 and 5:30 P.M., which was also during the period when her baby most often showed signs of distress. The mother's responses in this period could have been influenced telepathically by the baby, but they might also have been due to a physiological synchronization with her baby's feeding cycles. Nevertheless, excluding both these periods from the analysis, there were still significantly more letdowns that coincided with the baby's needs than would have been expected by chance: 8 as opposed to 1.7.

This preliminary study has given encouraging results, but much further research is needed. Most of the women in this study were first-time mothers, and only one of them returned to work while still breast-feeding. For future studies, it would be best to recruit experienced mothers, rather than mothers with their first baby, and also mothers who intend to return to work while still breast-feeding.

CHAPTER 6

The Natural History of Telephone Telepathy

Here is the questionnaire that I used in my surveys in Britain, the United States, Germany, and Argentina. Of course, in the German and Argentine surveys, I used translated versions.

SEEMINGLY TELEPATHIC TELEPHONE CALLS

A Questionnaire

1. Have you ever thought of somebody just as the telephone rang, or just before, and it was indeed the person you had been thinking of? (Exclude anticipations that could have an ordinary explanation, and include only those that seemed telepathic.)
   ○ Yes   ○ No
   (If no, answer only questions 2, 3, 7, and 8.)
2. Your age?
   ○ Under 18   ○ 31–50   ○ 71+
   ○ 19–30   ○ 51–70
3. Sex
   ○ Male   ○ Female
4. How often had you had the experience of seemingly telepathic telephone calls? (Please check one only.)
   ○ Almost every day   ○ At least once a month   ○ Less than once a year
   ○ At least once a week   ○ At least once a year
5. Has this ever happened with a mobile phone?
   ○ Yes   ○ No   ○ Don't have one

6. With whom have you had these experiences? (If more than one person in a given category, please put the number instead of a check.)

- ○ Father
- ○ Mother
- ○ Son
- ○ Daughter
- ○ Brother

- ○ Sister
- ○ Spouse
- ○ Partner
- ○ Male friend
- ○ Female friend

- ○ Male colleague
- ○ Female colleague
- ○ Employee
- ○ Employer
- ○ Others (please specify)

7. Have you ever found that you could think about somebody, wanting them to call you, and they would phone you soon afterwards in a way that seemed to be telepathic?
   ○ Yes   ○ No
8. Have you had any other kinds of telepathic experience?
   ○ Yes   ○ No
   If yes, please give a brief description:

I handed out the questionnaires in my lectures or seminars, usually after the lecture and before the question-and-discussion period. Everyone present was given a copy, and asked to fill it in then and there. Pens or pencils were supplied to people without them. There was a pause while people filled in the forms, which were then collected. The great majority filled in the questionnaire.

The total numbers of people who took part in this survey were as follows:

Argentina	220 women	114 men
Britain	134 women	59 men
Germany	496 women	169 men
U.S.	332 women	167 men
Totals:	**1,182 women**	**509 men**

In response to question 1, an average of 92 percent of respondents said they had thought of someone as the telephone rang, or just before, in a way that seemed telepathic. In all countries, a statistically significant higher proportion of women than men said they had had this experience (Figure 6.1).

The age distribution of people in the survey was as follows:

Under 18	2 percent
19–30	11 percent
31–50	46 percent
51–70	37 percent
Over 70	4 percent

In response to question 4, most people said this experience happened weekly or monthly, but some 10 percent said it happened daily (Figure B.1).

Most people who took part in the survey did not have mobile phones, but

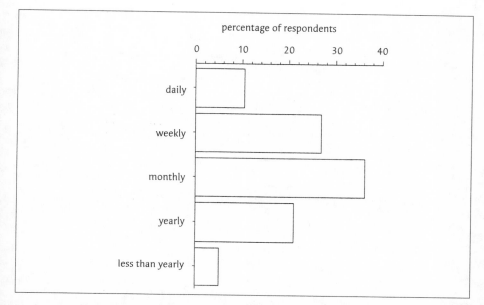

Figure B.1 *The frequencies with which respondents in the questionnaire surveys said they had seemingly telepathic experiences in relation to telephone calls. The data refer to the combined results from Argentina, Britain, Germany, and the United States.*

a total of 265 people said they had had the experience of seemingly telepathic telephone calls with mobile phones. This is a sufficiently large number to make it clear that the phenomenon does not depend on any particular type of telephone technology, and occurs both with signals traveling through copper wires and also in the form of radio waves.

The responses to question 6, "With whom have you had these experiences?" are summarized in Figure B.2. By far the commonest responses were with friends, followed by mothers, spouses, partners, and colleagues.

However, these figures could be misleading. Typically, people have either a spouse or a partner, and if these two categories were combined, they would exceed mothers. In future questionnaires, it would probably be best to have a single category of "spouse or partner" rather than two separate categories. Also, people have only one mother, and usually only one spouse or partner, but they may have several friends. Hence if the "friends" category were broken down into individual friends, "friends" might not be so preponderant when compared with mothers, spouses, and partners.

As discussed in chapter 6, more people responded to same-sex friends than to opposite-sex friends, but both women and men responded more to mothers than to fathers, and to a lesser extent, both responded more to sisters than

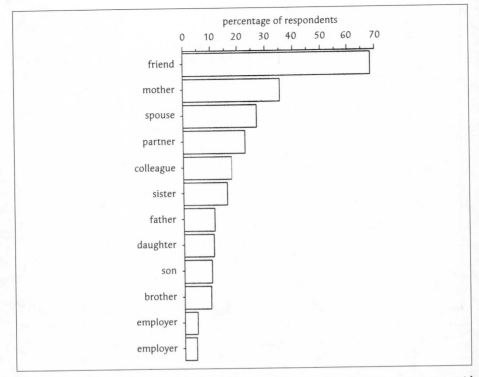

Figure B.2 *Categories of callers with whom respondents in the questionnaire surveys said they had had seemingly telepathic experiences. The data refer to the combined results from Argentina, Britain, Germany, and the United States.*

brothers. By contrast, mothers responded slightly more to daughters than to sons, and fathers slightly more to sons than to daughters (Figure B.3).

One reason for the greater responses to mothers and sisters than to fathers and brothers may be that people tend to form tighter emotional bonds with mothers than with fathers, or with sisters than with brothers. A more mundane explanation might be that women tend to phone other family members more frequently than men do, and hence there may be more chances for their calls to be anticipated.

Experimental Research on Telepathic Telephone Calls

As described in chapter 6, in my experiments on telepathy in connection with telephone calls, each subject had four potential callers. In some cases the subjects nominated all four callers themselves; in others the subjects nominated

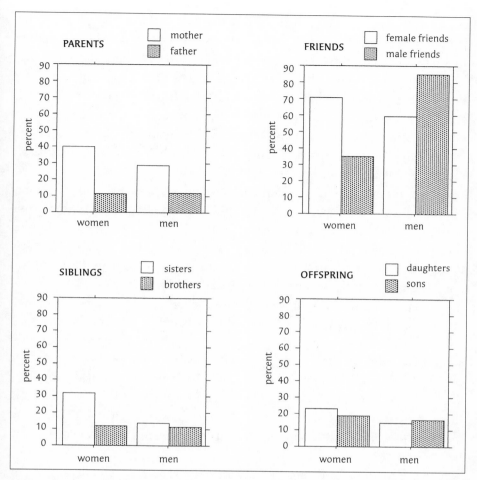

Figure B.3 *Seemingly telepathic responses to telephone calls from male and female friends and family members by women and men. The data refer to the combined results from Argentina, Britain, Germany, and the United States.*

two or three, and the other callers were provided by my research associate, and were strangers to the subjects.

My research associate Pam Smart and I recruited subjects through advertisements in local newspapers or through Internet recruitment agencies. We paid subjects for taking part (usually at a rate of £10 per trial). They received the same payment whether or not their guesses were right. We asked people to take part in an initial series of ten trials, and some subjects were then asked to take part in a further series of ten trials. (Some subjects were unable to complete the whole series owing to changes in their circumstances.)

At a prearranged time, the subject received a call from one of these four people. Before answering the phone, he or she had to guess who was calling. In trials that were not videotaped, the caller answered the phone by saying "Hello, [name]" before the other person had spoken. The caller reported immediately afterward what this guess had been. In videotaped trials, the subject sat in a chair in the field of view of the camera, and was filmed continuously on time-coded videotape for fifteen minutes before the time prearranged for the call. The subject spoke to the camera what his or her guess was before picking up the telephone.

Each of the four callers for a given subject was assigned a number between 1 and 4, and before each trial the experimenter selected one of the four callers at random by throwing a die from a dice cup. (We used professional casino-quality dice and dice cups, purchased in Las Vegas.) This selection of the caller was carried out less than fifteen minutes before the call was due, when subjects being filmed were already on camera.

The probability of the subjects' guesses being right by chance was 1 in 4, or 25 percent. In a total of 571 unfilmed trials completed by September 2002, 231 guesses were correct (40 percent) and 370 wrong. This result was extremely significant statistically, with odds against chance of quadrillions to one (by the binomial test, $p = 4 \times 10^{-16}$). By the same date, we had completed a total of 283 videotaped trials, with 127 correct guesses (45 percent). Again, there were very significantly more correct guesses than the 25 percent expected by chance, with odds against this result being due to chance of trillions to one ($p = 3 \times 10^{-13}$).

In a series of 100 videotaped trails with Sue Hawksley, who lives in Wakefield, Yorkshire, England, the callers included several friends and also her mother. With her mother, her success rate was at the chance level of 25 percent, and with her sister it was slightly higher, at 29 percent. But with her friends, the success rates were considerably greater, and with one it was 75 percent (Table B.4).

In a second videotaped series of 85 trials, two of Sue Hawksley's callers were strangers and two were friends who had taken part in the first series (Gayle and Jayne). With these friends her success rate was 66 percent, and with the strangers only 18 percent (Figure 6.3). The difference in her scores with friends and strangers was highly significant statistically (by the 2×2 contingency test, chi-squared $= 19.2$, $p = 0.00001$). In this series her overall success rate was 45 percent, very significantly above the chance level, with odds against this result being due to chance of 25,000 to 1 (by the binomial test, $p = 0.00004$).

Table B.4. *Results of Sue Hawksley's telephone telepathy trials with different callers: her mother, Emma; her sister, Gillian; her friends Gayle and Kay (who are sisters); and Jayne. There was also one trial with her daughter Laura.* All trials were videotaped and took place between September 2000 and March 2001 in Wakefield, Yorkshire.

Caller	Total Calls	Right	Wrong	Percent Right
Emma	16	4	12	25
Gayle	20	13	7	65
Gillian	22	6	15	29
Jayne	20	15	5	75
Kay	21	10	11	48
Laura	1	0	1	0
TOTALS	**100**	**49**	**51**	**49**

In these series of trials with Sue Hawksley, as in trials with other subjects, the callers were all in different places: some at home, some at work, and some in other locations. In a further experiment with Sue, all four callers were gathered together in the same place, in a hotel called the Holmfield Arms, a mile from her home in Wakefield. I was there myself to coordinate the experiment. We used a private room for making the calls. Three of the callers were friends (Gayle, Kay, and Jayne). The other caller was my research associate Pam Smart, who had only met Sue once before, and was one of the "strangers" in the previous series of trials. Two independent cameramen filmed all the trials using synchronized video cameras. One was in the Holmfield Arms, and filmed me throwing the die to select the caller for each trial, and then filmed the caller as she made the call. The other cameraman was in Sue Hawksley's house. During the course of a day we carried out seventeen trials, with the results shown in Table B.5. The pattern of results was similar to that in Sue Hawksley's other trials: the scores with her friends at levels well above chance, while with Pam Smart she was exactly at the chance level.

Sue Hawksley told us that in some trials she felt much more confident about her guesses than in others. In order to explore whether these feelings were related to the accuracy of the guesses, in 144 of the videotaped trials, Sue said to the camera how confident she was about her guess before answering the telephone. Her confidence ratings were later transcribed from the videotape. There were three grades: "confident," "not very confident," and "just

Table B.5. *Results of a telephone telepathy experiment on June 15, 2001, in Wakefield, Yorkshire, England.*
One cameraman filmed the subject, Sue Hawksley, continuously throughout each trial at her home. Another cameraman filmed the callers in another location a mile away. The subject's overall result of 8 correct guesses out of 17 trials was significantly above the chance level (by the binomial test, $p = 0.04$).

Caller	Trials	Right	Wrong	% Right
Gayle	5	2	3	40
Jayne	5	3	2	60
Kay	3	2	1	67
Pam	4	1	3	25
TOTALS	17	8	9	47

guessing." The results showed that when she was thought she was just guessing, in fact she was, with only 29 percent success, not significantly higher than the chance level of 25 percent. When she was not very confident, she was right 35 percent of the time, significantly higher than chance, but not much higher. But when she felt confident, she was spectacularly successful, correct 82 percent of the time, with odds against this result being due to chance of billions to one (Table B.6).

Another subject who took part in an extended series of videotaped trials was Scott Reeves, who lives in London. Two of his callers were his parents, who live in Southport, Lancashire, 250 miles away, in the northwest of England; the other two were my associate Pam Smart and Carole Macaulay, neither of whom he had met. The prediction was that he would do better with

Table B.6. *The relationship between Sue Hawksley's confidence and her success in guessing who was calling in 144 videotaped trials.*
The probabilities (p) shown in the last column were calculated by means of the binomial test and give a measure of how significantly her success rate differed from chance. NS means "not significant."

Confidence	No. of Trials	Right	Wrong	% Right	p
Confident	28	23	5	82	4×10^{-10}
Not confident	95	33	62	35	0.02
Just guessing	21	6	15	29	NS

the familiar people, his parents, than with the people he had not met, Pam and Carole. This turned out to be the case. His success rate with his parents was 47 percent and with the other two callers 25 percent (Figure 6.3).

The data for individual callers show that he did better with his mother than with his father, and better with Carole than with Pam (Table B.7). In percentage terms, he was actually more successful with Carole than with his father, although with such small numbers of trials, this difference was not significant. One possible reason for his higher-than-expected success rate with Carole could be that he and she built up a friendly relationship on the telephone, so she soon became less of a stranger.

In order to investigate whether distance had any effect on telephone telepathy, we recruited subjects living in Britain who could nominate callers in countries at least a thousand miles away. They also nominated callers in Britain. Table B.8 shows their success rates with these two categories of callers. (For some of these subjects, one or more of their four callers were strangers, but the data for their calls with strangers are not included in this table, since the comparison of interest here is between familiar people who are geographically nearer or farther away.) The overall success rate with overseas callers was 61 percent, which was higher than that with callers in Britain, 36 percent. There is no suggestion here that telepathy is diminished by distance. The greater success with the people farther away may well have been because they were mostly close friends or family members with strong bonds to the subjects.

Table B.7. *Telephone telepathy experiments with Scott Reeves as subject, carried out between June 2001 and January 2002.*

His callers were his mother and father (Brenda and Brian Reeves), Pam Smart, and Carole Macaulay. All these trials were videotaped. His guesses were correct in 12 out of 30 trials, an overall success rate of 40 percent. (Statistical significance by the binomial test: $p = 0.05$).

Caller	No. of Trials	Right	Wrong	% Right
Mother	7	4	3	57
Father	10	4	6	40
Carole	7	3	4	43
Pam	6	1	5	17
TOTALS	**30**	**12**	**18**	**40**

Table B.8. *Telephone telepathy trials with subjects living in Britain who had callers living at least 1,000 miles away, compared with other callers in Britain, also nominated by the subjects.*
Calls from strangers are not included in this table.

Subject	Overseas Callers In:	Overseas Right	Overseas Wrong	British Right	British Wrong
Claire Morsman	Australia/NZ	7	7	2	6
Kama Murray	South Africa	3	1	0	4
Marina Theofrastos	South Africa	2	0	0	1
Rebecca Harlow	South Africa	1	1	1	1
Tope Adebanji	Nigeria	3	1	1	0
Dhuha Awad	Yemen	4	2	0	1
Esther Leoneis	Greece	2	2	4	1
TOTALS		22	14	8	14
% right		61		36	

CHAPTER 8

A Questionnaire Survey About the Sense of Being Stared At

In order to find out more about the circumstances in which people experienced the sense of being stared at, I handed out the following questionnaire in lectures I was giving. As with the questionnaire on pages 307–308, this was usually done after the lecture and before the question-and-discussion period. Everyone present was given a copy, and asked to fill it in then and there, and supplied with a pen or pencil if they did not have one. There was a pause while people filled in the forms, which were then collected. The great majority of people present filled in the questionnaire.

THE FEELING OF BEING STARED AT

A Questionnaire

1. Have you ever felt that someone was looking at you from behind, and turned around to find they were? (Exclude experiences that could have an ordinary explanation.)
   ○ Yes   ○ No
   If no, omit questions 4 to 7. If yes, please answer all questions.
2. Your age?
   ○ Under 18   ○ 31–50   ○ 71+
   ○ 19–30   ○ 51–70

3. Sex:
   ○ Male   ○ Female
4. How often had you had the experience of being stared at from behind? (Please check one only.)
   ○ At least once a week   ○ At least once a month
   ○ At least once a year   ○ Less than once a year
5. With whom have you had these experiences?
   ○ Father   ○ Sister   ○ Female friend
   ○ Mother   ○ Spouse   ○ Male stranger
   ○ Son   ○ Partner   ○ Female stranger
   ○ Daughter   ○ Colleague   ○ Others (please specify)
   ○ Brother   ○ Male friend
6. In what situations have you had these experiences?
   ○ In the street   ○ In a theater, lecture   ○ At home
   ○ In a car   theater, etc.   ○ Others (please specify)
   ○ In a café, bar, or club   ○ In a train or bus
7. Have you ever had this kind of experience with an animal?
   ○ Yes   ○ No
   If so, what species?
8. Have you ever found that you could stare at someone from behind and make them turn around?
   ○ Yes   ○ No
9. What kinds of emotions or intentions have you found affect other people when you are staring at them?
   ○ Wish to attract their   ○ Anger   ○ Curiosity
      attention   ○ Sexual desire   ○ Others (please specify)
10. Have you ever found that you could stare at an animal from behind and make it react?
    ○ Yes   ○ No
    If so, please give further details.
11. Please give a brief description of any particularly memorable occasion on which you have felt yourself being stared at, or have affected someone by staring at them.

The respondents were students at Cambridge University (36 in all), participants in a scientific symposium in Sweden (34), and citizens in Huntington, New York (50); Atlanta, Georgia (30); Arlington, Virginia (53); and Asheville, North Carolina (126). Of these respondents, 175 were women and 154 men. The age distribution of the respondents was:

Under 18	4 percent
19–30	22 percent
31–50	36 percent
51–70	35 percent
Over 70	2 percent

More women (81 percent) than men (74 percent) answered yes to question 1, and a similar sex difference showed up in all the locations. Those who said yes then supplied further details of their experiences, as follows.

In response to question 4, about the frequency of these experiences, the responses were as follows:

Weekly	18 percent
Monthly	33 percent
Yearly	30 percent
Less than yearly	19 percent

The answers to question 5 are summarized in Table B.9, below, and shown in Figure 8.1. The highest proportion of respondents said they had been stared at by male strangers (76 percent), followed by female strangers (54 percent). Next in order came female friends, male friends, colleagues, spouses, mothers, partners, fathers, and other family members.

Table B.9. *Percentages of respondents who had had the experience of being stared at from behind, who had reacted to different categories of starers.*

Figures are given for all respondents, and also separately for women and men. The figures in this table are based on responses from 154 women and 113 men. The statistical significance of the difference between the responses of men and women (calculated on the basis of 2 × 2 contingency tables) is shown in the p column. The figures in the column are measures of the probability (p) that this difference between men and women is a matter of chance. The lower the probability values, the greater the odds against chance. Some differences were not statistically significant (NS).

Starer	All	Women	Men	p
Male stranger	76	87	64	< 0.0001
Female stranger	54	48	62	0.02
Female friend	32	28	38	NS
Male friend	27	26	27	NS
Colleague	24	32	13	0.003
Spouse	18	22	12	0.03
Mother	16	17	15	NS
Partner	14	24	12	0.02
Father	12	14	11	NS
Daughter	10	16	3	0.0005
Sister	9	11	6	NS
Son	7	9	4	NS
Brother	3	5	2	NS

There were several interesting sex differences in these responses. When women were being looked at by strangers, they reacted more to male strangers than to female strangers. And in relation to friends, men said they had reacted more to looks of female than male friends. In response to looks from spouses, partners, colleagues, and daughters, women reacted significantly more than men.

The answers to questions 6, 8, and 9 are summarized in chapter 8, and detailed results are shown in Figures 8.2 and 8.3. In response to question 8, significantly more women (88 percent) than men (71 percent) said they had found they could stare at others and make them turn around, as discussed in chapter 8.

In response to question 7, 55 percent of the respondents said they had felt they were being looked at by an animal. Out of the 329 respondents, 79 said this had happened with a dog; 59 with a cat; 9 with a horse; 6 with a deer; 5 with a bird; 3 with a bear; 2 with a snake; and 1 each with a goat, pig, monkey, squirrel, mouse, dolphin, iguana, and sea turtle. Thus the list included mammals, birds, and reptiles, but no amphibians, fish, or insects and other invertebrates.

In response to question 10, again 55 percent said they had found they could stare at an animal from behind and make it turn around. Most reports concerned cats and dogs, but some people said this had happened with horses and with birds.

CHAPTER 13

Challenges by Skeptics About the Sense of Being Stared At

ROBERT BAKER

The largest skeptical organization in the world is CSICOP, the Committee for the Scientific Investigation of Claims of the Paranormal, based in Amherst, New York. In 2000, the CSICOP magazine, the *Skeptical Inquirer*, published two articles claiming that the feeling of being stared at was illusory. Both attempted to refute my own research on the subject.

The first article was by Robert Baker, a CSICOP Fellow and retired psychology professor in Kentucky, who carried out two "demonstrations" designed to disprove that people could tell when they are being stared at. For his first demonstration, Baker selected people who were engrossed in eating or drinking, watching TV, working at computer terminals, or reading in the University of

Kentucky library. He unobtrusively positioned himself behind them and stared at them. He then introduced himself and asked them to fill in a response sheet.

Baker's prediction was that people engrossed in an activity would "never" attend to a sensation of being stared at. The response Baker expected people to give was: "During the last five minutes I was totally unaware that anyone was looking at me." Sure enough, 35 out of 40 people gave this response. But five did not. Two people reported that they had been aware that they were "being observed and stared at," and three reported they felt something was "wrong." Baker noted that while he was staring at these particular subjects, "All three stood up, looked around, shifted their position several times and appeared to be momentarily distracted on a number of occasions."

The answers of these five people went against Baker's prediction, so he retrospectively introduced another criterion. He ruled that subjects should be able to say *where he had been sitting* when he was looking at them. None could. He regarded their inability to do so as a "good reason to believe that they were . . . not aware that they were being viewed."[2] But this begs the question. A sensitivity to being stared at does not necessarily imply remembering the position of a starer several minutes later.

To complete his analysis, Baker "discarded" the results from the two people who said they knew they had been stared at. He regarded them as "suspect" because one claimed she was constantly being spied on, and the other claimed he had extrasensory ability. But if the sense of being stared at really exists, people with paranoid tendencies might be more sensitive than most,[3] and so might people who claim to have extrasensory abilities.

In his second "demonstration," Baker, together with a student, looked at subjects from behind at random intervals. The subjects were asked to write down when they thought they were being looked at. Baker told them that they would be stared at for five one-minute periods during a 20-minute trial. In accordance with his expectations, he found that their guesses were no better than chance.

Why were these results so different from the consistently positive and statistically significant effects obtained by myself and others? There were several important differences in procedure.

In my own experimental design, in a series of 20 trials there were more or less equal numbers of control and looking trials, whereas in Baker's there were 15 control and only 5 looking one-minute periods. This peculiar feature precluded a straightforward statistical analysis of the results. Each subject was allowed only five guesses as to when they were being looked at. If guesses were entirely random, misses would be three times more probable than hits.

In my experiments, each trial lasted only about ten seconds, but Baker used sixty-second trial periods. In preliminary tests, I found that subjects gave the highest percentage of correct guesses when they were asked to guess quickly, without spending much time thinking about their responses.

Baker also introduced three different sources of distraction for his subjects:

1. Beside each time on the specimen score sheet shown in Baker's paper, there was a pair of unexplained numbers, for example: "0801 1&2; 0802 2&3."[4] I wrote to Baker to ask for a clarification, but his reply confused matters further. He said that the times shown on his specimen time-sheet "were not on the subject's time-sheet at all—since they, of course, would differ from subject to subject. The 1&2 indicates the first minute, the numbers 2&3 indicates the second minute of the time-period, etc."

   If I had been one of Baker's subjects, I would have been at a loss to understand his instructions. If I thought I was being stared at, to start with I would have had to calculate from the clock in which minute this happened. Then I would have had to decide where to write my response. If I felt I was being stared at in the seventh minute, would I write my response on the line labeled "6&7" or on the line labeled "7&8"?

2. The instructions published by Baker were self-contradictory. He wrote that the subjects were told that there would be five one-minute staring periods. Yet the specimen instruction sheet stated that subjects would be stared at "five times for two minutes each." Baker now concedes that this was an error.[5] To confuse matters further, in his article the one-minute staring periods were also described as "five-minute periods."[6]

3. Not only did Baker instruct his subjects to guess when they were being stared at, but they were also asked to compare their guesses with their responses in other periods so that they could change their previous guesses if they wanted to. This instruction might well have helped to distract subjects still further from their immediate feelings.

   Like Baker, I predict that those who follow his experimental methods (including his ambiguous instructions) are likely to replicate his negative results. But I also predict that my own positive results should be replicable by those who use similar methods to my own.[7]

DAVID MARKS AND JOHN COLWELL

The second article in the *Skeptical Inquirer* was by two British psychologists, David Marks (also a CSICOP Fellow) and John Colwell.[8] It was based on two experiments by Colwell and his colleagues, carried out at the University of North London.[9] In their principal experiment, they used methods based on my own procedures, and followed the randomized sequences of 20 looking and not-looking trials given on my website. Far from refuting my findings, they replicated them, and obtained strikingly significant positive results (Figure 11.4).

They then tried to dismiss the positive results of this experiment by technical arguments about my randomized sequences. The sequences I then provided on my website were "counterbalanced" in the light of comments from other skeptics about problems that could arise from "structureless" randomizations.[10] For each sequence of 20 trials, another sequence was the opposite, so that every time in one sequence there was a looking trial, in the other there was a not-looking trial, and vice versa.

Marks and Colwell speculated that because the subjects were given feedback, their success in the staring trials might be due to an "implicit learning" of structures hidden in my randomized sequences, so that they could somehow guess whether a looking or not-looking trial was coming next. But Marks and Colwell offered no evidence that the participants really did detect any hidden structures in the randomized sequences. They did not take the trouble to test their own hypothesis, which they could have done by examining the participants' score sheets to see if the guesses really did follow the patterns they predicted. When I asked Colwell for copies of the score sheets in order to find out if the facts fitted their hypothesis, he refused to let me see the data.

Marks and Colwell also failed to mention a fatal flaw in their speculation, perhaps hoping that readers would not spot it. If implicit learning had taken place, it should have enabled participants to improve equally in looking *and* not-looking trials. But this is not what happened. Improvements occurred *only* in the looking trials.

Although their argument failed to fit their own data, Marks and Colwell claimed that their pattern-detection hypothesis invalidated all my staring experiments. But not only was their hypothesis refuted by their own findings, it was irrelevant. They based their criticisms of my work on a brief account by a journalist in a popular science magazine. They were apparently unaware of the detailed papers on the subject that I had already published in peer-reviewed scientific journals. If they had read these papers, they would have seen that their pattern-detection hypothesis had already been refuted.

First, in more than 5,000 of my own trials, the randomization was indeed "structureless," and was carried out by each starer before each trial by tossing a coin.[11] The same was true of more than 3,000 trials in German and American schools.[12] Thus the highly significant positive results in these experiments cannot be explained, as they claimed, as "an artifact of pseudo randomization."[13] Also, in the computerized experiment in the New Metropolis science museum in Amsterdam experiment (described on pages 176–178), the sequence of looking and not-looking trials was determined by a randomization program within the computer that provided structureless random sequences. In these trials, involving more than 18,700 subjects, the results were positive and astronomically significant. In these tests there could have been no implicit learning of the kind postulated by Marks and Colwell.

Second, when I adopted the modified sequences that Marks and Colwell describe as pseudo-random, I changed the experimental design so that feedback was no longer given to the subjects. Since the pattern-detection hypothesis depends on feedback, it cannot account for the fact that in more than 10,000 trials without feedback, there were still highly significant positive results.[14]

Colwell and his colleagues, with Marks's advice, tried to clinch the matter by means of a second experiment, in which they used structureless randomizations. But this experiment differed from the first experiment in another important respect: one of Colwell's academic colleagues did all the staring. (In the first experiment, which gave positive results, a graduate student had done the staring.) Sure enough, the results showed no effect of staring. They jumped to the conclusion that that this was because of the structureless randomization. In their article, Marks and Colwell did not mention that a different person did the staring in the second experiment. All this experiment showed was that Colwell's colleague was an ineffective starer. Thousands of similar trials using structureless randomizations carried out by myself and independently replicated by others have given extremely significant positive results.[15]

There is already experimental evidence that different starers can obtain very different results. In staring tests carried out through closed-circuit television, Richard Wiseman, a skeptic, obtained results at chance levels when he was the starer. In the same experiment, another starer, Marilyn Schlitz, obtained statistically significant positive results (see below).

CCTV Experiments and Experimenter Effects

Richard Wiseman, a British Fellow of CSICOP, started his research on the staring effect by carrying out some CCTV staring experiments in which students served as starers and subjects. As in the research on staring by Colwell and his colleagues, discussed above, the first experiment gave significant positive results.[16] Again like Colwell and his colleagues, Wiseman tried to dismiss this result as an artifact of the randomization procedure, but did not actually test his hypothesis using his own data. I asked him to supply me with the data so I could find out if his artifact theory was true or not. He first told me that the data were "inaccessible," but later managed to retrieve the results for some of the subjects, which he kindly passed on to me. I found that they did not support his artifact theory.[17]

In his subsequent CCTV experiments, Wiseman and his colleagues did the staring themselves. Then, as they expected, they found there was no significant effect.

Fortunately, this is not the end of the story. Marilyn Schlitz, a psychologist from California who had obtained consistently positive results in CCTV staring experiments, went to Wiseman's laboratory in England, where they carried out a joint experiment under identical conditions. Half the student subjects were allocated at random to Schlitz, the other half to Wiseman. Schlitz obtained statistically significant positive results with herself as the experimenter and looker. Meanwhile, Wiseman obtained nonsignificant results with himself as the experimenter and looker.[18]

Thus there was a striking "experimenter effect." Such effects are well known in psychology and medicine.[19] Generally speaking, experimenters tend to obtain the results they expect, which is why many psychology experiments and clinical trials are carried out under "double blind" conditions, where neither experimenters nor subjects know who is receiving which treatment. Certainly Wiseman and Schlitz had very different expectations, she taking the possibility of staring effects seriously, and he taking the approach that, in his words, it was a "waste of time but here we go."[20]

Such experimenter effects are not symmetrical. The failure of the subjects to detect Wiseman's stares implies only that Wiseman was an ineffective starer. His negative expectations could well have influenced the way he looked at the subjects. By contrast, the detection of Schlitz's stares by the participants under conditions that excluded sensory cues implies the existence of an unexplained sensitivity to stares.

A Brief History of Early Theories of Vision

As we saw in chapter 13, in the ancient world there was a long-running debate about the nature of vision, with far-ranging implications for the understanding of the nature of the mind. There were four main theories: the intromission theory, in which images moved into the eye, but nothing moved out; the extramission theory, according to which attention moved out; theories combining intromission and extramission; and theories about the medium through which vision took place.

David Lindberg has described the history of this debate in an excellent book, *Theories of Vision from Al-Kindi to Kepler*, which I recommend to anyone who is interested in the details. Here I give only a brief summary of the developments of ideas that led up to the currently orthodox theory of vision, first proposed by Johannes Kepler in 1604.

Ancient Greece and Rome

The atomist philosophers, starting with Leucippus and Democritus in the fifth century B.C., put forward the earliest version of materialism, the doctrine that reality consists of indivisible particles of matter in motion—in other words, of atoms moving in a void. They proposed that material particles streamed off the surface of things in all directions. Vision depended on these particles entering the eye, where they caused visual sensations. In order to account for coherent images, they supposed that the particles were joined together in thin films that traveled into the eye. The Roman atomist Lucretius (who died around 55 B.C.) called these films *simulacra*, and compared them to the smoke thrown off by burning wood, or the heat from fires, or the skins cast off by insects or snakes when they molt.[1]

This intromission theory raised fundamental problems that proponents of rival theories delighted in pointing out. For example, how can material simulacra pass through each other without interference? And how can the image of a large object like a mountain shrink enough to enter the pupil? This theory also failed to account for what happens once the films have entered the eye.

How do they account for seeing? Also, this theory made vision into a passive process, and hence ignored the active role of attention.

Nevertheless, some atomists admitted that influences could move both ways, not just into the eyes, but also outward from the looker. Democritus explained the evil eye on the same principle as vision: the action at a distance was mediated by moving material images charged with hostile mental contents that "remain persistently attached to the person victimized, and thus disturb and injure both body and mind."[2]

Early in the fifth century B.C., members of the Pythagorean school proposed an early version of the extramission theory, suggesting that a visual current was projected outward from the eye, and that the eye had "fire" within it. One reason for this belief in inner light was that people can see light with their eyes closed as a result of a blow — as in "seeing stars" after being hit on the head.

The philosopher Plato (427–347 B.C.) adopted the idea of an outward-moving visual current, but proposed that it combined with daylight to form a "single homogeneous body" stretching from the eye to the visible object. This extended medium was the instrument of visual power reaching out from the eye. Through it, influences from the visible object passed to the soul. In effect, Plato combined intromission and extramission theories with the idea of an intermediate medium between the object and the eye.[3]

Aristotle (384–322 B.C.), who ranks with Plato as the greatest of Greek philosophers, was originally Plato's student. He followed Plato in emphasizing the importance of an intermediate medium between the eye and the object seen, but he rejected both the intromission and extramission theories. Nothing material passed in or out of the eye during vision. The intermediate medium he called the "transparent." Its properties were shared by air, water, and many solid objects, and also by the heavenly firmament, through which we see the stars. He thought of light not as a material substance, but as a "state of the transparent," resulting from the presence of fire or some other luminous body. As a state of the medium, rather than as a substance, light required no time for propagation, but instantaneously connected the eye to the visible object. So although Aristotle sometimes seemed to be supporting the idea that there was an intromission of influences from the visible object to the eye, he did not mean that they actually moved in time from one to the other. Rather, the visible object was the source or cause of the instantaneous change of state of the transparent through which influences were transmitted to the soul of the observer.

Like Aristotle and Plato, the Stoic school of philosophy in ancient Greece and Rome emphasized the importance of the medium between the observer and the visible object. Like Plato, the Stoic philosophers thought that an optical spirit flowed out from the eye and combined with daylight to form a visual cone. This cone, with its point inside the eye, was the medium of vision. Some suggested that this medium became an instrument of the soul and acted as an extension of the perceiver. As the Roman Stoic Cicero (106–43 B.C.) put it, "the air itself sees together with us."

The Stoic theory was adopted by Galen (c. A.D. 129–199), a Greco-Roman physician who had a profound influence on medicine for some 1,400 years. Like Cicero, he thought that the air itself became an instrument of perception, and "sight reaches out through the air to the coloured body."[4] But as a physician, Galen added a wealth of anatomical detail to his theory of vision, and concluded that the lens was the chief organ of sight in the eye.

The final major contribution of classical antiquity was that of the mathematicians, starting with the great geometer Euclid (active c. 300 B.C.). Euclid's approach was strictly mathematical and excluded practically all aspects of vision that could not be reduced to geometry. He adopted an extramission theory according to which rays proceeded outward from the eye in a cone. The vertex, or point, of the cone was in the eye, and the rays were assumed to move outward until they intercepted the object. Euclid, of course, recognized that light played a part in vision, but he said very little about the way it was related to the visual rays projecting outward from the eyes.

Euclid's geometrical approach was taken further by other mathematicians, most notably by Claudius Ptolemy (active A.D. 127–148). Ptolemy thought that the visual flux coming out of the eyes consisted of ether, or what was called the *quintessence*, or fifth element (over and above earth, air, fire, and water).[5] He rejected Euclid's idea of discrete rays coming out of the eyes with gaps between the rays, and thought of the visual cone as continuous. The visual cone was modified by light, and the perception of color depended on the presence of light.

All these theories of vision had strengths and weakness, and the different schools of thought coexisted for well over a thousand years. The debate continued within the Arab world, especially between the ninth and thirteenth centuries A.D., and it was mainly through Arabic sources that these ideas were transmitted to medieval Europe.

Islamic Theories of Vision

The translation of Greek philosophical, mathematical, and medical texts into Arabic reached its culmination in the ninth century A.D., and led to a great intellectual ferment in the Islamic world. In this period, science became an international enterprise for the first time. The Islamic world stretched from Spain and Morocco to the borders of China. As well as drawing on the Greek traditions, mainly through Alexandria, in Egypt, it was also enriched by the cultures of Persia, India, central Asia, and China. This great civilization provided an essential transition between the civilizations of antiquity and the dawn of the modern era in the West.

One of the pioneers in the process of assimilating and developing the Greek tradition was Al-Kindi (c.801–c.866), who lived in Baghdad. He saw his own task as to communicate, correct, and complete this inherited body of learning. In this spirit, he wrote some 260 books on all branches of study, including one on optics. But optics was not just one subject among many; Al-Kindi saw the radiation of power or force as fundamental to all nature: "It is manifest that everything in this world . . . produces rays in its own manner like a star. . . . Everything that has actual existence in the world of the elements emits rays in every direction which fill the whole world." In an astonishing vision of interconnectedness, he thought that radiation bound the world into a vast network in which everything acted on everything else to produce natural effects. Stars acted on Earth, and magnets, fire, sound, and colors acted on objects in their vicinity. Even words conceived by the mind could radiate power and produce effects outside the mind.[6]

Thus for Al-Kindi the laws of radiation were the laws of nature, and optics was fundamental to all other sciences. Although he was aware of the different schools of thought about the nature of vision, he rejected the intromission theories, and adopted a modified version of Euclid's theory, with visual power issuing forth from the eye. Like Ptolemy, he did not accept the idea of distinct rays, but proposed that the visual cone was a continuous beam of radiation, sensitive throughout.[7] He did not think of this radiation as an actual movement of material substance out of the eye, but rather as a transformation of the medium.

Al-Kindi's treatise on vision became a popular textbook in Islam, and influenced the course of thinking for centuries. But some Muslim scholars rejected the extramission theory in favor of versions of the Aristotelian theory, most notably Avicenna (980–1037), while others followed Galen in concentrating on the anatomy of the eye.

Alhazen (965–1039) put forward a new theory of vision that brought together ideas from the rival schools of thought into a brilliant synthesis. He adopted the anatomical insights of Galen and his followers, the Aristotelian idea of a transparent medium, and the mathematical approach of Euclid and Al-Kindi. His principal innovation was to reverse the direction of the influences traveling in the visual cone. Instead of radiation moving out of the eye, light moved in. He thus laid the foundations of the intromission theory of vision that became the orthodox scientific view in the early seventeenth century.[8] But although his theory dealt impressively with the way that influences entered the eye, he had much less to say about what occurred when they arrived there. He thought the sensitive organ in the eye was the lens, but had no explanation as to how the lens's sensitivity could result in vision itself.

The Middle Ages and the Renaissance

Astronomy and optics were the sciences that flourished most in medieval Europe. The development of ideas in these fields was strongly influenced by the translation of texts from Arabic and Greek into Latin, and intellectual fashions changed as more material became available. Up until the end of the twelfth century, the main influences were from Plato and the Platonic tradition, and the extramission theory of vision was predominant. The influence of this theory increased when translations of Al-Kindi from Arabic and of Ptolemy from Greek became available, with their mathematical analysis of visual rays issuing from the eye.

By the thirteenth century, a flood of new translations included most of the works of Aristotle, together with the writings of his Arabic commentators, and also the optical writings of Alhazen. Practically all the points of view and arguments from the classical and Islamic worlds were now available to European scholars in major centers of learning like Paris and Oxford.

Several important scholars contributed to the new debate about the nature of vision. The most influential of these was Roger Bacon (c.1220–c.1292), an English Franciscan friar. He based his theory of vision on Alhazen, with a cone or pyramid of radiation entering the eye, and elaborated the geometry of the rays and of visual perspective. But Bacon was not trying to promote the intromission school of thought at the expense of the others. He wanted to achieve a synthesis, and did so by including Aristotelian ideas about the transparent medium, and by acknowledging the existence of visual rays passing out from the eye through this medium to the visible object.

For the next two hundred years Bacon's theory continued to be influential. But Aristotelians increasingly dominated the medieval universities, and although there were many scholastic discussions of the Aristotelian approach, there were few original contributions.[9]

In the Renaissance there was no radical break with the medieval theories of vision, but in four areas (see page 200), technological advances contributed to

Johannes Kepler's theory of the retinal image, and hence to modern science. First, the development of linear perspective, already apparent in the paintings of Giotto (c.1266–1337), and explicitly formulated by the Florentine artist Brunelleschi (1377–1446). Second, advances in the study of anatomy in general, and an improved understanding of the structure of the eye in particular, with a recognition of the true shape of the lens, previously regarded as a sphere. Third, the study of the camera obscura. And, fourth, from the study of spectacle lenses, the recognition that double convex lenses cause rays of light to converge.

All these advances provided essential ingredients for Kepler's synthesis, which was in many ways a culmination of the medieval tradition of optics. In the words of David Lindberg, "Kepler presented a new solution (but not a new kind of solution) to a medieval problem, defined some six hundred years earlier by Alhazen. By taking the medieval tradition seriously, by accepting its most basic assumptions but insisting on more rigour and consistency than the medieval perspectivists themselves had been able to achieve, he was able to perfect it."[10] Yet his synthesis led to new problems, still unsolved today, as discussed in chapter 13.

Notes

Introduction: The Seventh Sense and the Extended Mind
1. Matthews, 1996.
2. Horgan, 1996.
3. Kuhn, 1970.
4. Inglis, 1977, pp. 148–49.
5. Michell and Rickard, 1977, p. 16.
6. Popper and Eccles, 1977.
7. Electromagnetic senses, in McFarland, 1981.
8. Downer, 1999.
9. Baker, 1980.
10. Droscher, 1971.
11. Ibid.
12. An example of this kind of controversy occurred in Britain in the autumn of 2001. It started innocently enough when the Royal Mail issued a set of stamps to commemorate the hundredth anniversary of the Nobel Prize. Several Nobel laureates were asked for their comments, which the Post Office published in a booklet when the stamps were issued. A Nobel laureate in physics, Brian Josephson, a professor at Cambridge University, mentioned that he thought developments in quantum theory "may lead to an explanation of processes still not understood within conventional science such as telepathy." This comment stirred up a hornet's nest, and he was soon being denounced by angry academics and other opponents of "the paranormal." For example, David Deutsch, a physicist at Oxford University, told the *Observer* newspaper, "Telepathy simply does not exist. The Royal Mail has let itself be hoodwinked into supporting ideas that are complete nonsense" (McKie, 2001). It turned out that Deutsch was so sure of his opinion that he had felt no need to study the evidence for telepathy (Carr, 2001). And James Randi, a professional debunker from the United States, told listeners on BBC radio that it was "a refuge of scoundrels" to try to explain telepathy in terms of quantum physics (BBC Radio 4 *Today* program, October 2, 2001). Josephson's Nobel Prize is for quantum physics; Randi is a conjurer with no scientific credentials.
13. For example, the same David Deutsch who dismissed Brian Josephson's ideas (see note above) is a leading proponent of parallel universes (Deutsch, 1997).
14. E.g., Deutsch, 1997.
15. Broad and Wade, 1985.
16. Sabbagh, 1999.

17. The cases of W. J. Levy (J. B. Rhine, 1974) and S. G. Soal (Markwick, 1978).

18. Certainly experimental research in psychic research and parapsychology is more rigorous in terms of methodology than in any other area of science. In a recent survey of journals in various fields of science, I found that 85 percent of the experiments in psychic research and parapsychology involved blind methodologies, compared with 6 percent in the medical sciences, 5 percent in psychology, 1 percent in biology, and none at all in physics and chemistry (Sheldrake, 1998b, 1998c).

19. Gardner 1983, p. 57.

20. Ibid., p. 58.

21. For example, in the United States at the beginning of the twenty-first century, there were fewer than ten professional scientists working full-time in parapsychology, all of whom were privately funded. The worldwide circulation of the main journal in the field, the *Journal of Parapsychology*, was less than 800 (Hansen, 2001). Meanwhile, there are several well-funded and powerful organizations whose main purpose is to propagate a negative attitude to all psychic phenomena, such as CSICOP, the Committee for the Scientific Investigation of Claims of the Paranormal. This organization does not carry out research, but is primarily concerned with debunking. The CSICOP magazine, *Skeptical Inquirer*, has a circulation of some 50,000 and calls itself "the magazine for science and reason." Many of its supporters are academics, and include several prominent scientists, such as the biologist Richard Dawkins, as well as influential figures in the scientific media like Sir John Maddox, the former editor of *Nature*, a leading scientific journal.

22. Piaget, 1973, p. 280.

23. Crick, 1994, p. 3.

24. The neurologist Wilder Penfield found that he could evoke vivid flashes of memory by stimulating the cerebral cortices of patients during brain operations, but although this stimulation could evoke memories, he did not think they were located in the part stimulated, and he also concluded that the memory "is not in the cortex" (Penfield, 1975).

Chapter 1. Picking Up Thoughts and Intentions

1. Frederic Myers, one of the pioneers of psychic research, introduced the term *telepathy*, in 1882. (Myers, 1882).

2. Gallup and Newport, 1991.

3. Blackmore, 1997.

4. E.g., Schouten, 1982.

5. Sheldrake and Smart, 1997; Sheldrake, Lawlor, and Turney, 1998; Brown and Sheldrake, 1998.

6. Sheldrake, 1999a, chapter 7.

7. Woodhouse, 1992, p. 54.

8. "It is tempting when one is riding a very well schooled horse, or a horse that knows one very well indeed, to think the horse is receiving telepathic messages. However, it may just be slight movements of the rider which are interpreted by the horse and acted upon" (Kiley-Worthington, 1987, pp. 88–89).

9. Pepperberg, 1999.

10. We are doing further experiments, and Aimée is monitoring N'kisi's ongoing acquisition of language, and continuing to study the way he uses it.

11. Gurney, Myers, and Podmore, 1886, chapter 6, case 37.

12. With the help of people to whom this happens quite frequently, it should be possible to do experimental tests by asking them to guess what tune they will hear on the radio before it is switched on. With a large enough sample of guesses, it should be possible to work out whether this is a matter of coincidence.

13. For a wide range of examples, see Eason, 1994, 1995.

14. Schwarz, 1972.

15. Ibid., p. 77.

16. Ibid., p. 152.

17. Ibid., p. 203.

18. Galton, 1883.

19. Penrose, 1989, pp. 424–27

20. *Penguin Dictionary of Psychology*, pp. 785–86.

21. Freud, 1955, pp. 175–93.

22. Ibid., 179–80.

23. For a review, see J. Ehrenwald, Psi, psychotherapy and psychoanalysis, in Wolman, 1977.

24. A pioneer in the exploration of telepathy in psychoanalysis was Jule Eisenbud (Eisenbud, 1970).

25. Mayer, 1996, p. 718.

26. Ibid.

27. Mayer, 2001.

28. See, for example, Whan, 2000.

29. Jung, 1963, pp. 137–38.

30. Here, for example, is a possible experiment that could be performed live on television. The popular TV quiz show *Who Wants to Be a Millionaire?* has a multiple-choice format, in which contestants have to choose among four possible answers for each question. For the purposes of this experiment, in some trials the answers could be shown on the screen to the viewers. In other trials the answers would not be shown. Do the contestants give a greater number of correct replies when the answers are known to millions of viewers than when they are not?

31. See Murphy, 1992.

32. Murphy and White, 1978, p. 52.

33. Ibid., p. 52.

34. Hawkins, 1983.
35. Ibid., p. 43.
36. Novak, 1976, pp. 135–36.

Chapter 2. Thought Transference in the Laboratory
1. Temple, 1989, chapter 5; Richet, 1923.
2. Gregory, 1919.
3. Quoted in Gurney, Myers, and Podmore, 1886, vol. 2, p. 324.
4. Gregory, 1919, p. 212.
5. Clements, 1983.
6. Wallace, 1874, chapter 10.
7. Gurney, Myers, and Podmore, 1886, vol. 2, p. 340.
8. Ibid., p. 344.
9. Gurney, Myers, and Podmore, 1886, vol. 1, chapter 2.
10. Ibid.
11. Ibid.
12. Ibid.
13. For a review, see Thouless, 1972, chapter 5.
14. Sinclair, 1930.
15. Radin, 1997, p. 97.
16. For a detailed review, see Radin, 1997.
17. J. B. Rhine, 1937, p. 56.
18. For a summary of these results, see Radin, 1997.
19. J. B. Rhine, 1937.
20. L. E. Rhine, 1967.
21. J. B. Rhine, 1954, p. 24.
22. J. B. Rhine, 1937, p. 115
23. Schmeidler and McConnell, 1958.
24. J. B. Rhine, 1954, p. 166.
25. Fenwick and Fenwick, 1998.
26. Ullman, Krippner, and Vaughan, 1973.
27. The image with the greatest correspondence to the transcript was 1, and that with the least 8. If the actual image used was in the top four, this was considered a hit; and if it ranked 5 or below, it was a miss. If telepathy did not occur in dreams, by chance about half the tests would be hits and about half misses. In other words, the average score would be 50 percent.
28. Radin, 1997, chapter 5.
29. Ibid., p. 78.
30. Radin, 1997.
31. E.g., Wiseman, Smith, and Kornbrot, 1996.
32. E.g., Parker, 2000.
33. In 1999, two researchers, one of them a well-known skeptic, Richard Wiseman,

claimed that the combined results of new ganzfeld studies were not significantly above chance (Milton and Wiseman, 1999). But they had arrived at this result by including a number of nonstandard experiments, including clairvoyance trials in which there were no senders, and they had also omitted some recent highly successful experiments. When these were included, the combined results were indeed statistically significant (Milton, 1999). Their analysis was flawed in a number of other ways (Storm and Ertel, 2001; see also Milton and Wiseman, 2001), and was the subject of an intensive discussion among experts, an edited version of which has been published (Schmeidler and Edge, 1999). For a comprehensive updated review, see Schlitz and Radin, 2002.

34. Broughton and Alexander, 1997.
35. Bem, Palmer, and Broughton, 2001; Storm and Ertel, 2000.
36. Bem et al., 2001.
37. Schlitz and Honorton, 1992.
38. Dalton, 1997.
39. Broughton and Alexander, 1997.
40. By contrast, dogmatic skeptics have simply ignored the evidence. For example, in 2001, Professor Lewis Wolpert, a biologist at London University, speaking as a scientific authority on a Discovery Channel television show, claimed that "there is no evidence for telepathy of any kind" (*Animal X*, Discovery Channel, U.S.A., August 31, 2001). And a few months later a well-known physicist at Oxford University, David Deutsch, asserted in the *Observer* newspaper that "telepathy simply does not exist" (McKie, 2001). These claims were untrue. But I doubt that assertions like these are deliberate lies. Rather, they are expressions of prejudice and ignorance.
41. For reviews of this research, see Schlitz and Braud, 1997, and Delanoy, 2001.
42. Delanoy and Sah, 1994.
43. Recordon, Stratton, and Peters, 1968.
44. In their published paper, Peters and his colleagues did not provide a statistical analysis. At my request, Jan van Bolhuis, assistant professor of statistics at the Free University of Amsterdam, has analyzed their results, using the binomial test, and the figures I quote in the text are the result of his calculations.
45. The only problem with these remarkably successful tests was that the boy's mother wanted to see the next card before she said "right" or "no" in response to the guess for the previous card. This left open the remote possibility that she was somehow passing information by an unconscious code in the intonation with which she spoke these words. But Peters and his colleagues thought this was extremely unlikely, and they could detect no trace of such a code in the tape recordings of the test sessions. Moreover, the boy was severely retarded mentally, and the test took place so fast that the use of a code seemed practically inconceivable. In addition, the tapes were listened to carefully by three magicians, all members of the Magic Circle, and they, too, were unable to detect any possible

code. I also listened to them myself, and could see no possibility of a code in the mother's words, or in any other possible sounds.

46. Recordon, Stratton, and Peters, 1968, p. 396.

Chapter 3. Telepathic Calls
1. Quoted in Stevenson, 1970, pp. 5–6.
2. L. E. Rhine, 1981, p. 88.
3. Ibid., p. 46.
4. Stevenson, 1970, p. 89.
5. Ibid., pp. 61–62.
6. Stoppard, 1985.
7. Eason, 1992.
8. Sheldrake, 2002.
9. Williams, 1960, p. 208
10. Long, 1919.

Chapter 4. Distant Deaths and Distress
1. Gurney, Myers, and Podmore, 1886, chapter 5.
2. Inglis, 1985.
3. Myers, 1903, p. xvi.
4. Ibid., p. xvii.
5. Inglis, 1977, p. 382.
6. Gurney, Myers, and Podmore, 1886, vol. 1, case 76.
7. Gurney, Myers, and Podmore, 1886, vol. 2, p. 723.
8. Ibid.
9. Quoted in Kelly, 2001.
10. For a helpful summary of these calculations, see Broad, 1962, chapter 5.
11. E.g., Stevenson, 1970; L. E. Rhine, 1981.
12. Stevenson, 1970, p. 17.
13. Ibid., p. 24.
14. Ibid., p. 25.
15. L. E. Rhine, 1981, p. 20.
16. Stevenson, 1970, p. 22.
17. Ibid., pp. 24, 183.
18. For a range of examples, see Sheldrake, 1999a.
19. Playfair, 1999, 2003.

Chapter 5. The Effects of Intentions at a Distance
1. *Country Life*, November 5, 1999.
2. Details of these experiments can be read in our published papers on the subject (Sheldrake and Smart, 1998, 2000a) and in Appendix B of Sheldrake, 1999a.

3. Sheldrake and Smart, 2000b.
4. Berger, 2001, p. 240.
5. Adamson, 1960, p. 28.
6. Ibid., p. 137.
7. Sitwell, 1946, p. 144.
8. Hygen, 1987.
9. Ibid.
10. Lang, 1911.
11. Twain, 1884.

Chapter 6. Telephone Telepathy
1. Van der Post, 1962, pp. 236–37.
2. Perhaps this percentage was inflated because some people who would have answered no did not bother to fill in and return the questionnaires. In fact, about 20 percent of the people surveyed did not return the questionnaire, so the real total of people surveyed was around 2,113. In the worst-case scenario, assuming that *all* those who did not fill in the form would have answered no, this would lower the percentage answering yes to 74 percent. But that is still a clear majority.
3. Sheldrake, 2000d; Brown and Sheldrake, 2001.
4. Sheldrake, 2000d; Brown and Sheldrake, 2001.
5. This figure includes the results from all the subjects we have tested, including those who showed no significant telepathic abilities.
6. Sheldrake and Smart, 2003a.
7. Sheldrake and Smart, 2003b.
8. By the binomial test, $p = 0.00004$.
9. By the binomial test, $p = 10^{-16}$.
10. Comparing the results with friends and strangers using a 2×2 contingency table, chi-squared = 25.65; $p = 0.0000002$ (2 tailed).
11. Cooper, 1982; Braude, 1979.
12. Sheldrake, 1999a.
13. Steiger and Steiger, 1992, p. 16.
14. By the binomial test, $p = 0.0000001$.

Chapter 7. The Evolution of Telepathy
1. Sheldrake, 1999a.
2. Morell, 1997.
3. Clutton-Brock, 1981.
4. Sheldrake and Smart, 1998; Sheldrake, Lawlor, and Turney, 1998; Brown and Sheldrake, 1999.
5. Wylder, 1978.
6. Blake, 1975.

7. The stress was not imposed on the rabbit by any specific stressful stimulus, but rather arose spontaneously in relation to its environment.

8. Peoc'h, 1997.

9. Long, 1919, pp. 101–5.

10. Ibid., p. 95.

11. For a more detailed discussion, see Sheldrake, 1999a, chapter 13.

12. Carlson, 2000.

13. Available at www.red3d.com/cwr/boids. See also a more complex model with "carnivorous boids" made by Ariel Dolan at www.aridolan.com/eFloys.html.

14. For an example in which a flock of pigeons was studied in three dimensions by the use of two cameras, see Pomeroy and Heppner, 1992. And for a review of research on flocks and other animal groups, see Parrish and Hammer, 1997.

15. Heppner, Convissar, Moonan, and Anderson, 1985.

16. Gould and Heppner, 1974.

17. E.g., Selous, 1931.

18. The conventional theory is that inherited differences in flock behavior are coded in the genes. Then somehow this "genetic program" for flocking behavior expresses itself in the formation of flocks, through individual-based programs, analogous to those in the artificial-life boids model. Apart from the difficulty of explaining flocking behavior in terms of such programs, there is also the problem that genetic programs are only metaphors. What genes actually do is code for the sequences of amino acids in proteins. How does the making of particular proteins cause brains to develop as they do? And then how do these proteins cause particular patterns of movement within flocks? In addition, these movements are supposed to be organized through some internal representation, inside the brain, of the birds' visual world, and how does this work? There are a lot of deep unanswered questions. The standard view is extremely speculative, and there is very little evidence for it.

19. Schechter, 1999.

20. "Our model combines features of the Navier-Stokes equation for a simple compressible fluid and a simple relaxational model for spins in a ferromagnet." See http://materialscience@uoregon.edu/toner.html.

21. Long, 1919.

22. Wilson, 1980.

23. Partridge, Schooling, in McFarland, 1981.

24. Huth and Wissel, 1992. For information on the Virtual Fishtank, an exhibit at the Boston Museum of Science, see www.mos.org.

25. See, for example, Niwa, 1994.

26. Partridge, Schooling, in McFarland, 1981.

27. Hölldobler and Wilson, 1994.

28. Von Frisch, 1975.

29. Marais, 1973. See also the discussion of this work in Sheldrake, 1994, chapter 3.

Chapter 8. The Sense of Being Stared At

1. Told me by A. R. Mansfield.
2. Sheldrake, 1994.
3. Sheldrake, 1994; Braud et al., 1993a.
4. Cottrell, Winer, and Smith, 1996.
5. Conan Doyle, 1884.
6. Poortman, 1959.
7. Haynes, 1973.
8. Braud et al., 1993a; Cottrell, Winer, and Smith, 1996.
9. The statistical significance of this difference between women and men was calculated using a 2×2 contingency table: chi-squared $= 15.15$; $p < 0.0001$.
10. Titchener, 1898.
11. The only significant exceptions are some recent experiments by skeptics, in which the skeptics themselves were the starers, as discussed in chapter 11 and Appendix B.

Chapter 9. Surveillance and Wariness

1. Matthews, 1996, p. 16.
2. Payne, 1981, p. 34.
3. Kokubo, 1998.
4. Yamamoto et al., 2000.
5. Payne, 1981, p. 72.

Chapter 10. Animal Sensitivity

1. D. McFarland, Defensive behaviour, in McFarland, 1981.
2. Morris, 1990, p. 69.
3. Willmer, 1999.
4. Morris, 1990.
5. Reichel-Dolmatoff, 1997, p. 115.
6. Boone, 1970, pp. 74–75.
7. Ehrenreich, 1997, p. 40.
8. Ibid, p. 43.
9. Ibid., p. 52
10. Corbett, 1986, pp. 179–81
11. Goodall, 2000, p. 47.
12. London, 1991, pp. 77–78.
13. Long, 1919, pp. 91–92.
14. Gould, 1989.

Chapter 11. Experiments on the Sense of Being Stared At

1. Titchener, 1898.
2. Ibid.

3. Coover, 1913. For a more detailed account, see Coover, 1917.
4. Poortman, 1939.
5. Poortman, 1959.
6. Poortman, 1959, did not analyze his own results statistically, but I have done so (Sheldrake, 1994) and found that they were indeed significant at the $p < 0.05$ level.
7. The results were never published, but were written up in an M.A. thesis (Peterson, 1978).
8. Only a brief summary of this research was published (Williams, 1983).
9. Sheldrake, 1981, p. 165.
10. By Michael Mastrandrea at Nueva Middle School, in Hillsborough, California.
11. The coordinators were Dr. Harris Stone and James Trifone.
12. Sheldrake, 1999b.
13. Sheldrake, 1998a.
14. Sheldrake, 2001.
15. Sheldrake, 1998a, 1999b, 2001. As well as projects in schools and colleges, a version of my staring experiment was included in a traveling art exhibition called "Do It" in art museums throughout North America, again with positive and significant results, showing the usual pattern. For example, at the Nickle Arts Museum at the University of Calgary, Canada, 37 looker-subject pairs carried out this experiment in early 1999. In the looking trials, 63 percent of the guesses were correct; in the not-looking trials, 50 percent; and in the overall totals, 56.5 percent. The subjectwise scores were $27 + 7 - 3 =$ for looking trials; $12 + 16 - 9 =$ for not-looking trials; and $23 + 7 - 7 =$ overall.
16. I am grateful to Professor Nicholas Humphrey for suggesting this method of analysis.
17. Coover based his conclusions only on the overall average scores, which were indeed close to chance levels. But when the performances of individual subjects were taken into account, not only was the overall result positive $(5 + 3 - 2 =)$, but that there was also a marked tendency for people to be right when they were actually being looked at $(7 + 2 - 1 =)$ while they were at the chance level in the not-looking trials $(5 + 5 - 0 =)$.
18. To prevent clues being given by differences in the way the signal was given to indicate the beginning of each trial, I used mechanical clickers, bells, or bleepers to signal the beginning of the trial. The results were the same whatever the kind of signal (Sheldrake, 1999b). Also, in many of the tests carried out in schools, all the pairs of students did their trials at the same time and the teachers gave a signal to the whole class. Since each pair was using a different randomization procedure, but all heard the same signal from the teacher at the beginning of each trial, this signal could not have conveyed to the subjects whether or not they were being looked at. The results were still positive and showed the usual pattern (Sheldrake, 1998a, 1999b).

19. Sheldrake, 2001.
20. Sheldrake, 2000a, 2001.
21. Sheldrake, 2000a.
22. For summaries of the data from other investigators, see Sheldrake, 1998a, 1999b, 2000a, 2001.
23. The statistical procedure was developed by Jan van Bolhuis, an assistant professor of statistics at the Amsterdam Free University.
24. Although the statistical significance of the results of the Amsterdam experiment is astronomical, and they provide a seemingly overwhelming confirmation of the reality of the sense of being stared at, the experiments were carried out unsupervised, and it is possible that some children cheated. But while some may have done so, I think it is very unlikely that cheating alone can explain the observed results. Nevertheless, it would be very desirable to conduct this experiment under more controlled conditions. Improved versions of this experiment could be set up relatively easily in other museums and schools, as well as on home computers. Also, the computer in the Amsterdam experiment was programmed to record only the numbers of people who did or did not have "eyes in the back of their heads." It did not record the results separately for looking and not-looking trials. In an improved version of this experiment, it would be important to make sure that these data were retained.
25. These experiments were carried out by my research associate Pam Smart with her sisters, nephews, nieces, and their friends in Ramsbottom, Greater Manchester, England. In the looking trials, the subjects' correct guesses were very significantly above chance levels, and in the not-looking trials they were not significantly different from chance. The overall scores from a total of 28 tests (made up of 20 trials each) were $17 + 7 - 4 =$ (i.e., 17 subjects were more often right than wrong; 7 were more often wrong than right; and 4 made an equal number of right and wrong guesses). This positive result was statistically significant ($p < 0.05$).
26. The scores were $23 + 10 - 4 =$.
27. The prison was in Willich. The scores were $9 + 3 - 1 =$.
28. BBC1 TV, *Out of This World*, first broadcast on July 30, 1996.
29. The management of the BBC insisted that the studio audience sign release forms in advance, warning them that they might be part of an experiment on secret observation. When they first entered the building we arranged for trainees to film them from behind pillars in a rather obvious way, in the hope that when the real experiment took place most would think it was already over.
30. Sheldrake, 1996.
31. I visited the Mind Science Foundation in San Antonio, Texas, in 1986, when William Braud and his colleagues were doing experiments on the effects of intention on subjects in separate rooms, measuring their skin resistance as a measure of emotional arousal. I spoke about my own preliminary research on the

sense of being stared at, using direct staring. Braud and his colleagues subsequently combined these two approaches in their pioneering CCTV experiments.
32. Braud, Shafer, and Andrews, 1990, 1993a, 1993b; Schlitz and LaBerge, 1994, 1997; Delanoy, 2001; Schlitz and Braud, 1997. For reviews, see Delanoy, 2001; Schmidt et al., in press.

Chapter 12. The Evil Eye and the Rise of Rationalism

1. Jones, 1992.
2. Dundes, 1992.
3. Ibid., p. 67.
4. At ICRISAT, the International Crops Research Institute for the Semi-Arid Tropics.
5. Dundes, 1992, p. 12.
6. Ibid., p. 13.
7. Budge, 1930, p. 13.
8. Huxley, 1990.
9. Elsworthy, 1895, p. 143.
10. Dundes, 1992, p. 112.
11. Ibid., p. 259.
12. Ibid.
13. Thomas, 1973, p. 79.
14. Ibid., p. 540.
15. Ibid., p. 535.
16. Ibid., p. 531.
17. Ibid., pp. 533–34.
18. Ibid., p. 684.
19. The last prosecution under the 1736 Witchcraft Act was the trial of the spiritualist medium Helen Duncan in 1944. As a result of her trial, the Witchcraft Act was replaced by the Fraudulent Mediums Act of 1951 (Cassirer, 1996).

Chapter 13. Are Images in the Brain, or Are They Where They Seem to Be?

1. Lindberg, 1981.
2. Ibid., p. 202.
3. Ibid.
4. For Descartes, the spiritual realm was that of God, angels, and human minds, but it excluded animals and everything else in the material world.
5. Descartes was deliberately and consciously rejecting the Aristotelian philosophy of the Middle Ages, which had recognized souls in all living beings, including all plants and animals. The Greek word for soul was *psyche*, from which words like *psychology* and *psychotherapy* and *psychic* are derived. The Latin word for the soul was *anima*, the root of the English words *animate* and *animal*. In this animistic view, against which Descartes was rebelling, human beings and animals

shared with plants a nutritive or vegetative soul that gave shape to the body as it grew and maintained its form. Humans also shared with animals an animal, or sensitive, soul that coordinated their sensations, movements, and instincts. In addition, humans possessed an intellectual or rational soul. Before Descartes, the rational mind was seen as part of a larger psychic system that pervaded the entire body and reached out beyond it. No one supposed that all aspects of this extended psyche were conscious. To use modern terminology, the conscious mind was part of a much larger psychic system that was largely unconscious.

6. Burtt, 1932, chapter 4.
7. Cartesian dualism is taken for granted by most educated people, but few would want to try to defend this position if challenged, because it leads to such insoluble problems. Two rare exceptions were the neurophysiologist Sir John Eccles and the philosopher of science Sir Karl Popper, who together wrote a book called *The Self and Its Brain: An Argument for Interactionism* (Popper and Eccles, 1977).
8. Wallace, 2000, pp. 28–29.
9. Ibid., p. 49.
10. The standard view of cognitive psychology can be described as the representational-computational view of mind. For a penetrating critique, see Shannon, 1993.
11. Kayser, 1997, p. 43.
12. Dennett, 1991, p. 33.
13. Wallace, 2000, p. 147.
14. Greenfield, 2000, pp. 12–15.
15. Piaget, 1974.
16. Winer and Cottrell, 1996.
17. Ibid.
18. Ibid.
19. Winer et al., 1996.
20. A higher percentage of schoolchildren and college students said they believed the intromission theory when they were asked purely verbal questions than when they were asked using pictures or computer animations, or by drawing their own diagrams (Cottrell and Winer, 1994; Winer et al., 1996). Winer and his colleagues suggested that this might be because in purely verbal responses the subjects were more likely to repeat what they had been taught, namely, the "correct" theory of vision, whereas the pictorial method accessed a "developmentally less advanced" and "more primitive" type of response (Winer and Cottrell, 1996b).
21. Cottrell, Winer, and Smith, 1996.
22. Winer and Cottrell, 1996b.
23. Winer et al., 2002.
24. Winer and Cottrell, 1996a.

25. E.g., Bergson, 1911; Burtt, 1932.
26. Quoted in Velmans, 2000, p. 112.
27. Ibid., p. 114.
28. Ibid., p. 115.
29. For a discussion of the way visual perception actually works in the real world, see Gibson, 1986. See also Noë, 2002.
30. The detection of this change in the background field may or may not attract the person's attention, just as a change in any other sense might do. For example, someone might turn around in response to a sudden, unexpected noise from behind. Whether the person turns depends partly on the intensity of the noise. Most people would respond to the sound of an explosion behind them; few would respond to a slight rustling sound. But the responses would also depend on people's emotional states, needs, and interests. For example, people's sensitivity to noises from behind is greater if they feel wary, and lesser if they feel secure. In a similar way, the sense of being stared at is affected by people's emotional state, and also by competing claims on their attention. The sense of being stared at, like telepathy and other aspects of the seventh sense, may primarily influence the emotions, with their associated physiological changes. Such emotional responses may well be unconscious. For an illuminating discussion of the role of emotions and their influences on feelings and consciousness, see Damasio, 2000.
31. Within science, fields of some kind are the only medium through which such influences could pass. Maybe, at some time in the future, new ways of thinking about interactions at a distance will be possible. But for the time being, some kind of field theory seems the only option. I recognize that this field hypothesis of the sense of being stared is still vague, and leaves many questions unanswered. But it seems to me the only feasible way of trying to understand this sense. Unless fields reach out of brains when we look at things, there is no way that staring could be detected in the absence of other sensory clues. And unless we have fields all around us, we would not be able to detect stares from behind. The only alternative to detecting stares through fields would be to suppose that we have stare-detecting sense organs in our skins, such as "eyes in the back of our heads." But if this were the case, the sense of being stared at should not work when people are clothed and their skin is covered. Also, people with long hair that covers the backs of their necks should be immune to the effects of staring from behind. But this is not the case. The sense of being stared at still seems to work when people are fully clothed, when they have long hair, and when no bare skin is visible.

Chapter 14. Remote Viewing

1. Inglis, 1985.
2. St. Barbe Baker, 1942, p. 41.
3. Puthoff and Targ, 1976.

4. Braude, 1979.
5. Radin, 1997, p. 101. Now that some of the SRI research has been declassified, some of the subjects have written their own stories about their experiences, notably McMoneagle, 1993, and Graff, 1998.
6. E.g., Millay, 1999.
7. Schlitz and Gruber, 1980, 1981.
8. Schlitz and Gruber, 1980, p. 315.
9. Radin, 1997, pp. 102–3.
10. Ibid, p. 103.
11. Ibid, p. 105.
12. Myers, 1997.
13. Inglis, 1985, pp. 38–39.
14. Targ and Katra, 1998, pp. 70–72.
15. Ibid., p. 49.
16. J. B. Rhine, 1937.
17. E.g., J. B. Rhine, 1937, 1954.
18. Taylor, 1998.

Chapter 15. Animal Premonitions
1. For a discussion, see Sheldrake, 1999a, chapter 15.
2. Newsom and Scott, 1999.
3. Sheldrake, 1999a, chapter 15.
4. Ibid.
5. Hampshire, 1999.
6. By Support Dogs, a British charity that specializes in training seizure-alert dogs (Support Dogs, P.O. Box 447, Sheffield S6 6YZ, England).
7. Edney, 1993.
8. Sheldrake, 1999a, chapter 6.
9. Chen et al., 2000.

Chapter 16. Human Forebodings
1. Saltmarsh, 1938.
2. Ibid., p. 56.
3. Barker, 1967.
4. Behe, 1988.
5. Ibid., p. 137.
6. Ibid., pp. 125–26.
7. Stevenson, 1960.
8. Cox, 1956.

Chapter 17. Exploring Precognition
1. Dunne, 1958, p. 96.
2. J. B. Rhine, 1954; L. E. Rhine, 1967.

3. Radin, 1997, chapter 7.
4. Ibid.
5. Targ and Katra, 1998.
6. Radin, 1997, chapter 7.
7. Sobel, 1996.
8. There is, however, one very interesting study on changes in hormone levels in the blood before being awakened at an unusually early time, carried out in Lübeck, Germany, by Jan Born and his colleagues (Born et al., 1999). In these studies, volunteers slept for three nights under laboratory conditions, with continuous monitoring of their brain activity and eye movements, and with blood samples being taken every fifteen minutes. They went to bed at midnight. They were told that on one of the three nights they would be awakened at 6:00 A.M., but that the other two nights they would be awakened at 9:00 A.M. In fact, on one of these nights they were awakened at 6:00 A.M. by surprise. When subjects knew they would be awakened early, there was a significant increase in the level of the hormone adrenocorticotropin over a period of an hour before they were awakened. There was a smaller increase in the control subjects, who were awakened at 9:00 A.M., and also in the subjects awakened at 6:00 A.M. by surprise. This hormone is related to stress responses, and shows that the subjects who expected to be awakened early were already responding physiologically well in advance. However, this study did not examine the phenomenon of spontaneous waking before the expected or surprise arousal at 6:00 A.M. Also, the fifteen-minute intervals between blood samples were too far apart to detect any increase in stress hormone levels just before waking in the subjects awakened unexpectedly.
9. Dunne, 1958, chapter 6.
10. *Oxford Shorter English Dictionary* (Oxford, England: Oxford University Press, 1975).

Chapter 18. Extended Minds and Modern Physics
1. Amoebalike cells are called amoebocytes, and form one of the three main families of cell types in multicellular animals, according to the classification of the cytologist E. N. Willmer (Willmer, 1970).
2. Ibid.
3. Radin, 1997; Jahn and Dunne, 1987.
4. Dossey, 1993, 2001; Astin, Harkness, and Ernst, 2000.
5. For details, see the websites http://noosphere.princeton.edu and http://www.boundaryinstitute.org/randomness.htm.
6. Laplace 1819 (reprinted 1951), p. 4.
7. For a much more detailed and comprehensive review, see Stokes, 1987.
8. See Smythies, 2000.
9. See, for example, Dunne's theory of serial time (Dunne, 1958).

10. Schmeidler, 1972.
11. Targ, Puthoff, and May, 1979.
12. Gleick, 1988.
13. Davies, 1984; Greene, 1999.
14. Hawking, 2001.
15. Smythies, 2000.
16. Taylor, 2000.
17. Taylor is, of course, aware of these problems and attempts to overcome them (Taylor, 2000).
18. Stanford, 1978.
19. Braud, 1981.
20. Braud understood that lability was related to randomness, and in this sense his ideas were in close agreement with Stanford's and with theories based on quantum physics.
21. For a more detailed discussion of Braud's theory, see Hansen, 2001, chapter 21.
22. Walker, 1974, 1984.
23. For a review of Walker's ideas, see Hansen, 2001, chapter 21.
24. Davies and Gribbin, 1991, chapter 7.
25. Josephson and Pallikari-Viras, 1991.

Chapter 19. Mental Fields
1. Brenner, 2001.
2. Thom, 1975, 1983.
3. For a detailed discussion of these ideas, see Sheldrake, 1981, 1988.
4. Ibid.
5. Creighton, 1978.
6. Karplus, 1995.
7. Anfinsen and Scheraga, 1975.
8. Zhou and Karplus, 1999.
9. "The topology of a protein's native state appears to determine the major features of its folding free-energy landscape" (D. Baker, 2000).
10. For a more detailed discussion, including possible experimental tests, see Sheldrake, 1988.
11. Freeman, 1999, p. 107.
12. Ibid., p. 117.
13. Melzack, 1992.
14. Mitchell, 1872, p. 352.
15. Feldman, 1940.
16. Sheldrake, 1994, chapter 5.
17. For a more detailed account of medical research on phantoms, see Sheldrake, 1994.

18. Weinstein and Sarsen, 1961.
19. Melzack, 1992.
20. Ibid.
21. Ibid.
22. Melzack, 1989, p. 9.
23. Ibid.
24. Ramachandran and Blakeslee, 1998.
25. Melzack and Bromage, 1973.
26. Bromage and Melzack, 1974.
27. As Poeck and Orgass, 1971, have shown, numerous problems arise when researchers try to fit the body schema into the brain, and the concept is usually used in a way that involves circular arguments.
28. E.g., Palmer, 1979.
29. Quoted in Blackmore, 1983, p. 48.
30. Moody, 1976. For an account of recent research on near-death experiences in patients with cardiac arrest, see van Lommel, 2001, and Parnia, 2001, and also www.horizon-research.co.uk.
31. Melzack, 1989, p. 4. See also Phillips, 2000, p. 11.

Appendix A. How to Take Part in Research
1. Sheldrake and Smart, 1998, 2000a, 2000b.

Appendix B. Details of Experiments and Surveys
1. Sheldrake and Morgana, in preparation.
2. R. Baker, 2000, p. 40.
3. Sheldrake, 1994.
4. R. Baker, 2000, p. 38.
5. R. Baker, personal communication, May 27, 2000.
6. R. Baker, 2000, p. 38.
7. Sheldrake, 1998a, 1999b, 2000a, 2001.
8. Marks and Colwell, 2000.
9. Colwell et al., 2000.
10. Like Marks and Colwell, Wiseman and Smith (1994) obtained an unexpectedly positive result in a staring experiment and then tried to explain it as an artifact of the randomization procedure, but in their case they attributed it to there being more looking trials preceding not-looking trials than vice versa. They advocated counterbalancing the sequences whereby each set of randomized sequences was balanced by another set which was the opposite, so that whenever there was a looking trial in one, there was a not-looking trial in the other, and vice versa.
11. Sheldrake, 1999b, Tables 1 and 2.

12. Sheldrake, 1998a.
13. In reply to my criticism of their claims in the *Skeptical Inquirer* (Sheldrake, 2000b), Marks and Colwell (2000b) tried to argue that the randomization by means of tossing coins could also have involved patterns that the subject could have detected! I asked Marks to explain to me how he thought this could have happened, but he seemed unable to do so.
14. Sheldrake, 1999b, Tables 3 and 4; Sheldrake, 2000a.
15. Sheldrake, 1999b, 2000a.
16. Wiseman and Smith, 1994.
17. Sheldrake, 2001.
18. Wiseman and Schlitz, 1997.
19. Rosenthal, 1976.
20. Quoted in Playfair, 2000, p. 15.

Appendix C. A Brief History of Early Theories of Vision
1. Lindberg, 1981, pp. 1–3.
2. Dodds, 1971.
3. Lindberg, 1981, pp. 3–7.
4. Ibid., pp. 9–11.
5. Ibid., p. 15.
6. Ibid., p. 19.
7. Ibid., p. 26.
8. Ibid., pp. 58–86.
9. Ibid., chapter 7.
10. Ibid., p. 203.

Abraham, R. 2000. A two-worlds model for consciousness. Proceedings of symposium: *Subtle Energies and Uncharted Realms of Mind* (July). Big Sur, Calif.: Esalen Institute.

Adamson, J. 1960. *Born Free*. London: Collins and Harvill Press.

Anfinsen, C. B., and H. A. Scheraga. 1975. Experimental and theoretical aspects of protein folding. *Advances in Protein Chemistry* 29: 205–300.

Astin, J. E., E. Harkness, and E. Ernst. 2000. The efficacy of "distant healing": A systematic review of randomized trials. *Annals of Internal Medicine* 132: 903–10.

Baker, D. 2000. A surprising simplicity to protein folding. *Nature* 405: 39–42.

Baker, R. 1980. *The Mystery of Migration*. London: McDonald.

————. 2000. "Can we tell when someone is staring at us from behind?" *Skeptical Inquirer*, March/April, 34–40.

Barker, J. C. 1967. Premonitions of the Aberfan disaster. *Journal of the Society for Psychical Research* 55: 189–237.

Behe, G. 1988. *Titanic: Psychic Forewarnings of a Tragedy*. Wellingborough, England: Patrick Stephens.

Bem, D. J., J. K. Palmer, and R. S. Broughton. 2001. Updating the ganzfeld database: A victim of its own success? *Journal of Parapsychology* 65: 207–218.

Berger, J. 2001. *The Parrot Who Owns Me*. New York: Villard Books.

Bergson, H. 1911. *Matter and Memory*. London: Allen and Unwin.

Blackmore, S. 1983. *Beyond the Body*. London: Granada.

————. 1997. Probability misjudgement and belief in the paranormal: A newspaper survey. *British Journal of Psychology* 88: 683–89.

Blake, H. N. 1975. *Talking with Horses: A Study of Communication Between Man and Horse*. London: Souvenir Press.

Boone, J. A. 1970. *The Language of Silence*. New York: Harper & Row.

Born, J., K. Hansen, L. Marshall, M. Mölle, and H. M. Fehm. 1999. Timing the end of nocturnal sleep. *Nature* 397: 29–30.

Braud, W. 1981. Lability and inertia in conformance behavior. *Journal of the American Society for Psychical Research* 74: 297–318.

Braud, W., D. Shafer, and S. Andrews. 1990. Electrodermal correlates of remote attention: Autonomic reactions to an unseen gaze. *Proceedings of Presented Papers, Parapsychology Association 33rd Annual Convention*, Chevy Chase, Md., 14–28.

————. 1993a. Reactions to an unseen gaze (remote attention): A review, with new data on autonomic staring detection. *Journal of Parapsychology* 57: 373–90.

———. 1993b. Further studies of autonomic detection of remote staring: Replications, new control procedures, and personality correlates. *Journal of Parapsychology* 57: 391–409.

Braude, S. 1979. *ESP and Psychokinesis: A Philosophical Examination.* Philadelphia: Temple University Press.

Brenner, S. 2001. *My Life in Science.* London: BioMed Central.

Broad, C. D. 1962. *Lectures on Psychical Research.* London: Routledge and Kegan Paul.

Broad, W., and N. Wade. 1985. *Betrayers of the Truth: Fraud and Deceit in Science.* Oxford, England: Oxford University Press.

Bromage, P. R., and R. Melzack. 1974. Phantom limbs and the body schema. *Canadian Anaesthetists' Society Journal* 21: 267–74.

Broughton, R. S., and C. H. Alexander. 1997. Autoganzfeld II: An attempted replication of the PRL ganzfeld research. *Journal of Parapsychology* 61: 208–26.

Brown, D., and R. Sheldrake. 1998. Perceptive pets: A survey in northwest California. *Journal of the Society for Psychical Research* 62: 396–406.

———. 2001. The anticipation of telephone calls: A survey in California. *Journal of Parapsychology* 65: 145–56.

Budge, W. 1930. *Amulets and Superstitions.* Oxford, England: Oxford University Press.

Burtt, E. A. 1932. *The Metaphysical Foundations of Modern Science.* London: Kegan Paul.

Carlson, C. 2000. Artificial life: Boids of a feather flock together. *Scientific American*, November, 94–95.

Carr, B. 2001. President's note. *Paranormal Review* 20: 11–13.

Cassirer, M. 1996. *Medium on Trial: The Story of Helen Duncan and the Witchcraft Act.* Stansted, England: PN Publishing.

Chen, M., M. Daly, S. Natt, and G. Williams. 2000. Non-invasive detection of hypoglycaemia using a novel, fully biocompatible and patient friendly alarm system. *British Medical Journal* 321: 1565–66.

Clements, H. 1983. *Alfred Russel Wallace.* London: Hutchinson.

Clutton-Brock, I. 1981. *Domesticated Animals from Early Times.* London: Heinemann.

Colwell, J. S. Schröder, and D. Sladen. 2000. The ability to detect unseen staring: A literature review and empirical tests. *British Journal of Psychology* 91: 71–85.

Conan Doyle, A. 1884. J. Habakuk Jephson's statement. *Cornhill Magazine* (January).

Cooper, J. 1982. *The Mystery of Telepathy.* London: Constable.

Coover, J. E. 1913. "The feeling of being stared at"—experimental. *American Journal of Psychology* 24: 570–5.

———. 1917. Experiments in psychical research at Leland Stanford Junior University. *Leland Stanford Junior Publications: Psychical Research Monograph no. 1,* 144–67.

Corbett, J. 1986. *Jim Corbett's India.* Oxford, England: Oxford University Press.

Cottrell, J. E., and G. A. Winer. 1994. Development in the understanding of perception: The decline of extramission perception beliefs. *Developmental Psychology* 30: 218–28.

Cottrell, J. E., G. A. Winer, and M. C. Smith. 1996. Beliefs of children and adults about feeling stares of unseen others. *Developmental Psychology* 32: 50–61.

Cox, W. E. 1956. Precognition: An analysis, II. *Journal of the American Society for Psychical Research* 50: 99–109.

Creighton, T. E. 1978. Experimental studies of protein folding and unfolding. *Progress in Biophysics and Molecular Biology* 33: 231–97.

Crick, F. 1994. *The Astonishing Hypothesis: The Scientific Search for the Soul.* London: Simon and Schuster.

Dalton, K. 1997. Exploring the links: Creativity and psi in the ganzfeld. *Proceedings of the Parapsychological Association 40th Annual Convention,* 119–31.

Damasio, A. 2000. *The Feeling of What Happens.* London: Heinemann.

Davies, P. 1984. *Superforce.* London: Heinemann.

Davies, P., and J. Gribbin. 1991. *The Matter Myth.* London: Viking.

Delanoy, D. 2001. Anomalous psychophysiological responses to remote cognition: The DMILS studies. *European Journal of Parapsychology* 16: 30–41.

Delanoy, D., and S. Sah. 1994. Cognitive and physiological psi responses to remote positive and neutral emotional states. In *Proceedings of Presented Papers of the 37th Annual Parapsychological Association Convention,* ed. D. J. Bierman. Fairhaven, Mass.: Parapsychological Association.

Dennett, D. 1991. *Consciousness Explained.* Boston: Little, Brown.

———. 1997. *The Fabric of Reality.* London: Allen Lane.

Dodds, E. R. 1971. Supernormal phenomena in classical antiquity. *Proceedings of the Society for Psychical Research* 55: 189–237.

Dossey, L. 1993. *Healing Words.* San Francisco: HarperCollins.

———. 2001. *Healing Beyond the Body.* Boston: Shambhala.

Downer, J. 1999. *Supernatural: The Unseen Powers of Animals.* London: BBC.

Droscher, V. B. 1971. *The Magic of the Senses.* London: Panther.

Dundes, A., ed. 1992. *The Evil Eye: A Casebook.* Madison: University of Wisconsin Press.

Dunne, J. W. 1958. *An Experiment with Time.* 3rd ed. London: Faber and Faber.

Eason, C. 1992. *A Mother's Instincts.* London: Thorsons.

———. 1994. *Psychic Power of Children.* London: Foulsham.

———. 1995. *Psychic Families.* London: Foulsham.

Edney, A. T. B. 1993. Dogs and human epilepsy. *Veterinary Record* 132: 337–38.

Ehrenreich, B. 1997. *Blood Rites.* New York: Metropolitan Books.

Eisenbud, J. 1970. *Psi and Psychoanalysis: Studies in the Psychoanalysis of Psi-conditioned Behavior.* New York: Grune and Stratton.

Elsworthy, F. 1895. *The Evil Eye.* London: Murray.

Feldman, S. 1940. Phantom limbs. *American Journal of Physiology* 53: 590–92.

Fenwick, P., and E. Fenwick. 1998. *The Hidden Door.* London: Headline.

Freeman, W. J. 1999. *How Brains Make Up Their Minds.* London: Weidenfeld and Nicholson.

Freeman, W. J., and W. Schneider. 1982. Changes in spatial pattern of rabbit olfactory EEG with conditioning to odors. *Psychophysiology* 19: 44–56.

Freud, S. 1955. Psychoanalysis and telepathy. In *The Complete Psychological Works of Sigmund Freud,* vol. 18. London: Hogarth Press.

Gallup, G. H., and F. Newport. 1991. Belief in paranormal phenomena among American adults. *Skeptical Inquirer* 15: 137–46.

Galton, F. 1883. *Inquiries into Human Faculty and Its Development.* London: Murray.

Gardner, M. 1983. *The Whys of a Philosophical Scrivener.* New York: Quill.

Gibson, J. J. 1986. *The Ecological Approach to Visual Perception.* Hillsdale, N.J.: Lawrence Erlbaum Associates.

Gleick, J. 1988. *Chaos: Making a New Science.* London: Heinemann.

Goodall, J. 2000. *Reason for Hope.* New York: Warner Books.

Gould, L. L., and F. H. Heppner. 1974. The vee formation of Canada geese. *Auk* 91: 494–506.

Gould, S. J. 1989. *Wonderful Life.* London: Hutchinson.

Graff, D. E. 1998. *Tracks in the Psychic Wilderness: An Exploration of Remote Viewing, ESP, Precognitive Dreaming and Synchronicity.* Shaftesbury, England: Element Books.

Greene, B. 1999. *The Elegant Universe.* London: Cape.

Greenfield, S. 2000. *Brain Story: Unlocking Our Inner World of Emotions, Memories, Ideas and Desires.* London: BBC.

Gregory, W. 1919. *Animal Magnetism, or Mesmerism and Its Phenomena.* 5th ed. London: Nichols.

Gurney, E. F., W. H. Myers, and F. Podmore. 1886. *Phantasms of the Living.* London: Kegan Paul, Trench, Trubner.

Hampshire, M. 1999. Pets that saved our lives. *Daily Mail,* March 30, 40–42.

Hansen, G. P. 2001. *The Trickster and the Paranormal.* Philadelphia: Xlibris Corporation.

Hawking, S. 2001. *The Universe in a Nutshell.* London: Bantam.

Hawkins, L. 1983. The ice babies. *TV Times,* March 23.

Haynes, R. 1973. *The Hidden Springs: An Enquiry into Extra-Sensory Perception.* London: Hutchinson.

Heppner, F. H., J. L. Convissar, D. E. Moonan, and J. G. T. Anderson. 1985. Visual angle and formation flight in Canada geese (*Branta canadensis*). *Auk* 102: 195–98.

Hölldobler, B., and E. O. Wilson. 1994. *Journey to the Ants: A Story of Scientific Exploration.* Cambridge, Mass.: Harvard University Press.

Horgan, J. 1996. *The End of Science: Facing the Limits of Knowledge in the Twilight of the Scientific Age.* London: Little, Brown and Co.

Huth, A., and C. Wissel. 1992. The simulation of the movement of fish schools. *Journal of Theoretical Biology* 156: 365–85.

Huxley, F. 1990. *The Eye: The Seer and the Seen.* London: Thames and Hudson.

Hygen, G. 1987. *Vardøger: Vårt Paranormale Nasjonalfenomen.* Oslo: Cappelans Forlag (in Norwegian).

Inglis, B. 1977. *Natural and Supernatural: A History of the Paranormal from Earliest Times to 1914.* London: Hodder and Stoughton.

———. 1985. *The Paranormal: An Encyclopedia of Psychic Phenomena.* London: Granada.

Jahn, R., and B. Dunne. 1987. *Margins of Reality: The Role of Consciousness in the Physical World.* New York: Harcourt Brace Jovanovich.

Jennings, H. S. 1906. *Behavior of the Lower Organisms.* New York: Columbia University Press.

Josephson, B. D., and F. Pallikari-Viras. 1991. Biological utilization of quantum nonlocality. *Foundations of Physics* 21: 197–207.

Jung, C. G. 1963. *Memories, Dreams, Reflections.* New York: Random House.

Karplus, M. 1995. The Levinthal paradox yesterday and today. *Folding and Design* 2: 569–76.

Kayser, W., ed. 1997. *A Glorious Accident.* New York: Freeman.

Kelly, E. W. 2001. The contribution of F. W. H. Myers to psychology. *Journal of the Society for Psychical Research* 65: 65–90.

Kiley-Worthington, M. 1987. *The Behaviour of Horses.* London: J. A. Allen.

Kokubo, H. 1998. Contemporary active research groups in Japan for anomalous phenomena. *Japanese Journal of Parapsychology* 3: 19–63.

Kuhn, T. S. 1970. *The Structure of Scientific Revolutions.* 2nd ed. Chicago: Chicago University Press.

Lang, A. 1911. Second sight. *Encyclopaedia Britannica.* 11th ed. Cambridge, England: Cambridge University Press.

Laplace, H. 1819, reprinted 1951. *A Philosophical Essay on Probabilities.* New York: Dover.

Lindberg, D. C. 1981. *Theories of Vision from Al-Kindi to Kepler.* Chicago: University of Chicago Press.

London, J. 1991. *The Call of the Wild.* London: Mammoth.

Long, W. 1919. *How Animals Talk.* New York: Harper.

Marais, E. 1973. *The Soul of the White Ant.* Harmondsworth, England: Penguin Books.

Marks, D., and J. Colwell. 2000. The psychic staring effect: An artifact of pseudo randomization. *Skeptical Inquirer*, September/October, 41–49.

———. 2001. Fooling and falling into the sense of being stared at. *Skeptical Inquirer*, March/April, 62–63.

Markwick, B. 1978. The Soal-Goldney experiments with Basil Shackleton: New evidence of data manipulation. *Proceedings of the Society for Psychical Research* 56: 250–77.

Matthews, R. 1996. Sixth sense helps you watch your back. *Sunday Telegraph,* April 14.

Mayer, E. L. 1996. Subjectivity and intersubjectivity of clinical facts. *International Journal of Psycho-Analysis* 77: 709–37.

Mayer, E. L. 2001. On "telepathic dreams?": An unpublished paper by Robert J. Stoller. *Journal of the American Psychoanalytic Association* 49: 629–57.

McFarland, D., ed. 1981. *The Oxford Companion to Animal Behaviour.* Oxford, England: Oxford University Press.

McKie, R. 2001. Royal Mail's Nobel guru in telepathy row. *Observer,* September 30.

McMoneagle, J. 1993. *Mind Trek: Exploring Consciousness, Time and Space Through Remote Viewing.* Norfolk, Va.: Hampton Roads Publishing.

Melzack, R. 1989. Phantom limbs, the self and the brain. *Canadian Psychology* 30: 1–16.

———. 1992. Phantom limbs. *Scientific American,* April, 120–26.

Melzack, R., and P. R. Bromage. 1973. Experimental phantom limbs. *Experimental Neurology* 39: 261–69.

Michell, J., and R. Rickard. 1977. *Phenomena.* London: Thames and Hudson.

Millay, J. 1999. *Multidimensional Mind: Remote Viewing in Hyperspace.* Berkeley, Calif.: North Atlantic Books.

Milton, J. 1999. Should ganzfeld research continue to be crucial in the search for a replicable psi effect? Part I. Discussion paper and introduction to an electronic mail discussion. *Journal of Parapsychology* 63: 309–33.

Milton, J., and R. Wiseman. 1999. Does psi exist? Lack of replication of an anomalous process of information transfer. *Psychological Bulletin* 125: 387–91.

Mitchell, W. 1872. *Injuries of Nerves and Their Consequences.* Philadelphia: Lippincott.

Moody, R. A. 1976. *Life After Life.* New York: Bantam.

Morell, V. 1997. The origin of dogs: Running with the wolves. *Science* 276: 1647–48.

Morgan, T. H. 1901. *Regeneration.* New York: Macmillan.

Morris, D. 1990. *Animalwatching.* London: Cape.

Murphy, M. 1992. *The Future of the Body.* Los Angeles: Tarcher.

Murphy, M., and R. White. 1978. *The Psychic Side of Sports.* Reading, Mass.: Addison-Wesley.

Myers, A. 1997. *Communicating with Animals.* Chicago: Contemporary Books.

Myers, F. 1882. Report of the literary committee. *Proceedings of the Society for Psychical Research* 1: 147.

———. 1903. *Human Personality and the Survival of Bodily Death.* London: Longmans.

Newsom, S., and A. Scott. 1999. Wall of Death. *Sunday Times,* February 28.

Niwa, H. 1994. Self-organizing dynamic model of fish schooling. *Journal of Theoretical Biology* 171: 123–26.

Noë, A., ed. 2002. *Is the Visual World a Grand Illusion?* Thorverton, England: Imprint Academic.

Novak, M. 1976. *The Joy of Sports.* New York: Basic Books.

Palmer, J. 1979. A community mail survey of psychic experiences. *Journal of the American Society for Psychical Research* 73: 221–51.

Parker, A. 2000. A review of the ganzfeld work at Gothenberg University. *Journal of the Society for Psychical Research* 64: 1–15.

Parnia, S. 2001. Near death experiences in cardiac arrest and the mystery of consciousness. *Network: The Scientific and Medical Network Review*, August, 6–9.

Parrish, J., and W. Hammer. 1997. *Animal Groups in Three Dimensions.* Cambridge, England: Cambridge University Press.

Payne, P. 1981. *Martial Arts.* London: Thames and Hudson.

Penfield, W. 1975. *The Mystery of the Mind.* Princeton, N.J.: Princeton University Press.

Penrose, R. 1989. *The Emperor's New Mind.* Oxford, England: Oxford University Press.

Peoc'h, R. 1997. Telepathy experiments between rabbits. *Fondation Odier de Psycho-Physique Bulletin* 3: 25–28.

Pepperberg, I. 1999. *The Alex Studies: Cognitive and Communicative Abilities of Grey Parrots.* Cambridge, Mass.: Harvard University Press.

Peterson, D. M. 1978. Through the looking glass: An investigation of the faculty of extra-sensory detection of being looked at. Edinburgh, Scotland: Unpublished M.A. thesis, University of Edinburgh.

Phillips, H. 2000. Mind phantoms. *New Scientist*, July 8, 11.

Piaget, J. 1973. *The Child's Conception of the World.* London: Granada.

———. 1974. *Understanding Causality.* New York: Norton.

Playfair, G. L. 1999. Telepathy and identical twins. *Journal of the Society for Psychical Research* 63: 86–98.

———. 2000. Mediawatch. *Paranormal Review* 16: 15.

———. 2003. *The Twin Connection.* London: Vega.

Poeck, K., and B. Orgass. 1971. The concept of the body schema: A critical review and some experimental results. *Cortex* 7: 254–77.

Pomeroy, H., and F. Heppner. 1992. Structure of turning in airborne rock dove (*Columba livia*) flocks. *Auk* 109: 256–67.

Poortman, J. J. 1939. Het hegemonikon en zijn aandacht van den tweeden graad. *Tijdschrift voor Parapsychologie* 11: 97–120.

———. 1959. The feeling of being stared at. *Journal of the Society for Psychical Research* 40: 4–12.

Popper, K., and J. Eccles. 1997. *The Self and Its Brain: An Argument for Interactionism.* Berlin: Springer.

Puthoff, H. E., and R. Targ. 1976. A perceptual channel for information transfer over kilometer distances: Historical perspective and recent research. *Proceedings of the IEEE* 64: 329–54.

Radin, D. 1997. *The Conscious Universe.* San Francisco: Harper Edge.

Ramachandran, V. S., and S. Blakeslee. 1998. *Phantoms in the Brain.* London: Fourth Estate.

Recordon, E. G., F. J. M. Stratton, and R. Peters. 1968. Some trials in a case of alleged telepathy. *Journal of the Society for Psychical Research* 44: 390–99.

Reichel-Dolmatoff, G. 1997. *Rainforest Shamans.* Dartington, England: Themis Books.

Rhine, J. B. 1937. *New Frontiers of the Mind.* New York: Farrar and Rinehart.

———. 1954. *New World of the Mind.* London: Faber and Faber.

———. 1974. A new case of experimenter unreliability. *Journal of Parapsychology* 38: 218–25.

Rhine, L. E. 1967. *ESP in Life and Lab.* London: Macmillan.

———. 1981. *The Invisible Picture: A Study of Psychic Experiences.* Jefferson, N.C.: McFarland.

Richet, C. 1923. *Thirty Years of Psychical Research.* London: Collins.

Rosenthal, R. 1976. *Experimenter Effects in Behavioral Research.* New York: Wiley.

Sabbagh, K. 1999. *A Rum Affair: A True Story of Botanical Fraud.* London: Allen Lane.

Saltmarsh, F. H. 1938. *Foreknowledge.* London: Bell.

Schechter, B. 1999. Birds of a feather. *New Scientist,* January 29, 30–33.

Schlitz, M., and W. Braud. 1997. Distant intentionality and healing: Assessing the evidence. *Alternative Therapies* 3: 62–73.

Schlitz, M., and E. Gruber. 1980. Transcontinental remote viewing. *Journal of Parapsychology* 44: 305–15.

———. 1981. Transcontinental remote viewing: A rejudging. *Journal of Parapsychology* 45: 233–37.

Schlitz, M., and C. Honorton. 1992. Ganzfeld psi performance within an artistically gifted population. *Journal of the American Society for Psychical Research* 86: 83–98.

Schlitz, M., and S. LaBerge. 1994. Autonomic detection of remote observation: Two conceptual replications. Amsterdam: *Proceedings of Presented Papers, Parapsychology Association 37th Annual Convention,* Amsterdam, 352–60.

———. 1997. Covert observation increases skin conductance in subjects unaware of when they are being observed: A replication. *Journal of Parapsychology* 61: 185–95.

Schlitz, M., and D. J. Radin. 2002. Telepathy in the ganzfeld: State of the evidence. In W. Jonas and C. Crawford, eds., *Science and Spiritual Healing: A Critical Review of Research on Spiritual Healing, "Energy" Medicine and Intentionality.* London: Harcourt Health Services.

Schmeidler, G. R. 1972. Respice, adspice and prospice. *Proceedings of the Parapsychological Association*, no. 8. Durham, N.C.: Parapsychological Association.

Schmeidler, G., and H. Edge. 1999. Should ganzfeld research continue to be crucial in the search for a replicable psi effect? Part II. Edited ganzfeld debate. *Journal of Parapsychology* 63: 335–88.

Schmeidler, G. R., and R. A. McConnell. 1958. *ESP and Personality Patterns*. New Haven: Yale University Press.

Schmidt, S., R. Schneider, J. Utts, and H. Walach. 2002. Remote intention on electrodermal activity—two meta-analyses. *The Parapsychological Association 45th Annual Convention. Proceedings of Presented Papers*: 27–47. Durham, N.C.: The Parapsycholocical Association.

Schouten, S. A. 1982. Analysing spontaneous cases: A replication based on the Rhine collection. *European Journal of Parapsychology* 4: 113–58.

Schwarz, B. 1972. *Parent-Child Telepathy: A Study of the Telepathy of Everyday Life*. New York: Garrett Publications.

Selous, E. 1931. *Thought Transference or What? in Birds*. London: Constable.

Shannon, B. 1993. *The Representational and the Presentational*. New York: Harvester.

Sheldrake, R. 1981. *A New Science of Life: The Hypothesis of Formative Causation*. London: Blond and Briggs.

——. 1988. *The Presence of the Past: Morphic Resonance and the Habits of Nature*. New York: Times Books.

——. 1994. *Seven Experiments That Could Change the World: A Do-It-Yourself Guide to Revolutionary Science*. London: Fourth Estate.

——. 1996. An experiment with birds. In Christow-Bakargiev, C., and H. U. Obrist, eds., *Uccelli/Birds*. Rome: Zerynthia.

——. 1998a. The sense of being stared at: Experiments in schools. *Journal of the Society of Psychical Research* 62: 311–23.

——. 1998b. Experimenter effects in scientific research: How widely are they neglected? *Journal of Scientific Exploration* 12: 73–78.

——. 1998c. Could experimenter effects occur in the physical and biological sciences? *Skeptical Inquirer*, May/June, 57–58.

——. 1999a. *Dogs That Know When Their Owners Are Coming Home, and Other Unexplained Powers of Animals*. New York: Crown.

——. 1999b. The "sense of being stared at" confirmed by simple experiments. *Biology Forum* 92: 53–76.

——. 1999c. Commentary on a paper by Wiseman, Smith, and Milton on the "psychic pet" phenomenon. *Journal of the Society for Psychical Research* 63: 306–11.

——. 2000a. The "sense of being stared at" does not depend on known sensory clues. *Biology Forum* 93: 209–24.

——. 2000b. Research on the feeling of being stared at. *Skeptical Inquirer* (March/April): 58–61.

——. 2000c. The "psychic pet" phenomenon. *Journal of the Society for Psychical Research* 64: 126–28.

——. 2000d. Telepathic telephone calls: Two surveys. *Journal of the Society for Psychical Research* 64: 224–32.

——. 2001. Experiments on the sense of being stared at: The elimination of possible artefacts. *Journal of the Society for Psychical Research* 65: 122–37.

——. 2002. Apparent telepathy between babies and nursing mothers: A survey. *Journal of the Society for Psychical Research* 66: 181–85.

Sheldrake, R., C. Lawlor, and J. Turney. 1998. Perceptive pets: A survey in London. *Biology Forum* 91: 57–74.

Sheldrake, R., and P. Smart. 1997. Psychic pets: A survey in North-West England. *Journal of the Society for Psychical Research* 61: 353–64.

——. 1998. A dog that seems to know when his owner is returning: Preliminary investigations. *Journal of the Society for Psychical Research* 62: 220–32.

——. 2000a. A dog that seems to know when his owner is coming home: Videotaped experiments and observations. *Journal of Scientific Exploration* 14: 233–55.

——. 2000b. Testing a return-anticipating dog, Kane. *Anthrozoos* 13: 203–12.

——. 2003a. Experimental tests for telephone telepathy (in preparation).

——. 2003b. Videotaped experiments on telephone telepathy (in preparation).

Sinclair, U. 1930. *Mental Radio*. London: Werner Laurie.

Sitwell, O. 1946. *The Scarlet Tree*. London: Macmillan.

Smythies, J. 2000. The theoretical basis of psi. *Journal of the Society for Psychical Research* 64: 242–44.

Sobel, D. 1996. *Longitude*. London: Fourth Estate.

St. Barbe Baker, R. 1942. *Africa Drums*. London: Drummond.

Stanford, R. T. 1978. Toward reinterpreting psi effects. *Journal of the American Society for Psychical Research* 72: 197–214.

Steiger, B., and S. H. Steiger. 1992. *Strange Powers of Pets*. New York: Fine.

Stevenson, I. 1960. A review and analysis of paranormal experiences connected with the sinking of the *Titanic*. *Journal of the American Society for Psychical Research* 54: 153–71.

——. 1970. *Telepathic Impressions*. Charlottesville: University Press of Virginia.

Stokes, D. M. 1987. Theoretical parapsychology. *Advances in Parapsychological Research* 5: 77–189.

Stoppard, M. 1985. *Pregnancy and Birth Book*. London: Dorling Kindersley.

Storm, L., and S. Ertel. 2000. Does psi exist? Comments on Milton and Wiseman's meta-analysis of ganzfeld research. *Psychological Bulletin* 127: 424–33

Targ, R., and J. Katra. 1998. *Miracles of Mind: Exploring Nonlocal Consciousness and Spiritual Healing*. Novato, Calif.: New World Library.

Targ, R., H. E. Puthoff, and E. C. May. 1979. Direct perception of remote geographical locations. In C. T. Tart et al., eds., *Mind at Large*. New York: Praeger.

Taylor, J. 1998. A new theory for ESP. *Journal of the Society for Psychical Research* 62: 289–310.

———. 2000. Information transfer in space-time. *Journal of the Society for Psychical Research* 64: 193–210.

Temple, R. 1989. *Open to Suggestion: The Uses and Abuses of Hypnosis.* London: Aquarian Press.

Thom, R. 1975. *Structural Stability and Morphogenesis.* Reading, Mass.: Benjamin.

———. 1983. *Mathematical Models of Morphogenesis.* Chichester, England: Horwood.

Thomas, K. 1973. *Religion and the Decline of Magic.* Harmondsworth, England: Penguin.

Thouless, R. 1972. *From Anecdote to Experiment in Psychical Research.* London: Routledge and Kegan Paul.

Titchener, E. B. 1898. The feeling of being stared at. *Science New Series* 8: 895–97.

Twain, M. 1884. Letter. *Journal of the Society for Psychical Research* 1: 166–67.

Ullman, M., S. Krippner, and A. Vaughan. 1973. *Dream Telepathy.* London: Turnstone.

Van der Post, L. 1962. *The Lost World of the Kalahari.* London: Penguin Books.

Van Lommel, P. 2001. Near-death experience in survivors of cardiac arrest: A prospective study in the Netherlands. *Lancet* 358: 2039–45.

Velmans, M. 2000. *Understanding Consciousness.* London: Routledge.

Von Frisch, K. 1975. *Animal Architecture.* London: Hutchinson.

Walker, E. H. 1984. A review of criticism of the quantum mechanical theory of psi phenomena. *Journal of Parapsychology* 48: 227–32.

Wallace, A. R. 1874. *On Miracles and Modern Spiritualism.* London: Burns.

Wallace, B. A. 2000. *The Taboo of Subjectivity.* Oxford, England: Oxford University Press.

Weinstein, S., and E. A. Sarsen. 1961. Phantoms in cases of congenital absence of limbs. *Neurology* 11: 905–11.

Whan, M. 2000. Mercurius, archetype and transpsychic reality: C. G. Jung's parapsychology of spirit(s). In D. Barford, ed., *Lands of Darkness: Psychoanalysis and the Paranormal.* London: Rebus Press.

Williams, J. H. 1960. *Bandoola.* London: Hart-Davis.

Williams, L. 1983. Minimal cue perception of the regard of others: The feeling of being stared at. *Journal of Parapsychology* 47: 59–60.

Willmer, E. N. 1970. *Cytology and Evolution.* 2nd ed. London: Academic Press.

———. 1999. *The Sallow Bush.* London: Hamilton.

Wilson, E. O. 1980. *Sociobiology.* Cambridge, Mass.: Harvard University Press.

Winer, G. A., and J. E. Cottrell. 1996a. Does anything leave the eye when we see? *Current Directions in Psychological Science* 5: 137–42.

———. 1996b. Effects of drawing on directional representations of the process of vision. *Journal of Educational Psychology* 88: 387–96.

Winer, G. A., J. E. Cottrell, V. A. Gregg, J. S. Fournier, and L. A. Bica. 2002. Fundamentally misunderstanding visual perception: Adult's beliefs in visual emissions. *American Psychologist* 57: 417–24.

Winer, G. A., J. E. Cottrell, K. D. Karefilaki, and V. A. Gregg. 1996. Images, words and questions: Variables that influence beliefs about vision in children and adults. *Journal of Experimental Child Psychology* 63: 499–525.

Wiseman, R., and M. Schlitz. 1997. Experimenter effects and the remote detection of staring. *Journal of Parapsychology* 61: 197–207.

Wiseman, R., and M. D. Smith. 1994. A further look at the detection of unseen gaze. *Proceedings of Presented Papers, Parapsychology Association 37th Annual Convention*. Amsterdam, 465–78.

Wiseman, R., M. D. Smith, and D. Kornbrot. 1996. Exploring possible sender-to-experimenter acoustic leakage in the PRL autoganzfeld experiments. *Journal of Parapsychology* 60: 97–128.

Wolman, B. B., ed. 1977. *Handbook of Parapsychology*. New York: Van Nostrand Reinhold.

Woodhouse, B. 1992. *How Your Dog Thinks*. Letchworth, England: Ringpress.

Wylder, J. E. 1978. *Psychic Pets: The Secret World of Animals*. New York: Stonehill.

Yamamoto, M., et al. 2000. Study on analyzing methods of human body functions using various simultaneous measurements. *Journal of International Society of Life Information Science* 18: 61–97.

Zhou, Y., and M. Karplus. 1999. Interpreting the folding kinetics of helical proteins. *Nature* 401: 400–3.

Most people cited in this book were happy to have their real names used. Some requested pseudonyms and these are indicated by asterisks.

About the Author

DR. RUPERT SHELDRAKE is a biologist and author of more than sixty technical papers and nine books. A former Research Fellow of the Royal Society, he studied natural sciences at Cambridge University, where he took a Ph.D. in biochemistry, and philosophy at Harvard University, where he was a Frank Knox Fellow. He was a Fellow of Clare College, Cambridge, and director of studies in biochemistry and cell biology. He is currently a Fellow of the Institute of Noetic Sciences, near San Francisco, and lives in London with his wife and two sons.

His website is www.sheldrake.org.